LIBRARY IN A BOOK

CAPITAL PUNISHMENT

Third Edition

Harry Henderson

First Edition by Stephen A. Flanders

Facts On File, Inc.

CAPITAL PUNISHMENT, Third Edition

Facts On File, Inc.
132 West 31st Street
New York NY 10001

Library of Congress Cataloging-in-Publication Data
Henderson, Harry, 1951–
  Capital punishment / Harry Henderson— [3rd ed.].
    p. cm.— (Library in a book)
  Includes bibliographical references and index.
  ISBN 0-8160-5708-7
  1. Capital punishment—United States. 2. Capital punishment. I. Title. II. Series.
  KF9227.C2F53 2006
  345.73′0773—dc 22   2005013671

Facts On File books are available at special discounts when purchased in bulk quantities for businesses, associations, institutions, or sales promotions. Please call our Special Sales Department in New York at (212) 967-8800 or (800) 322-8755.

You can find Facts On File on the World Wide Web at http://www.factsonfile.com

Text design by Ron Monteleone

Maps and graphs by Jeremy Eagle

Printed in the United States of America

MP Hermitage   10   9   8   7   6   5   4   3   2   1

This book is printed on acid-free paper.

CONTENTS

PART III
APPENDICES

PART I

OVERVIEW OF THE TOPIC

CHAPTER 1

INTRODUCTION TO
CAPITAL PUNISHMENT

"Ladies and gentlemen, please stay in your places until your escort comes for you. Follow your escort, as instructed. Thank you."[1]

Whether they are journalists, the families of condemned prisoners, or murder victims' families looking for a measure of justice and closure, witnesses to an execution hear words like these when it is time to enter the execution chamber. The words mean that a person is to be killed by order of the state, pursuant to the verdict of two juries—one to find the condemned person guilty of a brutal murder, a second to judge that death rather than life in prison is the appropriate punishment. It is a death that is precisely specified and scheduled in a detailed warrant—yet in most cases, it has been delayed for years by repeated stays and appeals.

The witnesses to the execution, having been carefully searched, are escorted—or should one say guarded?—every step of the way to the viewing room. Now the escort says: "When the phone rings and I get the order to go, stand and follow me quickly." What will the witnesses to an execution see? Consider this account of an actual execution:

On April 21, 1992, time finally ran out for Robert Alton Harris, who had been convicted of the brutal murder of two teenagers. A lever was released, dropping cyanide into a pool of sulfuric acid. Deadly gas began to flood the tiny execution chamber at California's San Quentin Prison. Then, as a witness observed while watching Harris, strapped in the death chair:

> His head began to roll and his eyes closed, then opened again. His head dropped, then came up with an abrupt jerk, and rolled some more. It was grotesque and hideous, and I looked away. . . .
>
> He writhed for seven minutes, his head falling on his chest, saliva drooling from his open mouth. He lifted his head again and again. Seven minutes. A lifetime. Nine more minutes passed with his head slumped on his chest. His heart, a survivor's heart, kept pumping for nine more minutes . . .

Sixteen minutes after the cyanide gas had been released, Harris was pronounced dead. (Today, faster-acting injections are used.)

Most people will never witness an execution. Despite the urgings of some death penalty opponents (and a few supporters), executions are never televised. All that is usually shown on the 11 o'clock news is the scene outside the prison walls, where protesters calling for an end to state-sanctioned death often vie with supporters who see the ultimate penalty as ultimate justice for murder victims and their survivors.

Since the middle of the 20th century, capital punishment has become an important social, political, and legal issue. In 1972 the U.S. Supreme Court halted executions in the United States until new safeguards could be devised to protect the constitutional rights of the accused. In 1977 executions resumed under revised state laws. Today 38 of the nation's 50 states (and the federal government) have the death penalty although in many of the death penalty states actual executions are rare.

Since the 1960s, proponents and opponents of capital punishment have waged a fierce legal and political battle. At first the main terrain of the battlefield had to do with fairness. A growing number of research studies suggested that minorities (particularly blacks) and the poor were disproportionately condemned to death. In many cases there were questions about whether such defendants had received competent legal representation in accordance with the requirements of the Constitution.

States that had the death penalty quickly revised their statutes to provide more due process for defendants. After the new laws had survived a number of such challenges, the focus began to shift in the 1980s to questioning the death penalty's appropriateness for certain groups of people, such as persons under age 18 and the mentally disabled. Several key decisions have narrowed the scope of the death penalty: persons under 18 can no longer be executed nor can persons who are "substantially" mentally retarded.

Finally, in the late 1990s a powerful new challenge to the death penalty emerged—the risk of executing innocent people, forever cutting them off from any hope of justice or compensation. Aided particularly by the availability of DNA testing, more than 100 death row prisoners have been exonerated (declared to be not guilty) and released from prison as of 2004. This turn of events naturally suggested the likelihood that other innocent persons had been executed—but was it a significant risk? Did it outweigh the value of capital punishment as just retribution for crime and as a deterrent to the most brutal crimes?

Meanwhile, many experts have questioned whether capital punishment has any greater deterrent value than a sentence of life in prison without parole. It is also argued that the death penalty is much more expensive than life imprisonment and thus diverts scarce resources that could be used for fighting crime or helping victims.

Other observers have pointed to the fact that most of the world's advanced democracies have abandoned the death penalty, often decades ago. They argue that the death penalty is making the United States a moral pariah and is hindering the extradition of American suspects who have been captured abroad.

Despite these arguments, today most American citizens still support capital punishment in some form. Even some opponents of the death penalty have found their voices muted when they had to deal with the worst offenders, such as Oklahoma City bomber Timothy McVeigh. At the same time, however, the ongoing execution of hundreds of people every year raises both practical and moral questions as lawyers, judges, legislators, governors, and citizens continue to struggle with issues that will remain as long as there is capital punishment.

In exploring the issues surrounding the death penalty, this chapter presents a brief historical sketch tracing the development and use of capital punishment from the ancient world to the British political tradition, the influence of the Enlightenment, and the beginning of the American republic. The early efforts by death penalty abolitionists[2] and reformers throughout the 19th century are then summarized.

The historical background concludes with the first major legal challenges to the death penalty in the mid-20th century, leading up to the temporary suspension of executions in the 1970s. Although the abolitionists failed to end capital punishment for good, their efforts led to a surge in modern abolitionist groups.

The issues framed by the modern debate over capital punishment are the focus of the second major section. These issues include those raised by supporters of the death penalty, including deterrence, retribution, and the need to protect society. They are followed by the issues often raised by abolitionists: fairness, proportionality, cruelty, and perhaps most telling, the risk of killing an innocent person.

The third major section moves into the legal realm. It begins with a brief overview of how capital trials are conducted, the role of the jury, and the factors that must be considered in deciding whether to impose a death sentence. The often lengthy appeals process is also discussed. With that understanding of procedure in hand, it is then possible to look at the modern legal challenges to the death penalty, including such issues as racial bias, unfairness, inconsistency, the danger of "fatal error," and the appropriateness of executing people who may not be fully able to appreciate the gravity and consequences of their offense.

The concluding section provides some broad background about the use of capital punishment issues in political campaigns, international attitudes toward capital punishment (and how they may influence the American debate), and possible future trends.

HISTORICAL BACKGROUND

The infliction of death for the purpose of retribution has been a facet of human existence since earliest times. Even before the emergence of organized societies, individuals killed to avenge wrongs done to them and their families. These killings were acts of private retribution. There was no code that specified wrongful conduct or the penalties such behavior would incur.

The first criminal laws were an outgrowth of this practice of personal justice. These laws evolved as a means of codifying the compensation one individual or family owed another in order to right a personal wrong. The idea that this restitution involved a punishment imposed on behalf of the society as a whole, however, was yet to come.

As larger-scale social structures developed, wrongs or crimes were divided into public and private offenses. Public offenses, such as witchcraft or blasphemy against the official religion, were punished by the state, while private offenses were still answered by acts of personal retribution. This split system of justice eventually yielded to a unified scheme in which private retaliation was replaced by a concept of public justice. Behind the shift was an emerging recognition that every crime committed by any member of society was harmful to the interests of the entire society. With the public-private distinction removed, the individual relinquished the right to personal revenge. In return, the state assumed responsibility for the punishment of all crimes, including personal offenses. For ultimate crimes against the person, such as murder, personal vengeance had given way to lawfully derived and administered death sentences.

ANCIENT AND MEDIEVAL WORLD

Capital punishment was common throughout the ancient world. Death sentences were imposed for a wide variety of offenses. One of the earliest recorded sets of laws known to Western society, the Babylonian Hammurabi Code (ca. 1700 B.C.), decreed the death penalty for crimes as minor as the fraudulent sale of beer. Egyptians could be killed for disclosing sacred burial places. The Athenian leader Draco in the seventh century B.C. fashioned a criminal code that ordered the death penalty for most offenses. The severity of this code gave rise to the word *draconian*. Socrates' suicide several hundred years later to escape execution for the crime of flouting social mores is among the most famous events in Western intellectual history. The Torah, the law of the Hebrews, authorized death for more than a dozen offenses. And in the most famous execution in history, Jesus Christ was crucified as a rebel under the laws of the Roman Empire.

The Middle Ages and Renaissance saw little change in the widespread use of capital punishment. Death was the standard penalty for major crimes across Europe. The methods of execution used frequently were cruel and barbaric by modern standards, often involving some form of torture. The condemned were subject to such ordeals as burning at the stake, being broken on a wheel, or being crushed under heavy stones. Execution, in fact, represented the ultimate point in a continuum of corporal punishment that for minor offenses involved branding or flogging.

The reign of King Henry VIII was illustrative of this period. Apart from the famous beheading of several of the monarch's wives, as well as of Sir Thomas

Introduction to Capital Punishment

More, more than 70,000 executions took place during the first half of the 16th century in England. Over the next several centuries, Great Britain continued to add to its already large number of crimes punishable by death. By 1789, the British criminal law contained 350 capital crimes. The statutes were known popularly as the Bloody Code. Interestingly, the actual number of executions dropped substantially throughout this era. The reasons for this decline included the reluctance of judges and juries to convict persons of minor offenses that required the death penalty. (Britain also began to experiment with transportation to places such as Australia as an alternative to death for serious crimes.)

THE ENLIGHTENMENT

The emphasis on reason and humanity that marked the 18th-century Enlightenment brought about a transformation in the way capital punishment was viewed. The extensive use of the death penalty and the brutal manner in which it was administered were denounced by such leading thinkers as the French philosophers Montesquieu and Voltaire. In 1764, the Italian jurist Cesare Beccaria greatly advanced the entire field of criminal justice when he published his *Essay on Crimes and Punishment*. Widely translated and read, his book had an immediate and dramatic impact.

Beccaria criticized the use of torture, the imposition of harsh penalties for minor offenses, and the archaic state of the criminal law in general. He argued that the certainty of punishment was much more important to deterring crime than the severity of the sanction. He favored instead incarceration and hard labor for persons convicted of capital crimes.

Beccaria's writing served as the theoretical foundation for the major reforms in criminal law that occurred in the late 18th and early 19th centuries. In England, his ideas were taken up by the philosopher Jeremy Bentham, who advocated a complete revision of the British criminal code. Bentham's proposals, such as a reduction in the number of designated capital crimes, were presented in Parliament by another preeminent legal reformer, Sir Samuel Romilly. Although neither lived to see the result, their efforts sparked a reform movement that brought the number of capital crimes in Britain down to four by the mid-1800s.

EARLY REFORM MOVEMENTS IN AMERICA

The American colonies inherited the British system of law. Each of the colonies had its own criminal code, reflecting the distinctive circumstances of its founding. In early Puritan Massachusetts, the list of capital crimes included witchcraft, blasphemy, and adultery. In contrast, the Quaker influence in Pennsylvania limited the death penalty to crimes of murder and treason. Paralleling the trend in criminal law in the mother country, the number of criminal offenses in each of the colonies increased throughout their development. By the time of the American Revolution, all the colonies had severe criminal laws.

However legal historians, noting the relatively low rate of actual executions across the colonies, point out that these criminal codes were far harsher in word than in practice.

Americans in the first years of the nation were familiar with the new ideas on criminal justice taking hold in Europe. Beccaria's book had been published in New York City in 1773. In 1787 Dr. Benjamin Rush, a signer of the Declaration of Independence and surgeon general to the Continental Army, delivered an address at the home of Benjamin Franklin in Philadelphia. Rush called for an end to public executions as part of an overall reform of the criminal justice system. The same year he helped found the Philadelphia Society for Alleviating the Miseries of Public Prisons.

The society was instrumental in the development of the prison system in the United States. In 1790 the Walnut Street Jail in Philadelphia was converted into the nation's first modern penitentiary. The emergence of such penal institutions had a major impact on the use of capital punishment. Historically, one of the reasons societies had relied so heavily on the death penalty was that other punishment options sufficient to incapacitate serious offenders did not exist. The new prison facilities, funded by the state and staffed by professionals, changed this. For the first time, confinement became a realistic alternative punishment for many crimes.

Rush was the first prominent American to publicly urge the abolition of the death penalty. He published several influential essays in which he maintained that capital punishment was indefensible on either rational or religious grounds. Rush was joined by other legal reformers, most notably the state's attorney general, William Bradford, in a campaign to modernize Pennsylvania's criminal code. In 1794 the state became the first political entity to differentiate among degrees of homicide when it made first-degree murder its only capital offense.

Other states followed suit in a general movement to update the criminal law. Over the next two decades, state penitentiaries were constructed, and the number of capital offenses was cut considerably. While the efforts of those opposed to capital punishment helped make these reforms possible, the primary impetus for their implementation was the perceived need to curb excesses in the criminal justice system. The death penalty itself was widely accepted and remained in effect throughout the country.

THE FIRST AMERICAN ABOLITION MOVEMENT

Capital punishment in the United States has undergone many modifications since the early 1800s. Its use gradually has become more limited and constrained. However, the death penalty has endured as a basic fact of American jurisprudence. The debate over capital punishment throughout American history has been characterized by the struggle of a relative handful of groups and individuals to change the nation's broad and consistent support for the sanction.

The level of opposition has varied greatly. More often than not, its strength and success have been affected by other historical events.

The first concerted nationwide campaign against the death penalty took hold in the 1830s and 1840s. The movement initially formed around a desire to halt public executions. Public hangings of the time normally drew large crowds. Disturbed by the drunkenness and riots that often accompanied these events, by 1835 legislatures in five states had passed laws providing for private executions. A growing antigallows sentiment over the next 15 years caused another 10 states to enact similar measures.

This sentiment was fueled by a new generation of abolitionist leaders. Many had been inspired by the ideas and writings of the politician and lawyer Edward Livingston. In the early 1820s Livingston had drafted a new criminal code for the Louisiana Assembly that eliminated capital punishment. Although his proposals were not approved, his arguments against the death penalty were published and read throughout the nation.

The abolitionist cause was joined by such prominent reformers as Robert Rantoul, Jr., and John L. O'Sullivan and the writers John Greenleaf Whittier and Walt Whitman. The period also saw the formation of the first abolitionist organizations, most notably the American Society for the Abolition of Capital Punishment. The movement was effective in communicating its message to the American public. Written appeals, speeches, lectures, meetings, and debates were all part of the effort to generate understanding and support for abolitionist goals. Supporters William Cullen Bryant, editor of the *New York Post*, and Horace Greeley, founder of the *New York Tribune*, used their newspapers to reach a nationwide audience.

The campaign met with limited success. Maine implemented what was in effect a moratorium on executions in 1837. Ten years later, abolitionist forces achieved their most important victory to date when Michigan became the first state to completely abolish capital punishment. The sense that the movement was gaining momentum was short-lived, however. Although Rhode Island and Wisconsin repealed their death penalty statutes in the early 1850s, the attention of the country had turned elsewhere. After 1846, abolitionist activity faded as the Mexican War, the growing struggle over slavery, and the Civil War dominated the national agenda.

The diminished abolitionist movement made little real headway in the decades following the Civil War. Led by the dedicated reformer Marvin H. Bovee, opponents of capital punishment were able to persuade many state legislatures that mandatory death sentences for certain crimes should be replaced by discretionary sentencing procedures. By the 1890s, 21 states had switched to discretionary capital sentences. The abolitionists had believed that, given the option, courts would be more lenient in their sentencing patterns. In practice, the actual number of executions did not drop as juries continued to impose the death sentence.

Capital Punishment

The Progressive Era around the turn of the 20th century witnessed a burst of renewed abolitionist activity. In 1897 Congress approved a measure submitted by Representative Newton M. Curtis (R-N.Y.) that reduced the number of federal capital offenses to four. The first years of the 20th century saw a rejuvenation of abolitionist organizations. The ranks of capital punishment opponents included representatives from the new field of penology. The development of a more scientific approach to understanding criminal behavior contributed to the general inclination of the time for criminal law reform. Between 1907 and 1917, eight states repealed capital punishment, bringing the total number of abolitionist states to 12, or one-quarter of the Union.

CAPITAL PUNISHMENT AS STATUS QUO: THE 1920S TO THE 1950S

Abolitionist gains were halted by America's entry into World War I and then reversed. Historians believe that a series of sensational crimes in the years just after the war caused the reinstatement of the death penalty in four states. Members of the law enforcement community moved to the forefront of efforts to retain capital punishment.

Since the early 1920s, an interesting pattern has emerged in the debate over capital punishment. Certain kinds of events have tended to build support for the death penalty and others to generate opposition to the sanction. Not surprisingly, public support for capital punishment has been highest in the aftermath of particularly horrid or brazen crimes. Conversely, controversial executions have led to an upsurge in abolitionist activity.

In 1924 the renowned lawyer Clarence Darrow, an ardent foe of capital punishment, undertook to defend two young men, Nathan Leopold and Richard Loeb, accused of killing a neighborhood child. His stirring plea against their execution, which ultimately resulted in terms of life imprisonment, inspired abolitionists across the country. The following year Darrow, Sing Sing prison warden Lewis E. Lawes, and other leading opponents of the death penalty formed the American League to Abolish Capital Punishment. Membership picked up dramatically two years later following the execution of the Italian-born anarchists Sacco and Vanzetti. Supporters of the two men, alleging their murder convictions were politically motivated, fought an unsuccessful six-year legal battle to reverse their sentences. Their executions sparked worldwide protests. A picture secretly taken by a news photographer during the electrocution of Ruth Snyder in 1928 also raised many doubts as to the wisdom of capital punishment.

The revitalized abolitionist activity was quickly matched by growing cries for greater use of the death penalty. These pleas were driven by widespread alarm over a rise in violent crime. The St. Valentine's Day Massacre in 1929 became a symbol of the gangster violence of the Prohibition period. The kidnapping and murder of the Lindbergh baby in 1932 led to both federal and numerous state statutes making kidnapping a capital offense. In the wake of violent crime sprees

10

in their states, Kansas and then South Dakota legislators restored the death penalty.

As the United States entered World War II, the federal government and 42 of the 48 states had authorized capital punishment. This status did not change for almost 20 years. During this time, there was no real debate over the merits of the death penalty as the nation was preoccupied with the difficult challenges of the war, its cold war aftermath, and the conflict in Korea. The execution of Julius and Ethel Rosenberg for espionage in 1953 met with opposition, but at issue were their death sentences rather than the death penalty itself.

As the 1950s progressed, however, there was some resurgence of interest in the death penalty issue. The catalyst for resumed abolitionist efforts was the publication in 1954 of *Cell 2455 Death Row* by California death row inmate Caryl Chessman. The book, which characterized the prison system as a virtual school for crime and condemned the death penalty as little more than an act of vengeance, provoked a sympathetic response. Chessman, who published two more books about death row before his eventual execution in 1960, became a celebrated author as well as an international cause célèbre. His case served to galvanize a new affiliation of organizations and individuals opposed to capital punishment.

The territories of Alaska and Hawaii ended the death penalty in 1957. The following year, Delaware became the first state in 40 years to abolish capital punishment. In 1959 the American Law Institute, in its Model Penal Code, proposed significant changes in the way capital punishment was administered in the criminal justice system. Campaigns were mounted to eliminate the death penalty in California, New Jersey, Ohio, and Oregon.

In each state, however, abolitionist forces were unable to convince a majority of the public that the death penalty should go. Law enforcement organizations and officials, political figures, and others in favor of retaining capital punishment frequently cited statistics showing a steady increase in violent crime. In 1961 Delaware restored the death penalty after a series of highly publicized murders of elderly citizens. The same year Congress added skyjacking to the list of federal capital offenses.

THE FIRST LEGAL CHALLENGES

Historically, opponents of capital punishment had worked to eliminate the practice through the legislative repeal of death penalty statutes. To even the most optimistic abolitionist, though, it was increasingly evident there was little chance capital punishment would be ended through the legislative process in the foreseeable future. But as the strength of the civil rights movement grew during the early 1960s, it inspired a major switch in tactics on the part of the abolitionist movement. This shift was led by a small group of lawyers at the NAACP's Legal Defense and Education Fund (LDF). The new strategy was to move the struggle over capital punishment to the judicial arena.

Capital Punishment

The LDF was established in 1939 as a nonprofit organization to litigate civil rights issues and provide legal services to the poor. LDF lawyers were deeply involved in the civil rights movement, particularly in the South, where they frequently represented black defendants accused of capital crimes. Firsthand experience with the criminal justice system had convinced many of the attorneys that the death penalty was unfair and unworkable as well as morally wrong.

By 1965, the LDF, under director Jack Greenberg, had launched a nationwide legal attack on capital punishment. The immediate goal was to block every execution in America through a combination of lawsuits, appeals, and other court actions. At the same time LDF lawyers, headed by law professor Anthony G. Amsterdam, undertook a series of test cases designed to challenge the constitutionality of the death penalty. Their hope was that the Supreme Court would consent to hear one or more of these cases, rule the death penalty unconstitutional, and thus in one stroke outlaw capital punishment in the United States.

The LDF was subsequently joined by the American Civil Liberties Union (ACLU) and other legal organizations committed to ending the death penalty. Within two years, a coordinated series of legal actions across the country had achieved a freeze on executions in the United States. For the first time since the federal government started keeping statistics in 1930, no one was put to death in 1968. The moratorium continued over the next four years as the courts struggled to resolve the different legal challenges raised against capital punishment.

The legal campaign to have the death penalty declared unconstitutional seemingly had succeeded in 1972. In *Furman v. Georgia*, the Supreme Court struck down the nation's capital punishment laws. As Justice William O. Douglas noted in his opinion (and quoting former Attorney General Ramsey Clark):

> *It is the poor, the sick, the ignorant, the powerless, and the hated who are executed. . . . [The law] leaves to the uncontrolled discretion of judges and juries the determination of whether defendants committing these crimes should die or be imprisoned. . . . These discretionary statutes are unconstitutional.*

The court found that the statutes as written permitted the death penalty to be imposed in an arbitrary and capricious manner in violation of the Eighth Amendment's ban on cruel and unusual punishment.

The decision met with immediate criticism. President Richard Nixon and California governor Ronald Reagan were two of the most outspoken of the many political figures across the nation who denounced the ruling as an unwarranted intrusion on the prerogatives of the legislative branch of government. The Supreme Court was characterized as thwarting the will of the majority as expressed through its elected representatives. The Court, it was argued, had usurped to itself the right to make rather than interpret law.

Introduction to Capital Punishment

SALVAGING THE DEATH PENALTY

What seemed to be a sweeping abolitionist triumph would prove to be short lived. In *Furman*, the Court had not gone so far as to rule that capital punishment itself was unconstitutional but only that the haphazard way in which it was administered was constitutionally impermissible. Many states moved quickly to amend their capital punishment laws to conform to the procedural guidelines outlined in the *Furman* decision. In 1976, these revised laws received their crucial test when the case of *Gregg v. Georgia* reached the Supreme Court. In their decision, the justices held that the new statutes provided sufficient safeguards to ensure that the death penalty was employed in a constitutionally acceptable manner. The Court's ruling thus reinstated capital punishment in America. The nation's first execution in 10 years took place in January 1977 when Gary Gilmore was put to death in Utah by a firing squad.

Since that time, the Supreme Court has reaffirmed the principles in its *Gregg* decision and has failed to find any constitutional defect broad enough to sweep away all the state and federal death penalty statutes. However, as will be described later, the Court has invalidated a number of individual aspects of death penalty statutes on various grounds for not meeting the high standard of fairness and due process that is required before the ultimate sanction is imposed.

THE MODERN ABOLITION MOVEMENT

The failure to achieve a legal knockout of capital punishment also meant that abolitionists would return to the political arena. The death penalty was a major issue in the 1988 presidential campaign, where Republican George H. W. Bush attacked Democrat Michael Dukakis for being an opponent of capital punishment. During the 1990s, the number of executions would climb along with the crime rate. Political support for capital punishment was strong enough to compel leaders to demonstrate their public support for the sanction, such as when Arkansas governor and presidential candidate Bill Clinton interrupted his campaigning in 1992 in New Hampshire to return to the statehouse and deny the final appeal for clemency on behalf of Ricky Ray Rector, a man apparently suffering from serious brain damage.

Abolitionists have responded to this climate by organizing vigorously. In 1976, following the restoration of capital punishment, participants in the ACLU's Capital Punishment Project formed a new umbrella organization, the National Coalition to Abolish the Death Penalty (NCADP). Formed as a resource, coalition, and support agency for a nationwide campaign against capital punishment, the coalition now numbers about 140 affiliated organizations. A substantial number of the members are religious organizations. Most of the nation's major religious denominations have voiced their opposition to capital punishment. Additionally, many civil rights groups have long condemned what they view as the discriminatory manner in which the death penalty is disproportionately imposed on minorities in general and blacks in particular.

13

Today, like many other types of activists, death penalty abolitionists have taken to the World Wide Web, where even a small local group with limited resources can have a significant public presence, as well as forging links to kindred souls. In addition to the groups with an explicit agenda, there are also a variety of academics and others who compile news, research findings, and explore other resources on the death penalty. One of the largest sites belongs to the Death Penalty Information Center.

THE DEATH PENALTY PRO AND CON

As high-profile media coverage and the ongoing efforts of determined abolitionist groups have continued in recent years, certain basic issues surrounding capital punishment have been raised again and again. Proponents of the sanction focus on the need to deter crime, protect society, and promote a sense of proper retribution for the most serious crimes. Opponents, besides challenging these justifications for capital punishment, argue that the practice is unfair, cruel, expensive, and irreversible.

DETERRENCE

Deterrence is the idea that punishments imposed by society for criminal activity discourage its members from engaging in such behavior. Advocates of capital punishment contend that fear of death deters people from committing murder and other serious crimes. The average person will think twice before running the risk of possible execution. In addition, the death penalty is viewed by some as the only sanction severe enough to keep professional criminals from taking part in violent acts.

Deterrence is the most frequently made and most widely accepted argument in favor of the death penalty. It has generated intense debate and controversy. Opponents of capital punishment have attacked the deterrent value of the death penalty on a number of grounds.

They argue first that there is no conclusive evidence the death penalty has any impact on the rate of violent crime. At the least, they suggest, capital punishment is no more effective a deterrent than prolonged incarceration. Numerous studies have been conducted to gauge the actual effectiveness of the death penalty as a deterrent. Most often, murder rates are examined in states that have abolished capital punishment, or in states that have recently reinstated the sanction. The rate of murders prior to abolition or reinstatement is compared to the rate in subsequent years. The problem with this methodology is that many other variables can be involved. A general rise in the crime rate, a change in the state's demographics, or new types of violent crimes, such as gang wars, may complicate the picture. At any rate most experts agree that studies to date have not been able to conclusively show any specific deterrent value of capital punishment.

Abolitionists also stress that with deterrence, the certainty of punishment is much more important than the severity. Any fear of death is diminished, they contend, by the long delays between conviction and execution, the fact that death sentences are carried out in private, and the relatively low number of executions. Some proponents suggest that if this is a problem, it is caused by the abolitionists' own efforts to block executions by any means possible, and that the solution is to streamline the process and allow the number of executions to reach the point where the risk to the individual criminal is significant. But abolitionists, in turn, question whether Americans would truly want to live in a society where hundreds of people were executed each month rather than each year.

Abolitionists cite statistics showing that in a majority of murders the killer knew the victim. A rational consideration of future penalties has little or no bearing on situations where murders occur as a result of family quarrels or other emotional disturbances. Proponents respond that the death penalty is not applicable to these kinds of homicide but to premeditated first-degree murder. Crimes such as killing a police officer or a rival drug dealer are those which are said to be deterred by capital punishment. Public opinion has also reflected some erosion in support for the deterrence theory. A 2004 Harris poll found that while more than two-thirds of the population still supported the death penalty (at least for some cases), only 41 percent believed it was an effective crime deterrent.

If one assumes that capital punishment does produce some deterrence, another question that arises is how much more deterrence does capital punishment provide than another severe sanction such as life in prison without possibility of parole. How many of the "rational" criminals who would be deterred by death would not be deterred by the prospect of spending a lifetime in prison? This "incremental deterrence" also proves difficult to measure.

Finally, abolitionists argue that even if the deterrent effect of the death penalty were established, this would not in itself justify retaining capital punishment. They point out that if, as retentionists say, the specter of electrocution or lethal injection deters murder, then logically it should follow that burning at the stake or drawing and quartering would be even more effective at discouraging potential killers. But society has long renounced these methods of execution as barbaric. From the abolitionist perspective, if society can forego the deterrent value of these means of executions, its "evolving standard of decency" (frequently cited by the Supreme Court) ought to impel it to do without more modern, but still uncivilized, ways of putting people to death.

PROTECTING SOCIETY

In addition to deterrence there is the related concept of social protection. Both advocates and opponents of capital punishment agree that society has a right to protect itself from criminal activity. The debate is over the effectiveness of the death penalty as one of the means of protection.

Proponents claim that by imposing the death sentence for certain offenses, the law is sending a clear message about types of behavior that will not be tolerated. Capital punishment is a statement by society that it is willing and able to protect itself from brutal, violent crimes. The educational value of the death penalty is also noted. By defining premeditated murder as a capital offense, the law serves to develop a general abhorrence for the crime.

Abolitionists maintain that the selective and often arbitrary way in which the death penalty is administered undermines any message its use may be meant to deliver. They contend that death sentence statistics reveal that the criminal justice system disproportionately singles out the least advantaged members of society for execution. Those who are wealthier, more educated, and more socially connected rarely, if ever, receive the death penalty. In their view the message actually conveyed is that America has two standards of justice.

Finally, another aspect of social protection cited by death penalty advocates is its ability to incapacitate most violent offenders, ensuring that they can never commit another brutal crime. Opponents counter that the rate of recidivism, or return to criminality, among convicted murderers is very low. Moreover, dangerous individuals are just as incapacitated by life imprisonment without parole as by death. Further, modern "super-max" prisons can isolate the most violent offenders and minimize the chance they can harm guards or other inmates. (However, conditions in these institutions are themselves the subject of human rights concerns.)

RETRIBUTION

Retribution refers to the penalty a society exacts for wrongful behavior. It is the idea that persons should pay for their crimes.

The criminal law of a society reflects its value system or moral code. Proponents of capital punishment believe that the law should place less value on the life of a convicted murderer than on the life of an innocent victim. The law recognizes the necessity of this kind of distinction, justifying killings committed in self-defense or during the arrest of a dangerous felon. They conclude that the state has the right to execute certain grievous offenders in order to uphold and preserve greater societal values. This can be viewed both as a form of collective self-defense and as a declaration that the only fit restitution for taking a life in cold blood is the giving up of one's own life.

Proponents insist that there is no valid substitute for the death penalty. More serious offenses should be met with more severe penalties. If varying lengths of imprisonment are used to punish all crimes, then society risks losing sight of the distinction between murder and misappropriation of funds. Proponents insist that retribution is not revenge. The individual desire for revenge has been replaced in modern society by a concept of lawful punishment. It is important that the penalty for a crime fulfills society's sense that justice has been served. For certain horrifying and heinous crimes such as the September 11, 2001 attacks or the cruel dragging death of a black man or the brutal beating of a gay man in a hate crime, only the execution of the offender will satisfy the public that justice has been attained. Furthermore, continuing failure to satisfy the public's sense of justice may well lead to loss of respect for authority and persons taking justice into their own hands, such as through lynching.

Opponents of the death penalty do agree that retribution is an essential part of justice. However, the penalties imposed by society should not be based on vindictive or bloodthirsty motives that really amount to revenge masquerading as retribution. In a civilized society, the brutal nature of violent crime should not determine the limits of appropriate punishments. To do so would be to brutalize society itself. They contend that long periods of confinement will meet society's need for justice, while affording the offender some opportunity to become rehabilitated and possibly provide some form of restitution, however inadequate. Indeed, rehabilitation and restitution are hallmarks of an alternative view called "restorative justice," which is embraced by many religious opponents of capital punishment. In this view, the primary object of justice is to restore or repair the gaping wounds that have been inflicted by a heinous crime. Restorative justice thus focuses on having the offender take responsibility for his or her actions and use a lifetime in prison to work to provide some restitution to the victim's survivors and some good to society. The families of murder victims should also be provided with financial help, counseling, and other resources to help them resume meaningful, productive lives.

In an argument that parallels their attack on the deterrent value of capital punishment, abolitionists reiterate that the death penalty is not imposed in a uniform manner. Society is not protecting higher values or distinguishing between the relative seriousness of different offenses if it executes one person for murder but spares another for the same crime.

PROPORTIONALITY

Retribution also involves the issue of proportionality. In simple terms, the sentence should fit the crime. As for capital punishment, is death ever warranted as a penalty? If so, are there only certain crimes that merit its imposition?

Opponents of capital punishment would obviously answer no to the first question and thus consider the second question to be irrelevant. From the abolitionist perspective, an eye for an eye or a life for a life is neither a sound nor a workable principle of criminal justice. Punishments should correspond to the moral culpability of the offender, not the harm suffered by the victim.

Advocates of capital punishment point out, however, that moral culpability is related under the law to the impact a crime has on a victim. A person who commits murder is guilty of a more serious offense than an individual who merely injures another. Proponents maintain that death is the only form of retribution that matches the grievousness of certain crimes. Proponents are less in agreement about whether serious crimes that do not involve killing should nevertheless be subject to the death penalty. (In recent years, American courts have tended to restrict capital punishment to crimes that involve homicide, but the issue remains unresolved.)

BARBARITY

While opponents of capital punishment have tended to react to the arguments of proponents with regard to the social necessity of the death penalty, abolitionists also have taken the offensive by insisting that capital punishment, in any form and used for any reason, is inherently barbaric. The infliction of death, they maintain, has no place in an enlightened society. An execution, no matter how swift and painless, is still psychological, if not physical, torture. As opponents also observe, no method of execution is foolproof. For example, during the electrocution of Pedro Medina on March 25, 1997, a malfunction caused sparks, flame, and smoke to erupt from his head. Lethal injection has also run into problems when the condemned person, because of drug abuse, no longer has an easily accessible vein. Many abolitionist publications contain graphic accounts of such botched executions that caused evident pain and suffering to the condemned.

It is alleged that capital punishment brutalizes a society. Executions are seen as a form of institutionalized violence. In this view, use of the death penalty accustoms a society to violence, upholds violence as a way to solve social problems, and hardens people to the suffering of others.

Proponents counter that it is violent, wanton crime that tears apart the social fabric. Abolitionists are criticized for seeming at times to be concerned with the punishment of criminals but indifferent to the impact their actions have on society. The fact a given punishment may cause a prisoner anguish is not sufficient reason to abandon its use. After all, a life sentence without parole is also likely to produce anguish and psychological torture.

PUBLIC OPINION AND DEMOCRACY

The shifting debates over capital punishment are also reflected in surveys of public opinion, and thus in political pressure on lawmakers. Despite some recent erosion in support, most Americans still favor capital punishment, at least in some circumstances. Proponents of capital punishment often point to this continuing support to suggest that the death penalty reflects a democratic decision that should be respected.

Abolitionists respond in several ways. First, they assert that if capital punishment has become unconstitutional under evolving standards of cruelty or fairness, then the Constitution must prevail. That is, the democratic will of the people is limited by what the Constitution (as ultimately interpreted by the Supreme Court) says is permissible.

Further, death penalty opponents believe that enlightened public policy should lead public opinion on issues of justice and the law. If the best evidence from sociology, criminology, penology, and related fields shows that capital punishment is unfair, ineffective, and unnecessary and can be replaced by alternative forms of sentencing, then it should be eliminated.

Persons sharing this view tend to discount shifting public opinion as reflected in polls. They point to a correlation between the crime rate, perceived fear of crime or social instability, and support for capital punishment. Whether arising from the Red Scares of the 1920s and 1950s or the war on terrorism today, they believe fear should not be used as a justification for retaining failed policies.

Abolitionists also suggest that if the public were more informed about capital punishment and its alternatives, then the sanction's popularity would diminish significantly.

Death penalty advocates characterize these views as elitist and self-righteous. In a democracy, citizens, through their elected representatives, have the right and duty to determine the appropriateness of a given punishment. Judges and other experts who may not have personally experienced the devastation of violent crime should not function as self-appointed arbiters of right and wrong. Public opinion polls simply document the decision that the public continues to make, and that is reflected in the enactment and continued use of the death penalty across the nation. Retentionists also accuse abolitionists of hypocrisy. They note that in the 1960s, when surveys indicated an almost evenly divided public on the issue of capital punishment, abolitionists were quick to cite the results.

A number of abolitionists, while sharing the perception the public is uninformed about the realities of the capital punishment system, stop short of discounting the importance of public opinion to the functioning of the criminal justice system. They believe that they must continue the long struggle to educate and persuade a majority of Americans that the death penalty is unworkable and wrong. As this occurs, they expect the nation to gradually abandon capital punishment and they believe that this is already happening as the 21st century begins. Indeed, in 2004, only 125 death sentences were issued, the lowest number since the Supreme Court allowed capital punishment to resume in 1977.

EXECUTING THE INNOCENT?

The risk of executing an innocent person is generally considered the strongest practical argument against capital punishment. Abolitionists condemn the death penalty for its irreversibility. The death sentence, once carried out, is irrevocable. If society executes an innocent prisoner, there is no way to undo the error. In contrast, imprisonment always leaves the possibility of overturning a wrongful conviction. Although years lost to incarceration cannot be restored, it is possible to make some sort of compensation (although this is seldom done).

The possibility that innocent persons may be sentenced to death certainly exists. In 1987 professors Hugo Adam Bedau and Michael L. Radelet, both strong opponents of capital punishment, published in the *Stanford Law Review* a detailed study of death sentences in 20th-century America. They concluded that, between 1900 and 1985, 349 persons were incorrectly convicted of capital offenses and 23 innocent prisoners were actually executed. Abolitionists cite this and later studies, and the instances of persons wrongly sentenced since 1973 in particular, as proof that no amount of procedural safeguards can ensure that innocent persons will not be executed.

DNA HAS ITS SAY

The development of increasingly sensitive and sophisticated DNA testing of crime scene evidence in the 1990s has added an important new factor to the debate over the extent to which innocent persons may have been executed. Largely because of new DNA tests that failed to tie them to the crime for which they were convicted, 116 persons on death row have been exonerated and released between 1977 and 2004. (This compares to 928 persons executed during the same period.) Advocates (including volunteer groups of law students) continue to file legal petitions to obtain DNA tests for inmates, often facing obstacles such as uncooperative officials and decaying evidence that may be decades old.

Should every inmate for whom there is appropriate evidence be entitled to at least one DNA test using the most modern techniques? Many prosecutors oppose such a policy. Oregon prosecutor Josh Marquis, co-chairman of the capital litigation committee of the National District Attorneys Association, argues that

> *There are circumstances where enough is enough after going through 15 years of appeals. At some point there has to be finality. They have no disincentive for stopping. . . . In most of these cases, it's the last-ditch effort, the Hail Mary pass.*[3]

Many prosecutors are concerned about the cost of the tests but also argue that there has to be some finality in the legal process. There will always be improvements in forensic science, so what is to stop death penalty opponents from launching endless appeals and bogging down the system until it collapses under the weight?

Opponents of capital punishment reply that there is nothing worse than applying the ultimate sanction to an innocent person. They argue that no possible advantage of the death penalty can outweigh such an injustice. Further, a few cases where the prisoner has already been executed were reexamined in 2004 by DNA testing. There is a good chance that a few posthumous exonerations may give death penalty opponents proof that innocent people have indeed been executed. Richard Dieter, director of the Death Penalty Information Center, believes that:

> *There is no question that [such exonerations] could have a significant impact on the system. By putting a human face on a huge mistake, hesitation of the death*

penalty could turn into opposition—not because people morally perceive it as wrong but because they would see the system is flawed.[4]

However, thus far the growing perception that "the system is flawed" has not yet translated into a decisive rejection of the death penalty. In a July 2001 Harris poll, for example, an overwhelming majority of respondents said they believed that innocent persons were sometimes executed—indeed, on average they estimated that one in eight executed persons were innocent. However, although only 36 percent of respondents said they would continue to support capital punishment if a "substantial" number of innocent persons were being executed, apparently a majority still do not believe that this is the case.

Proponents make three additional points in rebuttal. They dispute the work of Bedau, Radelet, and others, saying that they overstate the number of cases where persons were demonstrably, factually innocent. They argue that the extensive safeguards now surrounding a capital trial in fact do work. The recent instances where it was found that innocent persons were sentenced to death, and their sentences overturned while they waited on death row, are taken as evidence of the effectiveness of the criminal justice system in catching such errors. Finally, they insist that even the theoretical possibility (indeed, likelihood) that at least a few innocent prisoners are being put to death is not sufficient grounds to abandon the death penalty. After all, innocent persons are also occasionally killed as a result of accidents during hot pursuits by police or by errors in judgment by law enforcement officers. Just as this is not a reason to abandon law enforcement, execution of the innocent is not a reason to abandon capital punishment. Society cannot place its concern for the wrongly condemned person above its legitimate and compelling interest in administering the death sentence for heinous crimes. Of course it is just the "compelling" nature of this societal interest that abolitionists challenge on all grounds discussed throughout this chapter.

FAIRNESS, CLASS, AND RACE

One of the most complex aspects of the debate over capital punishment is the question of fairness. The issues involved go to the very structure and nature of the American criminal justice system and invoke some of the most apparently intractable problems in our society.

Abolitionists charge that the death penalty is not applied in an even remotely impartial manner in the United States. Because the way it is administered is so fundamentally unfair, the practice of capital punishment should be discontinued. Moreover, abolitionists assert that the discretion built into the criminal justice system makes it impossible to ever achieve a truly consistent and unbiased use of the sanction.

Opponents of capital punishment point first to the fact that the death penalty is disproportionately imposed on the less advantaged members of society. The poor, the uneducated, and the socially unacceptable are more likely to face execution than those of more privileged backgrounds.

Abolitionists contend that justice is not blind where the death sentence is concerned. Juries are less sympathetic to persons from society's lower strata. Those of lesser means do not have access to the same quality of defense counsel as persons who can afford private representation. Key procedural issues may be overlooked by an inexperienced or overworked public defender.

The problem of the uneven distribution of justice becomes even more pronounced in the case of racial minorities. Blacks in particular make up a much larger share of the death row population (42 percent, as of 2005) than the percentage of the population as a whole (about 12 percent in 2005).

Further, as shown in a study, by professors David Baldus, George Woodworth, and Charles Pulanski of 2,000 murders committed in Georgia during the 1970s the race of offender and victim strongly influenced the likelihood of a death sentence. In cases in which someone who was black was convicted of killing someone who was white, the death penalty was given 22 percent of the time. When both offender and victim were white, the death penalty rate was only 8 percent, and only 1 percent when both participants were black. When someone who was white killed someone who was black, the rate of being given the death penalty was only 3 percent.

Abolitionists cite such statistics as striking evidence that the racism that still infects American society is manifested in harsher penalties for blacks than for whites. More importantly, because the criminal justice system allows district attorneys, judges, and juries great latitude in determining the fate of a given prisoner, there is no way to guarantee that bias or prejudice does not play a part in the decision made.

Some advocates of the death penalty believe that the statistics may exaggerate the role of racism and that other factors (such as the differing proportions of different kinds of homicide, such as drug-gang murders or street robberies versus domestic murders) may account for blacks committing a higher proportion of murders that qualify for the death penalty.

In general, advocates argue that the procedural safeguards built into the process for capital cases, such as bifurcated trials and appellate review, will diminish the effect of remaining racism.

Furthermore, proponents reject the idea that allowing the criminal justice system the discretion necessary to reach an individualized determination in each case (as required by the Supreme Court) results in unfair verdicts. This assertion is seen as an attack on a fundamental principle of American jurisprudence. If it were true, then all punishments arrived at under current procedures, and not just death sentences, potentially would have to be abandoned as fatally flawed. Rejecting the notion that capital sentences are inherently unfair, proponents stress the need for full enforcement of the safeguards already in place.

EXPENSE

The issue of expense has been another factor in the debate over capital punishment. It is commonly assumed that it costs less to execute a person than it does to imprison that individual for life. The reverse, however, is true.

As Richard Dieter of the Death Penalty Information Center notes:

> *There is no doubt that the death penalty costs more in all the steps leading up to an execution. Everything that is needed for an ordinary trial is needed for a death penalty case, only more so:*

> - *more pre-trial time will be needed to prepare: cases typically take a year to come to trial*
> - *more pre-trial motions will be filed and answered*
> - *more experts will be hired*
> - *probably two attorneys will be appointed for the defense, and a comparable team for the prosecution, compared to one in a non–death penalty case*
> - *jurors will have to be individually quizzed on their views about the death penalty*
> - *they are more likely to be sequestered*
> - *two trials instead of one will be conducted: one for guilt and one for punishment*
> - *the trial will be longer: the cost study at Duke University estimated that death penalty trials take 3 to 5 times longer than typical murder trials*
> - *and then will come a series of appeals during which the inmates are held in the high security of death row.*

> *It is only after an execution that the death penalty might actually cost less than a non–death penalty system. However, few cases result in execution, so the savings are relatively small.[5]*

Dieter points out that while executing someone permanently ends the state's expense for dealing with that person, only about 10 percent of cases with a death sentence actually result in execution—most are eventually overturned on appeal or converted to life sentences. As a result, putting large numbers of defendants through the death penalty process is much more costly than sentencing them to life in the first place.

Death row facilities where defendants often wait execution for 10 years or longer require more money to staff and maintain than regular prison facilities. The result is that capital cases are significantly more expensive over their entire course than cases of serious felonies that don't involve the death penalty. As a result, incarceration of a prisoner for 40 years is substantially less costly than going through the full legal process necessary to put a person to death.

Many localities are having difficulty meeting the costs involved in capital cases. Recognizing the growing concern over the availability of funding for the criminal justice system, the abolitionist movement has argued that capital punishment doesn't make economic sense. Instead of dedicating scarce resources to executing a relative handful of prisoners, it would be more worthwhile to sentence capital offenders to long prison terms and use the money saved to fully fund efforts such as victim-assistance programs.

Many advocates of the death penalty label these arguments as insincere. In their view, the high costs of capital punishment that abolitionists cite are due to the inordinate number of appeals filed by the abolitionists themselves as part of their campaign to block executions. Other proponents accept that procedural safeguards involved in capital punishment are necessarily more expensive, but insist that capital punishment's importance to the administration of justice is such that it should be underwritten regardless of the cost.

RELIGIOUS ARGUMENTS

From the earliest times religion has always been enlisted on both sides of the capital punishment debate. At least through the 19th century, the majority of Christians saw the death penalty as not only sanctioned by God, but even required by biblical injunctions. After all, Genesis 9:6 states that "Whosoever sheddeth a man's blood, so shall his blood be shed." (King James Version.) Most major American religious denominations thus supported capital punishment although the Quakers (Society of Friends) were staunch opponents of the death penalty as they were of war and other forms of violence.

By the middle of the 20th century, however, many mainstream churches had begun to reflect a more liberal theology that emphasized Jesus' message of forgiveness and redemption. The growing Civil Rights movement and concern over social issues also led to Christian (and Jewish) activists seeing capital punishment in the context of racial injustice and inequality.

Catholics in particular began to move to an anti–capital punishment stance. Finally, in 1995 Pope John Paul II's encyclical *Evangelium Vitae* (The gospel of life) demanded what has been called a "consistent pro-life ethic" that condemns capital punishment along with abortion, euthanasia, and unjustified war. According to many Catholic activists, capital punishment is part of a "culture of death" that sees violence as an expedient solution to social problems.

Although many conservative or fundamentalist denominations continued their strong support for the death penalty, the pending execution of "born again" murderer Karla Faye Tucker in 1999 in Texas brought appeals from both Pope John Paul II and prominent fundamentalist leader Reverend Pat Robertson.

LEGAL ISSUES: CAN IT BE FAIR?

Many of the political, social, and moral issues discussed in the previous section find their counterparts in the arena of the courtroom. The legal world, however, has its own strict, complex procedures for resolving questions of crime and punishment.

Capital punishment is inseparable from the law. The law defines the death penalty, authorizes its use, and specifies the circumstances under which it can be applied. Before considering the many legal issues that have arisen concerning capital punishment, it is useful to give a quick overview of the criminal justice system itself.

THE CRIMINAL JUSTICE SYSTEM

Capital punishment cannot exist outside of a criminal justice system. A person may kill another to avenge a wrong, but this is an act of private revenge. The idea of punishment implies there is an established standard of behavior to which persons are able and expected to conform. It suggests, as well, that society has both a means to determine whether a person has violated this standard and what penalties should be applied, depending on the infraction. The basic judicial system required to impose a punishment is necessarily the product of an organized society.

In a modern political state, such as the United States, the rules governing unacceptable behavior are specified in the law. In America, the law has two components. The first is statutory law. This refers to the statutes, or laws, that are enacted by a legislature, which can range from the Congress of the United States all the way down to a town council. These laws reflect the public policy wishes of the people as expressed by their elected representatives. What crimes are and the penalties for these crimes are defined by the statutory law.

This law, however, does not function in a vacuum. The courts modify and shape the law as they apply it to specific cases. The legal rules fashioned by courts in the process of deciding cases is known as common law. This second component of American law evolves over time as judges refer to prior cases and the precedents set by other justices to help them determine the appropriate ruling to make in a given instance.

America also has two distinct sets of laws. Each state has its own unique body of laws passed by its legislature. Historically, the preponderance of criminal activity has been a matter for state law. State criminal codes address offenses such as murder, rape, and kidnapping—all of which have merited the death penalty in a majority of states at one time or another. Today, court decisions have eliminated state capital offenses that do not involve murder.

Federal law, which is enacted by the U.S. Congress, traditionally has dealt with crimes that cross state lines (such as some kidnappings) or that affect the federal government or interstate commerce. Such offenses have included espionage, assassination of the president or other high officials, and air piracy. In 1994, Congress considerably expanded the range of federal offenses subject to the death penalty, including drug-related offenses. These new capital offenses include murders involving such factors as bomb attacks on government facilities, denial of civil rights, kidnapping or hostage-taking, killing of federal witnesses or informants, bank robbery, carjacking, murder for hire, racketeering, drug-related drive-by shootings, and sexual molestation of children. (See Chapter 2, The Law of Capital Punishment, for more details about what is covered by federal and state capital crimes legislation.)

The courts are where determinations of guilt or innocence are made and punishments meted out to the convicted. Corresponding to the distinction between state and federal law, there are state and federal court systems. Both systems are organized like a pyramid, with local, lower courts at the bottom, appeals courts above them, and a supreme court at the very top.

In most states, criminal cases are heard in local trial courts. (In some jurisdictions, more serious offenses are tried in statewide criminal courts rather than at the local or county level.) The appellate level of courts is the first stage where appeals of trial court rulings are heard. The appellate courts normally are concerned with issues of law. The decisions of the trial courts on issues of fact (and thus of the actual guilt or innocence of the defendant) are almost always considered final.

The state supreme court is the highest court in the state system. It reviews appeals from the lower courts, most often in connection with state constitutional issues. A state's supreme court is the final authority on its constitution. However, the rights guaranteed in the federal Constitution (such as the right to due process in the Fifth Amendment, the ban on "cruel and unusual punishment" in the Eighth Amendment, and the right to equal protection of the laws in the Fourteenth Amendment) take precedence over state constitutions and statutes. When such a constitutional question or a question of conflict between federal and state law arises, state court rulings can be appealed to the federal court system.

The federal court system has a similar structure. The basic trial court is the federal district court. Each state has at least one federal district court. These courts hear both federal cases and appeals from state courts involving questions of federal law and the Constitution.

The next level, the U.S. Court of Appeals, handles appeals of the decisions of the district courts. The United States is divided into 12 circuits, each of which takes appeals from several districts in a particular region of the country. As with the state appeals courts, the focus is on interpretation of the law. Findings of fact are ordinarily presumed complete and are not reviewed.

The U.S. Supreme Court is the court of last resort for the nation. Its decisions are binding on all federal and state courts. The Supreme Court hears limited appeals from the lower federal courts and from the highest state courts where a federal question is presented. The Court has the authority, through

Introduction to Capital Punishment

judicial review, to strike down legislation that it deems unconstitutional. (In such cases legislators have only two recourses: they can either revise their statutes to conform with the Court's guidelines, or try to pass an amendment to the Constitution.)

WHAT IS A CAPITAL OFFENSE?

A capital case begins of course with the arrest of a person for a serious crime (nearly always, murder). The district attorney reviews the facts of the case and decides whether it meets the jurisdiction's definition of a capital crime. This means determining whether the murder is a first-degree murder (or equivalent) in which the offender acted with deliberate intent, rather than spontaneously (as in a "crime of passion"). The crime must also have one or more "aggravating circumstances" to raise it to the status of capital offense. Such circumstances are specified in state and federal statutes. Some typical aggravating circumstances include:

- The crime was particularly vile, atrocious, or cruel.
- There were multiple victims.
- The crime occurred during the commission of another felony.
- The victim was a police or correctional officer in the line of duty.
- The offender was previously convicted of a capital offense or violent crime.
- The offender directed an accomplice to commit the murder or committed the murder at the direction of another person.

The death penalty is imposed most often for murders committed during the course of another major felony. These homicides are usually termed felony murders. In most states there is no need for the prosecution to prove intent on the part of the killer in a felony murder. The law assumes that persons who engage in serious felonies are responsible for the consequences of their actions and the dangerous situations they create. Defendants who kill, even accidentally, in the course of another felony may be found guilty of first-degree murder. It is only necessary to show that the offender intended to commit the original crime.

Historically, many states held accomplices to a felony murder to be equally liable for the crime, even if they did not participate in the actual homicide. In 1982, however, the Supreme Court, in *Enmund v. Florida*, prohibited states from sentencing to death accomplices to a felony murder unless it was shown that the accomplices took part in the killing, intended that the killing occur, or were involved in the employment of lethal force. (The Court later broadened its rule to make a defendant who was intimately involved with the crime and who showed "reckless disregard" for the victim's life to be liable to capital punishment even if the defendant did not directly use force.)

Capital Punishment

A few states still have death penalty statutes for crimes not involving homicide, such as kidnapping and child rape. However, recent Supreme Court decisions linking the death penalty to offenses involving the death of the victim make it extremely unlikely anyone will ever be sentenced under these laws.

Federal law provides for the death penalty for murder under a variety of special circumstances, including air piracy (skyjacking), certain drug-related murders, and sexual assault against children.

THE ROLE OF THE JURY

Most defendants opt to have their case heard by a jury. During the jury selection process (called voir dire), prospective jurors will be asked their opinions on the death penalty. The courts have ruled that mere opposition to the death penalty is not sufficient for someone to be automatically excluded from the jury, but if a juror's opposition is strong enough that it might affect his or her ability to determine the defendant's guilt, the juror will be excluded.

If the defendant is convicted of a capital offense, the Supreme Court has decreed that there must be a separate hearing called the penalty phase. This is like a mini-trial in which the issue is not guilt or innocence, but whether the defendant is to be sentenced to death or to some lesser sanction (usually life in prison). As in the main trial, the prosecutor and defense counsel both make opening statements, introduce and examine witnesses, and make closing arguments. The prosecution will try to show the aggravating circumstances that justify imposing the ultimate penalty. These are similar to the circumstances that justify making a capital charge in the first place, but are usually presented in an attempt to show the defendant acted in a particularly cruel or depraved way. The defense counsel try to counter the aggravating circumstances by introducing mitigating circumstances, such as the defendant's youth, lack of previous criminal record, extreme emotional circumstances, or lack of direct involvement in the crime. (For more on statutory aggravating and mitigating circumstances, see Chapter 2, The Law of Capital Punishment.)

In general, defendants in the penalty phase are entitled to the same rights to review and confront evidence that they had in the guilt phase. In *Powell v. Texas* (1989), for example, the Supreme Court ruled that a psychiatric exam used to prove the defendant's competency to stand trial could not be used later as evidence of his "future dangerousness" without prior warning.

Assuming the jury imposes the death penalty (and, depending on the state, the judge approves the sentence), the postconviction appeals process begins. Capital punishment statutes provide for an automatic review of every death sentence by a state appeals court. If this court upholds the death penalty, the defendant still has two other possible avenues of appeal. The first is postconviction proceedings in the state court system. Normally, these appeals culminate in a ruling by the state's highest court. However, if federal questions of law are involved, the defendant has the right to petition the federal courts for review. Appeals based on issues of federal law have the potential to reach the Supreme Court, and this is how the major issues involving capital punishment are ultimately settled. This entire appeals process may, and almost invariably does, extend over a number of years, even with recent Supreme Court rulings that have cut down on the number of appeals allowed and the ways in which issues can be raised.

There are three other important elements of the criminal justice system as it pertains to capital punishment. In criminal trials, the government's case is presented by a prosecuting attorney. Prosecutors have a substantial amount of discretion in the performance of their duties. A criminal proceeding has a number of key decision points. These include what charges to bring, whether to plea bargain, and what sentence, if any, to offer a defendant in return for a guilty plea. The choices a prosecuting attorney makes in a potential capital trial have a direct impact on the likelihood of a person facing a possible death sentence.

The ability of the prosecutor to influence a capital proceeding is balanced, at least theoretically, by the defendant's right to legal representation. It is a basic tenet of American jurisprudence that each person accused of a crime is entitled to a defense counsel. The capabilities of the defense attorney can have a major bearing on the outcome of the trial.

Finally, there is the penal system. Prisons fulfill several obvious roles in the administration of capital punishment. The area in which prisoners are held pending their execution, commonly known as death row, has held a certain fascination in American culture and lore. Since the 1930s, executions in America have been carried out within the relative privacy of prison walls. Less readily apparent is the fact that the development of modern penal institutions has provided society a range of possible punishments for serious crimes. It would not be possible, for instance, to advocate mandatory life sentences in lieu of the death penalty if appropriate confinement facilities were not available.

CRUEL AND UNUSUAL?

The debate over capital punishment has been waged primarily in the judicial system. In a series of court cases extending from 1972 to about 1990 (with a few later refinements), the Supreme Court has effectively set the parameters of capital punishment in America today. Summaries of the most significant Supreme Court decisions are provided in Chapter 2. Presented here are the basic issues that have driven the legal struggle over the role of capital punishment in American society.

The most basic legal controversy centers on whether capital punishment is inherently constitutional. This issue raises an even more fundamental legal question. How is the constitutionality of any given law determined? Since the early 19th century, the Supreme Court has exercised a power of judicial review or what is in essence the authority to strike down statutes it deems unconstitutional. The Court has the final say as to whether a legal measure conforms to the Constitution. Two elements normally are necessary for the Supreme Court to declare a law unconstitutional. The first is a clear and convincing argument that the law violates a specific constitutional provision. Historically, the Court has been reluctant to rule against the expressed will of the legislative branch of government without a compelling reason to do so. Second, the constitutional provision must be applicable to the law in question.

Most of the constitutional challenges to the death penalty have been based on one or more of the first 10 amendments. When these amendments, the Bill of Rights, were added to the U.S. Constitution in 1791, it was with the understanding that they applied only to federal law. State laws were beyond their reach.

As legal challenges to capital punishment mounted in the 1960s, one of the first issues that had to be resolved was whether the Bill of Rights could appropriately be applied to state death penalty statutes. The answer was found in the Fourteenth Amendment. This amendment, which was passed in 1868 in the aftermath of the Civil War, stipulates that states shall not "deprive any person of life, liberty, or property, without due process of law." In the course of the 20th century, the Supreme Court gradually interpreted this due process clause as extending all the due process guarantees in the Constitution, the first 10 amendments included, to state laws. In other words, the Supreme Court was empowered to review state laws for adherence to the fundamental individual rights articulated in the Bill of Rights.

In 1972, in *Furman v. Georgia*, the Supreme Court did precisely this when it held that the nation's capital punishment laws, both federal and state, were in violation of the Eighth Amendment. The Court found that the arbitrary and capricious way in which the death penalty was administered constituted cruel and unusual punishment, which the amendment bans. The Court, however, did not rule that capital punishment itself was unconstitutional. Only the random and freakish employment of the death penalty, and not the sanction itself, was ruled constitutionally indefensible. Many states quickly revised their death penalty statutes to respond to the objections raised in the *Furman* decision. Four years later, in *Gregg v. Georgia*, the Court reinstated capital punishment, holding that the new death penalty statutes contained safeguards that would ensure the sanction's use in a rational and fair manner.

APPROPRIATE APPLICATION OF THE DEATH PENALTY

Since 1976, the Supreme Court has declined to reconsider the basic legality of capital punishment itself. Instead, the Court has concentrated on narrower (but still very important) constitutional questions: what crimes merit the death penalty, and which members of society, if any, are eligible to receive a death sentence.

The Supreme Court has emphasized that a punishment must be proportionate to the crime committed. In applying this standard to the death penalty, the Court has overturned capital punishment statutes that allowed the death penalty to be imposed for rape and kidnapping. The Court indicated that the death penalty was a disproportionate and excessive response to offenses that did not involve the death of the victim. In apparently restricting the death penalty to crimes involving homicide, the Court has raised doubts as to the constitutionality of capital punishment for offenses such as espionage and treason, or for some of the many capital crimes newly created by Congress during the 1990s. Whether the death penalty is disproportionate for all nonhomicidal crimes has yet to be litigated.

Another tenet of American jurisprudence that has guided the Supreme Court's thinking on the death penalty is the belief that punishment should be related to the culpability of the defendant. Within a legal context, culpability implies the ability to exercise and take responsibility for one's conduct. There is widespread consensus in American society that juveniles are not sufficiently mature or informed to be held fully accountable for their actions. This consensus would seem to be supported by studies suggesting that in adolescents the brain structures that support judgment and impulse control are still undergoing development. What happens when a still-developing brain also has to cope with rapid hormonal changes and an environment that can include heavy peer pressure toward involvement in sex and drugs, media that glorifies violence, and even victimization by bullies? Such factors may have contributed to tragedies such as the Columbine High School shootings in 1999. In turn, the very horror and brutality shown in high-profile crimes committed by young people can spur proponents of capital punishment to argue that only the death penalty can protect society from the worst offenders. As a result, a debate has been waged over the age at which a juvenile may be considered an adult for the purposes of a capital trial. In a series of controversial decisions on this issue, the Court effectively set the age of 16 as the minimum age at which a person can be held responsible and executed for criminal offenses.

The question of what to do with 16- and 17-year-old murderers remained. These older teenagers can certainly commit serious crimes. However, they are still legally considered minors and thus presumably not mature enough to drink, vote, or even enter into contracts.

In defending the execution of older juveniles, however, Alabama attorney general Troy King argued that:

A bright-line rule categorically exempting 16- and 17-year-olds from the death penalty—no matter how elaborate the plot, how sinister the killing, or how sophisticated the cover-up—would be arbitrary at best, and downright perverse at worst.[6]

During oral arguments in 2004, Justice Anthony M. Kennedy seemed sympathetic to this argument. He also expressed concern that if 16- and 17-year-olds were exempted from the death penalty, gangs would recruit them to carry out murders against rivals.

In its March 2005 ruling, however, a narrow 5-4 majority of the Court (led by Justice Kennedy) ruled that executing persons for crimes committed before age 18 was no longer compatible with the Eighth Amendment. The majority saw support for its conclusion in the virtual disappearance of the juvenile death penalty in other nations, and in the fact that most U.S. states have also rejected the practice. The Court majority also agreed with the argument that juveniles cannot be presumed to have enough maturity to have the full culpability required for imposing the ultimate penalty. The minority, led by Justice Antonin Scalia, accused the majority of paying too much attention to the views of other nations and of imposing its own sense of morality on the people of the United States rather than letting juries weigh the culpability of defendants according to the particular circumstances of the case.

The Court likewise has ruled that it is unconstitutional to execute persons who are insane. The development of guidelines governing the execution of the mentally retarded has proven to be more difficult. In *Penry v. Lynaugh* (1989) the Supreme Court went only so far as to say that for a mentally retarded person who had been declared competent to stand trial, his or her condition of diminished mental capacity must be taken into account as a possible mitigating factor. In *Atkins v. Virginia* (2002) the Court revisited the issue. Noting the growing number of states that had banned execution of mentally retarded persons, the majority decided that such executions were now "unusual" and unconstitutional under the Eighth Amendment.

Further, the Court noted that because of the diminished capacity (and culpability) of substantially mentally retarded persons, the objectives of retribution and deterrence sought through the death penalty were unlikely to be achieved. Such persons would go into the execution chamber without the ability to fully understand the significance of what was about to happen to them.

The constitutionality of different methods of execution has also been litigated. The basic issue here is whether a method of execution is cruel enough or inflicts gratuitous pain to the extent it violates the Eighth Amendment ban on cruel and unusual punishment. In 1890 the Supreme Court decided the use of the newly invented electric chair was not cruel and unusual punishment. Interestingly, in 1925 the federal government substituted electrocution for hanging because it was viewed as more humane. The 1920s also saw several unsuccessful challenges to the introduction of the gas chamber. Proponents of lethal gas defended it as a swift and painless method of execution. More recently, inmates facing death by lethal injection sought unsuccessfully to block the procedure on the novel grounds that the Food and Drug Administration (FDA) had not approved the fatal drugs to be used.

Despite some continuing challenges, the Supreme Court has consistently taken the position that a given method of execution is not unconstitutionally cruel if it does not involve torture, barbarism, or the infliction of unnecessary pain and suffering.

Introduction to Capital Punishment

THE DEATH PENALTY AND RACE

One of the major roots to the movement beginning in the 1960s to challenge the death penalty in the courts was the civil rights movement. The question of race in capital sentencing came to a head in 1987 with the case of *McCleskey v. Kemp*. In its decision, the Supreme Court turned aside arguments that capital punishment in the United States was administered in a racially discriminatory manner in violation of the Fourteenth Amendment's requirement that the law be applied in a nondiscriminatory manner to all citizens. These arguments were based on statistical evidence that showed that blacks were significantly more likely than whites to receive the death penalty for similar crimes. (Although opponents suggested that the studies underplayed the importance of comparing crimes with similar aggravating factors and defendants with similar criminal records.)

The Court accepted the general accuracy of the information but found that broad statistical studies were insufficient to prove racial discrimination in a given specific case. *McCleskey* raised a line of questioning that goes to the very core of the American criminal justice system. In its decision, the Supreme Court indicated that in order to establish that racism played a part in a person receiving a death sentence, it was necessary to prove actual discrimination in the case at hand. As several of the dissenting justices pointed out, that was much easier said than done. In their view, the wide discretion provided prosecutors, judges, and juries frequently served to mask and give scope to the institutional racism that still infects the criminal justice process. How is it possible to prove that a certain prosecutor is more likely to offer a plea bargain agreement to a white defendant than to a black defendant? The Court majority acknowledged this problem but suggested that short of changing the entire American system of justice, which was both unreasonable and undesirable, the best answer was to surround the administration of capital punishment with extensive procedural safeguards.

PROCEDURAL ISSUES

The net effect of the Supreme Court's major rulings on capital punishment has been twofold. It is clear that the death penalty, at least from a legal perspective, is likely to remain in some form. After affirming that capital punishment is itself constitutional, the Court has gone on to define more precisely the circumstances and conditions under which it may be imposed. The Court as it is currently constituted has shown no inclination to reverse this course. In dealing with the various broad constitutional challenges to the administration of the death penalty, the Court gradually removed the remaining legal obstacles to a full resumption of executions in the United States. It is generally agreed that there are few if any remaining legal arguments against the death penalty that will affect more than a relative handful of death row inmates.

In recent years, a great deal of the legal debate over capital punishment has centered on procedural questions. There are several reasons for this. First, and

33

most importantly, has been a growing recognition throughout the criminal justice system that the death penalty is substantively different from other criminal sanctions. This has meant an enhanced focus on the procedural safeguards necessary to ensure that capital punishment is administered in a fair and appropriate way. Secondly, as broad or far-reaching constitutional challenges to the death penalty were whittled down following the reinstatement of the sanction in 1976, the only recourse left to defense attorneys was to challenge their clients' death sentences on technical or procedural grounds.

The Supreme Court has long taken the position that death is different from other punishments. The irrevocable nature of the death penalty has caused the Court to pay particular attention to procedural safeguards in capital cases. As early as 1932, the Court ruled that an indigent defendant had the right to a lawyer in a capital trial—a right only later emphasized as belonging to criminal defendants in all cases. Since the reinstatement of the death penalty in 1976, the Court has insisted on clear and objective standards to guide the administration of capital punishment.

In response to Supreme Court rulings, death penalty statutes across the nation now share several features. They all require a bifurcated, or split, trial proceeding. The bifurcated trial, as discussed earlier in this chapter, separates the determination of guilt or innocence from the decision as to what penalty will be imposed. This is done to ensure a convicted defendant has an opportunity to present mitigating evidence prior to sentencing. Death penalty statutes also require an automatic review of every death sentence by an appeals court.

The Court has effectively barred mandatory capital punishment laws, holding that automatic death sentences for certain crimes do not allow for individualized consideration of all the circumstances involved in a particular case. This same reasoning has led the Court to maintain that trial courts must permit defendants to introduce a wide range of evidence concerning mitigating factors on their behalf.

Much contention has centered around the kinds of evidence the prosecution in a capital case should be allowed to introduce to argue for the appropriateness of the death penalty and to counteract any mitigating factors. Generally, the Court has required that aggravating factors introduced by the prosecution be more narrowly defined and more directly relevant to the question of sentencing. In addition, if the prosecution tries to show that a defendant is particularly violent and likely to be dangerous in the future, the Court requires that the jury also be informed of any state law that would prohibit releasing the defendant on parole—that is, that a true "life without parole" sentence is available.

Another kind of prosecution evidence, victim impact statements that seek to show the extent of the harm done by a murder to the victim's relatives, received less consistent treatment by the Court. In *Booth v. Maryland* (1987), a 5-4 majority ruled that victim impact statements were unconstitutional because a jury must make an "individualized determination" based on the offender's particular circumstances, not those of the victim. Further, the idea that the killing of victims who were well loved and considered to be particular assets to the community should be punished more harshly than the killing of persons considered to be more marginal in society was repugnant to the majority.

However, in the 1991 case of *Payne v. Tennessee,* a 6-3 majority of the Court reversed its earlier finding. The justices now looked at the broad principle that crimes that cause more harm are typically punished more severely. (A theft of $50 may be a petty theft, while a theft of $50,000 is grand larceny.) In this view, the victim impact statement is simply another piece of evidence that the jury can consider when weighing the seriousness of the offense against the mitigating factors.

The most contentious procedural issue today concerns the misuse of the appeals process. The sheer volume of death penalty appeals threatens to overwhelm the criminal justice system. This volume can partly be attributed to the steady growth in the size of the death row population. It is also due to a deliberate strategy on the part of many opponents of capital punishment. It is their hope that by paralyzing the appeals courts with an excess of legal actions, the nation will eventually conclude capital punishment is unworkable. Many observers have seen a fundamental contradiction between the Court's insistence on the one hand that jurors and judges have the broad discretion they need in order to give each defendant individualized consideration and on the other hand that patterns of capital sentencing be rational and consistent rather than arbitrary and capricious.

According to Jim Liebman, a professor of law at Columbia University, the problem of procedural errors in capital cases has persisted despite the best efforts of courts and advocates. In reviewing all 5,760 death sentences issued between 1973 and 1995, Liebman found that 41 percent of the sentences (2,360) had been overturned because of sentencing errors. In more than 300 of these cases, aggravating circumstances that had been relied upon in choosing a death sentence were found not to have existed. About a third of the cases were overturned because appeals courts found that the defendant's attorneys had not represented them effectively. In about a fifth of cases, the prosecution had withheld exculpatory evidence.

David Elliott of the National Coalition to Abolish the Death Penalty argues that no one wins in such cases:

> *Remember that people on death row have relatives, and those relatives are losing a loved one. And the victim's relatives have to live through years of trials and hearings. And then there's the prisoner, [. . .] If he's executed because of a sentencing error, that's terrible, but even if the error is eventually corrected, he has lived under the threat of death for years. We have seen these people, and afterwards many of them have something resembling post-traumatic stress disorder. They can't adjust to the reality that they aren't going to die.*[7]

In 1994, in his dissent in the case of *Callins v. Collins,* Supreme Court Justice Harry Blackmun declared that

Capital Punishment

From this day forward, I no longer shall tinker with the machinery of death. For more than 20 years I have endeavored . . . along with a majority of this Court, to develop procedural and substantive rules that would lend more than the mere appearance of fairness to the death penalty endeavor. Rather than continue to coddle the Court's delusion that the desired level of fairness has been achieved and the need for regulation eviscerated, I feel morally and intellectually obligated simply to concede that the death penalty experiment has failed. It is virtually self-evident to me now that no combination of procedural rules or substantive regulations ever can save the death penalty from its inherent constitutional deficiencies.

The majority of the Court, however, has not agreed that the search for a truly fair capital justice system is hopeless. Throughout the 1990s executions continued at an increasing rate. In its recent procedural decisions, the Court has narrowed the circumstances under which defendants can file habeas corpus petitions, the appeal enshrined in the common law to require that authorities "bring forth the body" of a prisoner so that a judge can inquire into a possible miscarriage of justice. Such litigation raises one of the most fundamental questions of all: can a person be executed if convincing evidence of his or her innocence emerges after conviction?

In the 1993 case of *Herrera v. Collins,* the Supreme Court ruled by a 7-3 majority that it was constitutional to execute the defendant without the appeals court having to reopen the question of guilt or innocence. In his majority opinion, Chief Justice Rehnquist pointed out that while a defendant starts the legal process with a "presumption of innocence," this presumption disappears after conviction. Appeals courts exist, he said, "to ensure that individuals are not imprisoned in violation of the Constitution—not to correct errors of fact." No doubt practical considerations also played a role in the decision. After all, if defendants had a right to raise endless appeals based on supposed new evidence of innocence, they could postpone their execution indefinitely as each appeal received due consideration.

However, executing someone after being confronted by convincing evidence of his or her innocence is repugnant to most people. Speaking for the minority, Justice Blackmun insisted that

The Eighth Amendment prohibits "cruel and unusual punishments." This proscription is not static but rather reflects evolving standards of decency. I think it is crystal clear that the execution of an innocent person is "at odds with contemporary standards of fairness and decency." . . . [T]he protection of the Eighth Amendment does not end once a defendant has been validly convicted and sentenced.

The upshot of this decision and those that followed is that there must be a constitutional error, not just new evidence, before an appeal will be considered. Further, the Court set a high standard for overturning a conviction due to an error that prevented consideration of evidence of innocence. The evidence must be so convincing that "no reasonable juror" would have voted to convict if the evidence had been presented to the jury.

It remains to be seen whether the current wave of exonerations of death row prisoners on the basis of DNA tests will cause the Supreme Court to revisit this issue. Certainly, if such tests offer the opportunity to resolve the question of guilt or innocence once and for all, this may overcome the reluctance to allow a seemingly endless judicial process.

The first legal skirmish has already taken place. In July 2002 a U.S. district judge in Manhattan, New York, ruled in *United States v. Quinones* that the federal death penalty was unconstitutional because

> *[To this Court], the unacceptably high rate at which innocent persons are convicted of capital crimes, when coupled with the frequently prolonged delays before such errors are detected (and then often only fortuitously or by application of newly developed techniques), compels the conclusion that execution under the Federal Death Penalty Act, by cutting off the opportunity for exoneration, denies due process, and indeed, is tantamount to foreseeable, state-sponsored murder of innocent human beings.*

In December 2002, however, the U.S. Court of Appeals for the Second Circuit overturned the district court's ruling, citing the Supreme Court's failure to find that there is a "fundamental right to the opportunity for exoneration over the course of [his or her] natural life." A petition for rehearing was denied.

THE DEATH PENALTY IN POLITICS

Capital punishment first became a national political issue in the 1960 presidential campaign. The movement to spare California death row inmate Caryl Chessman had raised the level of public discussion on the issue. Of the major candidates canvassed on the subject during the primary season, only Senator Hubert H. Humphrey (D-Minn.) went on record as opposing the death penalty.

President Lyndon B. Johnson's administration became the first, and only, presidential administration to recommend ending the death penalty for federal crimes. Attorney General Ramsey Clark, in testimony before Congress, called on the United States to join the growing worldwide trend toward abandonment of the sanction. All of the presidential administrations since, however, have supported capital punishment.

Most political figures and public officeholders endorse capital punishment. The relatively few public figures who oppose the death penalty are normally found on the more liberal end of the political spectrum, while those who are more conservative are often its staunchest advocates. Political analysts believe that when the death penalty becomes an issue in a campaign, the candidate favoring capital punishment almost inevitably will benefit.

Most often, the death penalty has not been a dominant issue in major campaigns. The 1988 presidential race was an exception. Then vice president George H. W. Bush, the Republican nominee, campaigned extensively on his advocacy of the death penalty for the killers of law enforcement officers. He contrasted his position with the strong abolitionist stance of his Democratic opponent, Massachusetts governor Michael S. Dukakis. When Dukakis was asked during a presidential debate whether he would favor capital punishment if his wife were raped and murdered, his answer sounded weak and unconvincing to many viewers. Political experts agree that Bush's active support of capital punishment contributed to his eventual victory, as did his use of ads featuring Willie Horton, a furloughed convict who committed beatings and rapes while outside prison.

Perhaps with Dukakis's fate in mind, in 1992 both President Bush and his challenger Bill Clinton expressed their support for capital punishment. In 1994 Congress passed (and President Clinton signed) an omnibus crime bill that included an expansion of the federal death penalty to cover dozens of additional offenses. This expansion was further codified in 1996 in the Anti-Terrorism and Effective Death Penalty Act. Since then, the traditional Republican charge that Democrats are "soft on crime" has not gained much traction, and the death penalty did not figure significantly in the 2000 or 2004 presidential campaigns.

State legislatures have been the primary battlefield in the political fight over capital punishment. State legislators, who are responsible for fashioning the criminal codes that address most homicide offenses, are more immediately and directly affected by the views of their constituents on capital punishment. The most intense political debate over the death penalty took place in New York during the 1980s and early 1990s. For eight years, Governor Mario Cuomo, a staunch liberal Democrat, regularly used his veto pen to turn back death penalty legislation. In 1994, however, Republican George Pataki won the governor's seat, and in 1995 he signed a bill restoring capital punishment in New York, resulting in a major setback for the abolitionist cause.

INTERNATIONAL PERSPECTIVES

The trend worldwide among developed nations is toward a gradual decrease in the use of the death penalty. The United Nations has become increasingly active on the issue of capital punishment. Although the organization has not taken a formal abolitionist position, many studies, reports, and resolutions have called on member nations to progressively restrict the number of offenses for which the death penalty may be imposed. In 1971 the General Assembly adopted a resolution that articulated an ultimate goal of eliminating capital punishment in all countries. In 1997 the UN Commission on Human Rights voted to call upon member countries to abolish their death penalty. (The United States was among the eight nations voting in opposition.) Additional protocols to several international agreements now bind their signatories to work to abolish the death penalty: these include the International Covenant on Civil and Political Rights, the American Convention on Human Rights, and the European Convention on Human Rights. The United States has not signed these or similar agreements.

This worldwide abolitionist effort seems to have made considerable progress in the past 30 years. As of 2003, 70 countries had no penalties of capital punishment for any crime, while 24 countries still had laws on the books but had not executed anyone for the past 10 years. Seventy-eight countries continue to actively use capital punishment. According to Amnesty International (the international human rights organization), the four most prolific users of the death penalty in 2003 were China (at least 726 executions), Iran (108), the United States (65), and Vietnam (64).

The United States is now the only Western nation that routinely practices capital punishment. In recent years, Amnesty International thus focused much of its abolition effort on ending the death penalty in the United States.

Many Americans cherish what they consider to be a distinctively American approach to individual liberty and responsibility. To some extent the capital punishment debate parallels the debate over gun control. Conservatives believe in giving the individual the means to kill another person but hold the individual accountable with his or her life for the misuses of that liberty. Liberals take a more utilitarian approach and argue for restricting both the state's and the individual's capacity to kill.

At any rate, as the debate in the 2004 election campaign over world opinion on the U.S. intervention in Iraq has shown, appeals to international opinion seem to have a polarizing effect on domestic politics. If international views are to have an effect on the capital punishment debate, it is likely to be an indirect one. For example, if a growing number of countries refuse to extradite prisoners who face capital charges in the United States, federal authorities may be less inclined to seek capital punishment. Judges may also decide to take international as well as domestic opinion into account when considering whether a particular application of capital punishment is now "cruel or unusual."

CAPITAL PUNISHMENT IN THE 21ST CENTURY

What might the future of capital punishment in the United States look like? The new century may have brought the beginnings of a shift in the wind of public attitudes toward the death penalty. The most significant development began not in the judicial or legislative branch of government, but in the executive branch.

In Illinois in 2000, Republican governor George Ryan, having learned about errors in many of the state's capital cases, declared a moratorium on executions:

> *Until I can be sure that everyone sentenced to death in Illinois is truly guilty; until I can be sure, with moral certainty, that no innocent man or woman is facing*

a lethal injection, no one will meet that fate, [. . .] I cannot support a system which, in its administration, has proven so fraught with error and has come so close to the ultimate nightmare, the state's taking of innocent life.[8]

Governor Ryan also established a commission that recommended a number of changes in the state's criminal procedures, including the videotaping of all police interrogations and the restructuring of police lineups to minimize incorrect identifications. Maryland governor Parris Glendenning soon followed suit and declared his own moratorium, although it was later reversed.

Although the growing moratorium movement has not spread to other states or to the federal system, it has given new impetus to abolitionists. They can now argue that even if a government does not yet want to abolish capital punishment, it would still be prudent for it to halt executions until it can investigate possible innocent cases, offer inmates DNA testing and other opportunities to bring forth evidence, and review procedures to make sure innocent persons are not slipping through the cracks of the system.

Meanwhile, the Supreme Court continued chipping away at the scope of the death penalty. In *Ring v. Arizona* (2004) the Court declared that only a jury, not a judge, can impose a death sentence. This decision followed an earlier precedent stating that any facts that are used in enhancing a sentence must be found by the jury, not determined by the judge.

As of 2004, therefore, the use of capital punishment in the United States appears to be declining considerably, both in the number of executions and of new death sentences. It is possible, of course, that a new surge in crime, social unrest, or terrorism may harden support for the death penalty. But failing that, the gradual erosion of public support may eventually translate into the political will to abolish capital punishment in at least some states. This, in turn, might eventually lead to it becoming increasingly "unusual" in Eighth Amendment terms. Combined with arguments based on the risk to innocent persons, the day might come when capital punishment is effectively declared to be unconstitutional.

---

[1] This and the other quotes in this section are from Michael Kroll, "The Unquiet Death of Robert Harris." *The Nation*, vol. 255, July 6, 1992, p. 1 ff.

[2] For purposes of this book, *abolitionist* is used to refer to someone who wants to abolish the death penalty. This usage should not be confused with the 19th-century abolitionists who sought to abolish slavery.

[3] Quoted in "When DNA Meets Death Row, It's the System That's Tested." *The America's Intelligence Wire*, December 12, 2003, n.p.

[4] Quoted in "When DNA Meets Death Row, It's the System That's Tested."

[5] Quoted in Richard C. Dieter, "Testimony of Richard Dieter Before the Legislative Commission Subcommittee to Study the Death Penalty." Death Penalty Informa-

tion Center. Available online. URL: http://www.deathpenaltyinfo.org/article. php?scid=7&did=258. Posted on April 18, 2002.

[6] Quoted in "Is It Wrong to Put a Juvenile on Death Row? Families of Victims, Offenders Weigh in on Pending Supreme Court Case." *The Christian Science Monitor,* October 13, 2004, p. 15.

[7] Quoted in Dave Lindorff, "Unjust Executions." Salon.com. Available online. URL: http://archive.salon.com/news/feature/2003/05/06/sentencing_errors. Posted on May 6, 2003.

[8] Quoted in Carl W. Cannon, "The Problem with the Chair: A Conservative Legal Case Against Capital Punishment." *National Review,* vol. 52, June 19, 2000, n.p.

CHAPTER 2

THE LAW OF CAPITAL PUNISHMENT

This chapter begins by summarizing the main factors that are considered in deciding to impose the death penalty. This is followed by a summary of federal offenses for which the death penalty can be imposed. (This list was greatly expanded by Congress in the 1994 Omnibus Crime Bill.) Next comes a summary of the status of capital punishment in the 38 states that currently have the death penalty. (See Chapter 6, How to Research Capital Punishment, to learn how to find the latest information and statistics on capital punishment.) The remainder of the chapter presents summaries of the key Supreme Court decisions that have provided the guidelines that have shaped the administration of capital punishment during the past 35 years.

Early in the 21st century a number of important legal trends have begun to reshape many of the procedures and rules used to administer capital punishment. These include responses by state legislatures to Supreme Court decisions that allow only juries to impose the death penalty and that seem to be gradually removing classes of persons (such as the young and the mentally disabled) from eligibility for capital punishment. Another important trend may lead to an increase in state moratoriums on executions (the first was in 2000 in Illinois) out of concern about executing innocent persons.

FACTORS IN IMPOSING THE DEATH PENALTY

One of the implications of the Supreme Court's decision in *Furman v. Georgia* (1972) was that if a procedure for capital sentencing was not unconstitutionally "arbitrary and capricious," it had to be systematic in its protection of the rights of the defendant. In practice, the states tried to meet this requirement by establishing a bifurcated procedure in capital trials. In this scheme, if the defendant is convicted of a capital offense during the guilt phase (the main trial), a separate hearing called the sentencing phase is then held. During this second mini-trial the prosecution and defense counsel first give opening statements (although the defense can reserve its statement until after the prosecution presents its evidence). Following the opening statements is the case-in-chief, in which first the prosecution and then the defense present their witnesses and evidence. As in the main trial, each side has the right to cross-examine opposing witnesses.

AGGRAVATING AND MITIGATING FACTORS

The purpose of the witnesses and evidence presented during the penalty phase is to establish aggravating and mitigating factors (or circumstances) for the jury to consider in deciding whether to impose a death sentence or a sentence of life in prison.

The prosecution tries to demonstrate the existence of one or more aggravating factors that allow and justify imposition of the ultimate penalty of death. Aggravating factors can involve the circumstances of the offense, the status of the victim, or the attitude or state of mind of the offender. Each state's penal code specifies the aggravating factors that can be used. For example, the fact that a murder was committed in the course of another major felony such as robbery or rape is nearly always considered an aggravating circumstance.

The prosecution often also seeks to show the defendant's "future dangerousness"—the likelihood that the defendant will commit further violent crimes, either while in prison or if eventually freed. Such evidence might include a record of repeated violent felonies or bad prison disciplinary records.

The defense, in turn, tries to offer mitigating factors that, while not absolving the convicted defendant of culpability for the crime, reduce his or her culpability to the point where death is not an appropriate sanction. For example, a defendant's suffering from a serious mental or emotional disorder (although short of legal insanity) can be considered a mitigating circumstance in virtually all jurisdictions.

If the prosecutor has raised the issue of future dangerousness, the defense must be allowed to counter it. They may do this by showing that the defendant behaved well while in prison.

The justification for considering mitigating factors was expressed by Supreme Court Justice Sandra Day O'Connor in her concurring opinion in *California v. Brown* (1987), when she noted that

> *evidence about the defendant's background and character is relevant because of the belief, long held by this society, that defendants who commit criminal acts that are attributable to a disadvantaged background, or to emotional and mental problems, may be less culpable than defendants that have no such excuse. The sentence imposed at the penalty stage should reflect a reasoned moral response to the defendant's background, character, and crime.*

Although each state specifies a list of statutory mitigating circumstances, the Supreme Court has ruled that the defendant can introduce any testimony or evidence relevant to mitigation of the offense. Aggravating circumstances are more circumscribed. For example, many states have aggravating circumstances involving "heinous" or "brutal" actions. The courts have required that states use a "narrowing construction" to prevent the overapplication of such subjective characterizations.

WEIGHING THE FACTORS

After closing statements the jury must determine whether any aggravating or mitigating factors have been established by the evidence and testimony presented. Most states require that at least one aggravating circumstance must be proven beyond a reasonable doubt in order for the jury to consider imposing the death penalty. For mitigating factors, however, the standard in 12 states and the federal system is simply that "the preponderance of the evidence" show the existence of a mitigating circumstance. The remaining states have no explicit standard.

Once aggravating and mitigating circumstances have been established, the jury must weigh them in order to determine the appropriate sentence. This is not a simple process of counting to see whether there are more aggravating than mitigating circumstances, but rather a consideration of how credible, important, substantial, or persuasive the factors on each side are in their totality. The Supreme Court has left it to the states to determine exactly how this is to be done. In eight states and the federal system, a death sentence is indicated if the aggravating circumstances outweigh the mitigating circumstances. (The burden of proof is on the prosecutor, but there is no specific standard of proof, just the judgment of the jury.) In 12 states a death sentence is to be imposed unless the mitigating factors outweigh the aggravating factors. The burden of proof is thus on the defense, although again, there is no specific standard of proof.

The majority of states require that the jury impose a death sentence if the aggravating factors outweigh the mitigating ones. However, a considerable number of states allow for discretion such that the death penalty can be rejected even if the weighing process would indicate its appropriateness.

STATUTORY AGGRAVATING CIRCUMSTANCES

The following statutory aggravating circumstances have been enacted by the legislatures of one or more states. In order for a death sentence to be imposed, the penalty phase jury must find that one or more of these circumstances apply to the murder in question.

These "aggravators" are divided into three categories: those relating to the nature or circumstances of the offense, those relating to the identity of the victim, and miscellaneous other factors.

NATURE OR CIRCUMSTANCES OF OFFENSE

arson   intentional burning of an occupied dwelling, commercial building, vehicle, or other property

battery, aggravated   beating that causes serious injury to the victim

burglary   breaking and entering with intent to commit a felony (usually theft)

carjacking   forcibly taking a vehicle from its owner or possessor

drug trafficking   buying or selling of narcotics, often as part of a conspiracy

escape   from the custody of a law enforcement officer or correctional facility

hijacking   forcibly seizing control of a car, bus, aircraft, ship, or train (sometimes specifically called carjacking, bus hijacking, plane hijacking, ship hijacking, or train hijacking)

kidnapping   unlawful seizing or holding of a person, often for ransom

robbery   use of force or threat of force to commit larceny (theft)

sexual offenses   such as rape, statutory rape, compelled anal or oral intercourse, sodomy, and deviant sexual behavior with a minor

train wrecking   damaging or destroying railway equipment or deliberately causing a railroad accident

Note that the general crimes of arson, burglary, kidnapping, rape, and robbery are considered aggravating offenses in the majority of death penalty states. The more esoteric offenses such as carjacking are considered aggravators in only a few states at this time.

IDENTITY OF VICTIM

elected official	victim was an elected state or local official
firefighter	victim was a firefighter or paramedic
handicapped person	victim had a physical or mental disability
hate crime	victim was targeted because of race, religion, ethnicity, or, in some states, sexual orientation
informant	victim was a police informant killed in connection with information
judge	victim was a judge or magistrate
juror	victim was a juror killed in connection with a case

law enforcement officer	victim was a police or correctional officer
parole or probation officer	victim was a parole or probation officer
pregnant woman	victim was pregnant
prosecutor	victim was a prosecutor killed in connection with a case
witness	victim was killed for being witness or potential witness to a crime
youth victim	victim was a youth (age varies by state but is generally considered 11 years of age or younger)

Note that murder of law enforcement officers, firefighters, witnesses, prosecutors, and judges is an aggravating circumstance in a majority or substantial minority of states. Among the other victim characteristics, age is the most common aggravator.

OTHER

assault weapon	use of automatic (or certain semiautomatic) firearm
authorized release from custody	defendant on work release, leave, etc. from prison
disrupting government function	when resulting in death
drive-by shooting	(sometimes specified as gang-related)
explosives	used in commission of offense
great risk to others	defendant should have realized action caused extreme danger
in custody	defendant already in custody at time of offense
lying-in-wait	attacked from ambush or hiding
multiple homicides	mass murder or serial killing
ordered killing	committed upon the order of another person
parole or probation	defendant on parole or probation at time of offense
pecuniary (monetary) gain	murder motivated by desire for money
prior felony or homicide	defendant has serious prior conviction
terrorism	Following the September 11, 2001, attacks many states have added terrorism as an element in the definition of first degree murder or felony murder.

torture	defendant inflicted great pain or suffering on victim
unlawfully at liberty	defendant failed to return from authorized release

STATUTORY MITIGATING CIRCUMSTANCES

Mitigating circumstances authorized by one or more states include the following. Note that a mitigating circumstance is considered by the penalty jury only if deemed relevant and if evidence of its existence is offered in court. The Supreme Court has required that the jury consider a wide range of relevant mitigating evidence before imposing sentence, not just the mitigating circumstances specified by statute.

age   usually applies to defendants under 18 or over 75 years old

another proximate cause   a factor other than defendant's action had a direct role in causing the victim's death

codefendant spared death penalty   equally culpable codefendant was not sentenced to death

cooperation with authorities   defendant cooperated with authorities in investigating this offense or another one

extreme duress   defendant subject to extreme force or domination by another person

extreme mental or emotional disturbance   defendant is not retarded or insane, but is under the influence of an extreme, temporary mental state or emotion such as anger

impaired capacity   substantial mental impairment, due to mental disease or defect sufficient to prevent defendant from appreciating the wrongfulness of conduct or from conforming conduct to the law; some jurisdictions include impairment brought about by alcohol or drug intoxication

mentally retarded   not insane, but substantially limited in mental capacity. (In 2002 the U.S. Supreme Court ruled that substantially mentally retarded persons cannot be sentenced to death.)

minor participation   defendant played little role in the actual killing

moral justification   defendant believed killing was morally justified

no future threat   defendant unlikely to commit another murder if given life in prison

no reasonable forseeability   defendant could not reasonably foresee that the conduct would cause harm

no significant prior criminal history   defendant does not have a conviction for a serious crime

traumatic-stress syndrome defendant suffers from mental disorientation caused by extreme stress or abuse; can be mitigating if trauma had been previously caused to the defendant by the victim or through wartime service

victim's consent victim consented to being killed or to participating in activity that led to his or her death

FEDERAL CAPITAL OFFENSES

The following federal crimes are punishable by death. Citations in parentheses refer to the United States Code. (Many of these provisions were added by Congress as part of the 1994 Omnibus Crime Bill.) In all cases except treason and espionage, the activity must involve murder or the causing of death. Note that this summary is adapted from the Bureau of Justice Statistics's report *Capital Punishment* 2002.

Provisions are divided into three categories: those relating to the status of the victim, those involving the status of the offender, and those involving the nature of the criminal offense itself.

VICTIM STATUS

children, molestation of, murder related to (18 U.S.C. § 2245)

children, sexual exploitation of, murder related to (18 U.S.C. § 2251)

court officer or juror, murder of (18 U.S.C. § 1503)

federal judge or law enforcement official, murder of (18 U.S.C. § 1114)

foreign official, murder of (18 U.S.C. § 1116)

law enforcement official, family member, retaliation murder (18 U.S.C. § 115(b)(3) by cross-reference to 18 U.S.C. § 1111)

law enforcement official, state or local, or other person aiding federal investigation, murder of (18 U.S.C. § 1121)

law enforcement official, state or local, murder of, related to continuing criminal enterprise (21 U.S.C. § 848(e))

member of Congress, important executive official, or Supreme Court Justice, murder of (18 U.S.C. § 351 by cross-reference to 18 U.S.C. § 1111)

president or vice president, assassination of, or kidnapping resulting in death of (18 U.S.C. § 1751 by cross-reference to 18 U.S.C. § 1111)

state or local law enforcement official, murder of, while aiding in federal investigation, 18 U.S.C. §1121

state correctional officer, murder of (18 U.S.C. §1121)

U.S. national, murder of in foreign country (18 U.S.C. § 1119)

U.S. national, murder of in foreign country, related to terrorism (18 U.S.C. § 2332)

witness, victim, or informant, murder to prevent testimony by, (18 U.S.C. § 1512); retaliatory murder of, (18 U.S.C. § 1513)

DEFENDANT STATUS

federal prisoner, murder by (18 U.S.C. § 1118)
federal prisoner, escaped and sentenced to life, murder by (18 U.S.C. § 1120)

STATUS OF ACTIVITY

aircraft hijacking, death resulting from (49 U.S.C. §§ 1472–1473)
aircraft, motor vehicles, or related facilities, destruction of, resulting in death (18 U.S.C. §§ 32–34)
airport, international, killing in (18 U.S.C. § 37)
aliens, smuggling of, murder related to (8 U.S.C. § 1342)
bank robbery, murder or kidnapping related to (18 U.S.C. § 2113)
carjacking, murder related to (18 U.S.C. § 2119)
civil rights offenses, resulting in death (18 U.S.C. §§ 241–242, 245, 247)
commerce, foreign or domestic, destruction of property in, resulting in death (18 U.S.C. § 844 (i))
continuing criminal enterprise, murder related to (21 U.S.C. § 848 (e))
drug-related drive-by shooting, murder committed during (18 U.S.C. § 36)
espionage (18 U.S.C. § 794)
explosives, transportation of, death resulting from (18 U.S.C. § 844 (d))
federal government facility, murder committed in (18 U.S.C. § 930)
firearm, use of during violent or drug-trafficking crime, murder committed during (18 U.S.C. § 924 (i))
first-degree murder, involving federal jurisdiction (18 U.S.C. § 1111)
genocide (18 U.S.C. § 1091)
government property, destruction of, resulting in death (18 U.S.C. § 844 (f))
hire, murder for (18 U.S.C. § 1958)
hostage-taking, murder during (18 U.S.C. § 1203)
injurious articles, mailing of with intent to kill or resulting in death (18 U.S.C. § 1716)
kidnapping, murder during (18 U.S.C. § 1201)
maritime navigation, murder committed during offense relating to (18 U.S.C. § 2280)
maritime platform, murder committed during offense relating to (18 U.S.C. § 2281)
racketeering offense, murder during (18 U.S.C. § 1959)
rape, murder related to (18 U.S.C. § 2245)

torture, murder involving (18 U.S.C. § 2340)
treason (18 U.S.C. § 2381)
train, willful wrecking of, resulting in death (18 U.S.C. § 1992)
weapon of mass destruction, murder by use of (18 U.S.C. § 2332a)

Note that the U.S. military also provides for capital punishment under the Uniform Code of Military Justice (UCMJ), found in U.S.C. Title 10, Chapter 47. The method of execution is lethal injection. Life without parole can be given as an alternative. As of 2004 seven inmates were on the military death row, but no executions have been performed by the military since 1961.

SUMMARY OF CAPITAL PUNISHMENT BY STATE

The following section summarizes information about capital punishment for each of the 38 states that have the death penalty. Each entry consists of the following:

- offenses for which the state can ask for the death penalty: *First-degree murder* generally means premeditated or deliberated murder; *felony murder* means murder committed in the course of another felony. References to *aggravating factors* or *aggravating circumstances* refer to one or more of the aggravating circumstances discussed earlier. Some factors, such as killing a police officer, are recognized in most states, while others, such as an incarcerated person killing a fellow inmate, are found in only a few states. Note that while some states don't specify first-degree murder, in practice, the offense must generally meet the standards for first-degree murder.

- whether the state forbids execution of persons who are sufficiently mentally disabled (definition varies with state)

- whether the state also has life without parole (this is included because life without parole is frequently considered an alternative to capital punishment)

- the state's method of execution (A few states offer alternative methods.)

- Note that in *Ring v. Arizona* (2002) the U.S. Supreme Court ruled that death sentences can be imposed only by juries. States that allowed judges to hand down death sentences or use juries only in an advisory role have had to revise their legislation.

- Also note that in *Roper v. Simmons* (2005) the U.S. Supreme Court set a minimum age for the death penalty of 18 (at the time of the offense.)

Note that this material is drawn from information supplied by the Bureau of Justice Statistics's *Capital Punishment* 2002, the Death Penalty Information Center, and other sources.

The Law of Capital Punishment

ALABAMA

Capital offenses: intentional murder with one of 18 aggravating factors
Mentally disabled: no
Life without parole: yes
Method of execution: electrocution, lethal injection

ARIZONA

Capital offenses: first-degree murder with at least one of 10 aggravating factors
Mentally disabled: yes
Life without parole: yes
Method of execution: lethal injection; persons sentenced before November 15, 1992, can choose lethal gas instead.

ARKANSAS

Capital offenses: capital murder with at least one of 10 aggravating circumstances; treason
Mentally disabled: yes
Life without parole: yes
Method of execution: lethal injection; persons whose offense was committed before July 4, 1983, may choose electrocution instead

CALIFORNIA

Capital offenses: first-degree murder with special circumstances; perjury causing execution; train-wrecking; treason
Mentally disabled: no
Life without parole: yes
Method of execution: lethal injection unless inmate chooses lethal gas

COLORADO

Capital offenses: first-degree murder with at least one of 15 aggravating factors; treason
Mentally disabled: yes
Life without parole: yes
Method of execution: lethal injection

CONNECTICUT

Capital offenses: capital felony with eight categories of aggravated homicide
Mentally disabled: yes
Life without parole: yes
Method of execution: lethal injection

DELAWARE

Capital offenses: first-degree murder with aggravating circumstances
Mentally disabled: yes
Life without parole: yes
Method of execution: lethal injection; persons who committed the offense before June 13, 1986, may choose hanging instead

FLORIDA

Capital offenses: first-degree murder; felony murder; capital drug-trafficking; capital sexual battery
Mentally disabled: yes
Life without parole: yes
Method of execution: electrocution; lethal injection

GEORGIA

Capital offenses: murder; kidnapping with bodily injury or ransom where the victim dies; aircraft hijacking; treason
Mentally disabled: yes
Life without parole: yes
Method of execution: lethal injection

IDAHO

Capital offenses: first-degree murder with aggravating factors; aggravated kidnapping
Mentally disabled: no
Life without parole: yes
Method of execution: lethal injection or firing squad selected by the director of the Department of Corrections; firing squad will be used if lethal injection is "impractical"

ILLINOIS

Capital offenses: first-degree murder with one of 15 aggravating circumstances
Mentally disabled: no
Life without parole: yes
Method of execution: lethal injection

INDIANA

Capital offenses: murder with one of 16 aggravating circumstances
Mentally disabled: yes
Life without parole: yes
Method of execution: lethal injection

KANSAS

Capital offenses: capital murder with one of eight aggravating circumstances
Mentally disabled: yes
Life without parole: yes
Method of execution: lethal injection

KENTUCKY

Capital offenses: murder with aggravating factors; kidnapping with aggravated factors
Mentally disabled: yes
Life without parole: yes
Method of execution: lethal injection

LOUISIANA

Capital offenses: first-degree murder; aggravated rape of victim under age 12; treason
Mentally disabled: no
Life without parole: yes
Method of execution: lethal injection

MARYLAND

Capital offenses: first-degree murder either premeditated or during commission of a felony, if certain other requirements are met.
Mentally disabled: yes
Life without parole: yes
Method of execution: lethal injection; persons whose offenses occurred before March 25, 1994, may choose lethal gas instead

MISSISSIPPI

Capital offenses: capital murder; aircraft piracy
Mentally disabled: no
Life without parole: yes
Method of execution: lethal injection

MISSOURI

Capital offenses: first-degree murder
Mentally disabled: no
Life without parole: yes
Method of execution: lethal injection or lethal gas

MONTANA

Capital offenses: capital murder with one of nine aggravating circumstances; capital sexual assault.
Mentally disabled: no
Life without parole: yes
Method of execution: lethal injection (hanging eliminated March 1997)

NEBRASKA

Capital offenses: first-degree murder with a finding of at least one statutorily defined aggravating circumstance
Mentally disabled: yes
Life without parole: yes
Method of execution: electrocution

NEVADA

Capital offenses: first-degree murder with one of 14 aggravating circumstances
Mentally disabled: no

Life without parole: yes
Method of execution: lethal injection

NEW HAMPSHIRE

Capital offenses: capital murder (six categories)
Mentally disabled: no
Life without parole: yes
Method of execution: lethal injection; lethal gas if lethal injection cannot be given

NEW JERSEY

Capital offenses: purposeful or knowing murder by one's own conduct; contract murder; solicitation by command or threat in furtherance of a narcotics conspiracy
Mentally disabled: yes
Life without parole: yes
Method of execution: lethal injection

NEW MEXICO

Capital offenses: first-degree murder with one of seven aggravating circumstances
Mentally disabled: yes
Life without parole: no
Method of execution: lethal injection

NEW YORK

Capital offenses: first-degree murder with one of two aggravating factors
Mentally disabled: yes, except for murder by a prisoner
Life without parole: yes
Method of execution: lethal injection

NORTH CAROLINA

Capital offenses: first-degree murder
Mentally disabled: yes
Life without parole: yes
Method of execution: lethal injection

OHIO

Capital offenses: aggravated murder with at least one of nine aggravating circumstances
Mentally disabled: no
Life without parole: yes
Method of execution: lethal injection

OKLAHOMA

Capital offenses: first-degree murder with at least one of eight aggravating circumstances
Mentally disabled: no
Life without parole: yes
Method of execution: lethal injection; electrocution if lethal injection is found unconstitutional; firing squad if electrocution is held unconstitutional

OREGON

Capital offenses: aggravated murder
Mentally disabled: no
Life without parole: yes
Method of execution: lethal injection

PENNSYLVANIA

Capital offenses: first-degree murder with one of 18 aggravating circumstances

Mentally disabled: no
Life without parole: yes
Method of execution: lethal injection

SOUTH CAROLINA

Capital offenses: murder with one of 10 aggravating circumstances
Mentally disabled: no, but mental disability can be considered as a mitigating factor
Life without parole: yes
Method of execution: lethal injection or electrocution

SOUTH DAKOTA

Capital offenses: first-degree murder with one of 10 aggravating circumstances
Mentally disabled: yes
Life without parole: yes
Method of execution: lethal injection

TENNESSEE

Capital offenses: first-degree murder with one of 15 aggravating circumstances
Mentally disabled: yes
Life without parole: yes
Method of execution: lethal injection

TEXAS

Capital offenses: criminal homicide with one of eight aggravating circumstances
Mentally disabled: no
Life without parole: no
Method of execution: lethal injection

UTAH

Capital offenses: aggravated murder;
Mentally disabled: no, but can be a mitigating factor
Life without parole: yes
Method of execution: lethal injection or firing squad

VIRGINIA

Capital offenses: first-degree murder with one of 13 aggravating circumstances
Mentally disabled: no
Life without parole: yes
Method of execution: inmate may choose lethal injection or electrocution; lethal injection is used if inmate fails to choose

WASHINGTON

Capital offenses: aggravated first-degree murder
Mentally disabled: yes
Life without parole: yes
Method of execution: inmate may choose lethal injection or hanging; lethal injection used if inmate fails to choose

WYOMING

Capital offenses: first-degree murder
Mentally disabled: no
Life without parole: yes
Method of execution: lethal injection; lethal gas to be used if lethal injection is held to be unconstitutional

THE DEATH PENALTY AROUND THE WORLD

Overall, there has been a strong international trend since the 1970s to abolish capital punishment, with most European (and some other) nations giving up the practice. The following information about each nation's current possession or use of the death penalty as of 2005 is based on data gathered by Amnesty International.

NATIONS THAT HAVE NO DEATH PENALTY FOR ANY OFFENSE

Andorra, Angola, Australia, Austria, Azerbaijan, Belgium, Bhutan, Bosnia-Herzegovina, Bulgaria, Cambodia, Canada, Cape Verde, Colombia, Costa Rica, Croatia, Cyprus, Czech Republic, Denmark, Djibouti, Dominican Republic, East Timor, Ecuador, Estonia, Finland, France, Georgia, Germany, Guinea-Bissau, Haiti, Honduras, Hungary, Iceland, Ireland, Italy, Ivory Coast, Kiribati, Liechtenstein, Lithuania, Luxembourg, Macedonia (Former Yugoslav Republic), Malta, Marshall Islands, Mauritius, Micronesia (Federated States), Moldova, Monaco, Mozambique, Namibia, Nepal, Netherlands, New Zealand,

Nicaragua, Niue, Norway, Palau, Panama, Paraguay, Poland, Portugal, Romania, Samoa, San Marino, São Tomé and Principe, Serbia and Montenegro, Seychelles, Slovak Republic, Slovenia, Solomon Islands, South Africa, Spain, Sweden, Switzerland, Turkmenistan, Tuvalu, Ukraine, United Kingdom, Uruguay, Vanuatu, Vatican City State, Venezuela.

NATIONS WITH THE DEATH PENALTY ONLY FOR EXCEPTIONAL CRIMES

The following nations have the death penalty only for offenses such as treason or other crimes against the state or in the military: Albania, Argentina, Armenia, Bolivia, Brazil, Chile, Cook Islands, El Salvador, Fiji, Greece, Israel, Latvia, Mexico, Peru, Turkey.

NATIONS WITH A DISUSED DEATH PENALTY

The following nations have the death penalty on the books but have not used it recently, and may have policies to minimize or eliminate its use: Algeria, Benin, Brunei, Burkina Faso, Central African Republic, Congo Republic, Gambia, Grenada, Kenya, Madagascar, Maldives, Mali, Mauritania, Nauru, Niger, Papua New Guinea, Russian Federation, Senegal, Sri Lanka, Suriname, Togo, Tonga, Tunisia.

NATIONS WITH THE DEATH PENALTY

The following nations have the death penalty and have used it in recent years: Afghanistan, Antigua and Barbuda, Bahamas, Bahrain, Bangladesh, Barbados, Belarus, Belize, Botswana, Burundi, Cameroon, Chad, China, Comoros, Congo (Democratic Republic), Cuba, Dominica, Egypt, Equatorial Guinea, Eritrea, Ethiopia, Gabon, Ghana, Guatemala, Guinea, Guyana, India, Indonesia, Iran, Iraq, Jamaica, Japan, Jordan, Kazakhstan, Korea (North), Korea (South), Kuwait, Kyrgyzstan, Laos, Lebanon, Lesotho, Liberia, Libya, Malawi, Malaysia, Mongolia, Morocco, Myanmar, Nigeria, Oman, Pakistan, Palestinian Authority, Philippines, Qatar, Rwanda, Saint Christopher and Nevis, Saint Lucia, Saint Vincent and Grenadines, Saudi Arabia, Sierra Leone, Singapore, Somalia, Sudan, Swaziland, Syria, Taiwan, Tajikistan, Tanzania, Thailand, Trinidad and Tobago, Uganda, United Arab Emirates, United States, Uzbekistan, Vietnam, Yemen, Zambia, Zimbabwe.

THE DEATH PENALTY AND EXTRADITION

Many European (and a number of other) nations will not extradite suspects on capital charges to nations such as the United States that have the death penalty, unless they receive assurance that capital punishment will not be sought. The specifics in each case are given in the extradition treaties between the nations.

REPRESENTATIVE SUPREME COURT DECISIONS

In the case of *Furman v. Georgia* (1972) the U.S. Supreme Court declared that the "arbitrary and capricious" administration of capital punishment violated the Eighth Amendment's ban on "cruel and unusual punishment." Those states that had death penalty statutes quickly revised them in an attempt to satisfy the requirements implied in the Court's decision. The Court's decision in *Gregg v. Georgia* broadly affirmed that the revisions were sufficient to allow executions to proceed. In the ensuing decades, however, several important constitutional challenges were made concerning particular aspects of the legal procedures in capital cases. In the cases described below, these challenges were decided, sometimes resulting in further procedural safeguards for defendants during the sentencing and appeals process.

The following list summarizes the main issues dealt with in these cases. Decisions in boldface are discussed in separate entries in this chapter, while others are mentioned briefly:

accomplice, capital punishment for: **Enmund v. Florida,** *Tison v. Arizona*

aggravating circumstances: *Blystone v. Pennsylvania,* **Godfrey v. Georgia, Clemons v. Mississippi**

assistance of counsel, ineffective: **Burger v. Kemp,** *Strickland v. Washington*

counsel, right to (in appeals): *Murray v. Girratano*

counsel for indigent defendants: *McFarland v. Scott*

double jeopardy: **Bullington v. Missouri**

Eighth Amendment, cruel and unusual punishment (general): **Furman v. Georgia, Gregg v. Georgia**

execution methods: **Heckler v. Chaney,** *Fierro v. Gomez, Gomez v. Fierro, Francis v. Weshaber, Provenzano v. Moore*

future dangerousness and parole: **Barefoot v. Estelle,** *Simmons v. South Carolina*

innocence, actual as basis for appeal: **Herrera v. Collins, Schlup v. Delo,** *Sawyer v. Whitley, Murray v. Carrier,* **United States v. Quinones**

international law and treaties, applicability of: **Medellín v. Dretke**

jury as sole capital sentencer: **Ring v. Arizona,** *Walton v. Arizona, Apprendi v. New Jersey, Summerlin v. Stewart*

jury instructions: **Caldwell v. Mississippi**

jury qualifications for capital cases: **Witherspoon v. Illinois,** *Davis v. Georgia, Adams v. Texas, Wainwright v. Witt, Lockhart v. McRee*

juveniles, capital punishment for: ***Thompson v. Oklahoma, Roper v. Simmons***

lesser included offenses: ***Beck v. Alabama***

mandatory death sentences: ***Woodson v. North Carolina***, *Roberts v. Louisiana* (1977), *Summer v. Shuman*

mental incompetence or retardation: Estelle v. Smith, ***Ford v. Wainwright, Penry v. Lynaugh, Payne v. Tennessee, Atkins v. Virginia, Riggins v. Nevada***

mitigating circumstances: ***Lockett v. Ohio***, *Eddings v. Oklahoma, Skipper v. South Carolina, Mills v. Maryland, McKoy v. North Carolina, Buchanan v. Angelone*

non-murder crime, capital punishment for: ***Coker v. Georgia***, *Eberheart v. Georgia*

parole eligibility: *Simmons v. Siuth Carolina*

proportionality review: ***Pulley v. Harris***

race discrimination in death sentencing: ***McCleskey v. Kemp***, *Ham v. South Carolina, Ristaino v. Ross, Turner v. Murray*

shackling of defendant in penalty phase: ***Deck v. Missouri***

victim impact statements: ***Booth v. Maryland***, *South Carolina v. Gathers*, ***Payne v. Tennessee***

WITHERSPOON V. ILLINOIS, 391 U.S. 510 (1968)

Background

William G. Witherspoon was convicted in 1960 for the murder of a Chicago police officer. An Illinois law specified that persons could be excluded from serving on a jury for a capital crime if they opposed or had "conscientious scruples" against the death penalty. This "scrupled juror" rule was invoked by the prosecutor at Witherspoon's trial to dismiss any prospective members of the jury who voiced misgivings about capital punishment. Witherspoon contested his conviction and challenged the constitutionality of the procedure by which Illinois selected juries in capital cases. After Illinois courts rejected his appeals, the Supreme Court granted his request for review.

Legal Issues

Witherspoon's counsel maintained that—in violation of the Sixth Amendment—the question of his client's guilt or innocence had not been determined by an impartial jury. His argument rested on the contention that jurors without scruples against capital punishment are more inclined to vote for guilt than those with qualms about the sanction. He asked the Court to overturn Witherspoon's conviction on the grounds that it was obtained from a biased or "prosecution prone" jury.

The attorney general of Illinois responded that a state had a right to ensure that jurors were able to meet their responsibilities under the law. In defense of the scrupled juror statute, it was alleged that jurors who opposed capital punishment would be reluctant to convict a defendant of a capital offense out of concern the death penalty would be imposed. It was also noted that there was no substantive evidence that "death qualified" juries that excluded opponents of capital punishment were more likely to convict.

Decision

In a decision announced June 3, 1968, the Supreme Court did not specifically address Witherspoon's claim that his conviction was the result of a biased jury. As Justice Potter Stewart noted in his majority opinion, available data was "too tentative and fragmentary" to conclude that death qualified juries were more likely to find a defendant guilty. The Court instead focused on the narrower question of Witherspoon's punishment. Justice Stewart declared that the Constitution did not permit jury selection procedures that in effect produced a "hanging jury." The Court reversed Witherspoon's death sentence, ruling in his case that the systematic exclusion of jurors who had merely voiced ambiguous feelings about the death penalty had deprived him of his constitutional right to an impartial hearing. The Court concluded that an appropriate inquiry had to be conducted to determine a potential juror's level of opposition to capital punishment before that person could be excluded from jury duty. Only those persons who indicated that they would automatically vote against imposition of the death penalty could legitimately be disqualified.

Impact

Witherspoon was the first time the Supreme Court significantly impacted the procedures by which states administered the death penalty. The decision raised the hopes of abolitionists who looked to the Court to eventually outlaw capital punishment. The immediate impact of the *Witherspoon* ruling, because it applied retroactively, was to open a new avenue of appeal for many of the approximately 430 persons under death sentence nationwide at the time. However, it was quickly recognized that the ruling left their actual convictions intact affecting only the penalty, and many states moved to implement new, constitutionally acceptable jury selection procedures with the intent of resentencing their death row inmates. These efforts were superseded in 1971 when the Court held, in *Furman v. Georgia*, that the nation's death penalty statutes as written were unconstitutional.

After the restoration of the death penalty in 1976, the Court returned to the issue of juror selection at capital trials in a number of subsequent decisions. That same year the Court stated in *Davis v. Georgia* that the exclusion of even a single juror in violation of the principles determined in *Witherspoon* invalidated the death sentence imposed.

In response to the requirements outlined in *Furman*, capital trials had been bifurcated, or split into two separate parts: the regular trial, in which the guilt of the defendant was determined and (if the defendant was convicted) a separate sentencing phase. While *Witherspoon* had declared that jurors could not be removed simply for opposing capital punishment, what degree of opposition was tolerable in the sentencing phase? In *Adams v. Texas*, 448 U.S. 38 (1980), the Court ruled that jurors could not be excluded simply because they could not take an oath guaranteeing that their beliefs about capital punishment would have *no* effect on their deliberations.

However, in *Wainwright v. Witt*, 469 U.S. 412 (1985) the Court ruled that a juror who was not absolutely opposed to capital punishment could still be removed if he or she appeared to have a degree of opposition sufficient to "prevent or substantially impair the performance of his duties in accordance with his instructions and his oath."

Defense attorneys then raised an argument that exclusion of jurors who were strongly opposed to the death penalty would result in a jury unacceptably biased toward death. In *Lockhart v. McRee*, 476 U.S. 162 (1986), the Court rejected this argument. It ruled that the practice of striking jurors who were unequivocally (or too strongly) opposed to the death penalty from the guilt phase of a capital trial did not abridge a defendant's Sixth Amendment rights, even if it were established that death qualified juries were somewhat more "prosecution prone" than average juries.

FURMAN V. GEORGIA, 408 U.S. 238 (1972)

Background

In 1965 the NAACP Legal Defense and Education Fund (LDF) launched a campaign to have the death penalty declared unconstitutional. By 1967 a series of legal challenges to death sentences across the nation had succeeded in halting all executions while the courts grappled with the difficult constitutional issues involved. After the Supreme Court ruled against several major challenges to capital punishment in May 1971, many in the abolitionist legal movement worried that the moratorium on executions was about to end.

However, the following month the Court announced it would review four cases to determine whether the death penalty constituted "cruel and unusual punishment in violation of the Eighth and Fourteenth Amendments." In two cases, *Aikens v. California* and *Furman v. Georgia*, the defendants contested their death sentences under state law for murder. The other two cases, *Jackson v. Georgia* and *Branch v. Texas*, questioned the constitutionality of imposing the death penalty for rape. Underscoring LDF arguments about racial discrimination in the imposition of capital punishment was the fact that in each of the four cases the defendant was black and the victim was white.

The Law of Capital Punishment

Legal Issues

LDF lawyers, who represented three of the defendants, presented a progression of interconnected arguments against the death penalty. They noted the Supreme Court's understandable reluctance to overturn well-established death penalty statutes in forty-one states but urged the Court to do so because the laws violated the cruel and unusual punishment clause of the Eighth Amendment. They called on the Court to continue its practice, first articulated in 1958, of viewing the amendment's prohibition of cruel and unusual punishment within the context of "evolving standards of decency."

Acknowledging that the existence of the death penalty in so many states suggested its use was acceptable to contemporary society, they contended that the public tolerated the sanction only because it was so infrequently imposed. A mere fraction of those who committed capital offenses were actually put to death. Those who were executed were disproportionately the poor, the disadvantaged, and minorities. They concluded that it was cruel and unusual to randomly single out a handful of persons for a penalty which society would not condone if evenhandedly and extensively applied.

Attorneys for the states responded that the people, through their elected representatives, should decide what penalties a state might employ. There was no clear and compelling reason for the Court to impose its judgment on legislative bodies. By any measure of contemporary standards, the death penalty could not be construed as cruel and unusual punishment. The idea that Americans in reality opposed capital punishment was characterized as a way to explain away the fact that the federal government and the majority of states had death penalty laws. If there were discriminatory practices in the actual imposition of the death sentence, then the issue was not capital punishment but equal protection under the laws as guaranteed by the Fourteenth Amendment. The small number of executions reflected the care with which the death penalty was used.

Recognizing the importance of the pending Supreme Court decision, numerous groups filed friend-of-the-court briefs. These included arguments against capital punishment from a range of civil rights and religious organizations.

Decision

The case from California had subsequently been dismissed after the California Supreme Court ruled the state's capital punishment statute unconstitutional in February 1972. The remaining three cases, officially reported under the name *Furman v. Georgia*, were decided on June 29, 1972. In a brief general opinion, the Court declared that the imposition of the death penalty in these cases would constitute cruel and unusual punishment.

In a departure from normal practice that reflected the widely divergent views of the justices on the issues involved, there was no majority opinion that explained the Court's reasoning. Instead, each of the five justices who voted for abolition wrote a separate concurring opinion. Justices Brennan and Marshall believed capital punishment in general was prohibited under the Eighth Amendment. The other members of the majority did not address the constitutionality of capital punishment itself, but rather the way in which current laws caused the death penalty to be imposed. Justices Douglas, Stewart, and White agreed that the nation's capital punishment statutes resulted in cruel and unusual punishment because of the arbitrary and capricious manner in which the death penalty was imposed.

Each of the dissenting justices likewise issued a separate opinion. Their general conclusion was that the majority had gone too far in trying to find a judicial solution to the troubling aspects of capital punishment. They believed the Court through judicial review had encroached upon the powers constitutionally provided to legislatures.

Impact

At the same time it announced the *Furman* decision, the Supreme Court issued orders that similarly reversed the death sentences in more than 100 other capital cases under appeal. The effect of *Furman* was to render the nation's capital punishment laws, as written, unconstitutional. The ruling spared from execution the approximately 630 persons on death row across the country.

The *Furman* decision provoked widespread reactions. Although abolitionists hailed the landmark judgment, the prevailing response was negative. Political leaders nationwide, most notably President Richard Nixon and California governor Ronald Reagan, strongly criticized the Court's action. Many stated their intention to find a way to reinstate capital punishment.

In his dissent, Chief Justice Burger noted that the lack of a clear majority consensus on the ultimate constitutionality of the death penalty meant that the full scope of the *Furman* ruling was unclear. He suggested that legislatures could enact capital punishment measures tailored to satisfy the objections stated in *Furman* by "providing standards for juries and judges to follow in determining the sentence in capital cases or by more narrowly defining the crimes for which the penalty is to be imposed." Over the next several years numerous states followed this course in amending their death penalty laws. In 1976, in *Gregg v. Georgia*, the Supreme Court restored capital punishment by upholding the constitutionality of the revised statutes.

GREGG V. GEORGIA, 428 U.S. 153 (1976)

Background

In 1972 the Supreme Court struck down the nation's capital punishment laws. These statutes had allowed juries in capital cases an essentially unrestricted discretion to determine whether a person received the death sentence. The Court found in *Furman v. Georgia* that the resulting arbitrary and capricious manner in which the death penalty was imposed violated the Eighth Amendment ban on cruel and unusual punishment.

By 1976, 35 states had enacted death penalty measures that attempted to conform to the guidelines established in the *Furman* decision. That same year the Supreme Court agreed to review five cases that challenged the constitutionality of the new laws in several states. Its ruling would possibly determine whether capital punishment would be reinstated in the United States. Two of the cases concerned mandatory death sentences and are reviewed separately under *Woodson v. North Carolina*. The other three cases, *Gregg v. Georgia, Proffitt v. Florida,* and *Jurek v. Texas,* involved defendants convicted of murder.

Legal Issues

In *Furman,* the Supreme Court had stopped short of concluding that capital punishment was inherently unconstitutional. This left open the possibility that death penalty statutes could be designed that would pass judicial scrutiny. The states argued that they had implemented procedures that met the Court's requirement for clear sentencing standards in capital cases. These included a bifurcated, or split, trial proceeding in which guilt or innocence was determined during a first phase and the sentence then imposed during a separate second phase. Juries were provided certain criteria to follow in deciding which convicted capital offenders would receive the death penalty.

Attorneys for the defendants contended that neither these nor any other procedures that could be adopted by the states would ensure capital punishment was administered in a rational and fair way. They asserted the Court should take the final step of declaring the death penalty itself unconstitutional, alleging the sanction was no longer compatible with contemporary standards of decency and as such was a violation of the Eighth Amendment ban on cruel and unusual punishment.

Decision

In a historic judgment delivered on July 2, 1976, the Court ruled that capital punishment did not invariably violate the Constitution and upheld death penalty laws that set objective standards for juries to follow in their sentencing decisions. The Florida, Georgia, and Texas statutes were found to be within constitutional limits. The Court chose to present its basic reasoning in *Gregg v. Georgia,* making it the lead case that would be cited for the decision.

The seven members of the majority were unable to agree on an opinion. In the Court's ruling, Justices Stewart, Powell, and Stevens noted that passage of the death penalty measures by so many states after *Furman* undercut the argument that society no longer endorsed the sanction. The different majority opinions in general indicated the Court would uphold capital punishment laws that met several key conditions: clear standards to guide juries in their sentencing decisions; consideration of any mitigating factors prior to sentencing; and automatic review of each death sentence in a state appellate court.

Impact

Although *Gregg v. Georgia* reinstated the death penalty, the ruling did not overturn *Furman*. Instead, the decision reflected the Supreme Court's judgment that the defects previously identified in the administration of the death penalty had been remedied. More than 460 persons had been sentenced to death under post-*Furman* statutes, and *Gregg* cleared the way for a resumption of executions. The first execution in 10 years was carried out in 1977.

On the same day the *Gregg* decision was released, the Supreme Court determined in *Woodson v. North Carolina* that mandatory death sentences were unconstitutional. Together, *Furman* and *Woodson* made it clear the Court would not consent to giving a capital jury either too much or too little discretion in arriving at a sentence. Other states consequently moved to amend their death penalty laws to conform to the guided-discretion statutes approved in *Gregg*.

The 7-2 vote in *Gregg* suggested the Supreme Court was not likely to significantly modify its core stance on capital punishment in the foreseeable future. In subsequent decisions, the Court has focused on further defining the circumstances under which the death penalty is a constitutionally acceptable punishment.

WOODSON V. NORTH CAROLINA, 428 U.S. 280 (1976)

Background

In 1972 the Supreme Court ruled that death penalty statutes that did not contain specific sentencing standards were unconstitutional. Relying on the precedent established in *Furman v. Georgia*, the North Carolina Supreme Court overturned the provision of that state's capital punishment law that granted the jury tremendous leeway on when to impose the death penalty. In 1974 the North Carolina legislature attempted to resolve the question of sentencing procedures in capital trials by passing a new statute that removed all discretion, making the death penalty mandatory for first-degree murder. The state's highest court subsequently upheld death sentences two defendants had received under the new law following their murder convictions. The defendants appealed, and in 1976 the U.S. Supreme Court agreed to hear their case, *Woodson v. North Carolina*, as part of a broad review of the constitutionality of various state capital punishment laws enacted in response to the *Furman* decision.

Legal Issues

The basic question before the Supreme Court was whether mandatory death statutes provided a constitutionally acceptable response to the rejection in *Fur-*

man of unbridled jury discretion in sentencing decisions. Attorneys for the states involved argued that mandatory sentences would prevent arbitrary and freakish inconsistencies in the imposition of capital punishment. Defense lawyers countered that mandatory statutes did not take into account the unique circumstances of a given case and would still result in indiscriminate sentencing patterns. They further contended that there was no workable way to address the concern raised in *Furman* and called upon the Court to abolish capital punishment outright.

Decision

The Supreme Court announced its decision in *Woodson v. North Carolina* on July 2, 1976, the same day it delivered its landmark *Gregg v. Georgia* ruling. The court declared North Carolina's capital punishment law unconstitutional because it did not provide "objective standards to guide, regularize, and make rationally reviewable the process for imposing a sentence of death." In a companion case, *Roberts v. Louisiana*, 428 U.S. 242 (1976), the Court struck down that state's mandatory death penalty statute for similar reasons.

The 5-4 majority in *Woodson* stressed the fact that since the early 19th century the United States had gradually moved away from mandatory sentences. An automatic death sentence was seen as inconsistent with "evolving standards of decency" and consequently constituted cruel and unusual punishment under the Eighth Amendment. The Court stated that "particularized" consideration had to be given to the relevant aspects of a convicted defendant's character and record before a death sentence could be imposed.

Impact

In its simultaneous release of the *Gregg* and *Woodson* decisions, the Supreme Court staked out a carefully defined position on capital punishment. In *Gregg,* the Court found that the death penalty per se was not unconstitutional and upheld death penalty statutes that provided for guided jury discretion in sentencing decisions. With its ruling against mandatory sentences in *Woodson*, the Court, in effect, had endorsed a bifurcated, or split, trial process in capital cases where conviction and punishment were determined in separate hearings.

Woodson established the important precedent that a defendant was entitled to an individualized sentencing determination. In later decisions the Supreme Court extended this principle to include a defendant's right to present a broad range of mitigating evidence prior to sentencing. The Court continued to rule against mandatory death sentences. The following year, in *Roberts v. Louisiana*, 431 U.S. 633 (1977)—a different Roberts—a Louisiana statute that mandated the death penalty for persons convicted of killing a police officer was overturned. The Court did not accept the argument that the process of convicting a person of a special and narrowly drawn category of crime could serve as a substitute for "particularized" consideration. In 1987, the Court nullified, in *Summer v. Shuman,* a Nevada law that required the death penalty for murders committed by prisoners serving life sentences without possibility of parole.

While mandatory death sentences for particular crime circumstances had been banned by the Court, the justices took a different position with regard to mandating a death penalty based on aggravating circumstances found at the time of sentencing. In *Blystone v. Pennsylvania,* 494 U.S. 299 (1990), the Court ruled by a 5-4 margin that providing for a mandatory death sentence if the jury finds one aggravating circumstance and no mitigating circumstances was not a violation of the Eighth Amendment. Such a system did not interfere with the consideration of all relevant mitigating evidence, but only directed what was to be done if none was found. The dissenters objected, saying that any such mandatory aspect of the sentencing process deprived the jurors of the ability to make an individual determination of whether any aggravating circumstance they found was sufficient to warrant imposing the death penalty.

COKER V. GEORGIA, 433 U.S. 584 (1977)

Background

Anthony Coker escaped from a Georgia correctional institution where he was serving consecutive life sentences for murder, rape, and kidnapping. He subsequently raped an adult woman during an armed robbery. Georgia's death penalty statutes authorized capital punishment for rape if one or more of the following aggravating circumstances was present: the defendant had previously been convicted of a capital offense; the rape occurred during the commission of another capital felony (including armed robbery); or the crime was particularly vile or horrible, involving torture, depravity, or aggravated battery. After his conviction for rape and armed robbery, Coker was sentenced to death by a jury that found the first two aggravating factors applied. When Georgia's highest court affirmed the sentence on automatic appeal, Coker petitioned the Supreme Court to declare the death penalty for rape unconstitutional.

Legal Issues

In *Gregg v. Georgia* the Supreme Court upheld the constitutionality of capital punishment laws that provided for a consideration of aggravating and mitigating circumstances prior to sentencing. The question in *Coker v. Georgia* was not whether Georgia's statutes were procedurally flawed but whether death was an appropriate punishment for rape, even with aggravating circumstances. Coker's counsel noted that the rape had not involved the loss of life and contended the sentence was disproportionate to the crime committed. Such an excessively harsh penalty violated the Eighth Amendment's ban on cruel and unusual punishment.

State attorneys argued the case was beyond the reach of proper judicial review. The Court should not substitute its policy judgment for that of the state legislature. Rape was not a minor crime, and it was the considered reasoning of Georgia's elected representatives that there were times the offense merited the ultimate sanction.

Decision

The Supreme Court ruled in favor of Coker on June 29, 1977. The Court followed its normal practice of determining the constitutionality of a given punishment. A punishment was cruel and unusual under the Eighth Amendment if it was incompatible with "evolving standards of decency." Measured against contemporary American sensibilities, a sentence of death was wholly disproportionate to the offense of raping an adult woman. The Court cited the fact that Georgia was the only state to authorize the death sentence for rape. The 7-2 majority also underscored the difference between murder and crimes such as rape where the defendant, whatever the aggravating circumstances, had not taken the victim's life.

Impact

Coker was the first time the Supreme Court specifically limited the authority of either federal or state government to impose the death penalty for a specific type of crime. In a summary opinion released at the same time, *Eberheart v. Georgia*, the Court also overturned the death penalty for kidnapping when homicide was not involved. The two decisions served to suggest the Court was drawing a clear link between death as a punishment and crimes involving loss of life. This apparent linkage raised serious doubts about the constitutionality of capital punishment for other crimes such as treason, espionage, and airplane hijacking that might not result in immediate death. The Court has yet to rule on these questions.

Note that 36 of the 38 death penalty states also have life sentences without the possibility of parole, which can ensure that extremely violent offenders will not be able to endanger the public in the future. Further, the use of "three strikes" laws (such as in California) for repeat violent offenders can provide for greatly enhanced sentences for dangerous criminals. (However, such laws have been criticized when they include nonviolent felonies as third strikes.)

LOCKETT V. OHIO, 438 U.S. 586 (1978)

Background

Sandra Lockett drove the getaway car in a pawnshop robbery during which the owner was killed. Ohio laws required the death penalty for a conviction of aggravated murder (such as murder in the course of committing a robbery), unless the sentencing authority determined that at least one of the following three mitigating circumstances existed: the victim induced or facilitated the crime; the defendant was under duress, coercion, or strong provocation; or the crime resulted from the defendant's mental deficiency short of actual legal insanity. Lockett was found guilty of committing murder during the course of another major felony. At the penalty phase of her trial, the judge determined that none of the mitigating factors applied and imposed the death penalty. After the state courts turned down her appeals, Lockett successfully petitioned the Supreme Court to review the constitutionality of Ohio's sentencing procedures.

Legal Issues

The applicable Ohio statute attempted to conform to the requirement for individualized sentencing determinations mandated by the Supreme Court in *Woodson v. North Carolina*. The state contended that its procedures allowed for a balanced weighing of aggravating and mitigating elements prior to sentencing. Defense lawyers argued that Ohio's limited list of mitigating factors actually denied their client a fair hearing by preventing her from offering a wide range of pertinent information on her own behalf. For example, the court had not learned of Lockett's youth, her history of drug addiction, or her lack of previous serious criminal activity. As a consequence, her rights to due process and an individualized sentence had not been guaranteed.

Decision

The Supreme Court overturned Lockett's death sentence on July 3, 1978. The Court held that the Ohio statute in question unconstitutionally limited the presentation of mitigating evidence in violation of the Eighth and Fourteenth Amendments. In a related ruling, the justices left standing lower court orders that struck down comparable laws in New York and Pennsylvania.

In the principal opinion for the majority, Chief Justice Warren E. Burger stated that a death penalty statute could not preclude a sentencing authority from considering "as a mitigating factor, any aspect of the defendant's character or record or any of the circumstances of the offense that the defendant proffers as a basis for a sentence less than death." In keeping with the Court's traditional emphasis on the unique nature of capital cases, Burger observed that the death sentence differed profoundly from other penalties in its irreversibility. The nonavailability of corrective remedies once the sentence was carried out underscored the need for individualized treatment in the imposition of the death penalty.

The Law of Capital Punishment

Impact

The immediate effect of *Lockett v. Ohio* was to invalidate the death sentences of approximately 100 inmates on Ohio's death row. The decision cast serious doubts as to the validity of capital punishment laws in two dozen other states. State legislatures subsequently moved to align their statutes with the principle established in *Lockett*.

In later rulings, the Supreme Court continued to insist on the broadest possible consideration of mitigating factors prior to sentencing. In *Eddings v. Oklahoma* (1982), the Court nullified a death sentence on the grounds the sentencing judge had refused to consider the defendant's history of emotional disturbance and turbulent family background. Exclusion of testimony that the defendant would adjust well to prison life was cause for reversing the death sentence in *Skipper v. South Carolina* (1986). In 1988 the Court found, in *Mills v. Maryland*, that a jury did not have to unanimously agree a mitigating circumstance existed before considering it in sentencing. When some confusion arose concerning the latter ruling, the Court reaffirmed it in *McKoy v. North Carolina* (1990).

In *Buchanan v. Angelone* (1998), the Court was faced with the question of whether the jury must be explicitly told to consider any mitigating evidence that had been presented and must be instructed as to the meaning and use of such evidence. The Court decided by a 6-3 majority that such instructions were not required, that it was sufficient that the jury had been instructed to consider "all the evidence" in arriving at its sentence.

BECK V. ALABAMA, 447 U.S. 625 (1980)

Background

The defendant, Gilbert Beck, together with an accomplice, entered a house and tied up the victim during a robbery. Beck's accomplice suddenly struck and killed the victim. Beck was tried under an Alabama statute covering robberies in which the defendant intentionally killed the victim—making it a capital crime. At trial, Beck admitted that he had intended to rob the victim but denied that he had any intention of killing him.

Following an unusual Alabama law, the trial judge gave the jury only two options: Convict for the capital crime or acquit, freeing the defendant despite his admission to robbery. (Because the capital crime required an intentional killing, and ordinary robbery did not, the Alabama law did not consider robbery to be an "included" or alternative charge that covered the same circumstances.) The jury convicted Beck for the capital charge and he appealed.

Legal Issues

On appeal, Beck argued that by forcing the jury to choose all or nothing, the Alabama law impermissibly puts pressure on a jury that makes it more likely to convict. After all, the jury presumably does not want an admitted robber to go back on the street, which would be the consequence of acquittal on the capital charge.

Decision

When the case reached the U.S. Supreme Court the justices agreed with Beck and overturned his conviction. They noted that:

> *when the evidence unquestionably establishes that the defendant is guilty of a serious, violent offense—but leaves some doubt with respect to an element that would justify conviction of a capital offense—the failure to give the jury the "third option" of convicting on a lesser included offense would seem to inevitably enhance the risk of an unwarranted conviction.*

Impact

This case embodies the general principle that it is especially important when a defendant's life is at stake that the jury not be forced to a verdict not really justified by the facts. Therefore, if there is a lesser included offense that could be reasonably found from the facts in the case, the jury must be allowed to consider it as an option.

GODFREY V. GEORGIA, 446 U.S. 240 (1980)

Background

In *Gregg v. Georgia* the Supreme Court found that a provision of the Georgia code that allowed a person convicted of murder to be sentenced to death if the offense was "outrageously or wantonly vile, horrible or inhuman in that it involved torture, depravity of mind, or aggravated battery to the victim" was not unconstitutional. Robert Godfrey was subsequently found guilty of two counts of murder and a single count of aggravated assault. The defendant, experiencing marital difficulties, had shot his wife and his mother-in-law, killing both instantly. He also struck and injured his fleeing daughter with the barrel of a shotgun. At the sentencing phase of the trial, the jury relied on the provision in question in imposing the death penalty for each murder. The sentence was upheld by Georgia's highest court. The Supreme Court then agreed to consider Godfrey's charge that the definition of the aggravating circumstances for which he had received the death penalty was unconstitutionally vague.

Legal Issues

Godfrey v. Georgia presented the Supreme Court with two interrelated questions. The first was whether the Georgia law had been correctly applied in Godfrey's case. The court could rule that the evidence did not support the jury's finding of the aggravated circumstance without overturning the provision on which it was based. The Court could also hold that the language in the statute was so broad and imprecise, or unconstitutionally vague, that it violated a defendant's right to clear sentencing standards.

Decision

On May 19, 1980, the Supreme Court left standing the Georgia law but set aside Godfrey's death sentence imposed under the statute. In a plurality opinion announcing the judgment of the 6-3 majority, Justice Potter Stewart emphasized that a state that authorized capital punishment had a constitutional responsibility to design and apply its laws so as to avoid arbitrary and capricious infliction of the death penalty. In previous decisions, the Georgia Supreme Court had constrained use of the provision under which Godfrey was sentenced to instances involving serious physical abuse of the victim before death. The statute, however, had not been similarly limited in the case at hand. The Court concluded that there was "no principled way to distinguish this case, in which the death penalty was imposed, from the many cases in which it was not" and the sentence was thus improperly derived.

Impact

Godfrey marked the first time the Supreme Court directly addressed the constitutionality of a given aggravating circumstance. Although the Court did not overturn the provision in question, *Godfrey* made clear that the Court was exercising particular care to ensure the administration of capital punishment did not revert to the kinds of standardless death sentence determinations ruled unconstitutional in *Furman v. Georgia*. The Court established a very different yardstick for aggravating circumstances than it had for mitigating circumstances in *Lockett v. Ohio*. The two decisions indicated that constitutional safeguards for a defendant facing a possible death sentence required the widest possible consideration of mitigating factors and a very precisely drawn and applied set of aggravating conditions.

BULLINGTON V. MISSOURI, 451 U.S. 430 (1981)

Background

The defendant Robert Bullington was convicted of capital murder. In the trial's penalty phase, Bullington received life imprisonment rather than the death penalty. Bullington then appealed his conviction and was granted a new trial. The prosecutor announced that he would again seek the death penalty.

Legal Issues

Bullington filed a motion with the trial court requesting that the prosecutor not be allowed to seek the death penalty because his penalty had already been decided in the first trial. The trial court granted Bullington's request but the prosecutor then appealed. The appeals court upheld Bullington, the Missouri Supreme Court reversed (allowing the prosecutor to seek the death penalty), and the case then went to the U.S. Supreme Court.

The issue is whether the Constitution's prohibition against double jeopardy (wherein the state has only one chance to try a defendant for a given charge) also applies to the punishment phase of a trial.

Decision

In a previous case, *Stroud v. United States* (1919), the Supreme Court had ruled that a death penalty in a second trial following an original sentence of life imprisonment was not barred by the double jeopardy clause of the Constitution. With Bullington, however, the Court, in an opinion written by Justice Harry A. Blackmun, said that the modern division of capital trials into guilt and penalty phases made a difference. Because the penalty phase involves many of the same features as a trial for guilt (including introduction of evidence and examination of witnesses), the determination of a life sentence in the original penalty phase was equivalent to being acquitted of the death penalty. This meant that the prosecutor could not have another chance to secure a death sentence.

Impact

This case shows the complexity of dealing with bifurcated trials, which have both a guilt and a penalty phase. Today the penalty phase often involves time and resources comparable to those spent on a whole trial under the previous system.

ESTELLE V. SMITH, 451 U.S. 454 (1981)

Background

The defendant Ernest Benjamin Smith was indicted for capital murder. Prior to trial, he underwent a court-ordered psychiatric examination to determine whether he was competent to stand trial. He was deemed to be competent, tried, and convicted of capital murder. In the penalty phase of the trial, the prosecutor had the psychiatrist testify in order to show the defendant's future dangerousness, one of the arguments for imposing a death sentence. The defense objected that they had not been notified that the psychiatrist would testify.

The jury sentenced Smith to death, and he appealed. A Texas appeals court affirmed the conviction and sentence, so Smith went to federal court. The federal district court vacated the death sentence, and this was affirmed by the federal appeals court. The case then went to the U.S. Supreme Court.

Legal Issues

The issue is whether the prosecutor's use of psychiatric testimony in the penalty phase that is based on a court-required competency examination violates the defendant's constitutional rights.

Decision

Chief Justice Warren Burger's opinion for the Court held that use of the psychiatric testimony in the penalty phase violated both the defendant's Fifth Amendment right against self-incrimination and his Sixth Amendment right to assistance of counsel. In the competency exam, the defendant had not been advised of his right to remain silent or told that anything he said might be used against him. Therefore, evidence from the exam could not be used later in the penalty phase to show the defendant's future dangerousness any more than statements given in a police station house without a *Miranda* warning could be used at trial. Also, the defense counsel should have been told that anything the defendant said during the exam might be used against him later. Failure to do so deprived the defendant of his right to assistance of counsel.

Impact

Again, this case shows the importance of the separate penalty phase and the general trend to treat it as a full-fledged trial at which the defendant has all of the rights guaranteed by the Constitution.

ENMUND V. FLORIDA, 458 U.S. 782 (1982)

Background

Under Florida law, a killing committed during another major crime is a felony murder for which all the participants in the crime are legally responsible. Earl Enmund was convicted of the murder of two persons during the course of a robbery at their farmhouse. The Supreme Court of Florida upheld his death sentence, although the trial record revealed that Enmund's involvement in the crime was limited to waiting outside in a car for his two accomplices at the time the killings occurred. The state's highest court ruled this was sufficient to establish Enmund as a principal in the first-degree murder. Enmund's appeal that the Eighth Amendment barred capital punishment in cases where the defendant did not intend to take life was accepted by the Supreme Court.

Legal Issues

The question was not whether Enmund should have been convicted of a felony murder but whether he should receive the same sentence as those who were directly involved in the killing. Enmund maintained his punishment was

73

disproportionate to his peripheral role in the crime. Florida's counsel noted that the law has long recognized the joint responsibility borne by all accomplices to a given crime. Enmund actively took part in a felony that resulted in murder and then assisted the actual killers to escape.

Decision

By a 5-4 margin, the Supreme Court on July 2, 1982, reversed Enmund's death sentence. Writing for the majority, Justice Byron White stated that death was an excessive and disproportionate punishment for a defendant who aided and abetted in the commission of a felony that resulted in murder but who neither killed, attempted to kill, nor intended to kill the victim. Enmund's sentence was impermissibly cruel and unusual under the Eighth Amendment.

Impact

On its face, *Enmund v. Florida* seemed to establish a major new precedent that only those who were directly responsible for a homicide could receive the death sentence for the crime. Although the language of the decision was somewhat ambiguous, *Enmund* was widely viewed as prohibiting the execution of felons who neither actively participated in murder committed by their accomplices nor intended that the offense occur. Still, the Court's exact meaning in its use of the legal concept of intent was unclear.

The Supreme Court returned to the issue of intent in 1987. In *Tison v. Arizona* the Court held that an accomplice to felony murder was legally responsible for the crime if the person demonstrated a "reckless disregard for human life implicit in knowingly engaging in criminal activity known to carry a grave risk of death." Participation in such activity represented a "highly culpable mental state" which could be taken into account in capital sentencing judgments. While not exactly reversing *Enmund*, the new decision seemed to offer a standard that would be relatively easy for the prosecution to meet in many cases. Based on the fact that 26 states authorized capital sentences for accomplices to felony murders, many saw the decision as leading to an expanded use of the death penalty.

BAREFOOT V. ESTELLE, 463 U.S. 880 (1983)

Background

In 1978 Thomas A. Barefoot was convicted of the murder of a police officer in Texas. At a separate sentencing hearing, the jury decided that the death penalty should be imposed. The Texas Court of Criminal Appeals rejected Barefoot's contention that the state's use of psychiatric testimony to predict the future dangerousness of capital defendants was unconstitutional. Successive appeals to the U.S. Supreme Court, again to the Texas Court of Criminal Appeals, and then to a federal district court for the western part of Texas were likewise denied. Although the district court ruled against Barefoot's claim, it granted him a certificate of probable cause to appeal its judgment to the Fifth Circuit Court of Appeals. This appeal was filed in November 1982.

Texas authorities meanwhile set a new execution date of January 25, 1983. Another request for review and motion for stay of execution were subsequently turned down by the Texas Court of Criminal Appeals. In early January 1983, Barefoot petitioned the Fifth Circuit Court of Appeals for a stay of execution pending its consideration of his appeal of the district court ruling. The court of appeals heard arguments on this motion and, in turn, issued an order denying the stay.

On January 24, 1983, the Supreme Court agreed to consider Barefoot's contention that the court of appeals had erred in not granting a stay of execution while the appeal of the lower court's ruling was still pending. The Supreme Court's action halted the execution less than 11 hours before the scheduled time.

Legal Issues

Barefoot v. Estelle specifically addressed the narrow procedural question of the circuit court's actions in not issuing a stay of execution during a pending appeal. In a broader sense, however, the case illustrated the serious problems the mounting number of appeals in capital cases posed to the fair and timely administration of justice. The federal court system was struggling to distinguish substantive from frivolous appeals and to respond correctly to last-minute requests for stays of execution. The Supreme Court had to consider how best to balance the rights of defendants, the need for particular care in capital cases, and the necessity of workable appeals procedures.

Decision

On July 6, 1983, the Supreme Court ruled that the court of appeals had acted properly in its refusal to grant Barefoot a stay of execution even though the death row inmate's constitutional challenge to his sentence was technically still pending. In his majority opinion, Justice Byron R. White noted that the federal law governing the right to appeal prevented a prisoner from presenting his case to a federal appeals court unless the federal district court issued a certificate of probable cause (certifying that the appeal had substantial merit and was not frivolous). Once the certificate was granted, the appeals court "was obligated to decide the merits of the appeal." The appeals court was also required to issue a stay of execution if necessary to provide sufficient time to properly dispose of the appeal.

The majority found that the court of appeals had clearly considered the merits of Barefoot's appeal as part of its decision to deny his request for a stay of execution. The expedited process used by the appeals court, condensing the motions for appeal and stay of execution into one proceeding, was an acceptable handling of the case. Although the court of appeals had not specifically affirmed the fact it had ruled on Barefoot's appeal in its opinion, to conclude that the defendant had not had a full hearing "would be an unwarranted exaltation of form over substance."

The Supreme Court used *Barefoot v. Estelle* as a vehicle for issuing guidelines to the lower federal courts for the handling of appeals in death penalty cases. The subordinate courts were authorized to enact local rules that would implement these guidelines. In a general sense, the Court observed that appeals in the federal court system were only appropriate when a federal question was involved. Federal courts were not "forums in which to relitigate state trials." Similarly, repetitive appeals were not meant to function as a mechanism by which a defendant could delay an execution indefinitely. The appeals process was not a "legal entitlement" that a defendant had a right to pursue regardless of the substance of the issue in question.

The Court tightened the standards for separating meritorious from frivolous appeals. The different nature of the death penalty was a relevant consideration in deciding whether or not to grant an appeal, but the severity of the sanction did not justify automatic approval of an appeal in every case. A lower court should only allow an appeal to go forward if the petitioner had made a "substantial showing of the denial of a federal right" where the issues involved were at least "debatable among jurists of reason." When a court determined that these conditions were met, then the petitioner was entitled to a full hearing on the merits of the appeal. Circuit courts were encouraged to adopt and make known rules that would speed the appeals process. Expedited procedures were particularly appropriate in instances of second and successive appeals.

Impact

Barefoot was intended at least in part to relieve the burden on the Supreme Court of last-minute appeals in capital cases. The guidelines established by the Court, however, did not succeed in appreciably reducing either these appeals or the volume of death penalty-related legal actions in general. In subsequent years a number of justices, most notably William H. Rehnquist and Lewis F. Powell, Jr., have expressed their concern over the impact the growing number of appeals in death penalty cases was having on the entire criminal justice system. On several occasions, Justice Powell suggested publicly that if the issue could not be resolved, then the death penalty itself should be abandoned as unworkable.

In 1988, Chief Justice Rehnquist appointed then-retired Justice Powell to head a commission charged with finding ways to expedite the handling of capital appeals. The panel submitted its proposal for strict new limits on multiple appeals by death row inmates in 1989. Its recommendations have been incorporated into deliberations in the Senate over possible federal legislation in this area.

Underlying the debate over death-penalty appeals is the more basic struggle between proponents and opponents of capital punishment. Lawyers for death row inmates have a professional responsibility to pursue every possible avenue on the behalf of their clients. At the same time, many abolitionist groups believe that the generation of time-consuming and costly litigation will eventually lead the public to conclude that capital punishment is not worth the trouble its imposition causes. (Of course it could also lead to a political backlash resulting in legislation that seeks to drastically streamline the appeals process.)

While the Court had not overturned the use of "future dangerousness" testimony, it did require a balancing consideration. In *Simmons v. South Carolina* (1994), the petitioner had been sentenced to death. His attorney had asked the judge to instruct the jury that Simmons would be ineligible for parole because of his two previous convictions for violent crime. The judge refused to give this instruction, and when the jury spontaneously asked about it, he told them that parole "was not a proper issue for your consideration" and that "the terms life imprisonment and death sentence are to be understood in their plan [sic] and ordinary meaning." By a vote of 7-2 the Supreme Court overturned the conviction, noting that since the state had raised the issue of the defendant's future dangerousness in the first place, fairness required that the jury also be informed about the alternative of life without parole.

PULLEY V. HARRIS, 465 U.S. 37 (1984)

Background

Robert A. Harris was convicted by a California court of killing two teenage boys to use their car for a bank robbery. He was sentenced to death. California's capital punishment statute did not require that a state appellate court conduct a proportionality review to ensure that a given sentence was in line with other sentences imposed in the state for similar crimes. The California Supreme Court rejected Harris' claim that the lack of this special review rendered the state's death penalty law invalid under the Constitution. Harris then shifted his appeal to the federal court system. The court of appeals subsequently held that the proportionality review was constitutionally required and directed the California Supreme Court to undertake such an analysis within 120 days. Otherwise, the appeals court would reverse Harris' sentence. State officials appealed the decision to the U.S. Supreme Court.

Legal Issues

Harris' lawyers cited the Supreme Court's ruling in *Furman v. Georgia* that an arbitrary and capricious administration of the death penalty constituted cruel and unusual punishment under the Eighth Amendment. Without a comparative review of sentences, it was impossible to determine whether capital punishment was being imposed in an evenhanded and rational manner as required by the constitution. They argued that the Court's decisions in 1976 reinstating the death penalty had implicitly placed proportionality review on the level of a constitutional requirement. California officials maintained that there were already sufficient safeguards in the state's procedures to ensure the death penalty was consistently and fairly applied.

Decision

The Supreme Court sided with California. In a ruling announced January 23, 1984, the Court found that a state could carry out a death sentence without first conducting a proportionality review. The majority decision, written by Justice Byron White, stated that such a review was not required either by the Court's own death penalty precedents or by the Constitution's ban on cruel and unusual punishment.

Justice White observed that "any capital sentence may occasionally produce aberrational outcomes" but such inconsistencies were substantially different from the "major systemic defects" that led the Court to invalidate all existing death penalty laws in *Furman*. It was possible for a state to design a law that adequately protected against arbitrary executions without recourse to proportionality review. The fact the Court in 1976 had upheld Florida and Georgia statutes that included such review did not mean the procedure was indispensable. At the same time, the Court found that the Texas law, which did not contain proportional review, was also constitutional.

Impact

Pulley v. Harris had little direct effect on the pace of executions in California, where most death row inmates were far from exhausting their appeals. The decision had a more immediate impact in Texas, the only other state without proportionality review that also had a sizeable death row population. The proportionality question was the only substantive basis of appeal remaining for a number of prisoners there.

In his opinion, Justice White was careful to distinguish between ensuring a sentence was proportionate to the crime committed and the concept of proportionality review. He made it clear that the Court in *Pulley* was not retreating from the precedent established in cases such as *Coker v. Georgia* (where the death penalty was ruled an excessive punishment for rape) that capital punishment was only appropriate when it fit the crime.

CALDWELL V. MISSISSIPPI, 472 U.S. 320 (1985)

Background

During the closing arguments in the penalty phase of defendant Caldwell's capital murder trial, the defense attorney told the jury about the defendant's family's background, their struggle with poverty, and the positive elements of his character—all potentially mitigating factors against the death penalty. He also urged the jury to consider this evidence very carefully in carrying out its "awesome responsibility" for the defendant's fate.

The prosecutor, perhaps sensing a wavering on the part of the jury, assured jury members that they did not bear the whole weight of the decision. If they decided for death, that decision would be reviewed for correctness by the Mississippi Supreme Court. The defendant was sentenced to death.

Legal Issues

In their appeal, the defense argued that it was not proper for the prosecution to try to make the jury feel that they were not ultimately responsible for the sentence they gave to the defendant. Doing so might cause the jury to not give careful enough consideration to the mitigating factors raised by the defense.

Decision

The Mississippi Supreme Court upheld the conviction and (by a split decision) the death sentence as well. The case then went to the U.S. Supreme Court. Writing for the Court, Justice Thurgood Marshall ruled that it was not permissible to make the jury think that it was not fully responsible for its decision. It was also misleading to tell the jury that their decision was reviewable by the appeals courts because the latter normally do not review the jury's decision with regard to the facts of the case but only look for errors in procedure. The three dissenting justices did not really disagree with the underlying principle but felt that it was unlikely that the jury would have taken the prosecutor's remarks all that seriously as a diminishing of their responsibility.

Impact

The role of statements or instructions made to the jury can be critical in many cases. Although the official instructions given by the judge are the most important, courts also check to see that the trial jury is not being improperly influenced by misleading statements about their role.

HECKLER V. CHANEY, 470 U.S. 821 (1985)

Background

Generally, condemned prisoners have had only limited success in arguing that the actual means of execution are cruel or inhumane and thus not acceptable. In part this is because newer, allegedly less painful methods have been continually developed. Thus, when the Supreme Court was on the verge of considering the acceptability of the electric chair in 2000, Florida offered lethal injection as an alternative. A few years later, Georgia switched its sole means of execution from electrocution to lethal injection.

Capital Punishment

Legal Issues

Lethal injection has also been the subject of legal challenges. In the *Heckler* case a group of condemned prisoners first filed a claim with the Food and Drug Administration (FDA) arguing that the combination of drugs used in lethal injection had been misbranded and had not been approved for use as a means of execution. Further, they argued that the drugs would likely be administered in executions by untrained personnel, and they were therefore likely to cause an unacceptable level of pain and distress.

The FDA commissioner suggested that the agency likely did not have jurisdiction over the use of drugs in executions. Further, the agency's mandate was to protect the general public from harmful drugs, not to determine the acceptability of means of execution. The U.S. District Court for the District of Columbia agreed with the FDA's position and said that it had no jurisdiction over the agency's regulatory decision anyway. The Court of Appeals disagreed, saying that the FDA was mandated to investigate the potential misuse of a drug that could cause significant distress to a group of people (prisoners undergoing execution).

Decision

The U.S. Supreme Court then heard the case, and it was not very sympathetic to the prisoners' novel argument. The Court said not only that the FDA did not have jurisdiction over lethal injections but that it made no sense for an agency whose job it was to review drugs for safety and efficacy to evaluate drugs used for lethal injection.

Impact

The outcome of this case suggests that attempts to introduce federal regulatory agencies into the process of administering capital punishment are likely to fail. This does not mean, however, that the question of whether a means of execution is in itself unacceptably painful has not been considered by the courts.

In the case *Francis v. Resweber* (1947), the Supreme Court set a high standard for such scrutiny. Even though a first attempt at electrocution had been botched, the Court ruled that making a second attempt did not amount to cruel and unusual punishment so long as the state did not intend to cause unnecessary pain.

In *Provenzano v. Moore* the Supreme Court ruled that use of the electric chair was not unconstitutional. Although the Ninth Circuit Court of Appeals upheld a permanent injunction against the use of lethal gas *(Fierro v. Gomez)*, when the U.S. Supreme Court considered the issue in *Gomez v. Fierro* (1996), the Court vacated the injunction and returned the case to the lower court because California had adopted lethal injection as the default method of execution.

The Law of Capital Punishment

FORD V. WAINWRIGHT, 477 U.S. 399 (1986)

Background

In 1974 Alvin B. Ford killed a Florida police officer while robbing a restaurant. He was convicted of murder and sentenced to death the same year. There was no suggestion of mental incompetence at the time of the offense, during his trial, or at his sentencing hearing. After an extended period on Florida's death row, however, Ford began to show signs of serious mental disorder. His attorneys argued that he had gone insane and consequently should not be executed. At their request, the governor of Florida, following the procedures in state law for determining the competency of a condemned inmate, appointed a panel of three psychiatrists who interviewed Ford for approximately 30 minutes. When the panel reported, as required by state law, that Ford knew why he was to die, the governor signed a death warrant for his execution. After a series of unsuccessful appeals in state and lower federal courts, Ford's attorneys prevailed upon the Supreme Court to hear their claim that Florida's procedure for assessing the mental competency of convicted prisoners did not meet minimum due process standards.

Legal Issues

Ford's counsel argued that a 30-minute interview was insufficient to determine their client's sanity. State procedures, however, had stopped the attorneys from introducing additional information about his psychiatric condition. They contended that the fact Ford had not received an impartial hearing where all relevant evidence of his mental state could be considered was a violation of his due process rights under the Fourteenth Amendment. In a broader sense, *Ford v. Wainwright* raised the question of whether it was appropriate to inflict the death penalty on a person who was insane. Even if Ford were found to be mentally incompetent, there was no clear legal precedent that could preclude his execution.

Decision

On June 26, 1986, the Supreme Court blocked Ford's execution, at least until Florida implemented new procedures to evaluate his sanity. These procedures had to meet basic standards of due process. At a minimum, this meant designation of an impartial board or officer to consider all available evidence to include psychiatric presentations or legal arguments made on behalf of the prisoner.

The Court went on to rule that the Eighth Amendment prohibited the execution of death row inmates who had become so insane they no longer understood they were going to be put to death or the reason why. In his majority opinion Justice Thurgood Marshall wrote: "For centuries no jurisdiction has countenanced the execution of the insane, yet this Court has never decided whether the Constitution forbids the practice. Today, we keep faith with our common-law heritage by holding that it does." Marshall concluded that the basic meaning of a punishment was negated if a person no longer comprehended its purpose. Execution of the insane was closer to "mindless vengeance" than it was to retribution.

Impact

Ford's real significance was in the procedural safeguards it extended to prisoners who possibly suffered mental difficulties. Prior to the ruling, many states had essentially cursory procedures for testing for insanity. Interestingly, the Court also held that if a death row inmate who had been judged mentally incompetent was subsequently cured of the condition, then a state was free to go forward with the execution. While this was a logical consequence of the reasoning behind the decision, opponents of capital punishment pointed out the irony that an inmate who went insane had to remain insane to stay alive.

The decision was also important symbolically. The Court's statement that the Constitution did not allow the execution of the insane had no direct legal relevance because no state permitted such a proceeding. However, *Ford* represented a further incremental narrowing by the Court of the circumstances under which a person could be put to death.

MCCLESKEY V. KEMP, 481 U.S. 279 (1987)

Background

In October 1978, Warren McCleskey, a black man, was convicted of killing a white Atlanta police officer during an armed robbery. At the penalty phase of his trial, the jury of 11 whites and one black sentenced him to die in Georgia's electric chair. After McCleskey lost two rounds of appeals in state and federal courts, the NAACP Legal Defense and Education Fund (LDF) took over his case.

LDF attorneys filed a new appeal in Federal District Court challenging the constitutionality of Georgia's death penalty law on the grounds that it was administered in a racially discriminatory manner. In support of this claim, they cited a study conducted by Professor David C. Baldus of the University of Iowa. The Baldus study was a detailed and sophisticated statistical analysis of more than 2,000 murder cases in Georgia in the 1970s. The research indicated that black defendants were substantially more likely to receive the death sentence than white defendants. The disparity was even greater when the study compared the rate at which the death penalty was applied for black defendants who killed white victims as against white defendants who killed black victims. After the appeal was denied by both the district court and a circuit court of appeals, the Supreme Court agreed to hear the case.

Legal Issues

Since the early 1960s, the NAACP LDF had been engaged in defending black persons accused of capital crimes. At first, this activity was an outgrowth of the organization's involvement in the civil rights movement. Most of the court cases took place in the South. However, by the mid-1960s the LDF had committed to a nationwide campaign to abolish capital punishment.

The issue of possible racial bias against the defendant had been raised in several cases. In *Ham v. South Carolina* (1973), the Court had found that the defendant's counsel had the right to ask potential jurors about their possible racial biases if the facts of the case suggested bias might be a problem. (Ham was a civil rights activist who claimed that the charges against him were a frame-up.) In *Ristaino v. Ross* (1976), the Court did not extend this principle to a right to inquire about bias any time the defendant and victim were of different races. In *Turner v. Murray* (1986), however, the Court followed its common practice of requiring greater protection of rights in capital cases than in cases where the death penalty was not an issue. Here the Court ruled that in an interracial murder the defendant has the right to ask prospective jurors about racial bias.

Many LDF lawyers had concluded from personal experiences that the death penalty was imposed in a discriminatory manner. But trying to deal with possible individual bias on a case-by-case basis is very difficult. An alternative approach is to look not at individual behavior, but at outcomes—are minorities treated differently on a statistical basis than non-minorities?

In 1965 the organization initiated an exhaustive study of racial discrimination in the use of the death penalty for rape. The study revealed that black men frequently were sentenced to death for raping a white woman while white men who raped black women almost invariably were not. This statistical information was incorporated into a number of LDF challenges to capital punishment in the late 1960s and early 1970s. Although the Supreme Court did not specifically refer to racial bias in its 1972 decision striking down the nation's death penalty statutes, many of the opinions in *Furman v. Georgia* mentioned racial minorities as disproportionately affected by the capricious and arbitrary way capital punishment was administered.

When the Supreme Court reinstated the death penalty in 1976, patterns of racial discrimination in capital sentencing again became an issue. LDF's legal argument on behalf of McCleskey had two parts. First, the fact that black defendants convicted of murder were treated differently than white defendants convicted of murder was a violation of the equal protection clause of the Fourteenth Amendment. This clause requires that the laws be applied equally and uniformly to all. There cannot be one system of justice for whites and another for blacks. The LDF also maintained that the Baldus study demonstrated that Georgia's death penalty was not being imposed in an evenhanded manner. Although the law had been ruled constitutional by the Court in 1976, the actual practice of capital punishment in Georgia still singled out blacks for the harshest penalties. The LDF argued that the new death penalty statutes in Georgia were being applied in a way that did not meet the requirements the Court had established in *Furman* for fair and objective standards to guide capital sentencing decisions. McCleskey's counsel concluded this use of the death penalty was unconstitutional under the Eighth Amendment's ban on cruel and unusual punishment.

Decision

On April 22, 1987, a closely divided Supreme Court ruled against McCleskey. The 5-4 majority accepted the validity of the Baldus study but held that it was not enough to prove actual discrimination against the individual defendant in the case at hand. Writing for the majority, Justice Lewis F. Powell, Jr., allowed that the discretion provided to prosecutors and juries in the U.S. criminal justice system would inevitably lead to occasional abuses and disparities. For a defendant to show unconstitutional racial bias in a given death sentence, though, it was necessary to "prove that the decision makers in his case acted with discriminatory purpose." This proof required evidence specific to the case. A generalized study documenting "a discrepancy that appears to correlate with race" was insufficient.

The Court rejected the basic argument that statistics revealing a seeming disparity in sentencing were grounds for overturning Georgia's death penalty statute under the Fourteenth Amendment's equal protection provisions. The statistical evidence was not clear and convincing enough to warrant a finding of racial discrimination affecting the entire Georgia capital sentencing process. (An earlier appeals court had pointed out that the Baldus study did not break down cases by aggravating and mitigating factors and therefore may not have been a valid comparison of truly similar cases.) Similarly, the Baldus study by itself was not proof that the state's capital punishment system was arbitrary and capricious in application and that McCleskey's death sentence consequently was excessive in violation of the Eighth Amendment.

In previous decisions, the Court had approved the use of statistics in demonstrating instances of discrimination in areas such as employment. The majority found, however, that drawing an inference of prejudice in a specific trial from broad statistics was substantively different from inferring discrimination in a wide range of employment practices.

Justice Powell characterized the claim that Georgia juries were more prone to sentence a black man to death as an attack on the fundamental role discretion played in the criminal justice system. He contended that the discretion afforded to a jury was, in fact, a criminal defendant's core "protection of life and liberty against race or color prejudice." To the extent racism still infected the criminal justice system, the answer was to surround the process by which guilt and punishment were determined with procedural safeguards.

In an unusual step, the Court revealed several associated concerns that had guided its finding. McCleskey's claim, taken to its logical conclusion, meant that not only death sentences but potentially all criminal penalties were tainted with racism. Similarly, the methodology used in the Baldus study could be employed to allege patterns of discrimination involving other minority groups, gender, or any other arbitrary variables such as physical attractiveness. Absent the most compelling evidence, the Court was reluctant to reach a conclusion in the *McCleskey* case that might undermine the basic workings of the criminal justice system.

Impact

McCleskey v. Kemp is considered the most important Supreme Court decision on capital punishment since the death penalty was restored in 1976. The ruling removed what abolitionists had called their last sweeping challenge to the constitutionality of the death penalty itself. Numerous potential court challenges to capital punishment remained, but none would be applicable to more than a fraction of the death row population. The immediate effect of *McCleskey* for the approximately 1,900 persons on death row nationally was unclear. Although it was expected that the pace of executions would eventually quicken, the majority of the death row inmates had not exhausted their appeals on other issues.

Many opponents of capital punishment bitterly criticized the decision. They accused the Court of distorting established legal principles in order to avoid overturning numerous death sentences and creating disarray in the judicial system. Civil rights leaders also condemned the ruling. Legal experts pointed out that the Court had made it extremely difficult, if not impossible, to prove racial discrimination in the use of the death penalty. While it was possible to accumulate statistics evidencing a pattern of bias across a wide number of cases, it was an entirely different proposition to establish discriminatory intent in actions of a particular prosecutor, judge, or jury.

BOOTH V. MARYLAND, 482 U.S. 496 (1987)

Background

A 1983 Maryland law provided for the use of "victim impact statements" in death sentencing hearings. John Booth was subsequently convicted of two counts of first-degree murder. Together with an accomplice, he had bound, gagged, and stabbed to death an elderly couple in their Baltimore home during a robbery. At the sentencing phase of his trial, the prosecutor introduced a victim impact statement that described the personal characteristics of the victims and the emotional impact of their murders upon their family.

The state trial court refused to exclude the victim impact statement, rejecting the defendant's claim that its use in a capital case violated the Eighth Amendment. Based at least in part on the statement, the jury sentenced Booth to death. The Maryland Court of Appeals upheld the sentence, and Booth successfully petitioned the Supreme Court for review.

Legal Issues

Booth contended the victim impact statement was irrelevant to an appropriate consideration of the circumstances of his crime. Because of its inherently inflammatory nature, the statement had unduly influenced the jury in its deliberations. As a consequence, emotion rather than objective standards had guided the imposition of the death sentence in his case. This kind of subjective and capricious capital sentencing process was unconstitutional under the Eighth Amendment's ban on cruel and unusual punishment. Maryland officials maintained that a jury was entitled to consider any evidence that had a bearing on the sentencing decision. The victim impact statement served to inform the jury, as sentencing authority, of the full extent of harm caused by the crime.

Decision

On June 11, 1987, the Supreme Court invalidated the Maryland law in question. The Court found that the introduction of a victim impact statement at the sentencing phase of a capital trial was unconstitutional.

A capital sentencing decision, Justice Lewis F. Powell, Jr., wrote in the majority opinion, should center on the "blameworthiness" of the defendant. The victim impact statement created an unacceptable risk that a jury might impose the death penalty in an arbitrary and capricious manner in violation of the Eighth Amendment. A statement containing descriptions of the family's grief and suffering had the potential to divert a jury from its proper focus on the moral culpability of the defendant. Decisions on the death penalty had to be "based on reason rather than caprice or emotion." Many of the factors in a victim impact statement were irrelevant to the question of blameworthiness because they were unknown to the killer at the time of the crime.

Justice Powell pointed out that victim impact statements could lead to a double standard of justice. "We are troubled by the implication that defendants whose victims were assets to their community are more deserving of punishment than those whose victims are perceived to be less worthy."

In dissent, Justice Antonin Scalia emphasized the growing concern for victims' rights. He noted this concern stemmed from the feeling many citizens had that the criminal justice system increasingly failed to balance mitigating factors on behalf of a defendant against the harm that person caused to innocent members of society. He disputed the idea that blameworthiness was the only relevant consideration in death sentencing, observing that criminal codes routinely attached "more severe penalties to crimes based on the consequences to victims."

Impact

Justice Scalia's dissent was echoed by groups advocating the rights of crime victims. These organizations, which had become increasingly active in recent years, denounced *Booth v. Maryland* as a setback to legitimate efforts to furnish victims a more important role in the criminal justice process. At the time of the *Booth* ruling, 36 states and the federal government provided for the inclusion of victim impact statements in a variety of criminal proceedings. *Booth* made it clear that laws permitting the use of these statements at capital trials were unconstitutional.

South Carolina v. Gathers (1989) extended this principle to forbidding the prosecution from making statements about characteristics of the victim (such as his religiosity) that were not relevant to understanding the circumstances of the crime but suggested that the crime was more heinous because of the worthiness of the victim. However, *Payne v. Tennessee* (discussed later) represents an abrupt change of course for the Court on this issue.

BURGER V. KEMP, 483 U.S. 107 (1987)

Background

Christopher Burger was convicted for murder in Wayne County, Georgia, and sentenced to death on January 25, 1978. He brought a habeas corpus petition that asserted that he had been denied his constitutional right to "effective assistance of counsel" because his attorney "failed to make an adequate investigation of the possibly mitigating circumstances of his offense." The district court and the court of appeals successively turned down his claim.

Legal Issues

The Supreme Court has interpreted the "right to assistance of counsel" in criminal cases as specified in the Sixth Amendment to mean a right to a reasonably *effective* counsel. A lawyer, for example, who sleeps through most of the trial or is drunk cannot effectively assist the defendant, and such a defendant thus does not have the protection intended by the Constitution.

In *Strickland v. Washington* (1984), the Supreme Court declared that to make a claim of ineffective counsel, the defendant had to show the counsel was deficient, making mistakes or omissions that a reasonably competent professional would not make. The defendant also has to show that any such errors were so serious that they prejudiced the outcome of the case, thus depriving the defendant of a fair trial. In general, courts have interpreted this standard quite strictly in an attempt to prevent a flood of frivolous appeals.

In this case, the specific claim was that Burger's counsel was ineffective because he made no effort to investigate or establish mitigating circumstances (specifically, the defendant's troubled childhood in a drug-infested home) in the penalty phase. He also failed to put the defendant, his mother, and another witness on the stand to give testimony about these circumstances. This failure may have resulted in the defendant receiving the death penalty rather than a life sentence.

Decision

In his majority opinion, Justice Stevens agreed that a capital sentencing phase was sufficiently like a trial as to require similar standards of effective assistance of counsel. On the other hand, he noted that the earlier *Strickland* decision had insisted that evaluation of an attorney's performance must be "deferential" and strive to avoid second-guessing or speaking from hindsight.

87

Speaking for a 5-4 majority, Justice Stevens found that Burger's attorney had acted reasonably in evaluating evidence of the defendant's "unhappy childhood" and in deciding not to put witnesses relevant to that claim on the stand during the penalty hearing, including the defendant himself, whose lack of remorse and tendency to brag may have made him a poor witness. The Court went on to say that while the defendant's counsel "could well have made a more thorough investigation then he did," the court must address "not what is prudent or appropriate, but what is constitutionally compelled." Defendant's counsel did interview the relevant witnesses, and his decision not to use them was a "reasonable professional judgment." The Court majority thus denied Burger's petition. The four dissenters, led by Justice Harry Blackmun, disagreed that the defendant's counsel had adequately sought mitigating evidence, and also pointed out that the counsel rejected the free assistance of a lawyer who had known the defendant because the lawyer was black.

Impact

This decision shows the considerable reluctance of appeals courts to accept appeals based on ineffective assistance of counsel if counsel's actions are at all within the parameters of normal professional procedure. The justices in the appeals court and Supreme Court are concerned about avoiding being placed in the potential position of having to perform what might be called "quality control" on every criminal defense in a capital case.

THOMPSON V. OKLAHOMA, 487 U.S. 815 (1988)

Background

William Wayne Thompson was 15 when he participated in the murder of his brother-in-law in January 1983. The prosecution obtained an order allowing Thompson to be tried as an adult under the provisions of an Oklahoma statute that permitted such a proceeding if the court found the circumstances of the crime warranted the action, and there were no reasonable prospects for rehabilitation of the defendant in the juvenile system. The young man was convicted of first-degree murder and sentenced to death. After the Oklahoma Court of Appeals rejected his contention that the execution of a minor constituted cruel and unusual punishment in violation of the Eighth Amendment, Thompson successfully petitioned the Supreme Court for review.

Legal Issues

The question before the Supreme Court was whether it was appropriate to execute a defendant for a capital offense committed while the person was a juvenile. The issue was not the age of the defendant at the time the execution would be carried out. Thompson was 21 when the Court considered his case. Rather, the challenge to the Court was to determine whether a person at age 15 could be held fully accountable for criminal actions. American jurisprudence had gradually evolved to the belief that minors were not responsible in the same way as adults for their behavior. However, there was no clear precedent for deciding at what age a juvenile could, or should, be treated as an adult.

Decision

The Supreme Court on June 29, 1988, held that the execution under Oklahoma law of a defendant who was 15 at the time of the capital offense was unconstitutional. The five justices in the majority were unable to agree on a common opinion. In a plurality opinion, Justice John Paul Stevens stated the view of four of the five members of the majority that the execution of any person who committed a capital crime under age 16 offended contemporary standards of decency. It was excessive under the Eighth Amendment to punish with death a young person who was not yet "capable of acting with the degree of culpability" that would justify the ultimate penalty.

Justice Sandra Day O'Connor became the decisive, or swing, vote in the decision. Her opinion consequently expressed the basic consensus of the Court. She stopped short of declaring that all executions of defendants under 16 were unconstitutional. There was no conclusive evidence that the sentiment of society in general was against all such executions. However, she ruled that states could not sentence to death persons aged 15 or younger under capital punishment statutes that specified no minimum age standard for when the crime was committed.

Impact

Thompson v. Oklahoma effectively ended the execution of persons who committed capital offenses before the age of 16. No state had a capital punishment law that expressly allowed the execution of minors at this age, and none was considered likely to enact such a measure. The *Thompson* case had attracted international attention. Many opponents of capital punishment and others felt that the Supreme Court had not gone far enough in its decision. They argued that 18 should be the minimum age at which a person involved in a capital crime should be liable for the death penalty. Finally, in 2005 the Supreme Court agreed with this point of view, extending the minimum capital punishment age to 18 in *Roper v. Simmons.*

MURRAY V. GIRRATANO, 492 U.S. 1 (1989)

Background

A group of indigent (poor) Virginia death row prisoners filed a class action suit against state officials, asking that they be given court-provided counsel to represent them in their post-conviction appeals.

Capital Punishment

Legal Issues

The Supreme Court has interpreted the Constitution's due process clause as requiring that persons who cannot afford a lawyer be provided one to represent them from the time they are first arrested and questioned by police to their trial, acquittal, or conviction and sentencing. The issue is whether the Constitution also requires that convicted persons who cannot afford private counsel be provided with free counsel to represent them through the appeals process.

The federal district court agreed with the plaintiffs and ordered that the state develop a program to provide free counsel for indigent death row inmates who sought to appeal through the state court system. (They were not required to provide counsel for federal appeals of state convictions). A federal appeals court affirmed this ruling, so the state took it to the U.S. Supreme Court.

Decision

In a split decision, the plurality opinion, written by Chief Justice William Rehnquist, said that there was no constitutional due process requirement for attorneys to be provided for inmates seeking state post-conviction relief. Such proceedings are civil, not criminal, and are "collateral" and supplementary. Providing counsel for the main criminal proceedings is sufficient to fulfill the inmate's constitutional rights and to ensure a fair judicial system. Thus the judgment in favor of the inmates was reversed.

A dissenting opinion, shared by three justices and written by Justice John Paul Stevens, argued that unlike the case with lesser charges, in capital cases inmates prevailed on appeal about 60 to 70 percent of the time. This suggested that the regular criminal procedure is not doing a good job of preventing errors that could be fatal to inmates. It also implies that the constitutional guarantee of due process and fairness cannot be met without providing indigent inmates with meaningful access to the later stages of appeals, such as habeas appeals in federal courts.

Impact

As the dissenting opinion noted, about half of the death penalty states provide free counsel to help inmates with their appeals. Most of the rest provide some sort of state-funded resource center to serve such inmates. Because not providing such assistance appears to be "unusual," and unfair on some basic level, it is possible that this ruling will eventually be reversed, or at least made moot by the states providing adequate assistance.

PENRY V. LYNAUGH, 492 U.S. 302 (1989)

Background

In late 1979 Johnny Paul Penry was arrested for the rape and murder of a Texas woman. At a competency hearing before his trial, a clinical psychologist testified that Penry was mentally retarded. He was evaluated as having the mental age of six and one-half. His social maturity, or ability to function in the world, was described as that of a nine- or 10-year-old child. However the jury at the hearing found Penry competent to stand trial.

At the guilt–innocence phase of his trial, Penry's lawyers presented an insanity defense. The defendant was said to suffer from an organic brain disorder that resulted in an inability to learn and a lack of self-control. At the time of his offense, he did not grasp the difference between right and wrong and could not conform his behavior to the law. The prosecution countered with expert testimony that Penry was legally sane but had an antisocial personality. The jury rejected the insanity defense and convicted Penry of capital murder. During the penalty phase of his trial, he was sentenced to death.

The Texas Court of Criminal Appeals rejected the contention that Penry's sentence violated the Eighth Amendment. Although it denied a similar petition, a federal court of appeals noted that Penry's claim raised important issues. The Supreme Court subsequently decided to review the case.

Legal Issues

Penry's counsel argued first that Texas' capital punishment law was worded in such a way that it did not allow the jury to properly take into account the mental retardation of their client as a mitigating factor. The sentencing jury was instructed to include the evidence introduced at the trial in its deliberations. However, the aggravating circumstances presented to the jury were defined in such a way that Penry's limited mental ability was made essentially irrelevant. At a more fundamental level, defense lawyers contended that the Eighth Amendment ban on cruel and unusual punishment prohibited the execution of the mentally retarded. Penry was not fully responsible or culpable for his actions and should not be punished as if he were.

Decision

The Supreme Court agreed with Penry's lawyers on their procedural issue. On June 26, 1989, the Court reversed Penry's death sentence and instructed Texas officials to revise their sentencing procedures to ensure that full consideration was given to a defendant's mitigating evidence of mental retardation. The Court again stressed the point it first had made in *Lockett v. Ohio* that a state's capital sentencing process had to provide for inclusion of any mitigating factor relevant to a defendant's background, character, and crime.

By a 5-4 vote, however, the Court declined to state that the Eighth Amendment categorically barred the execution of the mentally retarded. Writing for the majority, Justice Sandra Day O'Connor observed that the broad consensus was against holding the severely retarded culpable for their actions. Retarded persons, though, were individuals whose abilities varied greatly. There was no basis to conclude that mentally retarded persons invariably lacked the capacity to act with the degree of responsibility that would justify use of the death penalty. Instead, the court must make an individualized determination as to whether the death sentence is appropriate in each instance where retardation is a possible factor.

After a new penalty hearing Penry was again sentenced to death. However on June 4, 2001 the Supreme Court overturned Penry's sentence by 6-3, ruling that the instructions concerning mental retardation given in the new hearing were still insufficiently clear.

Impact

The decision in *Penry v. Lynaugh* raised many difficult questions. Experts suggest that about 10 percent of the death row inmates are at least mildly retarded, but the evaluation of mental status is often inadequate. Further, there is no universally acceptable way to define mental retardation. In her opinion Justice O'-Connor noted that the concept of "mental age" was too imprecise to use to determine whether a particular individual can be held accountable for his or her actions. In the aftermath of *Penry*, state criminal justice systems struggled to find workable answers to the question of how retardation affects a person's ability to distinguish right from wrong and to act accordingly, or even to participate in a criminal proceeding.

In 2002 the Supreme Court essentially reversed *Penry* in *Atkins v. Virginia*, declaring it unconstitutional to sentence a significantly mentally retarded person to death.

CLEMONS V. MISSISSIPPI, 494 U.S. 738 (1990)

Background

The defendant, Chandler Clemons, was convicted of capital murder. During the penalty phase, the jury was told to consider two statutory aggravating circumstances: 1) that the murder was committed during the course of a robbery for pecuniary [monetary] gain, and 2) that the killing was "especially heinous, atrocious or cruel." The jury determined that both aggravating factors were present and that they outweighed any mitigating factors. Clemons was therefore sentenced to death.

Many court rulings have held that the "especially heinous, atrocious or cruel" language is unconstitutionally vague. However, the state is generally allowed to address that problem by supplying a "limiting construction" that prevents the aggravating factor from being applied inappropriately.

Legal Issues

Clemons appealed, and the Mississippi Supreme Court ruled that the death sentence was proper because the appeals court had provided a suitable limiting construction. They also said that beyond a reasonable doubt, if the especially heinous aggravating factor had been removed, the jury would still have decided in favor of the death penalty. The case then came to the U.S. Supreme Court.

The defense argued that the limiting construction was not good enough to undo the effects of the unconstitutionally vague language. Because only the jury could give the death sentence, the jury itself should have been asked to reconsider the case without using the improper aggravating circumstance.

Decision

In a divided opinion the Supreme Court upheld the death sentence. Writing for the majority, Justice Byron White said that the Constitution did not require that the jury have the final decision with regard to the death penalty. Therefore it was proper for an appeals court to remove the invalid aggravating circumstance and reweigh the remaining circumstances to see if the jury would have still decided on the death penalty. Alternatively, the court could determine whether the reference to the invalid aggravating circumstance was a harmless error that did not unduly influence the jury's decision.

In dissent, Justice Harry A. Blackmun said that it was not appropriate for an appeals court to reweigh aggravating and mitigating factors. Having only a written record, they do not have the same kind of direct experience of the case as the jury.

Impact

The question of how to address errors in sentencing procedures and instructions frequently arises. Those favoring reweighing or "harmless error" analysis believe that it maintains fairness for the defendant while not bogging down the judicial system in retrials and new hearings. However, recent decisions have emphasized the role of the jury, with *Ring v. Arizona* (2002) finally saying that only juries, not judges, can sentence someone to death. It is possible, therefore, that juries may be required to revisit more sentencing decisions where improper instructions had been given.

PAYNE V. TENNESSEE, 501 U.S. 808 (1991)

Background

Defendant Pervis Tyrone Payne was convicted by a jury of two counts of first-degree murder and one count of assault with intent to commit murder in the first degree. He was sentenced to death for each of the murders, plus 30 years for the assault. During the sentencing phase of his trial, Payne presented witnesses, including his parents, who testified to his good character, and a psychologist, who testified that Payne was mentally handicapped and had a low IQ score. The State in turn presented the mother of one of the victims, who testified to the severe effects of the crime on her two young grandchildren. In calling for the death penalty, the prosecutor referred graphically to the pain and suffering of the victims and the continuing effect of their death on their loved ones.

Following his conviction, the defendant appealed, arguing that the testimony of the victim's grandmother and the references to victim impact in the prosecutor's closing argument were prejudicial and violated the defendant's rights. The Supreme Court of Tennessee rejected the defendant's appeal, and the U.S. Supreme Court agreed to hear the case.

Legal Issues

The basic issue is whether the use of victim impact testimony violates the defendant's Eighth Amendment rights by prejudicing the factfinder through introducing emotional material that is not relevant to the defendant's culpability or blameworthiness. In *Booth v. Maryland* and *South Carolina v. Gathers*, the Supreme Court had banned victim impact testimony in capital trials for this reason.

Decision

In *Payne*, however, the Court effectively reversed its earlier opinions. Speaking for the majority, Chief Justice Rehnquist said that victim impact can indeed serve as evidence of the amount of harm caused by the crime, and that the criminal law had long recognized that different degrees of harm merit different amounts of punishment. For example, if a bank robber shoots a gun and kills a guard, he may well receive the death penalty, while if a robber in another case tried to shoot a guard but his gun jammed, he may not get the death penalty. Even though both defendants had an equal intent to kill, their actions had different effects. Hearing victim impact evidence, therefore, can help a jury decide the seriousness of the crime and use discretion in determining the penalty. Further, Justice Rehnquist noted that the defense had introduced considerable mitigating evidence concerning the defendant's character, and that it was unfair to deny the prosecution the ability to rebut such evidence by presenting the gruesome facts of the crime as evidence of the defendant's bad character.

Justices Marshall and Blackmun dissented. They reiterated the reasoning behind the Court's earlier decisions, and saw no reason to overturn them. Any value of victim impact evidence is outweighed by its prejudicial effect on the jury.

Impact

This decision seems to acknowledge the growing strength of the victim's rights movement and the desire of many states to give the victim's survivors a stronger role in the criminal justice system. If victim impact evidence is regularly introduced, it will tend to offset character evidence offered by the defense, and thus perhaps make the imposition of death sentences more likely.

RIGGINS V. NEVADA, 504 U.S. 127 (1992)

Background

David Riggins was charged by the state of Nevada with capital murder. However, because he told police and others that he heard voices and had trouble sleeping, Riggins was given a court-ordered psychiatric examination. The psychiatrist found Riggins to be competent to stand trial, but prescribed Mellaril, an antipsychotic drug, for him.

The defense asked the court to suspend administration of the drug during trial. Because an insanity defense was going to be used, the defense argued that giving Riggins the drug would mask his symptoms and not show the jury a true picture of his mental state at the time of the crime. This, they said, amounted to a denial of due process. The trial judge disagreed, Riggins was tried while under the influence of the drug, and he was convicted and sentenced to death. The Nevada Supreme Court upheld his conviction and sentence, saying that administering the drug did not deny Riggins any constitutional rights. The U.S. Supreme Court then considered the case.

Legal Issues

The issue is this: Under what conditions can a defendant be involuntarily medicated? In this case the psychiatrist had, after all, declared the defendant competent to stand trial. If someone is competent to be tried, it follows, presumably, that that person also be able to decide whether to be medicated. And what happens if medication affects the way the jury evaluates the defendant's mental state?

Decision

The opinion of the Court as written by Justice Sandra Day O'Connor begins with the assumption that the defendant has a right not to be involuntarily medicated. This means that the state should have been obligated to show a medical necessity for medication or demonstrate the need to administer it in order to protect the defendant's safety or that of others. The state could also have tried to show that the defendant needed the drug in order to be able to properly participate in his trial. However, the state had done none of these things. Therefore, the trial judge should have agreed with the defendant's motion to suspend the medication. Further, medical evidence suggested that the drug had impaired the defendant's ability to understand the proceedings, to testify effectively on his own behalf, and to communicate with his attorney. For all of these reasons the Supreme Court overturned the defendant's conviction.

Impact

This decision suggests that if a defendant is found to be competent to stand trial, a rather high burden must be met if forced medication is to be used. Given

Capital Punishment

the uncertainty and variation in the effects of many drugs used in psychiatry, it may be difficult to determine whether medication facilitates or impairs the ability of a defendant to receive a fair trial.

HERRERA V. COLLINS, 506 U.S. 390 (1993)

Background

The defendant, Leonel Torres Herrera, was convicted in 1982 for killing two police officers. At the trial, an eyewitness testified that he saw Herrera do the shooting, and one of the officers was able to corroborate this testimony before he died. In appealing the convictions, Herrera first claimed that these witnesses were unreliable. The Texas Court of Criminal Appeals rejected this appeal, and the U.S. Supreme Court refused to hear the case.

Herrera then raised a new appeal. This time he asserted that his brother, before his death in 1984, had admitted to his lawyer and his son that he, not Leonel, had killed the two officers. The state district court rejected the appeal, saying that no evidence of this claim was made in the original trial and that the appeals court would not consider facts not in evidence. The Texas Court of Criminal Appeals upheld the lower court's ruling, and the U.S. Supreme Court again refused to hear the case.

Finally, in 1992, Herrera raised a constitutional claim that because he was innocent of the crime and further, because police had covered up evidence of his innocence, his rights under the Eighth and Fourteenth Amendment had been violated. Although higher state and federal courts were skeptical of this argument, this time the case made it to the U.S. Supreme Court.

Legal Issues

The question here is whether the federal courts were obliged to consider a claim of actual innocence, even if it is presented many years (and appeals) after the offense had been committed.

Decision

By a 6-3 majority, the Court rejected Herrera's claim. Speaking for the majority, Chief Justice Rehnquist noted that Herrera's evidence consisted of affidavits from people no longer around to be cross-examined, and mainly consisted of hearsay. Even so, if the evidence had been offered at the original trial, it could have been legitimately weighed by the jury against other evidence that would lead to a verdict. But such evidence appearing years later "falls far short of that which would have to be made in order to trigger the sort of constitutional claim which we have assumed . . . to exist."

Speaking in dissent Justice Harry Blackmun said that "Nothing could be more contrary to contemporary standards of decency . . . or more shocking to the conscience . . . than to execute a person who is actually innocent." For the dissenters, the possibility of such a miscarriage of justice clearly outweighed any interest in maintaining orderly or workable court procedures.

Impact

The Court's findings in *Herrera* provoked considerable outrage on the part of death penalty opponents and the general public. The possibility of executing the innocent is a major argument frequently made by abolitionists, and many observers said they were shocked that the Court did not see a need to seriously consider a claim of actual innocence, even one presented belatedly.

Death penalty supporters generally replied that if the Court had found otherwise, defendants could launch last-minute appeals, based on tenuous or possibly fabricated evidence, and forestall their execution indefinitely. Courts should have strict procedures to ensure fairness in the death penalty process, but there has to be a closure somewhere.

SCHLUP V. DELO, 513 U.S. 298 (1995)

Background

The defendant Lloyd E. Schlup was convicted of capital murder for the killing of a fellow prison inmate. He was sentenced to death. After his state appeals failed, Schlup filed a petition for habeas corpus in which he claimed that his defense attorney had represented him inadequately by failing to call witnesses who could have shown his innocence. When this petition was denied, he filed a second one. This time he also asserted that he was actually innocent (did not commit the crime) and that the prosecutor had withheld evidence that could have shown his innocence. The district court denied his petition, saying that he had not met the standard of showing "by clear and convincing evidence that, but for a constitutional error, no reasonable juror would have found him guilty." Schlup's further appeal then reached the U.S. Supreme Court.

Legal Issues

The issue is whether the "clear and convincing" test (given by the Supreme Court in *Sawyer v. Whitley* [1992]) was too high a threshold to demand of inmates seeking to show their actual innocence. Schlup's appeal argued that he should have been held to a lower standard given in *Murray v. Carrier* (1986), which demanded only that the petitioner demonstrate that "a constitutional violation has probably resulted in the conviction of one who is actually innocent."

Decision

A divided Supreme Court opted for the lower *Murray* standard. The opinion of the Court, written by Justice John Paul Stevens, implied that the danger of convicting and executing an innocent person required that "if a petitioner . . . presents evidence of innocence so strong that a court cannot have confidence in the outcome of the trial unless the court is also satisfied that the trial was free of non-harmless constitutional error, the petitioner should be allowed to . . . argue the merits of his underlying claims." The dissenters suggested that having two different standards for evaluating claims of actual innocence would be confusing and that no need had been shown to intervene in how states dealt with particular cases.

Impact

Since the late 1990s the question of whether innocent persons are being executed has become perhaps the most vexing part of the death penalty debate. Because of the importance many advocates on both sides of the debate have placed on avoiding such ultimate injustice, it is likely that claims of actual innocence, which have often faced procedural hurdles, will receive hearing more readily in the future.

In another 1995 case *(Kyles v. Whitley)* the Court also applied the "reasonable probability" standard in granting a new trial where evidence that could have proved the defendant's innocence had been improperly withheld from the defense.

ATKINS V. VIRGINIA, 536 U.S. 304 (2002)

Background

Daryl Renard Atkins was convicted and sentenced to death for abduction (kidnapping), robbery, and capital murder. His attorneys appealed to the Virginia Supreme Court, arguing that Atkins's conviction should be overturned because he is mentally retarded. (At trial a psychiatrist had testified that Atkins was mildly mentally retarded with an IQ of 59.)

Relying on the Supreme Court decision in *Penry v. Lynaugh*, the Virginia court denied the appeal but did order a new sentencing hearing because the court had used the wrong verdict form.

In the new penalty trial Atkins was sentenced to death again. The sentence was appealed, but the Virginia Supreme Court upheld it. However, the U.S. Supreme Court then agreed to hear the case.

Legal Issues

The constitutional issue is whether executing a mentally retarded person amounts to cruel and unusual punishment prohibited by the Eighth Amendment. Although the Supreme Court had apparently already decided the issue in *Penry*, the Court has long held that applying the Eighth Amendment required attention to evolving standards in society. Had society now evolved to the point where executing retarded persons was no longer acceptable?

The Law of Capital Punishment

Decision

Justice John Paul Stevens wrote the opinion for a divided Court. In arriving at the conclusion that the death penalty should no longer be given to mentally retarded people, Stevens looked to the fact that an increasing number of states had already outlawed the death penalty in such cases.

Meaningful punishment requires that the person being punished understand his or her culpability for the criminal act, the reason for the punishment, and how it relates to his or her actions. The Court had already found that insane persons could not be executed *(Ford v. Wainwright)*.

Mental retardation also raises the question of whether punishment could have its intended effects. As the Court observed, retarded persons

> . . . *have diminished capacities to understand and process information, to communicate, to abstract from mistakes and learn from experience, to engage in logical reasoning, to control impulses, and to understand the reactions of others. . . . Their deficiencies do not warrant an exemption from criminal sanctions, but they do diminish their personal culpability.*

Impact

A number of ongoing strands are woven together in this decision. There is a widespread consensus that ultimate punishment should be reserved for persons whose culpability is undiminished and who can understand the consequences of their actions. The gradual narrowing of the scope of capital punishment as found in the actions of many death penalty states is also reflected in the Supreme Court's ongoing interpretation of the Eighth Amendment. When combined with the growing concern about the risk of executing the innocent, the result is that capital punishment is increasingly being scrutinized, questioned, and held to higher standards.

RING V. ARIZONA, 536 U.S. 304 (2002)

Background

In Timothy Ring's trial for murder and related offenses, the jury deadlocked on the charge of premeditated murder but found Ring guilty of murder occurring in the course of an armed robbery. Under Arizona law a judge holds a separate sentencing hearing in such cases in order to determine and weigh aggravating and mitigating circumstances. The death penalty can be imposed if the judge finds at least one aggravating circumstance and determines that no mitigating circumstances are sufficiently substantial to call for leniency. Following such a hearing, Ring's trial judge sentenced him to death.

Capital Punishment

Legal Issues

On appeal, Ring's attornies argued that Arizona's capital sentencing system violated the Sixth Amendment's guarantee of a jury trial because it allowed judges, not juries, to make factual determinations to be used for deciding whether to impose the death penalty.

The Arizona Supreme Court relied primarily on the U.S. Supreme Court's decision in *Walton v. Arizona* (1990), which had found that judges could make factual findings to be used in sentencing. They did this even though a later decision, *Apprendi v. New Jersey*, seemed to contradict *Walton* by requiring that juries, not judges, make factual determinations that could be used to increase the severity of a criminal sentence. The Arizona high court therefore upheld Ring's sentence, and he appealed to the U.S. Supreme Court.

The issue to be resolved was whether judges rather than juries could still make factual determinations used to impose death sentences. A subsidiary issue was whether an aggravating circumstance is simply a consideration to be used in sentencing or equivalent to an element used to prove an offense. (*Apprendi* had dealt with such elements).

Decision

The Court's 7-2 majority opinion, written by Justice Ruth Bader Ginsburg, ruled that with regard to determining aggravating circumstances in death penalty cases, it was *Apprendi*, not *Walton* that would control. That is, only juries could make such factual determinations, which are equivalent to proving elements of an offense. Indeed, for all practical purposes it must be the jury in the sentencing phase, not the judge, who imposes a death sentence.

Impact

Ring has had a major impact on the operation of capital punishment in the states where judges had previously made death sentences. Five states responded by passing legislation requiring jury verdicts for death sentences, and other states that had juries that only advised the judge as to sentencing have had to modify their systems as well.

The pending problem is whether the decision in *Ring* is to be applied retroactively to persons who had already been sentenced to death by a judge. The Arizona Supreme Court ruled in 2003 that *Ring* did not apply to cases in which all appeals had been completed, but that 27 cases in which final appeals had not yet been heard would be reviewed. (These cases included that of Timothy Ring, who was remanded for resentencing by a jury.)

Later in 2003 the federal Ninth Circuit Court of Appeals upheld the appeal in *Summerlin v. Stewart*, referring to *Ring*. The court's opinion said that *Ring* had made a substantial "watershed change" in legal procedures and thus should be applied retroactively. However, in June 2004 the U.S. Supreme Court disagreed, leaving existing death sentences in place.

UNITED STATES V. QUINONES, (205 F. SUPP. 2D [S.D.N.Y. 2002])

Background

Recent court decisions have made it somewhat easier for death row prisoners to make appeals based on their being innocent of the crime for which they have been convicted. However, there is also the potential for a more fundamental challenge to the death penalty based on the risk or even the likelihood that innocent persons have been or will be executed. In *United States v. Quinones* a group of defendants facing the federal death penalty act of 1994 challenged the law as being unconstitutional on that basis.

Legal Issues

This constitutional challenge to the federal death penalty is based on the fact that numerous errors have been found in capital cases, leading to the exoneration of a growing number of death row prisoners. However, the delays inherent in the system and resistance to requests for DNA tests likely mean that innocent people have been executed before they could prove their innocence. Because the finality of execution cuts off all possibility of exoneration, does it amount to a denial of constitutionally required due process?

Decision

Judge Jed Rakoff of the U.S. District Court in Manhattan, New York, found that the unacceptably high error rate, prolonged delays, and lack of consistency meant that the federal death penalty violated the constitution by denying due process. The Second Circuit Court of Appeals reversed the lower court's ruling, saying that the Supreme Court had never acknowledged a "fundamental right to the opportunity for exoneration over the course of [his] natural life." Indeed, the court pointed out that to recognize such a right would invalidate all death penalty statutes in the nation. The defendants appealed, asking for a new hearing before a panel of judges of the Second Circuit, but the request was denied in February 2003.

Impact

It is likely that this type of appeal will continue to be raised. (Indeed, in September 2002 another federal judge declared the federal death penalty to be unconstitutional on similar grounds.) If the appeal ultimately wins in several federal appeals circuits, the Supreme Court would eventually have to decide whether the death penalty, at least as currently administered, poses an unacceptable risk and denies fundamental rights to due process. The drastic nature of the consequences of such a ruling may make winning it all the more difficult.

ROPER V. SIMMONS, U.S. SUPREME COURT NO. 03-633 (2005)

Background

Defendant Christopher Simmons was convicted of a capital murder committed when he was 17 years old. The murder was clearly premeditated: Simmons even discussed it ahead of time with two friends, telling them he could get away with it because of his age. Simmons was tried as an adult. In the trial's penalty phase, the prosecution cited as aggravating factors the fact that the murder was committed for money, that the killing was an attempt to avoid being arrested (for burglary), and that the killing was "outrageously and wantonly vile, horrible, and inhuman."

The defense countered with mitigating circumstances, including the defendant's lack of a prior criminal record and his helping care for his two younger half-brothers and his grandmother. The defense also argued that Simmons's age should be considered as a mitigating factor, noting that 17-year-olds cannot legally drink, serve on juries, or even watch certain movies, because of their perceived lack of sufficient responsibility. The jury, however, recommended the death penalty, and the judge imposed it.

Legal Issues

On appeal Simmons obtained a new attorney who made several arguments, including the assertion that the previous attorney had not provided effective assistance at trial because he had failed to obtain psychiatric testimony that might have shown Simmons's impulsiveness and lack of control. The state appeals court rejected this argument and the Missouri Supreme Court affirmed Simmons's conviction.

However, after the U.S. Supreme Court ruled in *Atkins v. Virginia* (2002) that the Constitution prohibited the execution of the mentally retarded, Simmons appealed again to the Missouri Supreme Court. His attorneys argued that the same reasoning that concluded that a mentally impaired person cannot have the degree of culpability necessary to receive the death penalty should also apply to persons who have not reached age 18. The Missouri Supreme Court agreed with this reasoning and changed Simmons's sentence to life without parole. The prosecution then appealed that decision, and the U.S. Supreme Court agreed to hear the case.

The Law of Capital Punishment

The fundamental issue is whether the execution of a person for a crime committed before age 18 is considered "cruel and unusual" under the Eighth Amendment. It has long been held that this standard evolves according to the consensus of society, and the Court looks for evidence of that consensus in the actions of state courts and legislatures. In 2002 the Court decided that enough states had banned the execution of mentally retarded persons, and thus ruled in *Atkins* that the practice could no longer be tolerated under the Eighth Amendment. Would this same reasoning be applied to the execution of juveniles?

Decision

By a 5-4 majority, a sharply divided Court ruled that imposing the death penalty on a person who committed the crime before his or her 18th birthday was no longer compatible with the Constitution. The majority opinion, written by Justice Anthony Kennedy (joined by Justices John Paul Stevens, David H. Souter, Ruth Bader Ginsburg, and Stephen G. Breyer) noted that a majority of states no longer give the death penalty to juveniles, and that even in states that did so, such cases had become rare. Indeed, the United States stands virtually alone in the world in continuing to impose the death penalty on juveniles.

Under the Eighth Amendment, the death penalty must be reserved for those offenders who commit "a narrow category of the most serious crimes" and who have the extreme culpability necessary to be "the most deserving of execution." The majority concluded that juveniles, due to their immaturity, cannot be presumed to reach that extreme level of culpability.

The dissenters (Justices Antonin Scalia, Clarence Thomas, and Chief Justice Rehnquist) objected sharply to the majority's reasoning. Justice Scalia accused the majority of taking over the role of the nation's supreme moral arbiter and of taking excessive guidance from the practices of foreign countries. He said that juries should be entrusted with determining the culpability of juvenile offenders. In a separate dissent, Justice Sandra Day O'Connor took a milder position, saying that the majority had failed to show that there was truly a "national consensus" against executing juveniles.

Impact

The immediate result of the *Roper* decision is that 70 prisoners in 12 states had their death sentences overturned, although all will continue to serve some form of life sentence. As with *Atkins*, this decision seems to be part of a trend wherein the Supreme Court is increasingly restricting the applicability of the death penalty. It is possible the reasoning used in *Roper* and *Atkins* may be extended to defendants who may be presumed less than fully culpable for other reasons, although with age and IQ now taken care of, it is not clear what criteria might be used next.

Capital Punishment

DECK V. MISSOURI, U.S. SUPREME COURT, NO. 04-5293 (2005)

Background

The petitioner Carman Deck was convicted of capital murder and sentenced to death, but the sentence was set aside by the Missouri Supreme Court. During a second sentencing hearing, Deck was shackled with leg irons, handcuffs, and a belly chain. He was again given a death sentence. The defense counsel had repeatedly objected to the shackling, arguing that it would prejudice the jury by making the defendant appear to be extraordinarily dangerous. Deck appealed, but the state supreme court affirmed the second death sentence. Deck's appeal on constitutional grounds was heard by the U.S. Supreme Court.

Legal Issues

The U.S. Constitution guarantees defendants a fair trial at all stages in the proceedings. The issue is whether the potential prejudicial effect of visible restraints on the defendant outweighs the need to protect people in the courtroom from possible disruption or even violence.

Decision

By a comfortable 7-2 margin the Court majority, led by Justice Stephen Breyer, ruled that shackles could not be routinely used in the penalty phase of a capital trial. The opinion begins with the established idea that a defendant facing the choice of life or death must be afforded the same constitutional and procedural protections as in the trial's earlier guilt-or-innocence phase. Because of the likely prejudicial effect of seeing the defendant in shackles, such restraints can be used only if the authorities can justify it by "an essential state interest"—such as by showing why a particular defendant poses a substantial risk to the security and safety of the court.

Impact

This decision reaffirms the requirement that full constitutional protection be given to defendants in the penalty phase of a capital trial. A high standard must be met to justify actions that might prejudice the jury or impair the defendant's ability to present a robust argument against the death penalty.

MEDELLÍN V. DRETKE, U.S. SUPREME COURT, NO. 04-5928 (2005)

Background

José Ernesto Medellín, a Mexican citizen, was convicted of capital murder in a Texas state court. Medellín filed a federal appeal that argued that he had been deprived of access to the Mexican consulate as required by a treaty called the Vienna Convention, dealing with the legal rights of foreign nationals. The U.S. Court of Appeals for the Fifth Circuit rejected the appeal, ruling that Medellín would have had to raise the issue during his original trial. Further, the court said that the Vienna Convention did not provide for individuals to sue for enforcement. Meanwhile, the Mexican government won a ruling from the International Court of Justice that required that the state court consider the violation of Medellín's consular rights. The U.S. Supreme Court then agreed to rule on the dispute.

Legal Issues

The core issue here is whether state courts are bound to enforce rights granted by international treaties that the United States has signed or to comply with the related rulings of an international court.

Decision

Before the U.S. Supreme Court actually heard the case, President George W. Bush issued a memorandum ordering state courts to enforce the Vienna Convention, prompting a reconsideration of Medellín's state appeals. For this reason the Supreme Court dropped its consideration of the case. At the same time, the opinion of the Court suggested that it might well agree with the Fifth Circuit that Medellín's arguments under the Vienna Convention might not amount to a "cognizable" federal habeas corpus claim.

Impact

There are a variety of international treaties that might have an effect on legal proceedings within the United States. However as this case shows, it may be difficult for individuals to assert rights under these treaties in federal court. Politically, the question of how much deference should be given to international courts or treaties continues to be controversial.

CHAPTER 3

CHRONOLOGY

This chapter presents a chronology of significant developments in the history of capital punishment. Although some important earlier historical events are included, the main focus is on developments since the 1920s, when capital punishment in its modern form became a part of American life.

1700s B.C.

- The Code of Hammurabi decrees the death penalty for a variety of offenses, including the fraudulent sale of beer.

600s B.C.

- The legal code of Draco of Athens has numerous death penalties for even the most petty crimes, thus inspiring the word *draconian* to refer to excessive punishment.

circa 399 B.C.

- The execution of Socrates for heresy and "corruption of the young" illustrates a common use of capital punishment against offenders who attack religion and its close ally, the state.

circa A.D. 29

- In the execution that most shaped Western civilization, Jesus Christ is crucified by Roman authorities for sedition against the state. Abolitionists would note that Jesus forgave the two thieves who were executed with him, while death penalty supporters note that Jesus did not say the thieves should not die for their crime.

1500s

- In the evolving English legal system, only seven crimes are now officially punishable by death: treason, petty treason (murder of a husband by his wife), burglary, larceny, robbery, rape, and arson. Nevertheless, Henry VIII sets a new record for extrajudicial executions.

1612

- The draconian criminal code of the newly founded colony of Virginia extends the death penalty even to trading with American Indians or killing chickens. Later, colonies such as Massachusetts and New York will also use the death penalty for a variety of offenses, such as witchcraft, adultery, and blasphemy.

1682

- Countering the trend toward harsh laws in colonial America, Pennsylvania and New Jersey, settled mainly by pacifist Quakers, allow only treason and murder to be punishable by death. Later, however, more capital offenses are added.

1689

- The British Bill of Rights forbids cruel and unusual punishments, using language that will be adopted later in the Eighth Amendment to the U.S. Constitution.

1764

- Italian jurist Cesare Beccaria publishes his *Essay on Crimes and Punishment*. It is the first systematic look at deterrence and proportionality of punishment, and his ideas will influence early attempts to abolish capital punishment.

1785

- The Virginia legislature fails to abolish capital punishment by only one vote.

1789

- On the eve of the French Revolution, Dr. Joseph-Ignace Guillotin proposes a beheading machine that is eventually given his name. Like later methods of execution, the guillotine is touted as a humane alternative. It also expresses the Revolutionary ideal of treating people of all stations alike, rather than reserving some forms of execution for the nobility.

1791

- The first 10 amendments to the U.S. Constitution, known as the Bill of Rights, is adopted. Several of the amendments are concerned with the rights of criminal defendants to due process. The Eighth Amendment prohibits "cruel and unusual punishment." The Constitution elsewhere, however, assumes the legitimacy of capital punishment.

Capital Punishment

1794

■ Pennsylvania institutes the process of distinguishing different degrees of murder. Capital punishment is reserved for first-degree murders.

1833

■ Edward Livingston's "Introductory Report to the System of Penal Law Prepared for the State of Louisiana" calls for the abolition of capital punishment in that state. Livingston's proposals are rejected, but they greatly contribute to the growing debate over abolition.

1837

■ New Jersey introduces the right of jurors to impose at their discretion a lesser penalty than death for a capital crime.

1845

■ Death penalty opponents meet in Philadelphia to form the first national abolitionist organization, the American Society for the Abolition of Capital Punishment.

1846

■ Michigan becomes the first state to abolish the death penalty, except for treason against the state. A few years later, Rhode Island and Wisconsin will also abolish capital punishment.

1868

■ The Fourteenth Amendment is passed during the Reconstruction period following the Civil War. Its provisions for due process of the law and for equal protection of the laws will sometimes be used to challenge capital punishment.

1879

■ The Supreme Court applies the Eighth Amendment to a capital case for the first time. In *Wilkerson v. Utah*, the Court decides that a public execution of a murderer does not violate the amendment's ban on cruel and unusual punishment.

1890

■ The Supreme Court decision *In re Kemmler* finds that capital punishment is not inherently cruel and unusual and that the newly invented electric chair may be used.

Chronology

1895

- The American Federation of Labor calls for the abolition of the "revolting practice" of capital punishment.

1897

- The number of federal capital offenses reaches a low of three: treason, murder, and rape.

1910

- In *Weems v. United States*, the Supreme Court says that what constitutes "cruel and unusual punishment" is subject to change due to the "enlightenment" of public opinion. This "evolving standard" will be called upon by later justices as a justification for banning aspects of capital punishment.

1924

- *February 8:* A gas chamber is used for the first time in the execution of Gee John, a convicted tong (gang) murderer, in Nevada. Although electrocution remains the predominant mode of execution for some time, five other states construct gas chambers in the next five years.
- *September 10:* In a case that gains nationwide attention, Richard A. Loeb and Nathan F. Leopold, Jr., are sentenced to life imprisonment in Chicago for the murder of a neighborhood child. Their attorney, Clarence Darrow, had argued the execution of the two young men would serve no useful purpose. The success of this argument encourages opponents of capital punishment across the country.

1925

- *January 31:* President Calvin Coolidge signs a measure substituting electrocution for hanging in federal death sentences.
- *July 20:* The American League to Abolish Capital Punishment is formed in New York City by Clarence Darrow, Lewis E. Lawes, and other leading opponents of the death penalty. In its first year, the league enrolls more than 1,000 members nationwide and establishes affiliates in several states.
- *August 23:* Nicola Sacco and Bartolomeo Vanzetti are executed in Massachusetts for two murders that took place in 1920. The case, which commanded worldwide interest, had precipitated an unprecedented five-year legal battle over their guilt or innocence. Their executions contribute to an upsurge of abolitionist activity and lead to the formation of the Massachusetts Council for the Abolition of the Death Penalty.

1931

- *December 31:* The federal government begins to publish annual statistics on executions in the United States. It is reported that 155 persons were executed in 1930.

1932

- *March 1:* The baby son of Charles A. Lindbergh is kidnapped from his home in Hopewell, New Jersey. The body of the infant is found in the nearby woods two months later. The incident leads Congress to pass a federal kidnapping statute, popularly known as the Lindbergh Act, that makes the crime a capital offense. Similar "Lindbergh laws" are enacted in more than 20 states by the end of the decade.
- *March 13:* Kansas reinstates the death penalty following a series of violent crimes by Bonnie and Clyde (Bonnie Parker and Clyde Barrow), Charles "Pretty Boy" Floyd, and others.
- *November 7:* In a decision related to the Scottsboro case, the U.S. Supreme Court rules in *Powell v. Alabama* that failure to provide counsel to a defendant in a capital case violates constitutional due process protections.

1936

- *April 3:* After a sensational trial, Bruno Richard Hauptmann is executed in New Jersey for the kidnapping murder of the Lindbergh baby.

1937

- *January 4:* The American League to Abolish Capital Punishment initiates a drive to seek state laws preventing the execution of minors.
- *May 21:* In Galena, Missouri, approximately 500 persons pay an admission fee to the gallows to view the execution of Roscoe Jackson. It is the last execution in America that general spectators are allowed to attend.

1939

- *October 11:* The National Association for the Advancement of Colored People (NAACP) forms the Legal Defense and Education Fund (LDF) to provide legal assistance to the poor and to challenge racial segregation in the courts. This will lead to involvement in defending blacks in capital cases and in challenging the death penalty.

1944

- *November 13:* Pope Pius XII justifies the use of capital punishment.

Chronology

1945

- *January 31:* Private Eddie D. Slovik is executed by firing squad in the European theater of operations. He is the only U.S. soldier put to death for desertion during World War II.

1946

- *January 19:* President Harry S. Truman and the War Department limit imposition of the death penalty by military courts-martial.
- *October 1:* An international military tribunal at Nuremberg, Germany, sentences 12 former Nazi leaders to death. In subsequent Nuremberg trials, an additional 25 German war criminals receive the death penalty.

1947

- *January 13:* The U.S. Supreme Court, in *Louisiana ex rel Francis v. Resweber*, rules that a second attempt to execute an individual after a malfunctioning electric chair had halted the first try does not constitute cruel and unusual punishment under the Eighth Amendment.

1948

- *May 22:* Caryl Chessman is sentenced to death in California for a kidnapping crime he insists he did not commit. While on death row Chessman becomes a famous author and symbol of resistance to capital punishment.
- *July 14:* The U.S. Army ends mandatory death sentences for murder and rape.
- *October 19:* The United Nations Human Rights Commission rejects an amendment proposed by the Soviet Union to the International Bill of Rights that would ban the death penalty during peacetime.

1953

- *June 19:* Julius and Ethel Rosenberg are put to death for furnishing information about the atomic bomb to the Soviet Union. They are the first U.S. civilians executed for espionage.

1957

- *June 6:* The soon-to-be state of Hawaii, which had not executed anyone in more than 25 years, abolishes the death penalty for all crimes.
- *June 30:* Arthur Koestler's *Reflections on Hanging*, a highly critical study of the death penalty, is published in the United States.

Capital Punishment

1958

- **April 2:** Delaware governor J. Caldo Boggs signs into law a bill that abolishes capital punishment. The state is the first to eliminate the death penalty in 40 years.

1959

- **January 4:** The New York Committee to Abolish Capital Punishment is established.

1960

- **April 6:** The UN Economic and Social Council calls on Secretary-General Dag Hammarskjold to study the effect of the death penalty on crime.
- **April 9:** The death penalty is backed by Vice President Richard M. Nixon and opposed by Senator Hubert H. Humphrey in responses to a questionnaire sent to major presidential contenders by the Union of American Hebrew Congregations.
- **May 2:** After a protracted 12-year legal struggle, the internationally renowned death row author Caryl Chessman is executed at San Quentin, California.

1961

- **January 28:** In a study conducted at the request of the Governors Board of the American Bar Association (ABA), the American Bar Foundation finds that long delays in carrying out death sentences weaken public confidence in the law. The study urges uniform post-conviction procedures.
- **April 1:** A pioneering law article, "Testing the Death Penalty," by Los Angeles attorney Gerald Gottlieb, is published in the spring issue of the *Southern California Law Review*. In the article, Gottlieb suggests the traditional abolitionist tactic of persuading state legislatures to end capital punishment has met with only limited success. He argues that the death penalty should be attacked through the court system on the grounds that it violates the Eighth Amendment's prohibition of cruel and unusual punishment.
- **December 18:** Delaware legislators override a veto by Governor Elbert N. Carvel to reinstate the death penalty.

1963

- **March 14:** Georgia raises the minimum age for execution from 10 to 17.
- **March 15:** Victor Feuger is hanged in Iowa for kidnapping. He is the last federal prisoner executed in the United States until 2001.
- **October 21:** In a dissent to a U.S. Supreme Court decision to refuse to hear the case of *Rudolph v. Alabama*, Justice Arthur J. Goldberg, joined by Justices William O. Douglas and William J. Brennan, Jr., contends there are substan-

tive reasons to consider whether the Eighth and Fourteenth Amendments to the Constitution permit the death penalty for a convicted rapist who neither took nor endangered human life.

1964

- *May 2:* Attorney Melvin Belli charges that of 23 verdicts by Dallas juries entailing death sentences, seven were given after only four to seven minutes of deliberation.
- *November 4:* In a statewide referendum, Oregon voters approve abolition of the death penalty by a margin of 455,000 to 302,000.

1965

- *March 5:* Vermont ends the death penalty except for a second conviction for murder.
- *March 12:* West Virginia legislators vote to eliminate the death penalty for all crimes.
- *March 17:* The National District Attorney's Association urges the abolition of capital punishment.
- *June 1:* New York governor Nelson Rockefeller signs into law an abolition bill. However, the measure retains the death penalty for killing a law enforcement officer in the line of duty.
- *June 20:* The American Civil Liberties Union (ACLU) announces a nationwide drive to end capital punishment.
- *November 8:* The United Kingdom abolishes the death penalty for a trial period of five years.

1966

- *April 24:* The NAACP Legal Defense and Education Fund (LDF) announces an extensive survey on the use of the death penalty for rape convictions in the South.
- *June 29:* The Lutheran Church in America urges the abolition of capital punishment.
- *November 9:* Colorado voters reject a proposal to end capital punishment in the state.

1967

- *April 12:* California carries out its first execution in four years.
- *April 13:* The NAACP LDF and the ACLU challenge the constitutionality of Florida's death penalty laws in federal court. The court temporarily halts executions in the state pending its review of the class action suit.
- *June 2:* Luis Jose Monge dies in Colorado's gas chamber. Soon after, mounting legal challenges to the constitutionality of the death penalty bring about

a moratorium on its use. Monge becomes the last person (state or federal) executed in the United States until 1977.

- *June 27:* Charging there is a disproportionate number of blacks on San Quentin's death row, the NAACP LDF files a class action suit in federal court in San Francisco to block executions in the state.
- *November 27:* In response to a suit brought by the ACLU, a California superior court rules that the state's death penalty does not constitute cruel and unusual punishment even in cases where murder has not been committed.

1968

- *May 3:* NAACP LDF director Jack Greenberg releases statistics showing 90 percent of persons executed in the South for rape since 1930 were black.
- *June 3:* The U.S. Supreme Court, in *Witherspoon v. Illinois*, holds that persons who oppose the death penalty cannot automatically be excluded from juries in capital cases.
- *July 2:* The Johnson administration asks Congress to abolish the death penalty for all federal crimes and to reduce to life imprisonment the sentences of federal prisoners on death row. Attorney General Ramsey Clark urges the United States to join over 70 other nations that have abandoned capital punishment.
- *September 13:* The National Council of Churches issues a policy statement calling for the abolition of capital punishment.
- *November 18:* The California Supreme Court rules that the state's death penalty is constitutional, rejecting arguments that the law does not provide sufficient standards by which judges and juries should decide who receives a death sentence.
- *November 26:* A U.S. appeals court rules that North Carolina's provisions for imposing the death penalty are unconstitutional.

1969

- *February 15:* A Gallup poll survey finds growing support among whites for the death penalty for murder and opposition by a majority of blacks.
- *March 3:* The National Urban League urges abolition of the death penalty throughout the United States.
- *March 31:* New Mexico becomes the 13th state to abolish or severely limit capital punishment. The death penalty is retained only for killing a police officer or jail guard.
- *December 18:* Great Britain makes permanent its ban on capital punishment for all crimes except treason.

1970

- *January 31:* The American Psychiatric Association, in a brief to the U.S. Supreme Court, claims the threat of the death penalty may incite certain persons to crime rather than deter them.

- *October 8:* Congress enacts legislation that makes it a capital offense to cause a fatality by a bombing.
- *December 11:* Setting an important precedent, a federal appeals court in Virginia holds that the death penalty for rape when the victim's life is neither taken nor endangered is unconstitutional.
- *December 29:* Arkansas governor Winthrop Rockefeller commutes the death sentence of all 15 death row inmates in the state to life imprisonment.

1971

- *January 7:* The U.S. National Commission on Reform of Federal Criminal Laws, headed by former California governor Edmund G. Brown, issues a series of recommendations, including abolition of capital punishment.
- *January 20:* The World Council of Churches Central Committee, meeting in Addis Ababa, Ethiopia, urges the nations of the world to eliminate capital punishment as a violation of the "sanctity of life."
- *May 3:* The Supreme Court rejects two major constitutional challenges to the death penalty. Neither an absence of clear standards to guide the imposition of the death sentence nor the common practice of allowing a single jury to determine both guilt and penalty are found to be unconstitutional. The court does not address the basic constitutional question of whether the death penalty constitutes cruel and unusual punishment, thus the nationwide moratorium on executions remains in effect.
- *October 9:* Pennsylvania governor Milton Shapp and eight former governors from around the country file a friend-of-the-court brief with the U.S. Supreme Court that argues the death penalty does not deter murder.

1972

- *January 17:* The New Jersey Supreme Court in a 6-1 vote rules that the state's capital punishment statute as currently written is unconstitutional.
- *January 26:* A bill calling for the death penalty for drug pushers is defeated in the Georgia legislature.
- *February 18:* The California Supreme Court, in *People v. Anderson*, rules that the state's death penalty is unconstitutional. Among those whose sentences are changed to life imprisonment by the decision are Sirhan Sirhan, convicted assassin of Senator Robert F. Kennedy, and mass murderer Charles Manson. California governor Ronald Reagan charges that the court has set itself "above the people and the legislature."
- *April 26:* The United Methodist Church, at a convention in Atlanta, Georgia, adopts a doctrine of social principles that includes opposition to capital punishment.
- *June 29:* In a landmark decision in *Furman v. Georgia*, the U.S. Supreme Court rules that the death penalty, as imposed under current statutes, is unconstitutional. The court finds that the arbitrary and capricious manner in which the

Capital Punishment

death penalty is applied constitutes cruel and unusual punishment. The decision spares more than 600 persons on death row. In his dissent, Chief Justice Warren Burger notes that states could retain capital punishment by altering their laws to conform to the court's ruling. At a news conference, President Richard Nixon criticizes the Supreme Court decision and urges retention of the death penalty.

- *November 7:* A referendum to restore the death penalty is approved by a large margin of California voters.
- *November 22:* A Gallup poll finds that public support for capital punishment is at its highest point in nearly two decades. Of the persons questioned, 51 percent favored the death penalty for persons convicted of murder.
- *December 6:* The National Association of Attorneys General approves a resolution recommending the death penalty for violent crimes. The association notes that while the Supreme Court outlawed the death penalty in its present form, it did not rule that it is inherently cruel and unusual punishment.
- *December 8:* Governor Reuben Askew signs into law a measure making Florida the first state to reinstate capital punishment since the Supreme Court decision in *Furman v. Georgia.* The bill authorizes the death penalty for premeditated murder and the raping of a child under the age of 11.

1973

- *March 14:* President Richard Nixon in his State of the Union message advocates the imposition of the death penalty for a number of violent crimes.
- *July 26:* The Florida Supreme Court upholds the state's new capital punishment statute. The law provides for a separate sentencing procedure for capital crimes and automatic appeal of all death sentences.
- *December 31:* By the end of 1973, 23 states have enacted new death penalty statutes since the Supreme Court struck down capital punishment laws in June 1972. A total of 44 prisoners await execution across the nation.

1974

- *March 13:* The U.S. Senate approves legislation to reinstate capital punishment for a variety of serious crimes, but the legislation fails to emerge from the House Judiciary Committee.
- *November 21:* The National Conference of Catholic Bishops speaks out against capital punishment in a reversal of the traditional Roman Catholic Church position supporting the death penalty as a legitimate means of self-protection for the state.
- *December 31:* An additional six states by year's end have approved new capital punishment laws.

1976

- *April 28:* A Gallup poll shows that 65 percent of Americans favor the death penalty for convicted murderers, 28 percent are opposed, and 7 percent are undecided.

- *July 2:* The Supreme Court rules that the death penalty is not inherently cruel or unusual. In its landmark decision in *Gregg v. Georgia* and two related cases, the Court upholds the constitutionality of the new statutes in Georgia, Florida, and Texas. However, in *Woodson v. North Carolina* the Court rules that mandatory death penalty laws that do not allow for differences in defendants and circumstances are unconstitutional.
- *July 6:* Canada abolishes capital punishment for all but traitorous military crimes.
- *August 14:* The Southern Christian Leadership Conference passes a strongly worded resolution against capital punishment.
- *November 28:* The Law Enforcement Assistance Administration reports that 285 persons were sentenced to death in 1975, bringing the death row population at the end of the year to 479.

1977

- *January 17:* Gary M. Gilmore is executed by firing squad in Utah State Prison. It is the first execution in the United States since 1967. In what is to become a common practice, opponents of the death penalty conduct a vigil outside the prison.
- *February 15:* The ABA rejects a proposal calling for an end to capital punishment.
- *June 6:* The Supreme Court rules that states may not make the death penalty mandatory for the murder of a police officer. Citing its decisions in July 1976, the Court holds that judges and juries must be allowed to consider mitigating circumstances.
- *June 29:* In *Coker v. Georgia*, the Supreme Court finds that the death penalty for rape is unconstitutional. Citing the *Coker* decision in a summary opinion, the Court holds that the death sentence for nonhomicidal kidnapping is also unconstitutional.
- *August 3:* A federal appeals court in New Orleans reverses a Texas court ruling that TV camerapersons can film executions of condemned prisoners.
- *December 8:* Amnesty International announces a campaign for abolition of the death penalty.

1978

- *January 2:* Results of a study conducted by the Center for Applied Social Research show that murderers of whites are far more likely to be sentenced to death than murderers of blacks.
- *April 22:* The National Legal Aid and Defender Association announces it will not hold future conventions in states that have adopted the death penalty.
- *July 3:* The Supreme Court, in *Lockett v. Ohio*, requires that every person convicted of a capital offense be permitted to offer a broad range of extenuating evidence prior to sentencing.

- *December 31:* Opponents of capital punishment hail the absence of executions in 1978 but note there are 475 persons on death row.

1979

- *February 13:* The American Bar Association calls on the Supreme Court to require that free counsel be provided to persons who are appealing their state death sentences in federal court.

1980

- *February 12:* Serial killer Theodore R. Bundy is sentenced to death for the kidnapping and murder of a 12-year-old girl.
- *April 14:* Norman Mailer wins a Pulitzer Prize for *The Executioner's Song*, a fictionalized account of the last nine months of Gary M. Gilmore, the first person executed in the United States after a 10-year moratorium in 1977.
- *May 19:* In *Godfrey v. Georgia*, the Supreme Court sets aside death penalty statutes that are excessively broad or vague.
- *May 26:* Amnesty International calls for the creation of a presidential commission on capital punishment.
- *June 20:* In *Beck v. Alabama*, the U.S. Supreme Court rules that juries must be allowed to consider relevant "lesser included offenses" as an alternative to crimes that carry the death penalty.
- *July 22:* Delegates to the annual meeting of the American Medical Association (AMA) proclaim that physicians should not participate in the execution of prisoners.
- *November 13:* The Roman Catholic bishops of the United States object to the fact that the death penalty is more likely to be exercised unjustly against the poor who cannot afford adequate defense but uphold the principle of the state's right to impose capital punishment.

1981

- *March 15:* A Gallup poll reveals that two-thirds of all Americans, the highest percentage in 28 years, favor the death penalty for murder. Reflecting the level of support, 35 states have enacted new death penalty statutes since the Supreme Court invalidated current capital punishment laws in 1972.
- *May 4:* The U.S. Supreme Court for the first time extends constitutional protection against double jeopardy beyond the question of guilt to the sentence itself, ruling in *Bullington v. Missouri* that a defendant who had received a life sentence at a first trial could not be sentenced to death on retrial.
- *July 18:* The U.S. Supreme Court in *Estelle v. Smith* rules that a psychiatric examination for competency to stand trial cannot be used later as evidence for a death penalty without warning the defense.

Chronology

- *August 9:* Justice Department statistics show that more than half the prison inmates awaiting execution in 1980 were in Georgia, Florida, and Texas.
- *August 28:* The Food and Drug Administration (FDA) rejects a request by five condemned prisoners to use federal drug regulations to block their execution by lethal injection because the chemicals used are not federally approved.
- *September 28–October 2:* The World Medical Association issues a resolution condemning physician participation in capital punishment.
- *September 30:* France abolishes capital punishment.

1982

- *July 2:* The Supreme Court determines, in *Enmund v. Florida*, that death is an excessive and disproportionate punishment for a defendant who aided and abetted in the commission of murder but who had not killed, attempted to kill, or intended to kill the victim.
- *August 22:* The number of prisoners under death sentence in the United States exceeds 1,000.
- *December 7:* Charlie Brooks is executed by a combination of sedatives and drugs in Texas. He is the first person put to death by lethal injection.

1983

- *January 15:* In the first instance of a pontiff speaking out against capital punishment, Pope John Paul II condemns the death penalty in an address to the Vatican diplomatic corps.
- *May 9:* Associate Supreme Court Justice Lewis F. Powell, Jr., in a speech delivered in Georgia, says that unless Congress and the courts can find a speedier way to handle death penalty appeals, states should abolish capital punishment.
- *July 6:* In *Barefoot v. Estelle*, the Supreme Court holds that petitions for review in capital cases must raise issues that are at least "debatable among jurists of reason" and establishes guidelines for lower federal courts handling death penalty appeals.
- *October 11:* The Court of Military Appeals, the nation's highest military court, strikes down procedures used for sentencing members of the armed forces to death. The court notes the president can remedy the constitutional defects without new legislation.
- *October 15:* A federal appeals court panel orders the FDA to weigh evidence that drugs used for execution by lethal injection can cause "torturous pain."

1984

- *January:* President Ronald Reagan signs an executive order designed to correct defects in the administration of the death penalty under the Uniform Code of Military Justice.

- *January 23:* The Supreme Court, in *Pulley v. Harris*, rules that a state may carry out the death penalty without first conducting a "proportionality" review to ensure the sentence is in line with other sentences imposed in the state for similar crimes.
- *November 1:* Margie Velma Barfield, who was convicted of killing her fiancé and who confessed to killing three other people by poisoning, is executed by lethal injection in North Carolina. She is the first woman put to death in the United States in 22 years.

1985

- *March 20:* The Supreme Court rules in *Heckler v. Chaney* that the FDA is not required to approve the drugs used to execute prisoners by lethal injection.
- *June 11:* In *Caldwell v. Mississippi* the U.S. Supreme Court rules that a jury cannot be told that its decision in favor of capital punishment is not final and that it will be reviewed by appeals courts. Such instructions might make it easier for a jury to issue a death sentence without the most careful consideration of the evidence.
- *July 26:* Reflecting concern over a string of recent spying cases involving navy personnel, Congress approves a measure that would permit execution of military personnel for peacetime espionage.
- *September 11:* Charles Rumbaugh, convicted of committing robbery and murder when he was 17, is executed by lethal injection in Texas. The execution is the first in more than two decades for a crime committed by someone under age 18.
- *November 13:* A study conducted by the ACLU asserts that since 1900, 343 persons were wrongfully sentenced to death in America, 25 of whom were actually executed.
- *November 28:* A Gallup poll shows that American support of capital punishment for a variety of serious crimes has increased sharply over the last seven years. Seventy-five percent of Americans now favor the death penalty for murder.

1986

- *January 10:* James Terry Roach, who was 17 when he took part in the murder of a teenage couple, dies in South Carolina's electric chair despite international protests against the execution of offenders for crimes they committed while juveniles. Mother Teresa and UN Secretary-General Javier Perez de Cuellar are among those pleading for mercy.
- *February 23:* President Ronald Reagan signs a measure under which members of the armed forces convicted of espionage during peacetime could be executed.
- *April 15:* Amnesty International reports that there were more than 1,125 documented executions worldwide in 1985.

- *May 5:* The Supreme Court holds that dedicated opponents of capital punishment may be barred from juries in capital cases regardless of whether the move increases the likelihood of conviction.
- *June 26:* In *Ford v. Wainwright,* the Supreme Court rules that the Eighth Amendment bars the execution of persons presently insane. The Court requires states to establish procedures for determining sanity that meet minimum due process standards.
- *November 4:* A conservative backlash results in California Supreme Court Chief Justice Rose Bird and other liberal justices who had voted against capital punishment being voted out of office.
- *November 26:* New Mexico governor Toney Anaya, who leaves office in a few weeks, commutes the death sentences of all five persons awaiting execution in the state.

1987

- *February 18:* Amnesty International announces it is opening a worldwide campaign against the death penalty in the United States.
- *April 23:* In a controversial decision, the Supreme Court finds that Georgia's capital punishment law is constitutionally applied despite a wide statistical disparity between whites and blacks in the imposition of death sentences. The ruling in *McClesky v. Kemp* ends what opponents had called their last sweeping constitutional challenge to capital punishment.
- *June 15:* The Supreme Court annuls a Maryland law that provided for the use of "victim impact statements" at death sentence hearings. The decision in *Booth v. Maryland* is denounced by victims rights groups.
- *June 23:* The Supreme Court strikes down the last vestiges of the mandatory death penalty in the United States, holding that state laws making executions compulsory for murders committed by prisoners serving life terms without parole are unconstitutional.
- *June 26:* Continuing a busy year for death penalty jurisprudence, a narrow Supreme Court majority shows in *Burger v. Kemp* that it is unwilling to second-guess the effectiveness of tactics chosen by defense attorneys in deciding whether the defendant had "effective assistance of counsel."
- *September 26:* Pope John Paul II appeals for clemency in the case of Paula R. Cooper, an 18-year-old Indiana woman facing execution for a murder she committed when she was 15.
- *November 1:* A study published in the *Stanford Law Review* by professors Hugo Adam Bedau and Michael L. Radelet finds that 349 innocent persons were convicted and 23 put to death in 20th-century America.

1988

- *March 15:* Willie Jasper Darden, a convicted murderer whose case attracted worldwide attention, is executed in Florida.

- *June 29:* Addressing the issue of juvenile executions, the Supreme Court rules in *Thompson v. Oklahoma* that a state may not impose the death sentence for crimes committed by persons when they were less than 16 years old unless the state has specifically legislated the death penalty for minors.
- *July 31:* The Justice Department reports that of every 30 persons sentenced to death since capital punishment was reinstated in 1976, 10 left death row and one was executed.
- *August 1:* The movie *The Thin Blue Line* by filmmaker Errol Morris is released. The documentary film examines the possible innocence of Randall Dale Adams, on death row in Texas for murder of a police officer. The movie brings national attention to the case, and Adams is subsequently released.
- *October 12:* In the second presidential election debate, CNN newsperson Bernard Shaw asks Democratic candidate Michael S. Dukakis if he would still oppose the death penalty if Dukakis's wife were raped and murdered. Dukakis answers he would still oppose the death penalty. The appropriateness of the question, as well as Dukakis's response, generates considerable controversy.
- *November 22:* Congress adjourns after passing a comprehensive drug bill that includes the death penalty for homicides connected to drug-related crimes.

1989

- *January 24:* After numerous appeals and delays, serial killer Theodore R. Bundy is electrocuted in Florida.
- *February 6:* In his annual message before the midyear convention of the American Bar Association, Supreme Court Justice William H. Rehnquist urges reform of the system by which death sentences are reviewed in federal courts. Calling for changes to speed up the appeals process, he notes that the elapsed time between the commission of a capital crime and the date of execution averages eight years nationally.
- *February 28:* The Supreme Court, in its decision in *Dugger v. Adams*, turns down an appeal that argued that the trial judge had improperly instructed the jury about its role in sentencing.
- *May:* The United Nations Economic and Social Council passes a resolution calling for a ban on execution of mentally retarded or mentally incompetent people.
- *June 12:* In *South Carolina v. Gathers* the Supreme Court declares that it is unconstitutional to present "victim impact" evidence in the penalty phase of a capital trial.
- *June 23:* The Supreme Court, in *Murray v. Girratano*, rules that indigent inmates on death row do not have a constitutional right to a lawyer to assist them in a second round of appeals.
- *June 26:* In *Penry v. Lynaugh*, the Supreme Court rules that execution of the mentally retarded is not precluded by the Eighth Amendment, but the Court

requires states to establish clear standards for considering mental retardation as a mitigating factor. In two other decisions (*Stanford v. Kentucky* and *Wilkins v. Missouri*), the court holds that the execution of defendants who committed a capital offense at age 16 or 17 is not unconstitutional "cruel and unusual" punishment.

- *July 13:* The Indiana Supreme Court bars the execution of Paula R. Cooper for a murder she committed when she was 15 years old. Her death sentence had drawn appeals for leniency from a number of groups around the world.

1990

- *March 28:* The Supreme Court rules in *Clemons v. Mississippi* that having a crime being "especially heinous, atrocious, or cruel" considered as an aggravating death penalty factor is unacceptable. The court now considers such language to be too vague, even if qualified by additional jury instructions.
- *September 21:* A special committee of federal judges established by Supreme Court Chief Justice William H. Rehnquist submits its findings on the judicial system's handling of death penalty cases. The panel, headed by retired Supreme Court Justice Lewis F. Powell, Jr., recommends imposing strict limits on the multiple appeals filed by death row inmates. Chief Justice Rehnquist formally transmits the panel's proposal to the Senate Judiciary Committee for consideration.
- *December 15:* The UN General Assembly adopts the Second Optional Protocol to the International Covenant on Civil and Political Rights. It calls on all member nations to work to abolish capital punishment. The vote is 59 nations for, 26 against, and 48 abstaining.

1991

- *April 16:* In its decision in *McCleskey v. Zant*, the Supreme Court strictly limits the ability of death row prisoners to use habeas corpus petitions to challenge their death sentences in federal court. The Court states that a petitioner will get only one petition and generally cannot raise additional issues later.
- *May:* Ray Copeland, 76, becomes the oldest person to receive a death sentence, for a murder he committed when he was 71 years old.
- *June 24:* The Supreme Court refuses to consider the appeal of convicted murderer Roger Keith Coleman because he had been a day late in filing an appeal in Virginia state court. In *Coleman v. Thompson*, the Court rules that failure to properly use the state appeal system precludes a petitioner from taking the appeal to federal court. This decision becomes part of a broad trend to reduce the appeals rights of death row inmates.
- *June 27:* In *Payne v. Tennessee*, the Supreme Court, reversing its earlier trend, says that juries can take the character of the victim and the impact on his family into account when deciding a capital sentence.

- *June 30:* The parliament of Canada votes 148 to 127 to defeat a proposal to reintroduce capital punishment, which had been abolished in Canada in 1976.
- *October:* The Supreme Court of Canada, in a narrow 4-3 vote, allows accused murderer, rapist, and kidnapper Charles Ng and convicted murderer Joseph Kindler to be extradited to the United States. Previously, Canada, which had abolished capital punishment, had refused to extradite people to countries where they might be subjected to the death penalty. Lawyers for the accused had argued that Canada should demand assurances that the United States would not impose the death penalty before allowing extradition.

1992

- *April 21:* Robert Alton Harris is led to the gas chamber at San Quentin prison, California. Harris had fought a tenacious appeals battle. At the last minute, he received a stay of execution from the Ninth District Court of Appeals, but the U.S. Supreme Court, apparently angry at the lower court's continuing to follow a more liberal policy, swiftly overturns the stay and prohibits lower courts from entering any further stays. Harris becomes the first person to be executed in California in 25 years.
- *May 18:* The Supreme Court rules in *Riggins v. Nevada* that the state must show the necessity for giving a defendant psychiatric medication that may affect his ability to effectively defend himself in court.
- *May 20:* Roger Keith Coleman, who had been the subject of many appeals for mercy from around the world, is executed in Virginia for a murder many believe he did not commit.
- *June 22:* In *Sawyer v. Whittley* the Supreme Court seems to back off somewhat from its restrictions on federal appeals, ruling that certain issues could be raised even if they hadn't been raised earlier at the state level. The issues, however, are limited to procedural violations that prevented defendants from proving innocence of the crime, not mitigation of the sentence.
- *November 3:* Voters in Washington, D.C., overwhelmingly reject a referendum that would have introduced the death penalty into the District of Columbia.

1993

- *January 3:* Westley Allan Dodd, a three-time child killer, is hanged in a Washington state prison. This is the first hanging in the United States since 1965. Dodd had demanded to be executed, saying that if he were allowed to live he would try to escape and kill again. Offered a choice of hanging or lethal injection, he chose hanging as a more fitting death because he had strangled his youngest victim. Despite his wishes, death penalty opponents tried to block the hanging as cruel and unusual punishment and held a midnight vigil (facing death penalty supporters).

Chronology

- *January 23:* In *Herrera v. Collins* the Supreme Court refuses to allow Leonel Herrera to introduce new evidence that he said proved that his brother, not he, had killed a Texas policeman in 1981. The court ruled 6-3 that the deadline had long since passed for reexamining the factual part of the case. Justices Blackmun, Stevens, and Souter vigorously dissent, arguing that evidence of actual innocence must always be considered.
- *March 2:* Walter McMillen, a black man convicted in 1988 of killing a white teenager, is released after spending six years on death row. Evidence had emerged that key witnesses against McMillen had lied, possibly with the prosecution's knowledge or encouragement. The outcome is used by abolitionists to argue that an irrevocable penalty of death should not be imposed because some innocent persons will inevitably be executed. Death penalty supporters point out, however, that McMillen was after all exonerated.

1994

- *February 22:* In his dissent in the case of *Callins v. Collins*, Supreme Court Justice Harry Blackmun declares that the constitutional requirements for individual consideration of defendants and the avoidance of "arbitrary and capricious" sentencing decisions cannot be reconciled, and that he will "no longer tinker with the machinery of death."
- *June 30:* The Supreme Court rules in *McFarland v. Scott* that states must provide attorneys to help indigent death row prisoners with direct appeals of their sentences. An earlier ruling, *Murray v. Girratano*, had failed to extend this requirement to collateral civil appeals.
- *September 13:* A federal crime bill adds dozens of new federal capital offenses. Congressional Black Caucus members had tried to amend the bill by including the Racial Justice Act, which would have allowed defendants to use statistical evidence of racial disparities in death sentencing in their court appeals, but the amendment was defeated.

1995

- *January 23:* In *Schlup v. Delo* the Supreme Court establishes a more lenient standard for a petitioner seeking to establish actual innocence in an appeal. The evidence now need only be probable rather than clear and convincing.
- *March 7:* New York governor George Pataki signs a bill restoring capital punishment in the state. Pataki's predecessor Mario Cuomo had regularly vetoed each year's death penalty bill.
- *March 25:* Pope John Paul II issues the encyclical *Evangelium Vitae*. The document takes a tougher stand against capital punishment, saying that it is justified only in extreme cases where the criminal's guilt is certain and he or she poses an exceptional danger to society. Most Catholic observers believe that few if any executions in modern countries can meet this standard.

- *July 28:* A jury decides to give Susan Smith a life sentence rather than the death penalty. Smith was convicted of murdering her two young children, and her life was revealed to be a tangled web of molestation, manipulation, and compulsion that fascinated tabloid audiences. The jury's leniency is in sharp contrast to the results of a *Newsweek* poll that found 63 percent in favor of the death penalty for Smith.

1997

- *February 3:* The House of Delegates of the American Bar Association (ABA) calls for a moratorium on all execution in the United States. The ABA declares that the capital punishment system is "a haphazard maze of unfair practices with no internal consistency," and also points to racial bias in capital sentencing.
- *March 25:* Observers at the execution of Pedro Medina in Florida's electric chair are horrified when sparks and flames erupt from his head. Florida governor Lawton Chiles refuses to suspend pending executions but appoints a special medical examiner to investigate the mishap.
- *April:* The tally of prisoners awaiting execution on America's death rows now stands at almost 3,000 (50 of them women). Since the restoration of capital punishment in 1976, 372 men and one woman have been executed in the United States.
- *April:* The United Nations Commission on Human Rights votes to call upon member nations to abolish capital punishment. The United States joins China, Indonesia, and eight other nations in opposing the resolution.
- *June 13:* Timothy McVeigh is sentenced to death for the Oklahoma City bombing, the worst domestic terrorist act in American history. His case challenges abolitionists to remain consistent in their opposition to the death penalty.
- *October:* Mexico claims that the United States is in violation of international law for sentencing a Mexican national to death in Texas without allowing him to seek the help of the Mexican Consulate.

1998

- *February 3:* Despite pleas from many religious leaders, Karla Faye Tucker, a murderer who had become a born-again Christian, is executed in Texas.
- *April 2:* The Racial Justice Act is signed into law in Kentucky. It allows courts to consider statistical evidence of racial disparities in death sentencing and allows the defense to try to prove that a prosecutor's decision to seek the death penalty was motivated by racial factors.
- *October 29:* The Pennsylvania Supreme Court refuses to overturn the conviction of Mumia Abu-Jamal for the murder of police officer Daniel Faulkner in 1981. Abu-Jamal's case had been brought to public attention by a vocal group of supporters.

Chronology

1999

- *January 27:* Pope John Paul II, during his visit to St. Louis, Missouri, preaches a homily in which he calls the death penalty "cruel and unnecessary." The pope also asks Missouri governor Mel Carnahan, a supporter of the death penalty, to commute the death sentence of prisoner Darrell J. Pease. The governor first postpones the execution, but then commutes the sentence to life imprisonment.
- *February 5:* Anthony Porter is released from prison in Illinois. He had nearly been executed in September 1998, but his lawyers won a stay of execution to evaluate his mental competency. Using the time thus gained, investigators (including Northwestern University journalism students) turned up evidence that proved his innocence.
- *February 25:* White supremacist John William King is given the death penalty by a jury for taking part in the brutal murder-by-dragging of James Byrd, Jr., an African American, in June 1998. Many death penalty opponents have mixed feelings because the sentence is one of the rare instances in which a white man is condemned to death for murdering a black man. Many people consider it to be a just retribution for a terrible hate crime.
- *May 26:* Nebraska governor Mike Johans vetoes a bill that would have imposed a two-year moratorium on executions during which time the fairness of the death penalty would be studied. At the time it was passed, the bill was hailed as a sign of the strength of an emerging national death penalty moratorium movement.

2000

- *January 24:* The Supreme Court drops consideration of a challenge to Florida's electric chair as being cruel and unusual punishment (*Bryan v. Moore*, 99-6723) because the state has passed legislation offering inmates lethal injection as an alternative.
- *January 31:* Illinois governor George Ryan announces that there will be a moratorium on executions in the state until an inquiry into the operation of the death penalty has been completed. Since 1977, more death row inmates in the state have been exonerated than have been executed.
- *February 16:* At a press conference, President Clinton, who supports the death penalty, praises Illinois for its moratorium on executions. He says that the Justice Department is conducting a study to determine whether death sentences have been disproportionately given to blacks. Clinton also backs legislation that would give death row inmates access to DNA testing in cases where it might prove their innocence.
- *February 22:* The Supreme Court declines to hear the appeal of an Alabama death row inmate. Robert Lee Tarver had contended that the state's "antiquated" electric chair would expose him to an unacceptable risk of "excessive burning, disfigurement and . . . pain and suffering."

- *February 28:* Several hundred protesters block the Supreme Court building in Washington, D.C., demanding a new trial for death row inmate Mumia Abu-Jamal. A similar demonstration takes place in San Francisco at a federal courthouse, and protesters are arrested at both locations for blocking sidewalks.
- *April 18:* The Supreme Court overturns the death sentence of Michael Williams, ruling that the 1996 Death Penalty Act's ban on appeals by defendants who "fail to develop the factual basis of a claim in state court proceedings" cannot be applied in a case where the defendants made a "reasonable effort" based on their knowledge at the time.
- *May 19:* New Hampshire governor Jeanne Shaheen vetoes legislation that would have abolished the state's death penalty.
- *June 1:* Texas governor (and Republican presidential candidate) George W. Bush, having announced support for DNA testing in some death penalty cases, gives death row inmate Ricky Nolen McGinn a 30-day reprieve to allow for a DNA test.
- *June 12:* A study of 23 years of death sentences by Columbia University law professor James S. Liebman reveals only 5 percent of death row inmates were executed, while two out of three convictions were overturned on appeal, usually leading to reduced sentences after retrial or plea bargaining. In 7 percent of retried cases, however, the defendant was acquitted.
- *September 12:* The Department of Justice releases a report surveying the operation of the federal death penalty system since 1988. The report highlights racial and geographical disparities in the application of capital punishment.

2001

- *February:* The Supreme Court of Canada rules that prisoners held in Canada should not be extradited to countries that have capital punishment unless there is assurance that they will not be executed.
- *May:* Missouri becomes the 15th of the capital punishment states to ban the execution of the mentally retarded.
- *June 11:* Convicted Oklahoma City bomber Timothy McVeigh is executed by lethal injection after a delay caused by the FBI's failure to give evidence to defense attorneys. McVeigh and Juan Raul Garza become the first two federal prisoners to be executed since 1963.
- *October 5:* The Georgia Supreme Court becomes the first appellate court in the nation to ban electrocution as an unconstitutionally cruel and unusual punishment. The state switches to the statutory backup method of lethal injection.
- *December 18:* Mumia Abu-Jamal's death sentence is overturned by a federal district court in Pennsylvania. The court rules that jurors should not have been told that they would have to be unanimous in finding mitigating circumstances.

Chronology

2002

- *April:* The Illinois commission on the death penalty created by Governor George Ryan in 2000 issues its report. It includes a number of recommendations to limit the use of the death penalty and to provide safeguards against convicting innocent persons.
- *May:* Maryland Governor Parris Glendenning declares a moratorium on executions in Maryland pending the completion of a study of racial bias in the state's criminal justice system.
- *June:* German authorities are reported to be reluctant to supply the United States with information about the links between terrorist suspect Zacarious Mossaoui and the September 11 attacks because of the likelihood that he would face the death penalty.
- *June:* In *Atkins v. Virginia* the Supreme Court overturns the death sentence of a mentally retarded individual, Daryl Atkins, based upon a growing consensus against execution of the mentally handicapped making the practice now cruel and unusual under the Eighth Amendment.
- *June:* In another important ruling, the Supreme Court in *Ring v. Arizona* requires that only juries, not judges, decide whether to impose the death penalty. There will be considerable debate about whether the ruling will be applied retroactively to persons already sentenced.
- *July 1:* In *United States v. Quinones* a U.S. District judge declares the federal death penalty to be unconstitutional because of an "undue risk of executing innocent people." This potentially momentous decision is soon overturned by an appeals court.
- *August:* A Louisiana jury sentences Patrick O. Kennedy to death for repeatedly raping his eight-year-old stepdaughter. The U.S. Supreme Court had earlier ruled that the death penalty cannot be given for rape unless there is also murder, but it is unclear what it would say about the rape of a child.
- *August 14:* Javier Suarez Medina, a Mexican citizen, is executed in Texas. In protest, Mexican president Vicente Fox then cancels a trip to Texas. Medina had not been informed of his consular rights under the 1963 Vienna Convention.

2003

- *January:* Maryland attorney general J. Joseph Curran, Jr., urges that the state's death penalty be abolished because of the "intolerable risk" that innocent people would be executed.
- *January 11:* Illinois governor George Ryan announces that he is giving executive clemency to 167 of the state's death row prisoners. Most will receive life without parole. Four other prisoners get pardons.
- *February:* A Texas appeals court rejects a request by the PBS *Frontline* documentary series to videotape jury deliberations during the penalty phase of a capital case using an unobtrusive automatic camera.

- *November:* Washington, D.C., sniper John Allen Muhammad is sentenced to death in Virginia. He and accomplice Lee Boyd Malvo killed 10 people at random in October 2002. Malvo is convicted the following month, but receives a life sentence.

2004

- *March:* The International Court of Justice (World Court) finds that the United States has violated the rights of Mexican nationals on death row in nine states. Although the United States refuses to recognize it as binding, the decision gives new ammunition to international death penalty opponents.
- *March:* Wyoming and Dakota join the majority of death penalty states (now 31 of 38) that make 18 the minimum age (at the time of the crime) for imposing the death penalty.
- *June:* Maryland ends its short-lived moratorium and resumes executions.
- *June:* A New York state appeals court rules that the state death penalty is unconstitutional. The problematic language requires that the jury in the penalty phase be told that if it deadlocks on whether to impose death, the defendant will eventually be eligible for parole.
- *June:* Terry Nichols, Timothy McVeigh's accomplice in the Oklahoma City bombing, who had received a life sentence in federal court, receives another life sentence in state court after the jury deadlocks over the death penalty.
- *September 28:* The U.S. Supreme Court agrees to hear the appeal of death row prisoner Ronald Rompilla, who argues that the jury should have been informed that if he were sentenced to prison he would never be eligible for release.
- *October:* A series of investigative reports by the *Chicago Tribune* reveals that of 200 death row exonerations in the past 20 years, 55 cases (with 66 defendants) involved flawed forensic tests or errors in expert testimony.

2005

- *February:* In New York State a bill to correct the unconstitutional language in the state's death penalty statute bogs down in an assembly committee. A number of influential voices (including some previous supporters of the death penalty) now argue for letting the law lapse.
- *March 1:* In a 5-4 decision, the U.S. Supreme Court rules in *Roper v. Simmons* that the death penalty can no longer be given for crimes committed by an offender who is under 18 years of age.
- *April 17:* A CBS News poll finds that 39 percent of respondents believe that death is the appropriate penalty for murder. Life without parole also received 39 percent support. Only 6 percent favored a long sentence with possible parole, while 13 percent volunteered the answer "it depends." (Three percent had no opinion or offered other responses.)
- *May 23:* In *Deck v. Missouri* the U.S. Supreme Court rules by a 7-2 majority that the Constitution forbids the routine shackling of defendants during a

capital penalty proceeding. However, a prisoner can still be shackled if the state shows that he or she poses a credible threat to the court's security and safety.

- *May 23:* The Supreme Court declines to review the case of José Medellín, a Mexican citizen on death row in Texas who had been denied access to legal help from the Mexican consulate. The Court had apparently been satisfied by President Bush's order that state courts abide by a decision of the International Court of Justice that U.S. courts consider claims that the treaty rights of foreign nationals under the Vienna Convention had been violated. However, the issue of whether treaties trump state law is likely to be revisited in coming years.

CHAPTER 4

BIOGRAPHICAL LISTING

This chapter contains brief biographical sketches of selected persons who are important in the history of capital punishment in the United States. They include scholars, advocates, judicial and political figures, as well as inmates whose cases raised important issues or public controversy. The entries focus on the person's relationship to the issue of capital punishment and do not attempt to recount other areas of significance.

Mumia Abu-Jamal, black death row inmate and activist. Born Wesley Cook, Abu-Jamal had an early career as a Black Panther and journalist. He was convicted in 1982 for the murder of Philadelphia police officer Daniel Faulkner and sentenced to death. He has protested his innocence and what he considers the political nature of his trial and has become a cause célèbre in many leftist circles. Abu-Jamal's death sentence was overturned in December 2001 by a federal district court in Pennsylvania. The court ruled that jurors should not have been told that they would have to be unanimous in finding mitigating circumstances.

Anthony G. Amsterdam, prominent law professor and constitutional expert. Amsterdam directed the NAACP Legal Defense and Education Fund's campaign to have the death penalty declared unconstitutional. He is a leading figure in the legal struggle over capital punishment. Amsterdam has argued numerous capital cases before the Supreme Court.

Cesare Beccaria, 18th-century Italian jurist and legal reformer. Beccaria was the first modern writer to urge complete abolition of the death penalty. His book *Essay on Crimes and Punishment,* published in 1764, is considered the single most influential work on criminal justice reform. Beccaria argued that the certainty of punishment was more effective as a deterrent than the severity and that penalties should be proportionate to the crime. His ideas strongly influenced early American abolitionists.

Hugo Adam Bedau, chairman of the philosophy department of Tufts University since 1966. Bedau has been a leading opponent of capital punishment for the past 40 years. Among numerous other works, his anthology *The Death*

Penalty in America, first published in 1964 and revised periodically since, is considered the authoritative work on the subject.

Jeremy Bentham, British social philosopher and economist. Bentham's principle achievement was his attempt to create a systematic approach to social policy that became known as utilitarianism. According to this approach, social policies (including punishments for crime) should be based on the goal of creating the greatest amount of happiness for the greatest number of people. He suggested that the use of capital punishment should be limited if not totally eliminated because it did not serve the overall needs of society well.

Walter Berns, political scientist and supporter of capital punishment. Berns has served on the faculties of leading universities including Yale, Cornell, and Georgetown. From 1979 to 1986 he was a resident scholar at the American Enterprise Institute, a leading conservative think tank. His 1979 book *For Capital Punishment: Crime and the Morality of the Death Penalty* is a comprehensive defense of capital punishment. Berns insists that capital punishment is not "cruel and unusual," and is in fact a legitimate punitive (or retributive) response by society to persons who wantonly disregard the lives of others.

Rose Elizabeth Bird, chief justice of the California Supreme Court, 1977–86. A reform-minded liberal jurist, Bird was a stalwart opponent of California's capital punishment statutes, contending that the death penalty was disproportionately applied to blacks and other minorities. She and fellow liberal justices were targeted by a conservative campaign and voted out of office in 1986.

Harry Andrew Blackmun, associate justice of the U.S. Supreme Court, 1970–94. Blackmun generally supported capital punishment until the end of his judicial career. In *Furman v. Georgia* (1972), he sided with the minority in finding capital punishment as currently practiced to be constitutional. In *Gregg v. Georgia* (1976), he agreed with the majority in accepting the validity of revisions the states had made in their capital punishment laws in response to *Furman*. In the case of *Spaziano v. Florida* (1984), he sided with the majority in allowing a judge to override a jury's sentencing recommendation of a life sentence and impose the death penalty. However, in 1993 he told interviewers that he now believed the death penalty "comes close to violating the Equal Protection Clause of the Constitution," referring to evidence of racial bias in the imposition of the sanction. Finally, in his dissent in *Callins v. Collins* (1994), Blackmun said that there was no way to reconcile the constitutional requirements of individualized discretion and the need to avoid "arbitrary and capricious" decisions. He vowed that "from this day forward I will no longer tinker with the machinery of death."

Kirk Bloodsworth, the first American death row prisoner to be exonerated by DNA evidence. Bloodsworth was identified by five eyewitnesses as the person last seen with a nine-year-old girl who was raped and murdered in the woods of Baltimore County, Maryland. On March 8, 1985, Bloodsworth was convicted of rape, sexual assault, and first-degree murder. He received a death sentence but won a new trial when it was revealed that police had withheld evidence pointing to another suspect. Bloodsworth was retried, this time receiving two consecutive life sentences. Bloodsworth, however, who had become well versed in legal issues, read about a British case where a convicted killer had been freed after DNA evidence had been tested. Bloodsworth's attorney got the state to agree to such a test, and in June 1993 two tests revealed that the DNA found at the crime scene did not belong to Bloodsworth. He was released from prison that same month and later was given a pardon by the governor. Today Bloodsworth is an outspoken advocate for abolishing the death penalty. His biography, *Bloodsworth: The True Story of the First Death Row Inmate Exonerated by DNA*, was written by Tim Junkin.

SueZann Bosler, advocate for nonviolent reconciliation and abolition of the death penalty. In 1982 she testified on behalf of leniency for the man who had attacked her and killed her father. She is a board member of the organization Journey of Hope.

Marvin H. Bovee, politician and prominent 19th-century crusader against capital punishment. As a state senator, he led the successful fight to repeal the death penalty in Wisconsin in 1853. He subsequently dedicated himself over the next 30 years to ending capital punishment nationwide. At a time when the country was absorbed by the issues of the Civil War, his efforts generated little support. Nonetheless, his perseverance kept the question of capital punishment an object of public debate.

William J. Brennan, Jr., Supreme Court justice, 1956–90. Brennan is considered by most observers to be part of the liberal core of the Warren Court. In numerous opinions, Brennan argued that the death penalty constitutes cruel and unusual punishment under the Constitution and should be prohibited. Further, he believed that the killing of a human being by the State was "an absolute denial of the executed person's humanity," and agreed with his compatriot Harry Blackmun that the death penalty must be completely abolished.

Stephen B. Bright, director of the Southern Center for Human Rights in Atlanta and a director of the National Association of Criminal Defense Lawyers. He has handled numerous capital cases and appeals and has taught courses on capital punishment, criminal procedure, and international human rights at Yale, Harvard, and other universities. In 1998 he received the American Bar Association's Thurgood Marshall Award.

Edmund G. Brown, governor of California, 1959–67. Brown opposed the continuance of capital punishment in the state and sought without success to have the death penalty repealed. Brown subsequently headed the National Commission on Reform of Federal Criminal Laws, which issued a report in 1971 critical of capital punishment. In 1989, in his book *Public Justice, Private Mercy: A Governor's Education on Death Row*, he recounted how his involvement as governor with death penalty cases had shown him that capital punishment was both barbaric and ineffective.

Theodore R. Bundy, notorious serial killer, the subject of numerous books and a television miniseries, *The Deliberate Stranger*. The case of Ted Bundy fascinated and horrified America. An intelligent and attractive young man, he was also one of the most infamous serial killers in the nation's history. Sentenced to death in Florida in 1980 for the murder of a 12-year-old girl, Bundy was executed on January 24, 1989, after many appeals and delays. In his final days he reportedly confessed to killing at least 20 young women in five states. Bundy was frequently cited by advocates of capital punishment as an example of the kind of criminal who richly merited the death penalty.

Warren E. Burger, chief justice of the U.S. Supreme Court, 1969–86. Burger presided over several landmark rulings on capital punishment. He was in the minority when the Court declared the nation's death penalty laws unconstitutional in 1972. Four years later, Burger was part of the majority that authorized a resumption of executions.

George H. W. Bush, president of the United States, 1988–92. Considered a moderate Republican earlier in his political career, Bush moved toward the conservative wing of his party during his tenure as vice president in the Reagan administration. In the 1988 presidential campaign, he stressed his support for the death penalty in contrast to Democratic candidate Michael Dukakis's opposition to the measure. As president, Bush continued to call for wider use of capital punishment.

George W. Bush, president of the United States, 2001– . As governor of Texas, Bush presided over a state that death penalty critics have called a "death factory." While running for president in 2000, Bush said he was "not proud" that his state had executed 134 persons during his term, but that he believed that the penalty had been "fair and just" in each of these cases. In 1999 Bush experienced criticism after some reports suggested that Bush had mocked Texas inmate (and born-again Christian) Karla Faye Tucker on the eve of her execution. There was also some debate over how much time Bush actually spent reviewing capital cases for possible clemency. However, when Bush ran for a second term in 2004, the death penalty was not a prominent issue. In his 2005 State of the Union address, Bush suggested a possible moderation in his position: He called for expanded DNA testing to determine the possible innocence of death row inmates and for training defense attorneys so they could provide more effective representation in capital cases.

Albert Camus, French intellectual and author who won the Nobel Prize in literature. Camus wrote a powerful critique of the death penalty in 1957. His essay "Reflections on the Guillotine" contributed to the growing debate over capital punishment in the United States in the late 1950s. Camus's ideas and the responses they provoked became part of an ultimately successful effort to repeal the death penalty in France.

Truman Capote, American author. Capote was the best-known writer of his generation to oppose capital punishment. His controversial 1968 TV documentary *Death Row, USA* strongly criticized the practice.

George Cheever, 19th-century clergyman and a prolific writer on social issues. Cheever advocated the end of slavery but also vigorously defended capital punishment on biblical and moral grounds. His 1846 *Defense of Capital Punishment* is probably the leading defense of the death penalty in the 19th century from a Christian viewpoint.

Caryl Chessman, convicted murderer and successful death row author. In trouble with the law since his youth, Chessman was convicted in 1948 of kidnapping with bodily injury, a crime he insisted he did not commit, and was sentenced to death. While on death row in California, Chessman authored three books against capital punishment that won him an international audience. His case provoked the largest public outcry against the death penalty since the Sacco and Vanzetti trial 30 years earlier. After 12 years of legal maneuvering, Chessman was executed on May 2, 1960.

William Ramsey Clark, attorney general in the Johnson administration who became an outspoken social reformer. Clark was the first and only head of the Justice Department to call for the end of the death penalty. In testimony before Congress, he urged elimination of the federal death sentence. Since leaving office, Clark has remained a prominent and active opponent of capital punishment.

Bill Clinton, president of the United States, 1993–2000. As a law student and later an instructor at the University of Arkansas Law School, Clinton was an outspoken opponent of the death penalty. (His wife, Hillary Rodham Clinton, wrote a brief that helped free a mentally retarded man from death row.) As governor of Arkansas, Bill Clinton was at first reluctant to allow executions to take place and also freed a number of murderers before the end of their term. However, when one freed prisoner committed a new murder, the resulting backlash contributed to Clinton's being defeated for reelection in 1980. When Clinton won a new term in 1982, he emerged with a moderately pro–death penalty position, which he retained during two subsequent terms. When he ran for president in 1992, Clinton took a much stronger position in favor of capital punishment, perhaps in response to the 1988 debate debacle involving Democratic candidate Michael Dukakis, whose weak response on the issue had hurt him considerably. As president, Clinton supported an expansion of the federal death penalty in 1994, as well as urging tough new laws in the wake of the 1995 Oklahoma City bombing. However, toward the end of his term, Clinton began to share the growing misgivings about possible execution of innocent persons, as well as ongoing racial disparities in execution. He supported a detailed statistical survey on such matters that was released in 2000.

Lande Cohen, Canadian writer and supporter of capital punishment. His book *Law without Order: Capital Punishment and the Liberals* (1970) argues that while there should be strict procedural safeguards and execution should be humanely administered, the state may sometimes have to resort to capital punishment to protect itself from extreme violence or anarchy.

Mario M. Cuomo, governor of New York, 1983–94. Cuomo earned a national reputation for his forceful and outspoken opposition to capital punishment.

During his years in office he successfully resisted efforts to reimpose the death penalty in his state, vetoing reinstatement measures each year. (New York enacted a death penalty law in 1995 under Republican governor George Pataki.)

Newton M. Curtis, U.S. representative from New York, elected in 1890 and an active proponent of prison reform and the humane treatment of the mentally ill. Although Congress did not approve his abolitionist proposals, in 1897 it enacted his bill to greatly reduce the number of federal capital offenses.

George Mifflin Dallas, politician and prominent 19th-century activist against the death penalty. He was chosen to be the first president of the American Society for the Abolition of Capital Punishment.

Clarence S. Darrow, renowned defense attorney and advocate for controversial causes. Darrow was an ardent opponent of the death penalty. In a famous trial in 1924, he persuaded the judge to sentence Nathan Leopold and Richard Loeb, young men convicted of kidnapping and murder, to life imprisonment rather than death. The verdict infused new energy into the abolitionist movement nationwide. The following year he helped found the American League to Abolish Capital Punishment. Darrow continued to attack capital punishment in various lectures and in his autobiography in 1935.

Michael S. Dukakis, governor of Massachusetts and Democratic presidential candidate in 1988. His opponent, Vice President George H. W. Bush, sought to make their differences over capital punishment a major issue in the campaign. In a presidential debate, Dukakis fumbled when asked whether he would support the death penalty for someone who raped and killed his wife. Political analysts believe Dukakis's candidacy was seriously weakened by his opposition to the death penalty.

Herbert B. Ehrmann, defense attorney in the Sacco and Vanzetti case. As a result of his experience, he and his wife Sara became active in the movement to abolish capital punishment. He published two books critical of the Sacco-Vanzetti verdict, as well as articles on the death penalty and the criminal justice system.

Gary M. Gilmore, first person put to death following the Supreme Court's 1976 decision reinstating the death penalty. His case attracted worldwide attention and eventually became the subject of a Pulitzer Prize–winning book, *The Executioner's Song,* by Norman Mailer. Gilmore refused to contest his pending death sentence and twice attempted to commit suicide when appeals filed by various legal groups opposed to capital punishment threatened to block his execution. He was shot by a Utah firing squad on January 17, 1977.

Horace Greeley, prominent 19th-century newspaper editor and founder of the *New York Tribune* in 1841. He used the influential newspaper as a nationwide platform to campaign for a number of reform causes including the abolition of capital punishment. A frequent lecturer across the country, Greeley provided many rural Americans their first exposure to arguments against the death penalty.

Capital Punishment

Jack Greenberg, legal crusader against capital punishment. As director of the NAACP Legal Defense and Education Fund from 1961 to 1984, Greenberg coordinated the legal campaign against capital punishment that resulted in the Supreme Court striking down the nation's death penalty laws in 1972. He participated in several of the most important cases argued before the Court. Following the reinstatement of capital punishment in 1976, Greenberg maintained his organization's leading role in the legal fight against the death penalty.

Joseph-Ignace Guillotin, French doctor and inventor of the beheading machine that would later be named the guillotine. Interestingly, he developed his machine because he believed it would provide a uniform method of execution that could be applied to all classes of offenders, upholding the ideal of equality that fueled the French Revolution. In later years he was said to be uncomfortable with the fact the machine had been given his name.

Victor Hugo, noted 19th-century French author. His novels and other stories often exposed and attacked social injustices, and he had a particular interest in the harsh treatment of prisoners. Several of his works included negative portrayals of the death penalty, including *Last Days of a Condemned Man* and *The Death Penalty*, as well as his most famous work, *Les Misérables*.

Joe Ingle, minister and prison reformer. A minister of the United Church of Christ, the Reverend Ingle served as director of the Southern Coalition on Jails and Prisons since the 1970s. As part of this work he ministered to hundreds of prisoners on southern death rows and helped organize legal challenges to their sentences. Ingle was nominated for the Nobel Peace Prize in 1988 and 1989.

Arthur Koestler, renowned Hungarian-born author who became a British subject. Koestler was deeply involved in the successful campaign to abolish the death penalty in his adopted country. His 1955 book *Reflections on Hanging*, a critical study of the death penalty in Great Britain and an indictment of the practice in general, is considered among the classic works on the subject. Published in the United States in 1957, the book has had a major impact on abolitionist activity.

Lewis E. Lawes, warden of New York's Sing Sing prison for 20 years during the early 20th century. Lawes took part in hundreds of electrocutions. His firsthand experience with criminals and his study of death sentence statistics led him to conclude that capital punishment was misguided and wrong. A founder and later chairman of the American League to Abolish Capital Punishment, he presented his views in six books and numerous articles and speeches.

Nathan Leopold and **Richard Loeb,** infamous kidnappers and murderers of the 1920s. Leopold and Loeb were young men who considered themselves to be clever and superior persons, and decided to prove their superiority by committing the perfect crime. The result was the kidnapping and murder of a 14-year-old boy, for which they were soon arrested. With the facts of the crime in little dispute, famed attorney Clarence Darrow entered guilty pleas for both men but appealed to the judge to spare their lives. They received sentences of life plus 99 years. Loeb was stabbed to death in a prison dispute in 1936, but Leopold was paroled in 1958, the same year he published *Life Plus 99 Years*, in which he wrote about his rehabilitation.

Edward Livingston, Louisiana legislator and later secretary of state under President Andrew Jackson. As a member of the Louisiana Assembly in the early 1820s, Livingston introduced several new arguments against capital punishment: the risk of executing the innocent, the ineffectiveness of the death penalty as a deterrent, and the problems the sanction posed in the administration of justice. Livingston's writings had a major impact across the nation and in Europe. Considered by many the preeminent American abolitionist of his time, he raised issues that continue to shape the terms of the debate over capital punishment today.

Thurgood Marshall, associate justice of the U.S. Supreme Court, 1967–90. Although his proudest achievement was his successful argument against segregation in *Brown v. Board of Education* (1954), Marshall was also director of the NAACP Legal Defense and Education Fund from 1940 until 1961, where he led the organization's efforts to overturn capital punishment statutes. While on the Court, he consistently voted against capital punishment and dissented vigorously when the court majority reinstated capital punishment in the *Gregg* decision of 1976. Marshall frequently stated his belief that the death penalty is unconstitutional in all circumstances.

Claude Maturana, a French citizen convicted of murder in Arizona and sentenced to death despite serious questions about his mental health. (He was a paranoid schizophrenic.) Amnesty International expressed outrage when Arizona officials announced that Maturana would be treated with drugs to make him able to understand his pending execution. Many doctors considered it a violation of medical ethics to treat Maturana under such circumstances. He died in prison in 2002 before the case could be resolved.

Edwin Meese III, attorney general during the Reagan administration. As an assistant to the then-governor of California Ronald Reagan, Meese helped coordinate the successful referendum drive to restore the death penalty in the state. Meese has been an outspoken advocate of capital punishment.

John L. O'Sullivan, 19th-century American legislator and champion of American expansionism. (He coined the term *Manifest Destiny*.) O'Sullivan advocated repeal of the death penalty. He believed that capital punishment was incompatible with the "democratic genius" of the United States. O'Sullivan's 1841 report to the New York Assembly, written while he was a member, became one of the most influential abolitionist appeals of the time.

George Pataki, governor of New York, 1995 – . Started his political career as mayor of Peekskill, New York. In 1992 Pataki was elected to the New York State Senate. In 1994 he made the restoration of the death penalty and no parole for violent offenders centerpieces of his successful campaign for governor, defeating the incumbent, Mario Cuomo, a well-known liberal and death penalty opponent.

Albert Pierrepoint, British executioner who dispatched 450 people by the time of his retirement in 1956. After his retirement, he became an opponent of capital punishment and described his experiences in *Executioner: Pierrepoint*, published in 1974.

Lewis F. Powell, Jr., associate Supreme Court justice, 1972–87, who was nominated by President Richard Nixon. Considered the swing vote on many issues during his years on the Court, he cast the decisive vote in many important capital punishment decisions. Since the mid-1980s, Powell suggested that if a solution could not be found to the protracted appeals process in capital cases, then the death penalty should be abandoned as unworkable.

Helen Prejean, American nun who ministers to inmates on death row, particularly in the Louisiana State Penitentiary at Angola. Her book *Dead Man Walking* (later made into an Academy Award–winning movie) describes these painful and moving encounters. Prejean now serves as the national chairperson for the National Coalition to Abolish the Death Penalty.

Robert Rantoul, Jr., 19th-century death penalty abolitionist. The leading American opponent of capital punishment in the 1830s and 1840s, Rantoul served as president of the Massachusetts Society for the Abolition of Capital Punishment and assisted in reform efforts nationwide. In his writings, he strongly contested the inherent right of society to inflict the death penalty.

Ronald W. Reagan, governor of California (1967–74) and president of the United States, 1980–88. As governor of California, Reagan responded to the California Supreme Court's overturning of capital punishment in 1972 by leading a successful referendum to amend the constitution to restore the death penalty. As president, Reagan spoke out frequently in defense of the death penalty. He vigorously supported congressional legislation in 1988 that made drug-related murders a federal capital offense.

William H. Rehnquist, associate justice of the Supreme Court (1971–86) and chief justice (1987 –). Throughout his tenure on the Court, he has maintained that the issue of capital punishment should be settled in the legislative branch of government. He has criticized the lengthy appeals process involved in capital cases. (In 1992 he and his colleagues quashed a last-minute stay of execution of Robert Alton Harris and ordered the lower court not to issue any further stays.) As chief justice, Rehnquist has attempted to find ways to reduce the number of appeals. He has resisted making decisions that broaden protections for death row inmates retroactive and has refused to entertain appeals that should have been made in state courts.

Samuel Romilly, 18th- and early 19th-century British member of parliament and legal reformer. Influenced by the writings of French Enlightenment thinkers such as Jacques Rousseau as well as the pioneering criminological and legal work of Cesare Beccaria, Romilly became interested in comprehensive legal reform. He set out to eliminate the more than 200 capital offenses in the British law of the time, many of which would be only misdemeanors by modern standards. While only modestly successful, his work gave impetus to a reform movement that would have a significant impact on British use of the death penalty later in the 19th century.

Julius and **Ethel Rosenberg,** American communists who were tried and convicted in 1951 as part of a spy ring accused of providing secret information about the atomic bomb to the Soviets. The couple vigorously maintained their innocence but also appealed their conviction on the grounds they had been sentenced under a statute that had been enacted in 1946 although the acts they were accused of committing had taken place earlier, during World War II. While Supreme Court Justice William O. Douglas wanted to give them a stay of execution on that basis, the majority of the court disagreed and the Rosenbergs were executed on June 19, 1953.

Benjamin Rush, prominent Pennsylvania physician and a signer of the Declaration of Independence. Rush was the first prominent American to publicly oppose capital punishment. In 1787 he published *An Enquiry into the Effects of Public Punishments upon Criminals and upon Society,* the first of several essays calling for the complete abolition of the death penalty. Rush is credited with building support for the elimination of many death penalty statutes in the early 19th century.

George Ryan, Republican governor of Illinois who in 2000 declared a moratorium on executions in the state after concluding that the exoneration of 13 former death row inmates meant that it was likely that innocent persons would be (or had been) executed. Ryan also established a commission to address problems in the justice system that may lead to innocent persons being executed. The commission made its report in 2002, and in January 2003, just before leaving office, Ryan commuted the death sentences of 167 condemned inmates (mostly to life without parole) after having given pardons to four others. While Ryan has been praised by many observers for his unprecedented acts, critics have charged Ryan with ignoring the pleas of victims' families and of using his actions to distract attention from various corruption scandals.

Nicola Sacco and **Bartolomeo Vanzetti,** Italian-born anarchists who became the central figures in one of the most controversial trials of the 20th century. Maintaining their innocence to the end, the two men were executed on August 23, 1927, for the 1920 murder of a shoe factory paymaster and guard in South Braintree, Massachusetts. Their supporters claimed that guilt had been established on inconclusive evidence and that the two men were convicted at least in part because of their radical political beliefs. Defense attorneys filed numerous unsuccessful motions and appeals in state and federal court in what was the first instance of a now-common protracted legal struggle over a death sentence.

Antonin Scalia, associate justice of the U.S. Supreme Court since 1986. Scalia generally forms the core of the conservative wing of the Court, joined later in many decisions by Clarence Thomas. Scalia has been a consistent supporter of capital punishment and has voted against the appellant in most death penalty cases. In his dissent in *Booth v. Maryland* Scalia defended the role of victim impact statements in trials and sentencing procedures, arguing that without them jurors heard witnesses offering mitigating explanations for heinous crimes without a counter-balancing sense of the full suffering of the victims.

Henry Schwarzchild, prominent anti–death penalty activist. In the 1960s he was active in the civil rights struggle in the South. He was director of the American Civil Liberties Union Capital Punishment Project from 1975 to 1990. In 1976 he also founded and became first executive director of the National Coalition to Abolish the Death Penalty.

Thorsten Sellin, one of the leading criminologists of the 20th century; affiliated with the University of Pennsylvania. He based his opposition to the death penalty on a detailed study of the subject. He wrote numerous scholarly books and articles. Sellin's expertise led to frequent invitations to testify before legislative hearings on capital punishment.

Eddie Slovik, American soldier executed for desertion in France during World War II. This was the first execution for desertion since 1864. Military officers reviewing Slovik's death sentence argued that it was necessary to execute Slovik because of his lengthy criminal record and manifest cowardice, fearing that if they did not do so it could cause increased desertion just as the war effort was reaching its climax.

John A. Spenkelink, the second person to be executed after the Supreme Court reinstated the death penalty in 1976. Unlike Gary Gilmore, he fought his death sentence to the last moment. For this reason, many viewed his case as signaling a full resumption of executions in America. Numerous abolitionist individuals and groups joined in efforts to halt his execution. Spenkelink was electrocuted on May 25, 1979.

Potter Stewart, associate justice of the U.S. Supreme Court, 1958–81. Stewart was known for his pragmatic approach to jurisprudence, and coined the famous observation that while he might not be able to define pornography, "I know it when I see it." Because of his practicality and moderation, he was often responsible for carving out the middle ground on death penalty issues. In *Furman*, for example, he agreed that the death penalty was being administered in an unconstitutionally arbitrary and capricious way, but did not believe the sanction was inherently unconstitutional.

Scott Turow, best-selling novelist and attorney who has dealt with many capital cases and death penalty issues. His novels include *Presumed Innocent* (1987) and *Reversible Errors* (2002). In 2000 Turow brought his experience with capital punishment to his service on the Illinois death penalty reform commission. He says he understands the need many people feel for retribution for heinous crimes, but the risk of executing innocent people finally brought him to favor abolishing the death penalty. He summarizes his experience and thinking in his nonfiction book *Ultimate Punishment* (2002).

Biographical Listing

Ernest van den Haag, a leading conservative intellectual who wrote extensively about capital punishment beginning in the late 1960s. Van den Haag was widely viewed as a most influential advocate of the death penalty. He consistently maintained that the sanction is morally justified for some crimes and that it does, in fact, serve as a deterrent.

CHAPTER 5

GLOSSARY

This chapter presents a short glossary of terms that have particular application to the practice of capital punishment. It does not attempt to be an exhaustive treatment of legal terms in general.

abolitionist   A person, in the context of the death penalty debate, who opposes capital punishment and seeks to have it abolished.

actual innocence   A claim, usually made in postconviction appeals, that the defendant did not commit the crime. Such a claim is based on facts rather than procedural considerations.

affirm   A higher (appeal) court's finding that a lower court's decision was justified.

aggravating circumstance (or factor)   In a capital case, something that makes a murder more serious such that the death penalty can be asked for by the prosecutor or imposed by the jury. States often specify aggravating circumstances by statute. Examples include felonies such as arson, rape, or robbery committed in conjunction with the murder; crimes against certain types of victims (such as children or police officers), or crimes with particularly venal motives (such as monetary gain). If one or more aggravating circumstances specified by statute are found to apply, juries may also consider other aggravating factors that are not statutory but are particular to the case at hand.

allocution   In capital cases, the right of a convicted defendant to make a statement to the jury during sentencing. Normally the defendant will present mitigating evidence to be considered in favor of not applying the death penalty.

arbitrary and capricious   The claim that a punishment or procedure is administered without regard to the facts of individual cases, inconsistently, or irrationally.

bifurcated trial   Division of the legal process in a capital case into a regular trial to determine factual guilt and a special sentencing phase hearing to determine whether to impose the death penalty. Bifurcation was deemed necessary to comply with the ruling in *Furman v. Georgia*.

brutalization   The hypothesis that frequent executions may increase violent crime by demonstrating the use of violence as a way to solve problems.

Glossary

capital offense A crime subject to the death penalty.

capital punishment jurisdiction One of the 38 states and two federal jurisdictions that impose capital punishment.

certiorari A writ from the Supreme Court or another higher court to a lower court, ordering that the record of a case be turned over for review. The Supreme Court must "grant cert" before a prisoner's appeal will be heard.

clemency An act by an executive (state governor or the president) that reduces or eliminates a defendant's punishment.

commutation Reducing the length or severity of a sentence. Death sentences, if commuted, are usually reduced to sentences of life imprisonment.

concurring opinion An opinion in the Supreme Court that agrees with what the majority has decided to do, but gives different reasons or justifications.

court-appointed counsel Attorney appointed by the trial court to represent a defendant who cannot afford a private attorney.

court of appeals A state or federal court whose primary purpose is to review the appropriateness of verdicts or decisions made by lower courts.

cruel and unusual punishment According to the Supreme Court, this phrase from the Eighth Amendment to the Constitution should be interpreted as banning punishment that, according to the "evolving standards of decency," is no longer acceptable to society. Abolitionists argue that capital punishment is inherently cruel and unusual, but the Supreme Court has yet to agree.

death-qualified jury A jury whose members have all said they are willing to impose a capital sentence if the facts warrant it.

death row A portion of a maximum security prison housing persons who are under sentence of death. The total number of persons on death row throughout the nation is an important indicator of the extent of capital punishment and possibly of the time it takes to resolve appeals.

death warrant An order specifying the date and time for a prisoner's execution. The execution will be carried out unless a legal order is received to the contrary.

death watch cell A cell where a prisoner is held after receiving a death warrant with a specific date of execution.

deterrence The argument that punishment discourages criminal activity either by the person punished (special deterrence) or by others (general deterrence). With the death penalty, the argument is generally over whether it actually provides greater deterrence than would a sentence of life in prison without parole.

diminished capacity Mental impairment due to disease, defect, retardation, or intoxication that makes a defendant unable to properly appreciate the wrongness of an action or unable to comply with the demands of the law. Diminished capacity can be used as a mitigating factor in capital sentencing in some states.

dissent An opinion in the Supreme Court that disagrees with the majority's findings. While having no legal effect, a dissent sometimes influences later decisions.

double jeopardy clause   The provision in the Fifth Amendment to the U.S. Constitution that states that no person "shall be subject for the same offence to be twice put in jeopardy of life or limb." This means that a person cannot be retried for an offense for which he or she has been acquitted. Jeopardy is said to "attach" at this point. The Supreme Court has ruled that once a penalty phase jury has decided against capital punishment for a given offense, the death penalty cannot be given after a subsequent retrial and conviction.

due process   The right, guaranteed by the Fifth and Fourteenth Amendments, to fair consideration of one's arguments and evidence before a criminal penalty can be imposed.

effective assistance of counsel   The right, as interpreted by the Supreme Court, to have an attorney who is competent enough to represent the defendant effectively.

Eighth Amendment   Amendment to the U.S. Constitution, part of the Bill of Rights. Its prohibition on "cruel and unusual punishment" has become a key contention of opponents of the death penalty.

equal protection   A right, guaranteed by the Fourteenth Amendment, for all persons to be treated equally by the law and to have equal recourse to its protections. Opponents of capital punishment argue that racial and other disparities in the operation of the criminal justice system amount to a denial of due process.

error   A mistake made (or alleged to be made) in a criminal proceeding. Error is the basic element of an appeal to higher courts.

ex post facto law   A law that applies to actions that took place before the law was enacted, such as by making an act illegal, increasing a punishment, or changing the rules of evidence. Such laws are prohibited by the U.S. Constitution, but courts have held that laws that change only procedures can be applied to earlier cases if they do not substantially affect the outcome.

extrajudicial execution   A killing that is committed by someone other than the duly constituted authorities, such as a dictator's death squad, a vigilante group, or a lynch mob.

factfinder   The jury or judge who hears evidence and determines whether the facts amount to a crime for which the defendant is to be held accountable.

federal courts   The nationwide system of courts that includes district (trial) courts, circuit courts of appeals, and the U.S. Supreme Court.

felony   A serious crime punishable by a prison sentence.

felony murder   A murder committed in the course of committing another felony. Such a murder is often treated as a capital offense.

first-degree murder   Generally, murder that involves a deliberate intent to kill, though precise definitions vary by state. Normally only first-degree murders can be subject to the death penalty.

Fourteenth Amendment   Amendment to the U.S. Constitution adopted after the Civil War primarily to guarantee equal rights to the newly freed

Glossary

slaves. Its guarantee of equal protection of the laws has been a basis for challenging death sentences against blacks and other minorities.

future dangerousness   The determination by a jury whether a convicted defendant is likely to commit further murders or other serious violent crimes either in prison or if eventually released. A perception of high future dangerousness tends to tip the scales toward choosing the death penalty.

grand jury   A jury that determines whether to charge a person with a crime after reviewing evidence submitted by a prosecutor. One of the two possible sources for a capital murder prosecution is an indictment by a grand jury. In many jurisdictions the prosecutor can file a document called an "information" instead of using a grand jury. Where a grand jury has been used it has sometimes been challenged by minority defendants for excluding members of minority groups.

guilt phase   In a capital case, the first trial that establishes whether the defendant is guilty of the crime. If it does, the proceeding moves on to a penalty phase.

habeas corpus   Latin for "you have the body"; a request for an order from a court to the authorities to "bring forth" the case of a person who claims to be punished unjustly and to justify that person's conviction.

harmless error   In legal terms a mistake made during a judicial proceeding that did not affect the outcome of the case.

homicide   One person killing another. Homicides can be accidental, justifiable (as in self-defense), or criminal (murder).

incapacitation   The effect of a sentence of preventing further crimes by the incarcerated individual. In the case of execution, the person is permanently incapacitated and can no longer even commit crimes in prison. This is sometimes touted as a benefit of the death penalty.

individualized consideration   The requirement by the Supreme Court that juries or judges considering whether to sentence a defendant to death must take the particular circumstances of the defendant and the crime into account. Sometimes seen to be in conflict with the requirement not to be arbitrary and capricious in sentencing.

irrevocability   The fact that an executed person, unlike someone sentenced to a lesser penalty, cannot be compensated in any way if the conviction turns out to be wrongful. Combined with the possibility of execution of the innocent, irrevocability makes a powerful argument on behalf of abolitionists.

jury override   In capital sentencing, the right in some states for a reviewing judge to reverse the verdict given by the sentencing jury.

lesser included offense   A lesser offense that can be supported by the evidence in the case and that contains at least some of the same elements of the crime. The constitutional right to due process requires in a capital case that if a lesser included offense (such as second-degree murder or manslaughter) is applicable, the jury must be instructed that they can consider it.

147

Capital Punishment

life without possibility of parole A "true" life sentence from which the prisoner will not be released except perhaps through a pardon or a finding of actual innocence.

majority opinion An opinion in the Supreme Court that is agreed to by more than half of the nine justices. Generally, one justice takes responsibility for writing the opinion.

mandatory death statutes Laws that require a death penalty when certain criminal circumstances are found. Such laws were barred by the Supreme Court.

mitigating circumstance (or factor) Something that the jury can consider in favor of the defendant in deciding whether to impose death or a lesser sentence. Mitigating circumstances are often specified by state statute. Examples include extreme emotional disturbance, mental impairment, or the lack of a previous criminal record.

moratorium With regard to capital punishment, a decision by a state legislature or governor to halt all pending executions in the state. The purpose is generally to allow for the investigation of the fairness of operation of the death penalty; in January 2000, for example, the governor of Illinois imposed such a moratorium.

murder The unlawful and deliberate killing of a human being, with malice aforethought. There are generally different degrees of murder. An unlawful killing that lacks one of the elements of murder can be considered manslaughter.

penalty phase A separate hearing held after conviction on a capital charge to determine whether to impose the death penalty. This phase is required by Supreme Court decisions.

plurality opinion An opinion of the Supreme Court that is agreed to by more justices than any other. If the plurality and any concurring opinions make up a majority, the plurality opinion takes legal effect.

proportionality review The requirement in some jurisdictions that before a capital sentence is given, similar cases must be reviewed to see whether they also resulted in capital punishment.

recidivist A criminal who commits a crime again after being released from custody.

remand To send a case back to a lower court for reconsideration.

reprieve Temporary halt to enforcement of a sentence, such as a stay of execution.

retentionist A person who seeks to retain capital punishment.

retribution The infliction of punishment that is merited or deserved because of the offender's action.

reversible error A mistake made during a criminal proceeding that is serious enough to require that the conviction or sentence be overturned.

sanction A particular penalty, such as death or life in prison.

sentencing phase As required by the Supreme Court, a separate hearing held to determine the sentence to be imposed on a convicted defendant. The sentencing phase in a capital case is like a mini trial with witnesses and opening and closing arguments.

stay of execution   An order halting enforcement of an execution warrant, therefore preventing the execution from taking place. Typically the first execution date set is automatically stayed pending the resolution of direct appeals. Any further stays must be applied for from a court such as a federal appeals court or the U.S. Supreme Court. Contrary to what is commonly seen in the movies, execution preparations are designed to make sure that any last-minute stays are received and acted on.

three-tier system   A court system that has a lower level (trial court or court of general jurisdiction), an intermediate appeal court, and a final appeal court.

voir dire (Literally, to see and speak)   The process of interviewing prospective jurors by prosecutors and defense attorneys at the start of a trial. In capital cases jurors' attitudes toward the death penalty are examined to make sure they are willing to apply the ultimate sanction if warranted.

PART II

GUIDE TO FURTHER RESEARCH

CHAPTER 6

HOW TO RESEARCH
CAPITAL PUNISHMENT

Since the first edition of this book was published in 1991, the tools and methods available to the researcher have undergone considerable evolution. In particular, the World Wide Web now provides a way for advocacy groups, government agencies, and academics to make the results of their work available virtually instantly. Given the wealth of material available online, mastery of a few basic online techniques enables today's researcher to accomplish in a few minutes what used to require long, tedious hours in the library. Therefore, it makes sense to begin our exploration of resources relating to capital punishment by looking at some of the sources available on the Internet.

As valuable as the Internet is for the student and professional researcher alike, it is important to keep its limitations in mind. What's on the Net represents only a subset of the universe of materials. While some older papers or articles have been scanned or transcribed onto web pages, most material found on the Net will date from the mid-1980s or later—about the time that computer-readable academic publications and full-text databases of popular periodicals became available.

Most online documents will be short works: the full text of books is usually not available online, except for some historical and older works that are no longer under copyright. Therefore the library remains a very important tool for the researcher. Fortunately, the nearly universal use of online (and often, remotely accessible) library catalogs has also made libraries easier to use.

Web pages, like all intellectual products, reflect the agenda and possible biases of their creator. Many of the most useful web sites on capital punishment have been created by abolitionists, although some sites by supporters of the death penalty can also be found. In using sites built by advocates, it is necessary to be aware of possible bias in the selection and annotation of materials.

In traditional publishing, various "gatekeepers" controlled what was disseminated. General publishers evaluated the quality of writing in a manuscript and considered its likely reception by the public, while academic and scientific publishers applied standards of peer review in which scholars had to defend their methodology. Some material on the web, such as scientific papers and law school journal articles, have passed through such scrutiny or are backed by other official credentials from government or other agencies. But far more online material represents the efforts of individuals who simply have something to say and now have the means to say it. This is good in that it enables freedom of expression to a degree unprecedented in history. But it does mean that the researcher must carefully inquire into the background of the author, the sources used, and the methodology used to arrive at a given conclusion, particularly in studies that involve statistical evidence.

CAPITAL PUNISHMENT ON THE WEB

There are a number of web sites that offer extensive information and links relating to all aspects of capital punishment and the debate over the death penalty. Most can be divided into two categories: sites hosted by advocates of abolition or retention of the death penalty and sites provided by government or other agencies that do not take a position on the issue.

ADVOCACY SITES

Most advocacy sites on the web take an abolitionist stance. Since the death penalty is the status quo in America, organizations seeking to reform or abolish the sanction are strongly motivated to challenge it through education and advocacy efforts.

Abolitionists

The Death Penalty Information Center at http://www.deathpenaltyinfo.org is a good reference site provided one keeps in mind that the extensive materials offered reflect a strongly abolitionist (or at least reform) viewpoint. The offerings include summaries of state and federal death penalty provisions, news, reports, and fact sheets. Special "Issues" sections include costs, deterrence, innocence, juveniles, mental illness and retardation, and race.

Another abolitionist organization that offers an extensive web site is the National Coalition to Abolish the Death Penalty. Its site at http://www.ncadp.org/ offers news, statistics, and a featured campaign such as the release of a juvenile on death row whom the organization believes to be innocent. Researchers and advocates will particularly appreciate the extensive news summaries and the directories which provide contact information for both national and state anti-death penalty organizations.

The American Civil Liberties Union (ACLU) has a Capital Punishment Project dedicated to research and advocacy toward abolition of the death penalty. Its issue page for capital punishment is at http://www.aclu.org/DeathPenalty/

DeathPenaltyMain.cfm. It includes news, press releases and statements, various issue resource links, and newsletters.

The international human rights organization Amnesty International has made a major effort in recent years to abolish the death penalty in those countries that still employ the sanction. This effort has particularly focused on the United States. The Amnesty International USA Death Penalty site at http:// www.amnestyusa.org/ab/pages/death-penalty-index-eng offers news, fact sheets, press releases, and "actions" focusing on particular death row cases.

Another international human rights group called Derechos also has a strong advocacy against the death penalty. The group's web site at http://www.derechos. org/dp includes the usual facts and resource links but also a good variety of writings by and about death row inmates.

Lawrence M. Hinman's "Ethics Update" site has a useful page on "Punishment and the Death Penalty" at http://ethics.acusd.edu/death_penalty.html. Among other things, it offers an overview of the ethics of the death penalty in the form of a web-based Powerpoint slide presentation.

Pro–Death Penalty Sites

While defenders of capital punishment certainly have a presence on the web, they don't seem to have many extensive sites comparable to those of the abolitionists. However, the site "Pro-death penalty.com" at http://www.prodeathpenalty.com/ offers news and informational links similar to those provided by the abolitionist sites, as well as essays and articles by death penalty supporters, such as those opposing the efforts on behalf of Mumia Abu-Jamal. The host of this site also maintains a sister site on behalf of murder victims at http://www.murdervictims. com/. The site "Justice for All" at http://www.jfa.net/ also advocates on behalf of families of victims of murder and other serious crimes and links to the preceding site for death penalty information.

Finally, "1000+ Death Penalty Links," a page from the Clark County, Nevada, Prosecuting Attorney's Office at http://www.clarkprosecutor.org/html/ links/dplinks.htm, lives up to its name, offering an extensive array of reference links comparable to those at the Death Penalty Information Center but with a pro–death penalty viewpoint.

OTHER RESOURCE SITES

A variety of other sites are not clearly either anti– or pro–death penalty in viewpoint. Here are some examples:

Focus on the Death Penalty at http://www.uaa.alaska.edu/just/death/history. html is sponsored by the Justice Center at the University of Alaska, Anchorage, and focuses primarily on legal issues, with background material, statistics, and discussion relating to key death penalty cases. However, access to current news updates and reports as well as some historical information is also provided.

Capital Punishment

"Prof. David's Death Penalty Resources" by J. W. Vanderhoof at http://www.uncp.edu/home/vanderhoof/death.html was prepared for a class syllabus. It is a well-organized general guide to links and resources for the death penalty debate. It includes recorded lectures, archives relating to high-profile cases (such as the Jasper, Texas, hate crime trial and the Timothy McVeigh trial), excerpts and supplemental materials for PBS and NPR programs, newspaper articles, and other material.

GOVERNMENT AGENCIES AND STATISTICS

Much of the debate over capital punishment involves statistics. These range from polling and survey data to crime statistics to demographics of death row inmates. There are several important government agency sites that provide such statistics.

The U.S. Department of Justice Bureau of Justice Statistics offers complete and up-to-date statistics on every aspect of the criminal justice system. These include crime rates, statistics about criminal offenders, and statistics about every aspect of criminal procedure from arrests to sentencing to prison life. Statistics specifically related to capital punishment are found under "Corrections," at http://www.ojp.usdoj.gov/bjs/cp.htm. This page includes a summary of executions from the previous year broken down by state, by demographics, including race, and by method used. Reports are also available for prior years. Some statistics are also available in spreadsheet and tabular form.

Another important publication with Bureau of Justice Statistics information is the *Sourcebook of Criminal Justice Statistics*, which is available online at http://www.albany.edu/sourcebook/index.html. This annual publication gathers statistics from more than 100 sources and compiles them into more than 600 tables grouped into a number of files in Adobe Acrobat format. If your computer is not already equipped to read these files, you can download a free reader through the provided link.

The *Sourcebook* is divided into six main sections, each with a detailed table of contents. For example, Section 2, Public Attitudes Toward Crime and Criminal Justice-Related Topics, includes a subsection, Death Penalty, which in turn offers a number of files containing survey data, such as Attitudes toward the death penalty, by demographic characteristics, United States, 2001 (Table 2.47). Section 6, Persons Under Correctional Supervision, includes the subcategory State and Federal Prisoners Executed, which includes three tables with data from 1930 to 2003, with breakdowns by jurisdiction, offense, and race. The subcategory Persons Removed from Death Row is particularly interesting in view of the controversy over possible execution of innocent people.

Advanced researchers who are familiar with statistical data sets and software such as SPSS can find a treasure trove of data at The National Archive of Criminal Justice Data at http://www.icpsr.umich.edu/NACJD/. The Capital Punishment Resource Guide available there also explains how to find and interpret data relevant to the death penalty.

Another important source for crime data is the Uniform Crime Reports compiled by the Federal Bureau of Investigation (FBI). *Crime in the United States* and other reports can be obtained at the FBI web site at http://www.fbi.gov/ucr/ucr.htm.

The National Archive of Criminal Justice Data also offers data from the Inter-University Consortium for Political and Social Research (ICPSR), which has its own site at http://www.icpsr.umich.edu/index.html that provides a broad range of social science data.

Researchers on capital punishment issues will need to become familiar with penal systems. The Federal Bureau of Prisons site at http://www.bop.gov/ offers useful summaries under "Public Information." They include "Quick Facts and Statistics" on federal prison inmates. For state prison statistics, some information is available from the Bureau of Justice Statistics (under "Corrections."). Individual state prison systems can usually be found via a web search using the state name followed by "department of corrections," such as "California department of corrections." (For other statistics on capital punishment, also see Appendix A of this book.)

BIBLIOGRAPHIC RESOURCES

As useful as the web is for quickly finding information and the latest news, in-depth research still requires trips to the library or bookstore. Getting the most out of the library requires the use of bibliographic tools and resources. Bibliographic resources is a general term for catalogs, indexes, bibliographies, and other guides that identify the books, periodical articles, and other printed resources that deal with a particular subject. They are essential tools for the researcher.

LIBRARY CATALOGS

Access to the largest library catalog, that of the Library of Congress, is available at http://catalog.loc.gov. This page explains the different kinds of catalogs and searching techniques available.

Yahoo offers a categorized listing of libraries at http://dir.yahoo.com/Reference/Libraries. Of course for materials available at one's local public or university library, that institution will be the most convenient source.

Online catalogs can be searched not only by the traditional author, title, and subject headings, but also by matching keywords in the title. Thus a title search for "capital punishment" will retrieve all books that have those words somewhere in their title. (Of course a book about capital punishment may well not have that phrase in the title and perhaps instead refer to "death penalty" so it is still necessary to use subject headings to get the most comprehensive results.)

The most important LC subject heading is, of course "Capital Punishment." Its entry in the Library of Congress subject headings guide is as follows:

CAPITAL PUNISHMENT
Used for:
  Abolition of CAPITAL PUNISHMENT
  Death penalty
Narrower terms:
  Crucifixion
  Death row
  Discrimination in CAPITAL PUNISHMENT
  Electrocution
  Garrote
  Hanging
  Last meal before execution
  Stoning
Related terms:
  Executions and executioners
Broader terms:
  Criminal law

Note that there's no separate heading here for abolition of capital punishment. "Death Penalty" is not a valid LC subject heading but instead cross references to "Capital Punishment."

Once the record for a book or other item is found, it is a good idea to see what additional subject and name headings have been assigned. These in turn can be used for further searching.

BIBLIOGRAPHIES, INDEXES, AND DATABASES

Bibliographies in various forms provide a convenient way to find books, periodical articles, and other materials. Most book-length bibliographies published before the 1970s are not very useful except for finding historical and philosophical works since the shape of capital punishment in America was so radically changed by the Supreme Court decisions of the 1970s and early 1980s. More useful are the bibliographies or bibliographical notes found at the end of the recent overview or reference works found in the first section of Chapter 7 of this book.

Popular and scholarly articles can be accessed through periodical indexes that provide citations and abstracts. Abstracts are brief summaries of articles or papers. They are usually compiled and indexed—originally in bound volumes but increasingly available online. Some examples of printed indexes where you might retrieve literature related to capital punishment include:

• ATLA Religion Database—for religious works dealing with capital punishment
• Criminal Justice Abstracts
• Criminal Justice Periodical Index

- Index to Legal Periodicals and Books
- Social Sciences Citation Index
- Social Sciences Index
- Sociological Abstracts

Some of these indexes are available online (at least for recent years). Generally, however, you can access them only through a library where you hold a card, and they cannot be accessed over the Internet (unless you are on a college campus). Consult with a university reference librarian for more help.

There are two good indexes that have unrestricted search access, however. UnCover Web (http://www.ingenta.com) contains brief descriptions of about 8.8 million documents from about 26,000 journals in just about every subject area. Copies of complete documents can be ordered with a credit card, or they may be obtainable for free at a local library.

Perhaps the most valuable index for topics related to criminal justice is the National Criminal Justice Reference Service Justice Information Center, at http://www.ncjrs.org. It offers a searchable abstract database containing 180,000 criminal justice publications, and it can be a real gold mine for the more advanced researcher.

FREE PERIODICAL INDEXES

Most public libraries subscribe to database services such as Info Trac or EBSCO that index articles from hundreds of general-interest periodicals (and some moderately specialized ones). The database can be searched by author or by words in the title, subject headings, and sometimes words found anywhere in the article text. Depending on the database used, hits in the database can result in just a bibliographical description (author, title, pages, periodical name, issue date), a description plus an abstract (a paragraph summarizing the contents of the article), or the full text of the article itself. Before using such an index, it is a good idea to view the list of newspapers and magazines covered and determine the years of coverage.

Many libraries provide Internet access to their periodical databases as an option in their catalog menu. However, licensing restrictions usually mean that only researchers who have a library card for that particular library can access the database (by typing in their name and card number). Check with local public or school libraries to see what databases are available.

For periodicals not indexed by Infotrac or another index (or for which only abstracts rather than complete text is available), check to see whether the publication has its own web site (most now do). Some scholarly publications are putting all or most of their articles online. Popular publications tend to offer only a limited selection. Some publications of both types offer archives of several years' back issues that can be searched by author or keyword.

159

BOOKSTORE CATALOGS

Many people have discovered that online bookstores such as Amazon.com at (http://www.amazon.com) and barnesandnoble.com (http://www.bn.com) are convenient ways to shop for books. A lesser-known benefit of online bookstore catalogs is that they often include publisher's information, book reviews, and reader's comments about a given title. They can thus serve as a form of annotated bibliography.

On the other hand, a visit to one's local bookstore also has its benefits. While the selection of titles available is likely to be smaller than that of an online bookstore, the ability to physically browse through books before buying them can be very useful.

KEEPING UP WITH THE NEWS

It is important for the researcher to be aware of currently breaking news. In addition to watching TV news and subscribing to local or national newspapers and magazines, there are a number of ways to use the Internet to find additional news sources.

NEWSPAPERS AND NETNEWS

Like periodicals, most large newspapers now have web sites that offer headlines and a searchable database of recent articles. The URL is usually given somewhere in one's local newspaper. Yahoo! is also a good place to find newspaper links: see http://dir.yahoo.com/News_and_Media/Newspapers/ Web_Directories/.

Netnews is a decentralized system of thousands of newsgroups, or forums organized by topic. Most web browsers have an option for subscribing to, reading, and posting messages in newsgroups. The Google Groups site (http://groups. google.com) also provides free access and an easy-to-use interface to newsgroups. The general newsgroup for discussing capital punishment issues is alt.activism.death-penalty.

SEARCHING THE WEB

A researcher can explore an ever-expanding web of information by starting with a few web sites and following the links they offer to other sites, which in turn have links to still other sites. But since this is something of a hit-and-miss proposition, some important sites may be missed if the researcher only web surfs in this fashion. There are two more focused techniques that can fill in the information gaps.

WEB GUIDES AND INDEXES

A web guide or index is a site that offers what amounts to a structured, hierarchical outline of subject areas. This enables the researcher to zero in on a particular aspect of a subject and find links to web sites for further exploration.

The best known (and largest) web index is Yahoo! at http://www.yahoo.com. The home page gives the top-level list of topics, and the researcher simply clicks to follow them down to more specific areas.

In addition to following Yahoo!'s outline-like structure, there is also a search box into which the researcher can type one or more keywords and receive a list of matching categories and sites.

Web indexes such as Yahoo! have two major advantages over undirected surfing. First, the structured hierarchy of topics makes it easy to find a particular topic or subtopic and then explore its links. Second, Yahoo! does not make an attempt to compile every possible link on the Internet (a task that is virtually impossible, given the size of the web). Rather, sites are evaluated for usefulness and quality by Yahoo!'s indexers. This means that the researcher has a better chance of finding more substantial and accurate information. The disadvantage of web indexes is the flip side of their selectivity: the researcher is dependent on the indexer's judgment for determining what sites are worth exploring.

To explore capital punishment via Yahoo!, the researcher should browse Society and Culture, then Crime, Correction and Rehabilitation, and finally Death Penalty. At the time of writing, subtopics available under that heading include: Death Row, Execution Methods, Juvenile Death Penalty, Opposing Views, Supporting Views, and Web Directories. Clicking on a category opens a list of links, and there is also a list of individual sites.

The Mining Company's About.com (http://www.about.com) is rather similar to Yahoo!, but gives a greater emphasis to overviews or guides prepared by experts in various topics. To find information on capital punishment on About.com, browse to News & Issues, News, Crime and Punishment, Articles & Resources, Death Penalty (or try going directly to http://crime.about.com/od/death) or enter a direct keyword search such as "capital punishment." (Remember with guide sites it is often a good idea to supplement browsing with a direct search to ensure the most comprehensive results.)

New guide and index sites are constantly being developed, and capabilities are improving as the web matures. One example is Ask Jeeves, at http://www.ask.com. This site attempts to answer a researcher's plain-English question, such as "How many prisoners were executed in the United States in 1997?" It doesn't, alas, actually answer the question, but it does return a number of possibly useful links that it obtains by querying a whole series of search engines. (For the example question, the first link it found was "Bureau of Justice Statistics Capital Punishment Statistics," which would indeed have the desired information.)

There are also an increasing number of specialized online research guides that are similar to traditional bibliographical essays but with the added bonus of

161

having many of the materials discussed already linked so they are just a click away. The Boston University Library has a research guide to capital punishment at http://www.bu.edu/library/research-guides/cappun.html.

SEARCH ENGINES

Search engines take a very different approach to finding materials on the web. Instead of organizing topically in a top down fashion, search engines work their way from the bottom up, scanning through web documents and indexing them. There are hundreds of search engines, but some of the most widely used include:

- AltaVista (http://www.altavista.com)
- Excite (http://www.excite.com)
- Google (http://www.google.com)
- Hotbot (http://www.hotbot.lycos.com)
- Lycos (http://www.lycos.com)
- WebCrawler (http://www.WebCrawler.com)

Search engines are generally easy to use by employing the same sorts of keywords that work in library catalogs. There are a variety of web search tutorials available online. (Try "web search tutorial" in a search engine to find some.) One good one is published by Brightplanet at http://www.brightplanet.com/deepcontent/tutorials/search/index.asp.

Here are a few basic rules for using search engines:

- When looking for something specific, use the most specific term or phrase. For example, when looking for information about habeas corpus appeals, use the specific term "habeas corpus," since this is the standard term. (Note that phrases should be put in quotes if you want them to be matched as phrases rather than as individual words. We show all search terms in quotes to separate them from the rest of the sentence, but that doesn't mean quotes should be used in actual searches other than for phrases.)

- When looking for a general topic that might be expressed using several different words or phrases, use several descriptive words (nouns are more reliable than verbs). For example, "death row statistics." (Most engines will automatically put pages that match all three terms first on the results list.)

- Use "wildcards" when a desired word may have more than one ending. For example, prison* matches "prison," "prisoner," and "prisoners" (but not, for example, "inmate").

- Most search engines support Boolean (*and, or, not*) operators that can be used to broaden or narrow a search.

- Use AND to narrow a search. For example, "juvenile AND capital" will match only pages that have both terms.

- Use OR to broaden a search: "'capital punishment' OR 'death penalty'" will match any page that has *either* term, and since these terms are often used interchangeably, this type of search is necessary to retrieve the widest range of results.

- Use NOT to exclude unwanted results: "'death row' NOT Texas" finds articles about death row except for those that also mention Texas.

Since each search engine indexes somewhat differently and offers somewhat different ways of searching, it is a good idea to use several different search engines, especially for a general query. Several metasearch programs automate the process of submitting a query to multiple search engines. These include:

- Metacrawler (http://www.metacrawler.com)
- SurfWax (http://www.surfwax.com)

There are also search utilities that can be run from the researcher's own PC rather than through a web site. A good example is Copernic, a shareware (try before you buy) program available for download at http://www.copernic.com. (The Basic version is free.)

FINDING ORGANIZATIONS AND PEOPLE

Chapter 8 of this book provides an extensive list of organizations that are involved with the capital punishment issue, but new groups are emerging all the time. A good place to look for information and links to advocacy organizations is the major resource sites such as the Death Penalty Information Center and others mentioned at the beginning of this chapter. Web indexes such as Yahoo! also have a subtopic for organizations under "Capital Punishment" or "Death Penalty." If such sites do not yield the name of a specific organization, the name can be given to a search engine. Generally the best approach is to put the name of the organization in quote marks such as "Murder Victims for Reconciliation."

Another approach is to take a guess at the organization's likely web address. For example, the American Civil Liberties Union is commonly known by its acronym ACLU, so it is not a surprise that the organization's web site is at www.aclu.org. Note that noncommercial organization sites normally use the .org suffix, government agencies use .gov, educational institutions have .edu, and businesses use .com. This technique can save time, but doesn't always work.

There are several ways to find a person on the Internet:

- Put the person's name (in quotes) in a search engine and possibly find that person's home page on the Internet.

- Contact the person's employer (such as a university for an academic or a corporation for a technical professional). Most such organizations have web pages that include a searchable faculty or employee directory.
- Try one of the people-finder services such as Yahoo! People Search at http://people.yahoo.com or BigFoot at http://www.bigfoot.com. This may yield contact information such as e-mail address, regular address, and/or phone number.

LEGAL RESEARCH

While capital punishment is also a moral and ethical issue, the most decisive battles are generally those carried out in the legislative and legal arenas. Because of the specialized terminology of the law, legal research can be more difficult to master than bibliographical or general research tools. Fortunately, the Internet has also come to the rescue in this area, offering a variety of ways to look up laws and court cases without having to pore through huge bound volumes in law libraries (which may not be easily accessible to the general public, anyway).

FINDING LAWS

Since the vast majority of death sentences are passed under state laws, access to the relevant portions of state penal codes is a must for the legal researcher. The Cornell Law School Death Penalty Project provides a very useful set of links at http://www.lawschool.cornell.edu/library/death. These links include the state's constitution, laws, court opinions, and death penalty advocacy organizations.

This same site also provides links to recent federal legislation. While few federal prisoners have been executed, numerous federal death penalty offenses have been added in recent years. When federal legislation passes, it eventually becomes part of the United States Code, a massive legal compendium. Title 18 of the U.S. Code deals with Crimes and Criminal Procedure. Part I of this Title defines crimes and penalties and can be used together with the summary in Chapter 2 of this book, The Law of Capital Punishment, to look up specific sections that include the provision of the death penalty. (The Cornell Law School Death Penalty resource site at http://www.law.cornell.edu/topics/death_penalty.html provides a direct link to the sections of the U.S. Code Title 18 that involve the death penalty.)

The U.S. Code can be searched online in several locations, but the easiest site to use is probably the Cornell Law School at http://assembler.law.cornell.edu/uscode/. The fastest way to retrieve a law is by its title and section citation, but phrases and keywords can also be used.

KEEPING UP WITH LEGISLATIVE DEVELOPMENTS

Pending legislation is often tracked by advocacy groups, both national and those based in particular states. See Chapter 8, Organizations and Agencies, for contact information. The Cornell Law School Death Penalty Project site mentioned earlier also lists state organizations that provide information on legislation currently under consideration.

Proposed federal death penalty legislation normally turns up as part of a large bill often called an "omnibus crime bill," although there are other possible legislative vehicles, such as the Antiterrorism and Effective Death Penalty Act of 1996.

The Library of Congress Thomas web site (http://thomas.loc.gov) includes files summarizing legislation organized by the number of the Congress. (Each two-year session of Congress has a consecutive number: For example, the 109th Congress is in session in 2005 and 2006.) Legislation can be searched for by the name of its sponsor(s), the bill number, or by topical keywords. (Laws that have been passed can be looked up under their Public Law number.) Further details retrievable by clicking on the bill number and then the link to the bill summary and status file include sponsors, committee action, and amendments. Only the current session of Congress can be accessed from Thomas's main page, but earlier sessions can be searched by clicking on "Search Bills and Resolutions" under "Legislation." Sessions back to the 101st Congress (1989–90) can be accessed with "Simple Search"; summary and status information about bills introduced in prior sessions must be reached through "Advanced Search."

FINDING COURT DECISIONS

If legislation is the front end of the criminal justice process, the courts are the back. The Supreme Court and state courts make important decisions every year that shape the administration of the death penalty. Like laws, legal decisions are organized using a system of citations. The general form is: *Party1 v. Party2 volume reporter,* [optional start page] *(court, year)*.

Here are some examples:

Gregg v. Georgia, 428 U.S. 153 (1976)

Here the parties are Gregg (a condemned prisoner) and the state of Georgia. The case is in volume 428 of the U.S. *Supreme Court Reports,* beginning at page 153, and the case was decided in 1976. (For the Supreme Court, the name of the court is omitted.)

Fierro v. Gomez, 77 F.3d 301 (9th Cir. 1996)

Here the case is in the 9th U.S. Circuit Court of Appeals, decided in 1996.

A state court decision can generally be identified because it includes the state's name. For example, in *State v. Torrance,* 473 S.E.2d. 703, S.C. 1996, the S.E.2d refers to the appeals district, and the S.C. to South Carolina.

Once the jurisdiction for the case has been determined, the researcher can then go to a number of places on the Internet to find cases by citation and sometimes by the names of the parties or by subject keywords. A couple of the most useful sites are:

- **The Legal Information Institute** (http://supct.law.cornell.edu/supct) has all Supreme Court decisions since 1990 plus 610 of "the most important historic" decisions.
- **Washlaw Web** (http://www.washlaw.edu) has a variety of courts (including states) and legal topics listed, making it a good jumping-off place for many sorts of legal research. However, the actual accessibility of state court opinions (and the formats they are provided in) varies widely.

LEXIS AND WESTLAW

Lexis and Westlaw are commercial legal databases that have extensive information including an elaborate system of notes, legal subject headings, and ways to show relationships between cases. Unfortunately, these services are too expensive for use by most individual researchers unless they are available through a university or corporate library.

MORE HELP ON LEGAL RESEARCH

For more information on conducting legal research, see the "Legal Research FAQ" at http://www.cis.ohio-state.edu/hypertext/faq/usenet/law/research/top. html. For complex research projects, the researcher who lacks formal legal training may also want to consult with or rely on the efforts of professional researchers or academics in the field.

PUTTING IT ALL TOGETHER

It can be hard to know where to begin when there are so many kinds of information sources available. Unless one is researching a very specific topic, it is probably best to gain an overview and working knowledge of the topic by using some of the resource sites and web indexes and guides and then pursue specific interests by using bibliographical tools (library and bookstore catalogs and periodical indexes) to obtain appropriate books, news articles, and scholarly papers. When legal research is required, having the general knowledge, context, and citations in hand will save time and frustration.

CHAPTER 7

ANNOTATED
BIBLIOGRAPHY

This chapter presents a representative selection of books, articles, and Web documents related to many aspects of capital punishment. All sections have been reviewed for this revised edition and have been updated with books and articles published since 2000, including the most current reference works and handbooks. However, many historical accounts and legal and philosophical arguments from previous decades remain important, and the most relevant of these have been retained.

The 12 sections of this bibliography are organized under three broad topics as follows:

Reference and Background
Reference Works
Introductions, Overviews, and Collections
Historical and International Works
Accounts of Death Row and Executions
General Advocacy Works

Social and Legal Issues
Punishment, Retribution, and Deterrence
Race, Class, and Fairness
Special Cases: Youth, Mental Disability, and Gender
The Question of Innocence
General and Miscellaneous Legal Issues

Political and Cultural Issues
Public Opinion, Laws and Legislation, and Political Developments
Religious, Philosophical, Ethical, and Cultural Perspectives

REFERENCE AND BACKGROUND

Reference Works

This section includes encyclopedias, reference handbooks, bibliographies, and articles from online encyclopedias.

BOOKS

Grossman, Mark. *Encyclopedia of Capital Punishment.* Santa Barbara, Calif.: ABC-CLIO, 1998. An encyclopedia of topics, persons, court decisions, statistics, and other items relating to capital punishment. The book includes a bibliography and timeline.

Hall, Kermit L. *The Oxford Companion to the Supreme Court of the United States.* 2d ed. New York: Oxford University Press, 2004. Contains an overview of capital punishment jurisprudence but is most useful for learning how the Court works and for looking up general concepts that arise in reaching decisions.

Kronenwetter, Michael. *Capital Punishment: A Reference Handbook.* 2d ed. Santa Barbara, Calif.: ABC-CLIO, 2001. A comprehensive guide to capital punishment issues. Includes history, summary of issues, chronology, biographies, facts and documents, organizations, and a list of selected print and nonprint resources.

Latzer, Barry. *Death Penalty Cases.* 2d ed. St. Louis, Mo.: Elsevier Science & Technology, 2002. A collection of extensive excerpts from the decisions in 25 Supreme Court cases involving capital punishment, with a brief editorial introduction to each case. Each case is a separate chapter with a descriptive title that identifies the main issue involved.

Leone, Ugo, editor. *Death Penalty: A Bibliographic Research Guide.* Collingdale, Pa.: DIANE Publishing Co., 1995. A bibliographical survey and review of international research on capital punishment, covering the period 1979–86.

Palmer, Louis J. *Encyclopedia of Capital Punishment in the United States.* Jefferson, N.C.: McFarland & Co., 2001. A copious reference providing detailed entries on all relevant Supreme Court decisions, biographies of justices involved in death penalty litigation, federal, state, and foreign laws (about 200 countries), related legal and social issues, and much more.

Radelet, Michael L., and Margaret Vandiver. *Capital Punishment in America: An Annotated Bibliography.* New York: Garland Publishing, 1988. An annotated listing of more than 950 books and articles on capital punishment. The book includes citations to relevant congressional publications and brief synopses of major Supreme Court decisions.

Triche, Charles W., III. *The Capital Punishment Dilemma: 1950–1977: A Subject Bibliography.* Troy, N.Y.: Whitston, 1979. An extensive topical (but not annotated) bibliography of works dealing with the death penalty debate in the 1950s through the mid-1970s.

Web Documents

"Capital Punishment" in *Catholic Encyclopedia Online.* Available online. URL: http://www.newadvent.org/cathen. Posted in 2003. Overview from a Catholic perspective

"Capital Punishment Timeline." Clark County Prosecuting Attorney. Available online. URL: http://www.clarkprosecutor.org/html/death/timeline.htm. Updated in June 2004. A detailed chronology of events relating to the death penalty.

"Multimedia Resources on the Death Penalty." Death Penalty Information Center. Available online. URL: http://www.deathpenaltyinfo.org/article.php?did=142&scid=42. Posted in 2004. Describes a number of film, TV, and radio documentaries relating to the issue of capital punishment. Includes links to audio and video excerpts.

Introductions, Overviews, and Collections

This section consists of general introductions and overviews of capital punishment as well as collections of essays or papers. Although some of these works may be somewhat biased toward the pro or con side of the death penalty controversy, works that primarily serve an advocacy purpose will be found in the section "General Advocacy."

BOOKS

Acker, James R., Robert M. Bohm, and Charles S. Lanier, editors. *America's Experiment with Capital Punishment: Reflections on the Past, Present, and Future of the Ultimate Penal Sanction.* 2d ed. Durham, N.C.: Carolina Academic Press, 2003. A hefty collection of essays by distinguished experts, grouped under the following general topics: Part I, Introduction; Part II, Capital Punishment: Public Opinion, Law, and Politics; Part III, The Justice and Utility of the Capital Sanction; Part IV, The Administration of the Death Penalty; Part V, Terminal Stages of the Penalty of Death. Generally, the contributors in the later sections conclude that there are substantial defects in the justification and practice of the death penalty.

Baird, Robert M., and Stuart E. Rosenbaum. *Punishment and the Death Penalty: The Current Debate.* Revised ed. New York: Prometheus Books, 1995. A collection of essays in two parts. Part one deals with the justification for punishment in general in various frameworks of social philosophy. Part two focuses on capital punishment, in particular its history, the movement to abolish the death penalty, deterrence, execution of the innocent, the confrontation between capital punishment and contemporary social values, and the debate between Justices Blackmun and Scalia.

Bedau, Hugo. *The Death Penalty in America.* New York: Oxford University Press, 1997. An extensive collection including overviews, facts and statistics, and a variety of papers. Areas covered include: the death penalty vs. life imprisonment, deterrence and incapacitation, constitutionality (including "cruel and unusual punishment"), the part played by race and class in capital sentencing, and religious and moral arguments. A bibliography and case citations are included.

Bedau, Hugo Adam, and Paul Cassell, editors. *Debating the Death Penalty: Should America Have Capital Punishment? The Experts from Both Sides Make Their Case.* New York: Oxford University Press, 2004. Seven experts, including judges, lawyers, and scholars, debate the pros and cons of capital punishment. Topics include the appropriateness of punishment, deterrence, discrimination and unfairness in the legal system, and whether the possibility of executing innocent persons requires abandoning the death penalty.

Bohm, Robert M. *The Death Penalty in America: Current Research.* Cincinnati, Ohio: Anderson Publishing Company, 1991. A collection of studies by various researchers. Topics include statistical analysis of executions, deterrence, decision making by jurors in capital cases, recidivism by death row inmates paroled after the *Furman* decision, and public opinion on capital punishment. Some material is somewhat dated.

———. *Deathquest II: An Introduction to the Theory and Practice of Capital Punishment in the United States.* Cincinnati, Ohio: Anderson Publishing Company, 2003. Revised edition of a comprehensive legal textbook giving the history, issues, and court opinions relating to capital punishment. Includes extensive references and bibliography.

Capital Punishment. San Diego, Calif.: Greenhaven Press, 2004. A collection of pro and con essays on various aspects of the death penalty by authors including Justice Antonin Scalia and writer Scott Turow.

Gottfried, Ted. *Capital Punishment: The Death Penalty Debate.* Springfield, N.J.: Enslow, 1997. For young adult readers. A well-balanced presentation of the pro and con arguments regarding the death penalty, with good citations of cases and examples. Gottfried includes historical background, facts, and statistics, as well as a chronology, glossary, and bibliography.

Grabowski, John F. *The Death Penalty.* San Diego: Lucent Books, 1999. For junior high and older readers. An overview presenting issues relating to the death penalty, with pro and con arguments.

Harries, Keith, and Derral Cheatwood. *The Geography of Execution: The Capital Punishment Quagmire in America.* Lanham, Md.: Rowman & Littlefield, 1996. Begins with an overview and introduction to methodology. The authors give a historical, differential view of how particular constellations of practical and political considerations result in differences in the pace and methods of execution. They also present studies of race and gender in capital punishment and studies showing no discernable deterrent effect for the death penalty. The book also discusses the effectiveness and problems of life without parole.

Jacobs, George. *A Capital Case in America: How Today's Justice System Handles Death Penalty Cases, from Crime Scene to Ultimate Execution of Sentence.* Durham, N.C.: Carolina Academic Press, 2000. Uses details and recreations of six actual cases to show the factors involved in deciding when to charge capital murder, how to prosecute the case, the considerations affecting the jury's sentencing decision, and much more.

Koosed, Margery B. *Capital Punishment: The Philosophical, Moral, and Penological Debate over Capital Punishment.* New York: Garland Publishing Company, 1996. An overview of capital punishment issues from a variety of perspectives.

Lester, David. *The Death Penalty: Issues and Answers.* Springfield, Ill.: Charles C. Thomas, 1998. An overview of death penalty issues. Lester begins with an introduction to the operation of capital punishment, then discusses the results of research on topics such as public attitude, discrimination, juror behavior, and studies of deterrence. The book includes appendices summarizing surveys and studies.

Martinez, J. Michael, William Richardson, and D. Brandon Hornsby, editors. *Leviathan's Choice: Capital Punishment in the Twenty-first Century.* Lanham, Md.: Rowman & Littlefield, 2002. A wide-ranging collection of 18 essays on capital punishment from legal, sociological, theological, and philosophical viewpoints. Contributions reflect both pro– and anti–death penalty views. The last two chapters look at the possible future of capital punishment.

Pojman, Louis P., and Reiman Jeffrey. *The Death Penalty: For and Against.* Lanham, Md.: Rowman & Littlefield, 1998. The two authors debate each other over the philosophical proposition that the death penalty should be abolished in America. Each author then replies to the other's statement.

Rein, Mei Ling, Nancy R. Jacobs, and Mark A. Siegel, eds. *Capital Punishment: Cruel and Unusual?* Detroit: Thomson/Gale, 2004. A compact, fact-filled guide to capital punishment issues, including history, court rulings, legal issues, statutes and legislation, statistics, public attitudes, and international aspects. The book also includes a brief pro/con debate and listings of resources and organizations.

Streib, Victor L. *A Capital Punishment Anthology.* Cincinnati, Ohio: Anderson Printing Company, 1997. An anthology of critical writings on capital punishment. The book includes general contributions by noted writers in the field and Supreme Court justices, followed by sets of selections focusing on issues such as racial disparities, execution of the innocent, and various aspects of judicial procedure.

Turow, Scott. *Ultimate Punishment: A Lawyer's Reflections on Dealing with the Death Penalty.* New York: Farrar, Straus & Giroux, 2003. An attorney and best-selling novelist, the author vividly describes his dealings with capital cases as a young prosecutor and his later service on the Illinois commission that ultimately prompted the governor to commute dozens of death sentences.

The portraits of specific perpetrators and victims give a human dimension to what might otherwise be abstract concerns.

Winters, Paul A. *The Death Penalty: Opposing Viewpoints.* 3d ed. revised. San Diego: Greenhaven Press, 1997. A collection of readings from a variety of writers, arranged into a series of pro and con pairings. Topics include early consideration of the death penalty in England and America; justice, morality, and the execution of the innocent; the effectiveness of the death penalty as a deterrent; and fairness in the application of the death penalty to minority groups and the handicapped. Each reading includes an introduction and discussion questions. The book was written for junior and senior high school students, but is valuable for researchers at all levels.

Wolf, Robert V., and Austin Sarat, ed. *Capital Punishment: Crime, Justice, and Punishment.* Philadelphia: Chelsea House, 1997. For young adult readers. Provides a basic overview of capital punishment issues, introducing cases and arguments on each of the major topics.

ARTICLES

Ballard, Scotty. "Should the Death Penalty Be Abolished?" *Jet*, vol. 103, February 24, 2003, pp. 4–5. An overview of arguments for and against the death penalty, a summary of recent events, and statements by a variety of African-Americans, including radio talk host Larry Elder.

Liptak, Adam. "Fewer Death Sentences Being Imposed in U.S." *New York Times*, September 15, 2004, p. A16. A recent report from the Death Penalty Information Center and other data are used to summarize recent statistics and trends involving death row in the United States. The rate of death sentences has dropped from about 290 per year in the 1990s to 174 since the year 2000. Various possible explanations are given, including reaction to the publicity about exonerated death row inmates and greater care by prosecutors in determining whether to seek death sentences.

WEB DOCUMENTS

"Capital Punishment, 2003." U.S. Department of Justice, Bureau of Justice Statistics. Available online. URL: http://www.ojp.usdoj.gov/bjs/pub/pdf/cp03. pdf. Posted in November, 2004. This series of annual reports uses a variety of tables, charts, and bullet points to summarize the extent of executions in the United States, trends in capital sentencing and executions, provisions of capital punishment laws, death row demographics, and other developments.

"The Death Penalty in 2004: Year End Report." Death Penalty Information Center. Available online. URL: http://www.deathpenaltyinfo.org/DPICyer04. pdf. Posted in December 2004. Summarizes executions and other events relating to capital punishment in the United States. Also includes public opinion data and suggests gradually declining support for the death penalty under the impact of the ongoing exoneration of death row inmates. Note that earlier annual reports in this series are also available at the Death Penalty Information Center web site.

Historical and International Works

This section includes works that are primarily historical or that deal with international developments and perspectives on capital punishment. These works can provide a broader perspective on current issues.

BOOKS

Atholl, Justin. *Shadow of the Gallows*. London: John Long, 1954. A history of capital punishment in England.

Badinter, Robert, et al. *Death Penalty: Beyond Abolition*. Strasbourg: Council of Europe Publications, 2004. Reviews the successful campaign for the abolition of the death penalty in Europe, which has achieved almost complete success. Includes discussion of related issues such as the need to deal with the situation of murder victims' families and to provide effective penal alternatives to the death penalty. There is also discussion of the attempt to carry the campaign beyond Europe to nations that have observer status in the Council of Europe, notably the United States and Japan.

Banner, Stephen. *The Death Penalty: An American History*. Cambridge, Mass.: Harvard University Press, 2003. Explores in detail the evolution of capital punishment over 400 years of American history, including what crimes are punishable by death and the adoption of different methods of execution. The author then brings in the larger context of how the ritual of execution was enacted—originally public and with explicitly religious overtones, executions gradually became private and secular. The development of the modern debate over the death penalty is also covered.

Bowers, William J., Glenn L. Pierce, and John F. McDevitt. *Legal Homicide: Death As Punishment in America, 1864–1892*. Boston: Northeastern University Press, 1984. An important source providing extensive information on executions during the second half of the 19th century.

Chandler, David B. *Capital Punishment in Canada: A Sociological Study of Repressive Law*. Toronto: McClelland and Stewart, 1976. Discusses capital punishment and the social background to the debate over the death penalty in Canada.

Cooper, David D. *The Lesson of the Scaffold: The Public Execution Controversy in Victorian England*. Athens: Ohio University Press, 1974. Discusses social attitudes surrounding efforts to abolish capital punishment in Victorian England.

Darrow, Clarence. *Clarence Darrow on Capital Punishment*. Chicago: Chicago Historical Bookworks, 1991. Writings on capital punishment by the famous trial lawyer.

Ehrmann, Herbert B. *The Case That Will Not Die: Commonwealth vs. Sacco and Vanzetti.* Boston: Little, Brown, 1969. The account of an attorney for the defense in this famous and controversial case from the 1920s in which two immigrant anarchists were executed.

Evans, Richard J. *Rituals of Retribution: Capital Punishment in German Politics and Society Since the Seventeenth Century.* New York: Oxford University Press, 1996. Describes the role of capital punishment in German customary law, and then examines how the system broke down under the impact of social change during the early 19th century. Discusses the brief liberal triumph of 1848 in which the death penalty was abolished, its reinstatement by Bismarck in the 1880s, and the role of Social Darwinism in harsh treatment of criminals in the early 20th century, leading to Hitler's use of large-scale executions. Evans also discusses these events in the light of modern theories by Norbert Elias, Michel Foucault, and others.

Fogelson, Robert M. *Capital Punishment: Nineteenth Century Arguments.* New York: Arno Press, 1974. Describes arguments in the Massachusetts legislature during the 19th century on capital punishment.

Gatrell, V. A. C. *The Hanging Tree: Execution and the English People, 1770–1868.* New York: Oxford University Press, 1996. A history of public executions in England during the late 18th and early 19th centuries. Describes the reactions of crowds and literary observers such as James Boswell, Lord Byron, William Makepeace Thackeray, and Charles Dickens.

Great Britain Royal Commission on Capital Punishment. *Report of the Royal Commission on Capital Punishment: Presented to Parliament by Command of Her Majesty, Sept. 1953.* Westport, Conn.: Greenwood Publishing Group, 1980. Report of a commission charged with considering whether Britain's capital punishment system should be modified. The report is in three parts: I. Limitation or modification of the liability to suffer capital punishment; II. The alternative to capital punishment; III. Methods of execution. The report includes extensive appendixes.

Hood, R. *Death Penalty: A Worldwide Perspective.* 3d ed. New York: Oxford University Press, 2003. Analyzes worldwide data to determine the extent to which countries around the world administer their death penalty laws in compliance with international standards of fairness and human rights. Generally, developments reflect an ongoing worldwide trend toward abolition.

Jayewardene, C. H. S. *The Penalty of Death: The Canadian Experience.* Lexington, Mass.: D. C. Heath, 1977. Considers Canada's moratorium on and subsequent abolition of the death penalty.

Kennedy, Ludovic. *The Airman and the Carpenter: The Lindbergh Kidnapping and the Framing of Richard Hauptmann.* New York: Viking, 1985. The 1932 Lindbergh kidnapping case; presents the theory that Hauptmann's execution in 1936 was a mistake.

Koestler, Arthur. *Dialogue with Death.* New York: Macmillan, 1966. An account of Koestler's capture, incarceration, and death sentence during the Spanish Civil War.

Annotated Bibliography

Koestler, Arthur, and C. J. Rolph. *Hanged by the Neck: An Exposure of Capital Punishment in England.* London: Penguin, 1961. An expansion of Koestler's *Reflections on Hanging.*

Lawes, Lewis. *Man's Judgment of Death: An Analysis of Capital Punishment Based on Facts, Not Sentiment.* New York: Putnam, 1924. A Sing Sing prison warden's opposition to capital punishment. Lawes became a leading abolitionist of his time.

Lazarus, Edward. *Closed Chambers: The First Eyewitness Account of the Epic Struggles Inside the Supreme Court.* New York: Times Books, 1998. A former Supreme Court clerk reveals the culture, personalities, and struggles within the Court. Because of their urgency and complexity, death penalty cases play an important role in his account.

Levy, Barbara. *Legacy of Death.* Englewood Cliffs, N.J.: Prentice-Hall, 1973. History of the Sanson family, the official executioners of France for seven generations.

Linebaugh, Peter. *The London Hanged: Crime and Civil Society in the Eighteenth Century.* New York: Cambridge University Press, 1993. This historical study of capital punishment in 18th-century London concludes that the criminal law and capital punishment were tools used by the upper class to keep the lower classes in line. Many capital crimes reflected the generalized outrage of the poor about their miserable conditions. The upper class enacted new laws to protect their status as property owners and employers.

Mackey, Philip English. *Hanging in the Balance: The Anti–Capital Punishment Movement in New York State, 1776–1861.* New York: Garland Books, 1982. Recounts the history of New York State's death penalty law and attempts to reform it, from the American Revolution to the Civil War.

Mackey, Philip English, ed. *Voices against Death: American Opposition to Capital Punishment, 1787–1975.* New York: Burt Franklin, 1976. A collection of 26 statements by leading abolitionists throughout U.S. history.

Masur, Louis P. *Rites of Execution: Capital Punishment and the Transformation of American Culture, 1776–1865.* New York: Oxford University Press, 1991. A history that shows the institutionalization of capital punishment as reflecting major changes in American society from the nation's beginnings through the Civil War.

McGehee, Edward G., and William H. Hildebrand. *The Death Penalty: A Literary and Historical Approach.* Boston: D. C. Heath, 1964. Fifty opinions on capital punishment, covering several centuries.

McManners, John. *Death and the Enlightenment: Changing Attitudes to Death among Christians and Unbelievers in Eighteenth-Century France.* New York: Oxford University Press, 1981. Includes information on public executions and changing attitudes toward death.

Mikhlin, Aleksandr Solomonovich. *The Death Penalty in Russia.* Boston: Kluwer Law International, 1999. A survey and statistical study of the operation of capital punishment in Russia, including theories and regimes of punishment, the appeal and pardon process, and methods of execution.

175

Philipson, Coleman. *Three Criminal Law Reformers: Beccaria, Bentham, Romilly.* Montclair, N.J.: Patterson Smith, 1970. Examines the backgrounds, thought, and achievements of three thinkers who helped inaugurate the modern debate about crime, punishment, and public policy.

Playfair, Giles, and Derrick Singleton. *The Offenders: The Case against Legal Vengeance.* New York: Simon and Schuster, 1957. Presents six capital cases as examples of the ineffectiveness of legal vengeance.

Randa, Laura E. *Society's Final Solution: A History and Discussion of the Death Penalty.* Lanham, Md.: University Press of America, 1997. Begins with a history of capital punishment and then presents all of the major issues through selections written by a variety of people who must confront them. Writers include lawyers, teachers, lobbyists, and legislators.

Raper, Arthur F. *The Tragedy of Lynching.* Chapel Hill: University of North Carolina Press, 1933. A study of the causes, supposed and actual, of more than 3,000 lynchings that took place between 1889 and 1930. The book was prepared for the Southern Commission on the Study of Lynching.

Schabas, William A. *The Abolition of the Death Penalty in International Law.* 3d ed. New York: Cambridge University Press, 2002. Revised handbook on the applicability of international law to capital punishment, including human rights law, international humanitarian law, European human rights law, and inter-American human rights law. Includes extensive appendixes with documentation.

————. *The Death Penalty As Cruel Treatment and Torture: Capital Punishment Challenged in the World's Courts.* Boston: Northeastern University Press, 1996. The author argues on the basis of universal declarations of human rights and principles of international law that both sentencing procedures and methods of execution used throughout the world violate legal norms and that capital punishment should be abolished worldwide. Includes both historical background and detailed analysis of recent decisions.

Schabas, William A., Hugo Adam Bedau, and Peter Hodgkinson. *The International Sourcebook on Capital Punishment, 1997.* Boston: Northeastern University Press, 1997. A compendium of articles, book reviews, documents, and statistics dealing with capital punishment. The book is useful for comparative studies and reference.

Spear, Charles. *Essays on the Punishment of Death.* Littleton, Colo.: Fred B. Rothman, 1994. A collection of essays first published in 1845. The collection covers diverse aspects of capital punishment, including the effects of public executions on the prisoner and spectators as well as the impact on domestic life and comparison to other countries. It also includes discussion of Bible passages relating to capital punishment.

Spierenburg, Pieter. *The Spectacle of Suffering: Executions and the Evolution of Repression: From a Preindustrial Metropolis to the European Experience.* New York: Cambridge University Press, 1984. Explores the evolution of capital punishment debates in an international historical context.

Taylor, D. *Crime, Policing and Punishment in England, 1750–1914.* New York: St. Martin's Press, 1998. History of the development and operation of the criminal justice system in Great Britain, 1750–1914, including the role of capital punishment.

Thesing, William B. *Executions and the British Experience from the 17th to the 20th Century: A Collection of Essays.* Jefferson, N.C.: McFarland & Co., 1990. A collection of 10 essays examining the responses of various writers to the issue of capital punishment over a span of three centuries of British history. Writers discussed include Henry Fielding and Samuel Johnson as well as authors who use psychological or sociological insights.

Vila, Bryan, and Cynthia Morris. *Capital Punishment in the United States: A Documentary History.* Westport, Conn.: Greenwood Press, 1997. An extensive collection of primary sources relating to capital punishment. Areas included are the Bible and colonial America; the 19th-century death penalty abolition movement; the mid-20th-century; court cases of the 1960s and 1970s; the revival of both capital punishment and the death penalty debate starting in the late 1970s; and contemporary issues. Documents include court opinions, articles, and essays.

Woodward, Bob, and Scott Armstrong. *The Brethren: Inside the Supreme Court.* New York: Simon and Schuster, 1979. Looks at the workings of the Supreme Court from 1969 to 1975, including background on the *Furman* ruling.

ARTICLES

Bedau, Hugo Adam. "Bentham's Utilitarian Critique of the Death Penalty." *Journal of Criminal Law and Criminology*, vol. 74, 1983, pp. 1033–1066. Examines the work of political and economic philosopher Jeremy Bentham and his opposition to the death penalty.

Carro, Jorge L. "Capital Punishment from a Global Perspective: The Death Penalty: Right or Wrong?" *Vital Speeches*, vol. 62, August 1, 1996, pp. 629ff. Text of an address by a University of Cincinnati law professor who argues that the judiciary must resist public pressure for swift resolution of death penalty cases. Carro places the American legal issues in the context of the broad international movement to abolish capital punishment and recounts his experience practicing law in Cuba, where executions often followed sentencing by days or even hours.

"Conduct Unbecoming: Civilised Societies Don't Need the Death Penalty." *The Economist*, vol. 311, May 6, 1989, pp. 10–11. Assesses the need for capital punishment in an advanced society and concludes that relevant social objectives can be achieved by other means.

"The Cruel and Ever More Unusual Punishment." *The Economist* (U.S.), vol. 351, May 15, 1999, p. 95. Describes the growing international movement to abolish the death penalty, especially the efforts of the European Union. Only the United States and some Asian and Islamic countries continue to hold out. The U.S. public may support the death penalty, but it is unlikely that they would support the level of executions needed to achieve any possible benefit in deterrence.

Davis, David Brion. "The Movement to Abolish Capital Punishment in America, 1787–1861." *American Historical Review*, vol. 63, 1957, pp. 23–46. An account of the movement to abolish capital punishment between the Revolution and the Civil War.

"Death and the American." *The Economist* (U.S.), vol. 343, June 21, 1997, p. 32. Contrasts American and European attitudes toward the death penalty. Although popular sentiment in Europe is largely pro–death penalty, European politicians tend to put a damper on such attitudes while American politicians amplify and exploit them. The concept of just retribution seems to have a particular resonance in American culture.

De La Vega, Connie. "Going It Alone: The Rest of the World Has Abandoned the Death Penalty. Will the United States Follow Suit?" *The American Prospect*, vol. 15, July 2004, n.p. Also available online. URL: http://www.prospect.org/web/printfriendly-view.ww?id=7880 The great gap between the United States and other developed nations (particularly in Europe) can be seen most starkly in international denouncement of the execution of juveniles in the United States. In 2001 the Council of Europe demanded that the United States and Japan enact a moratorium on executions. The death penalty has also been increasingly raised in objections to extraditions of suspects to the United States.

Dieter, Richard C. "International Influence on the Death Penalty in the United States." *Foreign Service Journal*, vol. 80, October 2003, p. 31 ff. Also available online. URL: http://www.deathpenaltyinfo.org/article.php?scid=17&did=806. The head of the Death Penalty Information Center argues that the climate within the United States is turning against capital punishment and that world opinion is playing a significant role in this shift.

"Down with the Death Penalty." *The Economist* (U.S.), vol. 351, May 15, 1999, p. 20. Argues that the United States should join the majority of developed nations that have abandoned the death penalty. Of the three main arguments for capital punishment (deterrence, incapacitation, and retribution), the death penalty is ineffective or unnecessary for the first two and incapable of truly satisfying the third.

Evans, Richard. "Justice Seen, Justice Done? Abolishing Public Executions in 19th-century Germany." *History Today*, vol. 46, April 1996, pp. 20ff. Detailed study of reforms in Germany and throughout much of Europe that resulted in the abolition of public executions. Evans discusses conflicting opinions about whether the change was due to humanitarian impulses or fear by authorities that crowds would get out of hand or would sympathize too much with the offender.

French, Howard. "Japan Carries Out Executions in Near-Secrecy." *New York Times*. December 20, 1999, p. A14. Reports on the extremely secretive procedure for capital punishment in Japan. The only public news is a single terse sentence naming the condemned. The death penalty is popular in Japan, and the secrecy helps preserve the status quo by preventing activists and the media from developing a cause célèbre.

Gordon, John Steele. "Thomas Edison's Deadly Game." *American Heritage*, vol. 51, October 2000, p. 15. Recounts how the entrepreneurial inventor Thomas Edison promoted the electric chair as a way to discredit the alternating current of rival George Westinghouse. (Edison had built his pioneering power system using direct current.)

Grupp, Stanley. "Some Historical Aspects of the Pardon in England." *The American Journal of Legal History*, vol. 7, 1963, pp. 51–62. Provides historical background on the power of pardon and its effect on capital punishment in England before the 18th century.

Hill, Gary. "Capital Punishment: A World Update." *Corrections Compendium*, vol. 26, July 2001, p. 16. Presents a table showing the current status of nations with regard to the death penalty. The categories used are abolitionist for all crimes, abolitionist for ordinary crimes (not including wartime or crimes against the state), de facto abolitionist, and retentionist (having the death penalty).

———. "The Death Penalty: A European View." *Corrections Compendium*, vol. 28, March 2003, p. 8ff. Describes the strong anti–death penalty policies of the European Union and the Organization for Security and Cooperation in Europe (OSCE). The author notes that a majority of the population in most European countries actually favor capital punishment, but the indirect nature of European democracy minimizes single-issue politics.

Hongju, Harold Koh, and Thomas R. Pickering. "American Diplomacy and the Death Penalty." *Foreign Service Journal*, vol. 80, October 2003, p. 19ff. Also available online. URL: http://www.afsa.org/fsj/oct03/koh&pickering.pdf. The authors argue that the existence of the death penalty in the United States is a continuing obstacle to U.S. diplomatic efforts in a variety of contexts.

Kikuta, K. "Death Penalty in Japan: Why Hasn't It Been Abolished?" *International Journal of Comparative and Applied Criminal Justice*, vol. 17, Spring/Fall 1993, pp. 57–75. Gives reasons for Japan's insistence on retaining the death penalty. Kikuta suggests that strong public support for the sanction may be self-perpetuating. The author also suggests strategies for gradual abolition, such as promoting life sentences as an alternative.

Ndiaye, Bacre Waly. "Death Penalty Issue Addressed by Special Rapporteur." *UN Chronicle*, vol. 35, Summer 1998, p. 72. Presents the comments by the special rapporteur on death penalty issues to the United Nations Commission on Human Rights on January 22, 1998. Ndiaye observes that U.S. state authorities have virtually no knowledge of the requirements of international agreements in this area. He recommends that the United States adopt a moratorium on executions and permanently bar the execution of juveniles and the mentally disabled.

"Prisons and Executions—U.S. Model: A Historical Introduction." *Monthly Review*, vol. 53, July 2001, p. 1. Introduces a special issue of the publication devoted to a critique of the prison system from a liberal point of view. The overview points out that it was the United States, not Britain, that first developed the prison as an institution for the long-term incarceration and punishment of criminals. The availability of prisons was humane in that prison terms were used in lieu of the death penalty for a whole variety of crimes such as robbery, reserving execution for first-degree murder and a few other very serious crimes. The article also includes a radical leftist critique of the prison system and of the death penalty, including the roles of race, class, and social control.

Rosenzweig, Paul. "The Death Penalty, America, and the World." *Foreign Service Journal*, vol. 80, October 2003, p. 26ff. The author acknowledges that many countries around the world have abolished capital punishment and are putting increasing diplomatic pressure on the United States. However he argues that the United States should not simply bow to foreign pressure and change its legal framework.

Shapiro, Bruce. "Dead Reckoning: A World Effort to Force an End to the U.S. Death Penalty Is Gaining Momentum." *The Nation*, vol. 273, August 6, 2001, p. 14. The growing refusal of European and other countries to extradite defendants to the United States to face the death penalty expresses a strong international movement that the United States must take into consideration. Foreign-based and international abolitionist groups are growing more sophisticated in their intervention into U.S. politics, while American diplomats may be persuaded that maintaining capital punishment costs the nation more than it is worth.

"Singapore, World Execution Capital." *The Economist* (U.S.), vol. 351, April 3, 1999, p. 35. Reports on the high number of hangings in Singapore, which leads the world in proportional numbers of executions.

Weinstein, Henry. "Foreigners on Death Rows Denied Rights, U.S. Says." *Los Angeles Times*, December 10, 1998, p. A1. Reports on the violations of the rights of as many as 70 foreign nationals on U.S. death rows who were never allowed their right to consult their nation's consul as required by international agreements. This issue is coming to a head with executions of foreigners in Texas and California.

Zobel, Hiller B. "The Undying Problem of the Death Penalty." *American Heritage*, vol. 48, December 1997, pp. 64ff. Uses the 1901 case of Luigi Storti, the first person to die in the Massachusetts electric chair, to illustrate the ethical and legal problems involved in balancing the rights of the convicted and the desire for retribution—problems that persist to this day.

WEB DOCUMENTS

"Focus on the Death Penalty: History and Recent Developments." University of Alaska Anchorage Justice Center. Available online. URL: http://justice.uaa.alaska.edu/death/history.html. Updated on July 19, 2001. Provides some basic statistics and highlights of legal developments and cases up to 2001.

"International Standards on the Death Penalty." Amnesty International. Available online. URL: http://web.amnesty.org/library/Index/ENGACT500101998. Posted on December 1, 1998. An overview of applicable human rights principles, treaties promoting abolition, and model standards for countries that choose to have capital punishment.

"Ratification of International Treaties." Amnesty International. Available online. URL: http://web.amnesty.org/pages/deathpenalty-treaties-eng. Updated on September 14, 2004. Describes four international human rights treaties that include provisions promoting abolition of the death penalty.

Uschanov, T. P. "Capital Punishment in Modern British Law and Culture." Available online. URL: http://web1.pipemedia.net/~sar/bentley/cp-uk.html. Posted circa 1994. Gives an overview of the death penalty in Britain, including the law prior to 1957, the debate over the 1957 Homicide Act, the 1965 Murder Act (which totally abolished the death penalty), and subsequent attempts to reintroduce capital punishment.

Accounts of Death Row and Executions

Works in this section focus on the experience of death row inmates and the persons (such as prison officials, chaplains, or lawyers) who interact with them. There are also accounts and discussions of the actual procedure of execution.

BOOKS

Abbott, Geoffrey. *The Book of Execution: An Encyclopedia of Methods of Judicial Execution.* London: Headline, 1995. A graphically illustrated presentation of the many methods of judicial execution that have been devised in the course of human history.

Abu-Jamal, Mumia. *Death Blossoms: Reflections from a Prisoner of Conscience.* Farmington, Pa.: Plough Publishing House, 1997. A collection of short essays in which Abu-Jamal explores the deeper implications of imprisonment and justice, moving beyond the particulars of his own case found in his book *Live from Death Row.*

Arriens, Jan, ed. *Welcome to Hell: Letters and Writings from Death Row.* Boston: Northeastern University Press, 1997. A collection of letters from death row inmates to members of the pen friend group Lifelines. Alternately grotesque, tender, and surprising, the writings reveal the hidden face of capital punishment. A foreword by Sister Helen Prejean is included.

Bobit, Bonnie. *Death Row: Meet the Men and Women of Death Row.* Torrance, Calif.: Bobit Publishing, 2000. Although this annual compendium includes general facts and statistics about the death penalty, its main focus is on extensively profiling the individuals currently on death row throughout the United States, as well as persons who have been executed since the restoration of capital punishment in 1976.

Brandon, Craig. *The Electric Chair: An Unnatural American History.* Jefferson, N.C.: McFarland, 1999. A history of the electric chair, which has been used

181

to execute more than 4,300 individuals in 23 states since 1890, though its use has sharply declined in recent years. Brandon discusses how the chair's introduction was seen as a humane alternative to hanging and in part was the result of a rivalry between Thomas Edison and George Westinghouse.

Brasfield, Philip, and Jeffrey M. Elliot. *Deathman Pass Me By: Two Years on Death Row.* San Bernardino, Calif.: Borgo Books, 1983. Account of Brasfield's two years as an inmate on death row in Texas.

Brown, Larry K. *You Are Respectfully Invited to Attend My Execution: Untold Stories of Men Legally Executed in Wyoming Territory.* Glendo, Wyo.: High Plains Press, 1997. Stories of men executed in Wyoming during the days of the Old West. Brown does not directly discuss capital punishment issues, but his book is useful for exploring the role of capital punishment in the social and mythical world of the West.

Buchanan, William J. *Execution Eve.* Far Hills, N.J.: New Horizon Press, 1993. Describes the case in which golf star Marion Miley and her mother were murdered and three men were convicted of the slaying and sentenced to death in Kentucky State Prison. The author's father, who was a warden responsible for overseeing the executions, had serious doubts about the guilt of one of them. Through a series of bizarre manipulations, the warden attempts to force out the truth as the execution night wears on.

Cabana, Donald A. *Death at Midnight: The Confession of an Executioner.* Boston: Northeastern University Press, 1996. The author, a former prison warden and now a criminal justice professor, gives an account of his career and how he changed from a proponent of capital punishment to an abolitionist. As warden of the Parchman Penitentiary in Mississippi, he became friends with Connie Ray Evans, who was executed for murder. He became disillusioned when popular pressure led the state to step up the pace of executions. He argues that the death penalty discussion must move beyond the simplistic rhetoric usually used by politicians.

Capote, Truman. *In Cold Blood: The True Account of a Multiple Murder and Its Consequences.* New York: Random House, 1965. An extensive account of a 1959 multiple murder in Kansas that became a nonfiction classic.

Chessman, Caryl. *Cell 2455, Death Row.* Englewood Cliffs, N.J.: Prentice-Hall, 1954. The first of three works by a California inmate whose case became famous. Chessman describes his life on death row.

———. *The Face of Justice.* Englewood Cliffs, N.J.: Prentice-Hall, 1957. The third and final book of the celebrated death row author who was executed in 1960.

———. *Trial by Ordeal.* Englewood Cliffs, N.J.: Prentice-Hall, 1955. Describes Chessman's ongoing legal battles and stays of execution and the emotional toll that death row takes on prisoners, their families, and legal counsel.

Christianson, Scott. *Condemned: Inside the Sing Sing Death House.* New York: New York University Press, 1999. An investigative reporter and former criminal justice official reveals the secrets of Sing Sing prison's death house, responsible for executing more people than any other institution in the United States from 1891 to 1963. Includes reproductions of mug shots and excerpts from archives.

Davis, Christopher. *Waiting for It.* New York: Harper and Row, 1980. A biography of Troy Gregg. In 1976 the Supreme Court denied his death sentence appeal, upholding Georgia's death penalty law.

Diaz, Joseph. *The Execution of a Serial Killer: One Man's Experience Witnessing the Death Penalty.* Morrison, Colo.: Pancha Press, 2003. Describes the overwhelming psychological impact on the author, a young criminologist, when he witnesses the execution of a depraved serial killer.

Dicks, Shirley, ed. *Death Row: Interviews with Inmates, Their Families and Opponents of Capital Punishment.* Jefferson, N.C.: McFarland, 1990. The author's first of several books on capital punishment, written after her son was executed after what she believes was a wrongful conviction. The author interviewed experts, inmates, and the relatives of murder victims.

Drimmer, Frederick. *Until You Are Dead: The Book of Executions in America.* Secaucus, N.J.: Carol Publishing Group, 1990. A survey of executions in America from colonial times to the execution in 1989 of Ted Bundy. Drimmer describes the development of five methods of execution (hanging, firing squad, electric chair, gas, and lethal injection).

Duffy, Clinton T., with Al Hirshberg. *88 Men and 2 Women.* New York: Doubleday, 1962. A San Quentin warden's account of 90 executions, with strong arguments for the abolition of the death penalty.

Eliot, Robert G. *Agent of Death: The Memoirs of an Executioner.* New York: Dutton, 1940. An executioner in several states during the first decades of the 20th century recounts his experiences and his opposition to the death penalty.

Engel, Howard. *Lord High Executioner: An Unashamed Look at Hangmen, Headsmen, and Their Kind.* London: Robson Books, 1997. A vivid, compelling social history of the executioner: the person who carries out the collective will of the people by killing criminals using any of a variety of different methods. Writing from an abolitionist viewpoint, Engel describes the personalities of executioners and their way of life and work.

Gillespie, L. Kay. *The Unforgiven: Utah's Executed Men.* Salt Lake City: Signature Books, 1997. The author, a member of Utah's Board of Pardons, vividly describes his experiences interviewing most of Utah's death row inmates.

Hammer, Richard. *Between Life and Death.* New York: Macmillan, 1969. An account of the trial, incarceration, and appeal of John Brady, leading to the 1963 Supreme Court ruling in *Brady v. Maryland.*

Hearn, Daniel Allen. *Legal Executions in New York State: A Comprehensive Reference, 1639–1963.* Jefferson, N.C.: McFarland, 1997. A comprehensive reference to all cases of capital punishment in New York over a period of more than 300 years. Entries are arranged chronologically and include the facts of each case and the method of execution.

Jackson, Bruce, and Diane Christian. *Death Row.* Boston: Beacon Press, 1980. Interviews with 26 inmates on death row in Texas.

Johnson, Robert. *Condemned to Die: Life under Sentence of Death.* New York: Elsevier, 1981. Examines the effect of the death sentence on death row inmates and their families.

183

———. *Death Work: A Study of the Modern Execution Process.* 2d ed. Belmont, Calif.: Wadsworth, 1998. A detailed look at how capital punishment works today and how it affects the various participants—guards, executioners, and prisoners. The author argues that the death penalty has a hidden cost in psychological damage and brutalization to all involved and should be replaced by other forms of effective punishment.

———. *Poetic Justice: Reflections on the Big House, the Death House, and the American Way of Justice.* Thomaston, Maine: Northwoods Press, 2003. A criminologist and social scientist, the author turns to a new medium, poetry, to convey insights into America's system of justice and ultimate punishment. One theme is power and its abuse by both criminals and those charged with dealing with them. For example, the line between crime, criminal, and society is challenged in the poem "Police line: Do not cross."

Jones, Lou, and Michael Radelet. *Final Exposure: Portraits from Death Row.* Boston: Northeastern University Press, 1996. Photographer Lou Jones presents powerful images from death row with interviews and commentary. The presentation seeks to humanize the lives and deaths of the condemned and to challenge popular preconceptions.

Kunstler, William M. *Beyond a Reasonable Doubt? The Original Trial of Caryl Chessman.* New York: William Morrow, 1961. An account by a prominent advocate of the famous case of Caryl Chessman, executed in 1960. Chessman became renowned for several books he wrote while on death row.

Leslie, Jack. *Decathlon of Death.* Mill Valley, Calif.: Tarquin Books, 1979. Discusses three California cases that led to executions in 1955.

Levine, Stephen. *Death Row.* San Francisco: Glide Publications, 1972. Essays, the majority of which were written by death row inmates.

Lezin, Katya. *Finding Life on Death Row: Profiles of Six Inmates.* Boston: Northeastern University Press, 1999. A compelling narrative of six cases of death row inmates represented by Stephen Bright, director of the Southern Center for Human Rights. According to the author, these cases show how people with mental conditions such as schizophrenia or with drug problems that call their competency into question were improperly charged and often represented by incompetent attorneys. Judges, driven by political ambition, often refuse to consider mitigating factors such as retardation or a battered woman being in imminent danger. The legal techniques used by the center's attorneys to try to stop death sentences are explained.

Light, Ken (photographer), and Suzanne Donovan. *Texas Death Row.* Jackson: University Press of Mississippi, 1997. Uses striking photographs and a thoughtful essay to present the condemned prisoners, their jailers, and the social decisions represented by America's busiest death row.

Magee, Doug. *Slow Coming Dark: Interviews on Death Row.* New York: Pilgrim Press, 1980. Focuses on the lives of death row inmates before and after their death sentences.

Annotated Bibliography

———. *What Murder Leaves Behind: The Victim's Family.* New York: Dodd, Mead, 1983. Accounts of the impact of homicide on victims' families. The book is important for evaluating arguments in favor of capital punishment.

Mailer, Norman. *The Executioner's Song.* Boston: Little, Brown, 1979. A fictionalized account of the last months of convicted murderer Gary Gilmore, the first person executed following the reinstatement of capital punishment in 1976.

Malone, Dan, and Howard Swindle. *America's Condemned: Death Row Inmates in Their Own Words.* Kansas City: Andrews & McMeel, 1999. Presents the results of a 1995 survey of the nation's death row inmates by the *Dallas Morning News.* Seven hundred inmates responded to 75 questions about their crimes, experiences, and attitudes, resulting in a fascinating and comprehensive set of data.

Masters, Jarvis Jay, and Melody E. Chavis. *Finding Freedom: Writings from Death Row.* Junction City, Calif.: Padma Publishing, 1997. A collection of vivid, moving stories about life on death row, told by a convict who became a Tibetan Buddhist. The stories are told without polemics or an overt anti–capital punishment agenda.

Miller, Arthur S., and Jeffrey Brown. *Death by Installments: The Ordeal of Willie Francis.* Westport, Conn.: Greenwood Press, 1988. Study of the case of Willie Francis, who was executed in Louisiana in 1947 after a previous attempt to put him to death in the electric chair had failed.

Miller, Kent S., and Betty Davis Miller. *To Kill and Be Killed: Case Studies from Florida's Death Row.* Pasadena, Calif.: Hope Publishing House, 1991. A psychological and social profile of inmates on Florida's death row.

Moran, Richard. *Executioner's Current: Thomas Edison, George Westinghouse, and the Invention of the Electric Chair.* New York: Knopf, 2002. The electric chair was developed in the late 19th century and was a widely used form of execution to the middle of the 20th century. The author describes the invention and how it fit into the rivalry between Edison and Westinghouse and provides accounts of early electrocutions and the operation of this supposedly more humane method of execution.

Murray, Robert W. *Life on Death Row.* Phoenix, Ariz.: Albert Publications, 2002. A vivid account by an Arizona death row prisoner of the terror and minutiae of daily life—including being under execution warrant, wondering about the experience of lethal injection (no one lives to tell, of course), the routine of a super-max prison, and dealing with lawyers, guards, and the other people who control a prisoner's fate.

Nelson, Lane, and Burk Foster. *Death Watch: A Death Penalty Anthology.* Upper Saddle River, N.J.: Pearson Education, 2000. Gives a comprehensive overview of the challenges faced by prisoners and their attorneys in dealing with the death penalty. Topics covered include the arbitrary ways in which cases are selected for the death penalty, how the penalty is imposed and carried out, life on death row and on the verge of execution, and the difficult legal choices involved in trying to raise claims of actual innocence. (Author

Nelson is himself a former death row inmate, currently incarcerated for life without parole.)

Prejean, Helen. *Dead Man Walking: An Eyewitness Account of the Death Penalty in the United States.* New York: Vintage Books, 1994. The passionate account of the friendships between Prejean, a Roman Catholic nun, and two death row inmates, and her involvement in the crusade to end capital punishment. While her arguments against the death penalty are the conventional ones, readers quickly become involved with her depiction of the gritty reality of life on death row and the grim details of the far-from-painless execution process. The book inspired an Academy Award–winning movie.

Radelet, Michael L. *Facing the Death Penalty: Essays on a Cruel and Unusual Punishment.* Philadelphia: Temple University Press, 1989. A collection of essays that describe how condemned inmates and their families face impending execution and how lawyers and other professionals struggle to assist them. Writers include anthropologists, criminologists, a minister, a philosopher, and three condemned prisoners. The collection is generally abolitionist in attitude.

Reid, Don, and John Gurwell. *Eyewitness.* Houston: Cordovan Press, 1973. A journalist's eyewitness account of nearly 200 executions in Texas.

Smith, Edgar. *Brief against Death.* New York: Knopf, 1968. An autobiographical account of trial for murder, conviction, and years on death row.

Teeters, Negley K. *Hang by the Neck: The Legal Use of Scaffold and Noose, Gibbet, Stake, and Firing Squad from Colonial Times to the Present.* Springfield, Ill.: Charles C. Thomas, 1967. An excellent history of executions and execution methods in the United States.

Trombley, Stephen. *The Execution Protocol: Inside America's Capital Punishment Industry.* New York: Crown Books, 1998. Combines history with interviews, including one with the designer of the lethal injection apparatus. Trombley focuses on the method of execution and the people involved in implementing it.

United States—Breach of Trust: Physician Participation in Executions in the United States. New York: Human Rights Watch, 1994. Statements prepared by the Physicians for Human Rights, Human Rights Watch, American College of Physicians, and National Coalition to Abolish the Death Penalty. These groups strongly oppose participation of doctors in any aspect of the capital punishment process, viewing it as a serious breach of a physician's duty to "do no harm" under the Hippocratic Oath.

Whitman, Claudia, and Julie Zimmerman. *Frontiers of Justice: Death Penalty.* Brunswick, Maine: Biddle Publishing Co., 1997. A large collection of essays and articles by a variety of persons involved in working with death row inmates, relatives of murder victims, and other persons involved with capital punishment. The selections reflect a generally abolitionist point of view.

Williams, Nanon. *Still Surviving.* Gardena, Calif.: Breakout Publishing, 2003. Autobiography of a man who was convicted and sentenced to death at age 17 for a murder he insists he did not commit. He describes life on death row and the experience of having friends he has made there executed. Williams has an active support group seeking to raise funds for investigations and appeals.

ARTICLES

Anderson, George M. "Fourteen Years on Death Row: An Interview with Joseph Green Brown." *America*, vol. 176, March 29, 1997, pp. 17ff. Interview with Joseph Green Brown (now known as Shabaka) who was imprisoned on death row since his conviction for murder in 1974 and nearly executed in 1987. His sentence was reversed only 15 hours before his execution when the appeals court ruled that the prosecutor had knowingly allowed perjured testimony by the state's main witness. He describes his hasty trial and life in prison.

Blaustein, Susan. "Witness to Another Execution: In Texas, Death Walks an Assembly Line." *Harper's Magazine*, vol. 288, May 1994, pp. 53ff. Describes the prison complex at Huntsville, Texas, arguably the death capital of the United States with as many as two executions a week, and the rituals that are carried out by guards, executioners, protesters, and supporters of the death penalty.

Cheever, Joan. "A Chance Reprieve, and Another Chance at Life." *New York Times*, June 29, 2002, p. A15. Also available online. URL: http://www.deathpenaltyinfo.org/article.php?scid=17&did=301. Looks back at the 611 death row inmates who were released from death row by the Supreme Court's *Furman* decision in 1972. Eventually, 310 of them completed their reduced sentences or were paroled. The author suggests that the fact that the majority of them managed to stay out of prison after their release means that people should examine various sentencing alternatives to the death penalty.

Corum, Michael. "The Art of Hanging." *Wild West*, vol. 9, December 1996, p. 50. Describes techniques used in hanging during the 18th and 19th centuries. It is not easy to hang a person cleanly (avoiding strangulation or decapitation).

Creque, Stuart A. "Killing with Kindness." *National Review*, vol. 47, September 11, 1995, pp. 51ff. Advocates use of nitrogen asphyxiation (breathing pure nitrogen) as an alternative method of execution that would be painless and reliable, avoiding botched executions.

Dix, Tara K. "A Night Spent Waiting for Death to Come: College Students Join Vigil at Prison, Learn of Crime, Punishment." *National Catholic Reporter*, vol. 34, May 1, 1998, pp. 3ff. Describes the experience of an execution vigil by Indiana college students, woven together with the personal and legal details of the case of Gary Burris that had brought them there. The effect of the crime on the victim's family is also discussed.

Dorius, Earl F. "Personal Recollections of the Gary Gilmore Case." *Woodrow Wilson Journal of Law*, vol. 3, 1981, pp. 49–129. Diary account by a Utah assistant attorney general who was one of the state attorneys in the case that culminated in the execution of Gary Gilmore in 1977.

Egbert, Lawrence D. "Physicians and the Death Penalty." *America*, vol. 178, March 7, 1998, pp. 15ff. An anesthesiologist describes his investigation into the practice of lethal injection and declares his opposition to capital punishment.

Capital Punishment

Grogan, David, and Barbara Sandler. "Looking for a Lifeline: With His Days Numbered, Convicted Killer Girvies Davis Takes to the Internet." *People Weekly*, vol. 43, May 22, 1995, pp. 59ff. Describes the attempt by a death row inmate to use the Internet to arouse public support for his appeal for clemency. (Davis was executed at about the time the article was published.)

Hentoff, Nat. "Execution in Your Living Room." *The Progressive*, vol. 55, November 1991, pp. 16ff. Argues that while opponents of the death penalty are uncomfortable with televising executions for fear the public will support their continuance, banning the camera violates the First Amendment and is dangerous to civil liberties.

Hitchens, Christopher. "Scenes from an Execution." *Vanity Fair*, January 1998, pp. 30ff. A reporter witnesses, reacts to, and analyses the execution by lethal injection of a convicted murderer in Potosi, Missouri.

Kenworthy, Tom. "'I'm Going to Grant You Life'; Parents of Slain Gay Student Agree to Prison for His Killer." *Washington Post*, November 5, 1999, p. A02. Reports the dramatic moment when the parents of Matthew Shepard asked the court to spare the life of the convicted murderer of their son.

Kozinski, Alex. "Tinkering with Death: A Death-Penalty Judge Reflects: How Does It Feel to Send Another Man to Die?" *The New Yorker*, vol. 72, February 10, 1997, pp. 48ff. A U.S. Appeals Court judge describes the experience of hearing last-minute appeals from condemned prisoners. While he supports the death penalty, he acknowledges the difficulty and anguish of the position he and his fellow judges are put in by the system.

Lehman, Susan. "A Matter of Engineering: Capital Punishment as a Technical Problem." *The Atlantic*, vol. 265, February 1990, p. 26ff. Examines the technical aspects of electrocution.

"The Long Goodbye." *The New Republic*, vol. 210, June 6, 1994, p. 8. Editorial describes botched executions such as that of John Wayne Gacy, which showed that even the "humane" method of lethal injection could be botched. Such executions are cruel and unusual punishment that violates the Eighth Amendment and calls the entire institution of capital punishment into question.

Owens, Virginia Stem. "Karla Faye's Final Stop." *Christianity Today*, vol. 42, July 13, 1998, pp. 45ff. Account of the execution of Karla Faye Tucker, the convicted murderer who became a born-again Christian, and the focus for appeals for clemency by religious groups.

"Physician Participation in Capital Punishment." *JAMA, The Journal of the American Medical Association*, vol. 270, July 21, 1993, pp. 365ff. Statement and guidelines on medical participation in executions from the AMA's Committee on Ethical and Judicial Affairs. Definitions are provided to clarify the AMA's 1980 denunciation of the practice.

Prejean, Helen. "Letter from Death Row." *America*, vol. 180, February 13, 1999, p. 24. New Year's letter from Sister Helen Prejean, author of *Dead Man Walking*. She recounts her weeks spent with death row inmate Dobie Williams as he prepared for his execution.

Annotated Bibliography

Radelet, Michael L. "Poorly Executed." *Harper's Magazine*, vol. 290, June 1995, pp. 21ff. Describes six failed or botched executions that used lethal injection, lethal gas, and the electric chair.

Radelet, Michael L., Margaret Vandiver, and Felix Bernardo. "Families, Prisons, and Men with Death Sentences: The Human Impact of Structured Uncertainty." *Journal of Family Issues*, vol. 4, 1983, pp. 593–612. Discusses the psychological impact of the death sentence and appeals process on death row inmates and their families.

Schneider, Alison. "Through an Executioner's Eyes." *The Chronicle of Higher Education*, vol. 42, May 17, 1996, p. A6. Interviews Donald Cubana, author of *Death at Midnight: The Confession of an Executioner.* Cabana describes how he became an opponent of the death penalty while serving as warden of the Mississippi State Penitentiary. A young inmate whom he had befriended was executed, and what he saw as a senseless act led him to leave the corrections field.

Shapiro, Andrew L. "End of the Rope?" *The Nation*, vol. 258, June 6, 1994, pp. 772ff. Reports that an appeals court in the state of Washington has refused to prevent the hanging of convicted murderer Charles Campbell, declaring that this method of execution is not unnecessarily painful. The author disagrees and believes that given the risk of very painful botched hangings, they can no longer be justified in a civilized society.

Stumbo, Bella. "Executing the Murderer: The Victims' Families Speak Out." *Redbook*, vol. 186, November 1995, pp. 58ff. Recounts the responses of relatives of murder victims in five different cases. The emotions expressed differ greatly from case to case: some experience a degree of satisfaction, while others are disappointed or repelled by the process.

Truog, Robert D., and Troyen A. Brennan. "Participation of Physicians in Capital Punishment." *The New England Journal of Medicine*, vol. 329, October 28, 1993, pp. 1,346ff. Argues that participation of medical professionals in executions is a violation of fundamental principles of medical ethics. It is different from mercy killing, which is done on behalf of (and with the agreement of) the patient, rather than on behalf of the state. Medical societies should revoke the licenses of doctors who participate in capital punishment.

Weisberg, Jacob. "This Is Your Death; Capital Punishment, What Really Happens." *The New Republic*, vol. 205, July 1, 1991, pp. 23ff. Describes what people would see if they could actually view each of the five currently authorized methods of execution: hanging, the firing squad, the electric chair, the gas chamber, and lethal injection. All these methods of execution probably cause at least some pain, and any can be botched, leading to grotesque results.

WEB DOCUMENTS

"Angel on Death Row: The Real Life Case in 'Dead Man Walking.'" PBS. Available online. URL: http://www.pbs.org/wgbh/pages/frontline/angel. Downloaded on December 17, 1999. Web page with transcripts of interviews, links, and resources relating to a *Frontline* episode originally broadcast April 9, 1996. The page discusses the cases that made up the material for Sister Helen Prejean's book and the subsequent movie.

"The Execution." PBS. Available online. URL: http://www.pbs.org/wgbh/ pages/frontline/shows/execution. Downloaded on December 17, 1999. Web page with transcripts, video, interviews, links, and resources relating to a *Frontline* episode originally broadcast on February 9, 1999.

"Physician-Assisted Suicide and Capital Punishment: What Role Should Physicians Play?" Physicians Committee for Responsible Medicine. Medicine and Society Curriculum. Available online. URL: http://www.pcrm.org/issues/ Medicine_and_Society_Curriculum/med_soc_curr_4.html. Downloaded on December 8, 1999. Offers a pro-and-con look at physician participation in causing death through euthanasia, assisted suicide, and capital punishment. The page offers hypothetical cases for discussion.

General Advocacy Works

This section features works that present a broad range of arguments opposing or supporting the death penalty.

BOOKS

Bedau, Hugo Adam. *Death Is Different: Studies in the Morality, Law, and Politics of Capital Punishment.* Boston: Northeastern University Press, 1987. Ten essays explaining and refuting arguments in favor of the death penalty. Topics include retribution, deterrence, whether the convicted retains a right to life, and whether the death penalty is needed to buttress the social order. Includes a bibliography, a list of court cases, and extensive notes.

————. *Killing As Punishment: Reflections On the Death Penalty in America.* Boston: Northeastern University Press, 2004. A distinguished abolitionist's essays arguing against capital punishment from a variety of perspectives. Topics include the conviction and execution of innocent persons, the failure of executive clemency as a check on injustice, the choice between imprisonment and death, and moral and humanitarian attitudes toward cruel and unusual punishment as forbidden by the Eighth Amendment.

Berns, Walter. *For Capital Punishment: Crime and the Morality of the Death Penalty.* Lanham, Md.: University Press of America, 1991. Advocates the continuance of capital punishment based on the concept of justice as retribution.

Bessler, John. *Kiss of Death: America's Love Affair with the Death Penalty.* Boston: Northeastern University Press, 2003. This wide-ranging argument for ending capital punishment argues that executions serve no useful purpose and simply reflect what Bessler sees as the American preoccupation with vengeance and retribution. The author disposes of common arguments in favor of the death penalty and details its effects on law enforcement officers and the general public. Finally, he suggests that executions be televised so the public will be confronted by their brutal reality.

Bosco, Antoinette. *Choosing Mercy: A Mother of Murder Victims Pleads to End the Death Penalty.* Maryknoll, N.Y.: Orbis Books, 2001. The author describes the murder of her son and daughter-in-law and how she struggled with the crushing grief and came to decide that another intentional death (by the state) would only compound the wrong. She then goes on to make a general abolitionist case against the death penalty.

Brown, Edmund Gerald. *Public Justice, Private Mercy: A Governor's Education on Death Row.* New York: Knightsbridge Publishing Co., 1990. A former governor of California tells why he came to oppose capital punishment.

Carrington, Frank G. *Neither Cruel Nor Unusual.* New Rochelle, N.Y.: Arlington House, 1978. Defends the death penalty, refuting abolitionist reasoning step by step.

Cohen, Bernard L. *Law Without Order: Capital Punishment and the Liberals.* New Rochelle, N.Y.: Arlington House, 1970. Maintains that capital punishment is the cornerstone of any credible law enforcement system.

Costanzo, Mark. *Just Revenge: Costs and Consequences of the Death Penalty.* New York: St. Martin's Press, 1997. A comprehensive case for abolition of the death penalty. Costanzo begins by describing how the system actually works from trial to execution. He then addresses and refutes each pro–death penalty argument on the issues of cruelty, cost, fairness, deterrence, public support, and moral justification.

Davis, Michael. *Justice in the Shadow of Death: Rethinking Capital and Lesser Punishments.* Lanham, Md.: Rowman & Littlefield, 1996. Systematically looks at the major arguments for and against capital punishment, including deterrence, inhumaneness, considerations of medical ethics, proportional punishment, irrevocability, the purpose of punishment, and treatment of the insane. Davis comes to the conclusion that the United States should join most other developed nations in abolishing capital punishment.

Gray, Ian, and Moira Stanley, editors. *A Punishment in Search of a Crime: Americans Speak Out Against the Death Penalty.* New York: Avon Books, 1989. Contemporary writings and statements against capital punishment.

Haas, Kenneth C., and James A. Inciardi. *Challenging Capital Punishment: Legal and Social Science Approaches.* Newbury Park, Calif.: Sage, 1988. A collection of essays marshaling legal and sociological critiques of capital punishment.

Haines, Herbert H. *Against Capital Punishment: The Anti–Death Penalty Movement in America, 1972–1994.* New York: Oxford University Press, 1996. A detailed discussion of the rise of the modern anti–death penalty movement and the ongoing strategic debates within the movement over such issues as whether to promote a sentence of life without parole as an alternative, whether to form coalitions with groups such as "pro-life" activists, and the advantages and disadvantages of death penalty opponents also becoming involved in issues such as gun control and drug policy reform.

Capital Punishment

King, Rachel, *Don't Kill in Our Names: Families of Murder Victims Speak Out Against the Death Penalty*. New Brunswick, N.J.: Rutgers University Press, 2003. The author presents the stories of ten members of the Murder Victims' Families for Reconciliation, describing their suffering and how they came to oppose the execution of the murderers of their family members. The conclusions stress forgiveness over revenge and restorative over retributive justice.

Stassen, Glen Harold. *Capital Punishment: A Reader.* Cleveland: Pilgrim Press, 1998. A varied collection of readings on capital punishment, mainly from the abolitionist point of view. The readings are grouped into the following areas: justice as retribution or restoration; deterrence; fairness and equal treatment before the law; scriptural background to capital punishment; capital punishment from the point of view of a consistent ethic of the sacredness of human life; the need for restoring a just social order, and the role of religion and people of faith in transforming the capital punishment debate.

Articles

Bedau, Hugo Adam. "Dwindling Dominion." *The American Prospect*, vol. 15, July 2004, n.p. Also available online. URL: http://www.prospect.org/web/printfriendly-view.ww?id=7879 The author, a noted death penalty opponent, suggests that while a majority of Americans still support the death penalty in some form, they are less willing to apply it in a number of problematic circumstances such as to juveniles or mentally handicapped persons. The growing possibility that the execution of an innocent person will someday be documented is also likely to have a strong impact on support for capital punishment. The result may be a sort of virtual abolition of the death penalty even if it remains on the books.

Brown, Edmund G., and Dick Adler. "Private Mercy: As Debate over the Death Penalty Opens Again, a Former State Governor Reflects on the 36 People He Let Die." *Common Cause Magazine* vol. 15, July–August 1989, pp. 28ff. Former California governor Edmund G. Brown reflects on his experience of being the "court of last resort" for clemency appeals from death row prisoners. He describes how he changed from being an advocate of capital punishment to supporting its abolition.

Mead, Margaret. "A Life for a Life: What That Means Today." *Redbook*, June 1978, pp. 56–60. The noted anthropologist expresses her opposition to capital punishment.

Pallone, N. J. "Advocacy Scholarship on the Death Penalty." *Society*, vol. 26, November/December 1988, pp. 84–87. Reviews research advocating capital punishment.

Tremoglie, Michael. "Capital-Punishment Canards." *Insight on the News*, vol. 19, March 4, 2004, p. 52. A rebuttal of the major arguments against capital punishment. The author argues that liberal advocates of abolishing capital punishment ignore the benefit of execution in incapacitating people who might kill again once they are in prison. He also complains that the Death Penalty Information Center's tabulation of exonerated death row inmates includes those who were freed simply because the district attorney did not think it was worthwhile to retry them, as well as people with multiple felony records or who are reconvicted later. Finally, he says that people arguing about racial disparities in executions ignore the fact that blacks make up a disproportionate amount of both murder victims and perpetrators.

Will, George. "Reason and Death." *Washington Post*, October 30, 2003, p. A23. A noted conservative columnist compares the views of Massachusetts governor Mitt Romney (pro–death penalty) and lawyer/writer Scott Turow (abolitionist). Will suggests that Romney may come to agree with Turow in the long run.

Web Documents

Bedau, Hugo Adam. "The Case against the Death Penalty." Available online. URL: http://archive.aclu.org/library/case_against_death.html. Downloaded on November 28, 1999. A comprehensive statement of opposition to the death penalty, covering the standard arguments that capital punishment is not a deterrent, that it is unfair, irreversible, and barbarous, and that there are superior alternatives.

"Death Penalty and Sentencing Information in the United States." ProDeathPenalty.com Available online. URL: http://www.prodeathpenalty.com/DP. html. Posted on October 1, 1997. A lengthy article defending capital punishment against its critics. Topics include deterrence, the risk of executing the innocent, racism and the death penalty, the cost of capital punishment, procedural issues, and religious views on the death penalty.

"The Death Penalty: Questions and Answers." Amnesty International. Available online. URL: http://web.amnesty.org/library/Index/ENGACT500012000. Posted on April 12, 2000. Explains the organization's position on the death penalty, which it opposes in all instances.

Dieter, Richard C. "Testimony of Richard Dieter Before the Legislative Commission Subcommittee to Study the Death Penalty." Death Penalty Information Center. Available online. URL: http://www.deathpenaltyinfo.org/article. php?scid=7&did=258. Posted on April 18, 2002. The executive director of the Death Penalty Information Center offers the Nevada legislature a summary and assessment of studies of the costs and impacts of the death penalty. He argues that capital punishment represents a net expense to the state (thus depriving the public of money that could be used for other safety measures). The system is also highly inefficient because few people are finally executed; most avoid execution after a large amount of public expenditure on the legal system.

"Organizations Jointly Oppose Death Penalty." Available online. URL: http:// www.thetaskforce.org/media/release.cfm?releaseID=60. Posted on February 9, 1999. This is a statement against capital punishment by 11 worldwide groups representing lesbian, gay, bisexual, and transgender people, including the Lambda Legal Defense and Education Fund and the National Gay and Lesbian Task Force. The page includes quotes from group leaders and contact information for the groups.

SOCIAL AND LEGAL ISSUES

Punishment, Retribution, and Deterrence

Works in this section discuss theories of punishment and retribution relating to the death penalty and also the question of whether capital punishment has a deterrent effect or helps protect society.

BOOKS

Andenaes, Johannes. *Punishment and Deterrence*. Ann Arbor: University of Michigan Press, 1974. A collection of essays on methods of deterrence and their effectiveness.

Beccaria, Cesare, and Jane Grigson (translator). *Of Crimes and Punishments: The Groundbreaking Work That Began the Debate about Capital Punishment*. New York: Marsilio Publishers, 1996. Translation of an essay by an 18th-century Italian philosopher. In his systematic analysis of criminal justice, Beccaria raised most of the issues that would define the modern debate, including crime prevention, prompt punishment, and deterrence (he believed capital punishment did not function as a deterrent). Beccaria's ideas influenced Benjamin Franklin and Thomas Jefferson in America and Jeremy Bentham and Voltaire in Europe.

Jacoby, Susan. *Wild Justice: The Evolution of Revenge*. New York: Harper and Row, 1983. Discusses the meaning of justice and the corollary issue of revenge. Jacoby finds that revenge is legitimate but capital punishment is excessive and damaging to social morality.

Melusky, Joseph A., and Keith A. Pesto. *Cruel and Unusual Punishment: Rights and Liberties under the Law*. Santa Barbara, Calif.: ABC-CLIO, 2003. Provides a broad introduction to the problem of determining appropriate punishments for crimes and the interpretation of the Eighth Amendment ban on cruel and unusual punishment.

Moberly, Walter. *The Ethics of Punishment*. London: Faber and Faber, 1968. An in-depth examination of penal theory, including a section on the morality of capital punishment.

Montague, Philip. *Punishment as Societal Defense*. Lanham, Md.: Rowman & Littlefield, 1995. Develops a theory of punishment that is based on an extension of the individual right of self-defense to society's collective defense. Montague argues that this theory is superior to conceptions of punishment as deterrence or retribution and that it would justify the imposition of capital punishment in some circumstances.

Murphy, Jeffrie G., ed. *Punishment and Rehabilitation.* 3d ed. Belmont, Calif.: Wadsworth, 1994. Updated version of an anthology of articles outlining the major theories of punishment, including capital punishment. The anthology is useful for placing capital punishment within the general context of punishment and the social dynamics of justice.

Murphy, Jeffrie G. *Retribution Reconsidered: More Essays in the Philosophy of Law.* Boston: Kluwer Academic Publishers, 1992. The author further explores the retributive basis of the justice system through both political and moral philosophy. He reconsiders and qualifies his earlier theory of retribution.

Schonebaum, Stephen E. *Does Capital Punishment Deter Crime?* 2d ed. San Diego: Greenhaven Press, 2002. A collection of essays using arguments and facts to debate whether capital punishment reduces the incidence of violent crime. Suitable for junior high or older readers.

Sheleff, Leon Shaskolsky. *Ultimate Penalties: Capital Punishment, Life Imprisonment, Physical Torture.* Columbus: Ohio State University Press, 1987. Considers the justification for extreme penalties for heinous crimes.

van den Haag, Ernest. *Punishing Criminals: Concerning a Very Old and Painful Question.* New York: Basic Books, 1975. General discussion of the concept of punishment and the appropriateness of the death penalty.

Wilson, James Q. *Thinking About Crime.* Revised ed. New York: Vintage Books, 1983. Argues that criminal behavior is rational and can be deterred by appropriate sanctions. The supporting evidence offered is now dated but the clear statement of the issues remains valuable.

Articles

Anderson, Bruce. "A Hanging Matter: There Is a Sound Moral Case for Restoring the Death Penalty." *Spectator,* vol. 293, November 22, 2003, p. 18 ff. A British writer argues that advocates of the death penalty in the United Kingdom and United States should be more forthright despite the disdain of the elite. He suggests that using the death penalty as retribution for the worst crimes might actually dispose the public more favorably toward more humane treatment and rehabilitation for lesser offenders.

Archer, Dane, Rosemary Gartner, and Marc Beittel. "Deterrence, Brutalization, and the Death Penalty: Another Examination of Oklahoma's Return to Capital Punishment." *Criminology,* vol. 36, November, 1998, pp. 711–733. This study examines the immediate and possible delayed deterrent and brutalization effects of executions accompanying Oklahoma's return to capital punishment in 1990. The authors claim that there is a strong brutalization effect and possibly a delayed (lagging) deterrent effect.

Bailey, W. C. "Capital Punishment and Lethal Assaults against Police." *Criminology,* vol. 19, 1982, pp. 608–625. An analysis of state data nationwide,

1961–71, found little evidence to link the rate of murders of police officers and the presence of the death sentence. Sociodemographic factors had greater effect on the rate of lethal assaults on police.

Bailey, W. C., and R. D. Peterson. "Capital Punishment and Non-Capital Crimes: A Test of Deterrence, General Prevention, and System-Overload Arguments." *Albany Law Review*, vol. 54, 1990, pp. 681–707. Tests the theory that capital punishment may deter noncapital crimes by educating criminals about the general consequences of crime, by deterring felonies that might result in felony murder (and the death penalty), and by allowing reallocation of law enforcement resources due to reduced homicides. The authors' results find a "significant inverse relationship" between executions (and their publicity) and crime rates, lending support to this theory.

Bedau, Hugo Adam. "Justice in Punishment and Assumption of Risks: Some Comments in Response to van den Haag." *Wayne Law Review*, vol. 33, 1987, pp. 1,423–1,433. Criticizes an essay by death penalty advocate Ernest van den Haag on deterrence and retribution as justifications of punishment. A response by van den Haag follows the article.

Callahan, Sidney. "The Thirst for Revenge: Trying to Understand Capital Punishment." *Commonweal*, vol. 122, June 16, 1995, pp. 8ff. The columnist suggests that when the pragmatic arguments on both sides in the death penalty debate are stripped away, the core issue is whether society needs a symbolic ritual blood sacrifice to express its rejection of murder. This impulse should be rejected; life imprisonment offers sufficient moral sanction and social protection.

Cloninger, Dale O., and Roberto Marchesini. "Execution and Deterrence: a Quasi-Controlled Group Experiment." *Applied Economics*, vol. 33, April 15, 2001, p. 569. Statistical analysis of the correlation between the homicide rate and execution rate in Texas. The results suggest that execution has a deterrent effect but that increasing the rate of executions above normal increases deterrence marginally at best.

Davies, Christie. "Safely Executed." *National Review*, vol. 43, August 12, 1991, pp. 44ff. Argues that the death penalty for persons who commit murder after a string of other violent offenses would provide both deterrence and a sense of fit retribution. Since those executed would be career criminals, the chance of executing a truly innocent person would be minimized.

Gelernter, David. "What Do Murderers Deserve?" *Commentary*, vol. 105, April 1998, pp. 21ff. Gelernter, a computer scientist who was wounded by Theodore Kaczynski, known as the Unabomber, sees confusion about capital punishment as part of society's larger loss of moral moorings. He argues that the ultimate purpose of capital punishment is neither deterrence nor vengeance but the affirmation of society's moral rejection of murder. Gelernter includes discussion of the cases of Kaczynski and Karla Faye Tucker and the moral conclusions that might be drawn from them.

Goertzel, Ted. "Capital Punishment and Homicide: Sociological Realities and Econometric Illusions: Does Executing Murderers Cut the Homicide Rate or Not?" *Skeptical Inquirer*, vol. 28, July–August 2004, p. 23ff. The author compares traditional sociological research (which almost always finds no deterrence effect from capital punishment) with econometric mathematical modeling, which often does support the deterrence theory. He suggests that lack of fundamental knowledge and arbitrary tweaking of the econometric models accounts for the divergent results.

Goldberg, Steven. "So What If the Death Penalty Deters?" *National Review*, vol. 41, June 30, 1989, pp. 42ff. Argues that while conclusively showing the deterrent effect of capital punishment is very difficult, common sense suggests that the death penalty follows general experience that greater punishments do have greater deterrent effect. From a utilitarian viewpoint, imposing capital punishment will save more innocent lives than will be lost through mistaken convictions.

Grant, Robert. "Capital Punishment and Violence." *The Humanist*, vol. 64, January–February 2004, p. 25ff. Reviews the basic arguments for capital punishment (retribution and deterrence) and legal developments since the 1970s. Because the death penalty has never been shown to provide more deterrence than a life sentence, the only remaining plausible motive is retribution or revenge. However these motives are inhumane and only beget more violence. These outcomes should be resisted, and the focus of punishment should be on rehabilitation and restorative justice.

Green, Frank. "Some Murder Victims' Kin Reject Capital Punishment; Others Endorse the Sanction." *Richmond Times-Dispatch*, December 22, 2003, n.p. Also available online. URL: http://www.deathpenaltyinfo.org/article.php?scid=17&did=829. Describes the attitudes of a number of family members toward the idea of executing the murderers of their relatives. Examples include those victimized by Washington area sniper John Allan Muhammad.

Landsburg, Steven E. "Just Do It." *Forbes*, vol. 154, November 21, 1994, p. 166. Argues that the death penalty is justified. According to the author, poverty is no more an excuse for robbery or murder than lack of a sexual outlet is an excuse for rape. The legal system should use scarce resources more efficiently by confining and punishing violent criminals and not using prison space for lesser offenders. Authorities should be held responsible by the public for their choices and priorities.

Lowenstein, L. F. "Licence to Kill: Is There a Case for the Death Penalty?" *Contemporary Review*, vol. 252, January 1988, pp. 32–36. A study concluding capital punishment may be the only means of providing victims' relatives with a sense of retribution.

Pataki, George E., "Death Penalty Is a Deterrent." *USA Today*, vol. 125, March 1997, pp. 52ff. George Pataki, who defeated Mario Cuomo to become governor of New York, says he (unlike Cuomo) is a strong supporter of capital punishment, which he says is an essential part of a strategy for reclaiming society from the most violent and inhuman criminals.

Rapp, Geoffrey. "The Economics of Shootouts: Does the Passage of Capital Punishment Laws Protect or Endanger Police Officers?" *Albany Law Review*, vol. 65, Summer 2002, p. 1,051ff. Explores the idea that the increase in gun violence between police and civilians may be due to the reintroduction of capital punishment in New York. Suspects who have already killed someone may decide that they are already subject to capital punishment and have nothing to lose by shooting police officers. On the other hand, if capital punishment is a more likely sentence for killing a police officer, it may deter people from getting in gun battles with police. The discussion of statistical procedure is technical, and the results appear to be inconclusive or highly dependent on small shifts in the model, but the paper raises important issues and provides a useful review of previous research.

Stack, S. "Impact of Publicized Executions on Homicide." *Criminal Justice and Behavior*, vol. 22, June 1995, pp. 172–186. This study tested the hypothesis that blacks would be less receptive to the deterrent effect of publicized executions because they experienced themselves as outsiders to society and had little stake in conformity. The study results seemed to confirm this hypothesis, finding that publicized executions had significant deterrent effect on whites but not on blacks.

Stolzenberg, Lisa, and Stewart J. D'Alessio. "Capital Punishment, Execution Publicity and Murder in Houston, Texas." *Journal of Criminal Law and Criminology*, vol. 94, Winter 2004, p. 351ff. The author's study sought to determine the relationship (if any) between the frequency of executions, the amount of newspaper publicity about them, and the murder rate. The study found no discernable relationship. The paper also provides a useful overview of earlier research and a detailed discussion of methodology that points out some poorly understood problems, such as the need to take reciprocal effects into account (for example, the effect of an increasing murder rate and public fear on the decision to seek the death penalty).

Taylor, Stuart, Jr. "Does the Death Penalty Save Innocent Lives?" *National Journal*, vol. 33, May 26, 2001, p. 1,551. Although evidence for the death penalty providing additional deterrence is slim, common sense suggests that executing some murderers may save the lives of prison guards or inmates who might be killed by them in the future, and the death penalty may also deter some criminals from killing witnesses. Still, with all the problems in administering the death penalty and the difficulties in interpreting the writings of dueling experts, it is a tough call.

Tucker, William. "The Chair Deters." *National Review*, vol. 52, July 17, 2000, p. 42. The author admits that the deterrence argument is often overdrawn. The possibility of execution probably does not deter crimes of passion, but it can deter criminals from turning a robbery or other economic crime into murder. The death penalty, if used consistently but not overzealously, could paint a "bright line" that could stop many crimes from escalating to the ultimate violence.

van den Haag, Ernest. "Can Any Legal Punishment of the Guilty Be Unjust to Them?" *Wayne Law Review*, vol. 33, 1987, pp. 1,413–1,421. Argues that punishments should be set according to the differing needs of society for deterrence and retribution for a given crime, without reference to any claim of injustice on the part of the offender, who committed the act knowingly.

———. "Death and Deterrence." *National Review*, vol. 38, March 14, 1986, pp. 44ff. Offers new evidence to support the author's claim that the death penalty acts as a deterrent to murder.

Van Wormer, Katherine. "Those Who Seek Executions: Capital Punishment as a Form of Suicide." *USA Today*, vol. 123, March 1995, pp. 92ff. In an interesting and little-known argument against capital punishment, the author suggests that some criminals with suicidal feelings, such as Gary Gilmore, may commit murders in order to be given the death penalty. Capital punishment may thus put the public at greater risk.

Race, Class, and Fairness

This section includes works that deal with a central legal and moral challenge to the death penalty: the assertion that it is administered unfairly with regard to race or economic class.

BOOKS

American Civil Liberties Union. *American Civil Liberties Union Report on the Anniversary of* Furman v. Georgia *Three Decades Later: Why We Need a Temporary Halt to Executions*. Washington, D.C.: ACLU Capital Punishment Project, 2003. Argues that 30 years after the Supreme Court temporarily halted executions, the pervasive disparity and arbitrariness in the administration of the death penalty in the United States remains significant and unacceptable. Race, economic status, and geography still bear disproportionately on who receives the death penalty. Executions should again be halted until fairness can be guaranteed.

Baldus, David C., Charles A. Pulaski, and George Woodworth. *Equal Justice and the Death Penalty: A Logical and Empirical Analysis*. Boston: Northeastern University Press, 1990. Using an analysis of cases from 1972 to 1987, the author tests the proposition that the strengthened legal safeguards called for by the Supreme Court in 1972 and reaffirmed in 1976 can remove the arbitrariness and potential for discrimination from the death penalty process. Appendices contain further statistical information.

Carter, Dan T. *Scottsboro: A Tragedy of the American South*. Baton Rouge: Louisiana State University Press, 1969. An account of an Alabama case in which nine black men were wrongfully convicted of raping two white women. Presents the classic example of racism in the trying of capital cases.

Cole, David. *No Equal Justice: Race and Class in American Criminal Justice*. New York: New Press, 1999. The author, a professor of law and an attorney with the Center of Constitutional Rights, explores the role of race in the criminal justice system, including capital cases. He concludes that minorities are both disproportionately selected for capital prosecution and are afforded less constitutional protection.

Death Row U.S.A. Reporter: 1975–1988 and 1989–1997 Supplements. NAACP Legal Defense Educational Fund. Buffalo, N.Y.: William S. Hein, 1990. Describes cases and legal actions undertaken on behalf of minority inmates on death row.

Dicks, Shirley. *Congregation of the Condemned: Voices against the Death Penalty.* Reprint edition. Amherst, N.Y.: Prometheus Books, 1995. A collection of essays edited by a person whose son is on death row. The essays focus on the unfairness of the death penalty, arguing that it is imposed mostly on the poor, while wealthier persons convicted of similar crimes receive lighter penalties.

Fleury-Steiner, Benjamin D. *Jurors' Stories of Death: How America's Death Penalty Invests in Inequality.* Ann Arbor: University of Michigan Press, 2004. Presents an unusual perspective to the question of how race affects the administration of capital punishment. Actual accounts by black and white jurors in capital trials are surveyed, showing complicated ways in which race can play a part in their attitude toward minority defendants, who are often marginalized and rejected by people of both races.

Gray, Mike. *The Death Game: Capital Punishment and the Luck of the Draw.* Monroe, Maine: Common Courage Press, 2003. A hard-hitting book that examines a series of cases that show how a volatile mix of political pressure, police attitudes, and unreliable witnesses determine who will face capital charges and what might happen even to innocent defendants.

Gross, Samuel R., and Robert Mauro. *Death and Discrimination: Racial Disparities in Capital Sentencing.* Boston: Northeastern University Press, 1989. Traces the history of racial differences in sentencing for capital crimes.

Henson, Burt M., and Ross R. Olney. *Furman v. Georgia: The Death Penalty and the Constitution.* New York: Franklin Watts, 1996. An account for young readers of the historic Supreme Court decision that led to the declaration that capital punishment as practiced in the 1960s was unconstitutionally biased against blacks. The issues and appeals over the years since then are explained.

Jackson, Jesse. *Legal Lynching: Racism, Injustice and the Death Penalty.* New York: Marlowe, 1996. A general brief for the abolition of capital punishment. Jackson describes the history of capital punishment, rebuts arguments by death penalty supporters, and highlights the problem of execution of the innocent and what he sees as the inevitable expression of racism in the imposition of capital punishment. He concludes with a plea based on the dignity of life as expressed in the biblical tradition.

Kytle, Calvin, and David Z. H. Pollitt. *Unjust in the Much: The Death Penalty in North Carolina: A Symposium to Advance the Case for a Moratorium as Proposed by the American Bar Association.* Chapel Hill, N.C.: Chestnut Tree Press, 1999. Edited transcript of a symposium sponsored by North Carolinians Against the Death Penalty. Topics covered include race and class as factors in convictions, the demographics of capital punishment, and constitutional issues. In his contributions, author Pollitt draws on his experience teaching constitutional law and serving as a volunteer defense attorney representing poor and disabled clients in capital cases.

Annotated Bibliography

Lindorff, Dave. *Killing Time: An Investigation into the Death Row Case of Mumia Abu-Jamal.* Monroe, Maine: Common Courage Press, 2002. Lindorff, an investigative reporter, delves into the celebrated case of a death row inmate who claims that he has been framed for murder. What Lindorff finds through interviews with participants and examination of the court records casts doubt on both the prosecution and defense theories of the crime and suggests that the trial judge committed serious errors.

Marquart, James W., et al. *The Rope, the Chair, and the Needle: Capital Punishment in Texas, 1923–1990.* Austin: University of Texas Press, 1998. An analysis of data from original records that suggests that attitudes from the time of slavery and lynching drove the institutionalization of capital punishment and created a system with race, class, and gender bias.

McFeely, William S. *Proximity to Death.* New York: W. W. Norton, 1999. The author, a Civil War historian, tells the story of a group of blacks in Atlanta, Georgia, who were sentenced to death for killing a white man. Although they were probably guilty, a group of lawyers headed by Stephen Bright of the Southern Center for Human Rights argued that they should not have received a capital sentence because of the inflammatory racism that they had been exposed to and because the death penalty was itself unfair and racist in its application. The author paints a vivid portrait of his role as a witness and, later, as an advocate in fighting for the rights of death row inmates.

Nakell, Barry, and Kenneth A. Hardy. *The Arbitrariness of the Death Penalty.* Philadelphia: Temple University Press, 1987. A study that contrasts the death penalty process as described in law with the actual practice in North Carolina following the Supreme Court's upholding of reformed procedures in 1976. The authors conclude that disparate results in cases could not be explained by legal procedures alone but sometimes correlated with the identity of the prosecutor or the race of the defendant or the victim.

Rise, Eric W. *The Martinsville Seven: Race, Rape and Capital Punishment.* Charlottesville: University Press of Virginia, 1998. Explores a case in Martinsville, Virginia, where seven black men were convicted of rape and executed in 1951. The author, a professor of criminology and social justice, describes how community concern about crime impinged on due process, with the ever-present factor of race creating a disturbing equation. Rise also describes the battle of the NAACP and other groups against discriminatory application of capital punishment to blacks.

Russell, Gregory D. *The Death Penalty and Racial Bias: Overturning Supreme Court Assumptions.* Westport, Conn.: Greenwood Press, 1994. Uses statistical evidence to argue that the Supreme Court is wrong in its assumption that the process of selecting a "death qualified" jury does not bias the jury against the defendant. Russell's study results suggest that death qualification leads to a concentration of biased racial attitudes in particular.

Smead, Howard. *Blood Justice: The Lynching of Mack Charles Parker.* New York: Oxford University Press, 1986. Recounts a 1959 lynching in Mississippi.

Walker, S., C. Spohn, and M. DeLone. *Color of Justice: Race, Ethnicity, and Crime in America*. Belmont, Calif.: Wadsworth Publishing Co., 1996. Discusses the experience of African Americans, Hispanic Americans, Asian Americans, and Native Americans in the criminal justice system. The book covers a variety of topics in detail, including politics and the use of ethnic categories, geographical factors, myths about criminals and victims, and how race influences law enforcement, the courts, and the corrections system.

Weinglass, Leonard. *Race for Justice: Mumia Abu-Jamal's Fight against the Death Penalty*. Monroe, Maine: Common Courage Press, 1995. The author, chief counsel for Abu-Jamal's defense, describes an alternative theory of the crime and recounts discrepancies in the prosecution's case. He argues that the trial was essentially political and that Abu-Jamal is a victim of a deeply flawed justice system. The book includes court documents and contacts for advocacy.

ARTICLES

Amsterdam, Anthony G. "Courtroom Contortions: How America's Application of the Death Penalty Erodes the Principle of Equal Justice under Law." *The American Prospect*, vol. 15, July 2004, n.p. Also available online. URL: http://www.prospect.org/web/printfriendly-view.ww?id=7878. A noted death penalty abolitionist argues that capital punishment corrupts the law. The factors that determine who is given the death penalty (and who is ultimately executed) are arbitrary, capricious, and inherently unfair. For every case overturned because of a problem (such as incompetent defense lawyers) dozens more cases with the same problem are ignored. The death penalty has also been shown to involve pervasive racial discrimination. Courts have been slow to address these problems and as a result many people have died.

Arkin, Steven D. "Discrimination and Arbitrariness in Capital Punishment: An Analysis of Post-*Furman* Murder Cases in Dade County, Florida, 1973–1976." *Stanford Law Review*, vol. 33, 1980, pp. 75–101. A study of 350 homicide cases in Miami during the time capital punishment had been effectively halted by the Supreme Court. No conclusive evidence of racial discrimination is found.

Bonner, Raymond, and Marc Lacey. "Pervasive Disparities Found in the Federal Death Penalty." *New York Times*, September 12, 2000, p. A18. Also available online. URL: http://www.deathpenaltyinfo.org/article.php?scid=17& did=435. Reports that a comprehensive review has found considerable disparities in application of the federal death penalty. Prosecutions are concentrated on minorities (75 percent) as well as largely confined to a few parts of the country. (At the time of writing no federal executions had taken place since reinstatement of the death penalty in 1976. Since then there have only been two—Juan Raul Garza and Oklahoma City bomber Timothy McVeigh.)

Diamond, S. A., and J. D. Casper. "Empirical Evidence and the Death Penalty: Past and Future." *Journal of Social Issues*, vol. 50, Summer 1994, pp. 177–197.

Describes the utilization of social science data by the Supreme Court. The Court has largely ignored or discounted such evidence. The author suggests other areas of research (such as jury decision making) that might command the attention of courts.

Dispoldo, Nick. "Capital Punishment and the Poor." *America*, vol. 172, February 11, 1995, pp. 18ff. Argues that the death penalty pervasively discriminates against the poor, who cannot afford adequate counsel to deal with complex legal issues. Dispoldo also discusses the conflicting trends in recent Supreme Court decisions.

McFeely, William S. "A Legacy of Slavery and Lynching: The Death Penalty as Tool of Social Control." *The Champion*. November 1997, n.p. Available online. URL: http://www.nacdl.org/CHAMPION/ARTICLES/97nov03.htm. Posted in November 1997. Describes the use of the death penalty against African Americans during the slavery period and later during Reconstruction and the era of lynchings. McFeely suggests that many of the motives for using the death penalty for social control persist in the legal process even today.

Rabe, G. A. "Supreme Court and Evidence of Discrimination: A Comparison of Death Penalty and Employment Discrimination Cases." *Criminal Justice Policy Review*, vol. 9, 1998, pp. 209–231. Concludes that the Supreme Court has been willing to rely considerably on social science findings about discrimination when reviewing employment cases but has been very reluctant to accept similar findings in death penalty cases. The most likely reason is the Court's fear of the consequences of overturning the capital punishment system.

Roman, Nancy E. "Researchers Debunk Idea of Racial Bias: Some Researchers Now Say That Racial Bias in Death Sentences Doesn't Exist—Contrary to the Conventional Wisdom Behind the Proposed Racial Justice Act." *Insight on the News*, vol. 10, June 13, 1994, p. 17. Reports on a study of California murderers by Stephen Klein of the Rand Corporation. Once he controlled for the circumstances of the offense, any apparent disparity based on race of offender or victim disappeared.

Stark, Mike. "'Stop the Racist Death Penalty!' Racism on Federal Death Row Exposed." *The New Abolitionist*, November 2000, n.p. Also available online. URL: http://www.nodeathpenalty.org/newab017/index.html. Reports recent Department of Justice statistics that show that the federal death penalty is used disproportionately against minorities as well as being concentrated geographically in a few states such as Virginia and Texas. Legislation for a federal death penalty moratorium is being introduced. (As of 2004 it has not been passed.)

Swarns, Christina. "The Uneven Scales of Capital Justice." *The American Prospect*, vol. 15, July 2004, n.p. Also available online. URL: http://www.prospect.org/web/printfriendly-view.ww?id=7882. The author argues that race and poverty act as a double burden in determining who is sentenced to death. The continuing disproportionate results suggest ongoing bias by prosecutors, who have a great deal of discretion in deciding what charges to file. Meanwhile, the poor (who are often minorities) receive inadequate representation from overburdened public defenders and appeals advocates.

WEB DOCUMENTS

Dieter, Richard C. "The Death Penalty in Black and White: Who Lives, Who Dies, Who Decides." Available online. URL: http://www.deathpenaltyinfo. org/article.php?scid=45&did=539. Posted June 1998. Reports two studies that show pervasive racial bias continues in the administration of the death penalty. The fact that the overwhelming majority of district attorneys responsible for bringing capital charges are white is identified as a key contributing factor.

"Extreme Prejudice: Racism and the Death Penalty." Amnesty International Canada. Available online. URL: http://www.amnesty.ca/usa/racism.php. Downloaded on October 18, 2004. This report agrees with Supreme Court Justice Harry Blackmun, who said in 1994 that "even under the most sophisticated death penalty statutes, race continues to play a major role in determining who shall live and who shall die."

Smerconish, Michael, and Paul Palkovic. "Justice for Daniel Faulkner's Response to Amnesty International's Propaganda Piece for Mumia Abu-Jamal." Danielfaulkner.com Available online. URL: http://danielfaulkner.com/index amnesty.html. Downloaded on October 18, 2004. Detailed reply to Amnesty International's report favoring a new trial for Abu-Jamal, who was convicted in 1982 of murdering Faulkner, a Philadelphia police officer. The article attempts to rebut the report's main allegations, including its charges of police and judicial bias and its version of the facts of the case.

"United States of America: A Life in the Balance: The Case of Mumia Abu-Jamal." Amnesty International. Available online. URL: http://www.mumia.de/special/ a%20life%20in%20the%20balance.eng.pdf. Posted on February 17, 2000. This statement argues that Abu-Jamal's death sentence should be set aside and that he should be given a new trial. The reasons supporting this position include the alleged background of racism and police corruption in Philadelphia at the time Abu-Jamal allegedly killed police officer Daniel Faulkner, apparent bias on the part of the trial judge, poor representation and lack of resources for the defense, a racially biased jury, and conflicting evidence and testimony.

"United States of America: Rights for All—Killing with Prejudice: Race and the Death Penalty." Amnesty International. Available online. URL: http://web. amnesty.org/library/Index/engAMR510521999. Posted May 1, 1999. A detailed report on racial bias in the administration of the death penalty in the United States, with statistics and footnotes.

Special Cases: Youth, Mental Disability, and Gender

Works in this section discuss the application of the death penalty to juveniles, mentally disabled persons, and women. They raise questions of culpability and appropriate punishment.

Annotated Bibliography

BOOKS

Barfield, Velma. *Woman on Death Row*. Nashville: Oliver-Nelson, 1985. The author's account of her conviction for quadruple murder and her subsequent religious conversion before her execution in 1984.

Dicks, Shirley, ed. *Young Blood: Juvenile Justice and the Death Penalty*. Amherst, N.Y.: Prometheus Books, 1995. Presents a variety of essays that discuss the question of whether juveniles should face capital charges. Many of the writings describe particular cases and the experiences of young people facing the death penalty. A number of groups seeking to reform the juvenile justice system are profiled.

Eisenberg, James R. *Law, Psychology, and Death Penalty Litigation*. Sarasota, Fla.: Professional Resource Press, 2004. Directed primarily at mental health professionals, this is a comprehensive description of the work of forensic psychologists in determining the mental status and competency of defendants in capital cases. Includes a brief history of the death penalty and significant U.S. Supreme Court decisions, as well as an explanation of aggravating and mitigating factors and jury instructions used in the sentencing phase. There is also a discussion of ethical issues faced by professionals in capital cases.

Gillespie, L. Kay. *Dancehall Ladies: The Crimes and Executions of America's Condemned Women*. Lanham, Md.: University Press of America, 1997. Interesting (albeit rather lurid) accounts of American women who were condemned to die. Gillespie describes their crimes, personalities, and attitudes. Generally the book is arranged one chapter per case, each chapter titled using the words of the condemned.

Hale, Robert L. *A Review of Juvenile Executions in America*. Lewiston, N.Y.: Edwin Mellen, 1997. A study that examines the execution of juveniles in America starting in 1642. Hale identifies five periods characterized by the religious, legal, and political influences that determined which juveniles would be subject to the ultimate penalty. Includes tables, notes, references, and case citations.

Jones, Ann. *Women Who Kill*. New York: Holt, Rinehart and Winston, 1980. Studies women and homicide from several viewpoints, focusing on notable cases of female murderers.

Miller, Kent S., and Michael L. Radelet. *Executing the Mentally Ill: The Criminal Justice System and the Case of Alvin Ford*. Newbury Park, Calif.: Sage Publications, 1993. Discusses the question of whether a person should be executed even after becoming so mentally ill that he or she cannot comprehend the process. The centerpiece is the case of Alvin Ford, who was convicted of murder and then became psychotic while imprisoned on death row. Miller's psychological expertise is combined with Radelet's work on death penalty issues.

Naish, Camille. *Death Comes to the Maiden: Sex and Execution, 1431–1933*. New York: Routledge, 1991. The history of execution of women as illustrated by specific cases such as Joan of Arc and Anne Boleyn, with a focus on the

205

Middle Ages, the Renaissance, and the French Revolution. Naish also discusses the work of writers such as Jean Genet, Marguerite Yourcenar, and Bertolt Brecht in exploring the links between death and the erotic in the execution of prominent females.

O'Shea, Kathleen A. *Women and the Death Penalty in the United States, 1900–1998.* Westport, Conn.: Praeger, 1999. Presents the history of execution of women in America as well as the personal stories of women who have been executed or are awaiting execution on death row. O'Shea includes state-by-state summaries of the legal process and status of female death row inmates and statistical appendices.

Pucci, Idanna. *The Trials of Maria Barbella: The True Story of a 19th-Century Crime of Passion.* Translated by Stefania Fumo. New York: Vintage Books, 1997. The account of the first woman to be sentenced to die in the newly invented electric chair in America. She was convicted of killing the man who seduced her and then refused to marry her. This 1895 case became a cause célèbre that raised issues of capital punishment and women's rights, and her appeal was ultimately successful.

Reed, E. F. *The Penry Penalty: Capital Punishment and Offenders with Mental Retardation.* Lanham, Md.: University Press of America, 1993. Begins with the implications of the Supreme Court's *Penry* decision allowing execution of the mentally retarded. Reed offers arguments against the practice, drawing on case studies of both executed and pardoned retarded offenders.

Shipman, Marlin. *Penalty Is Death: U.S. Newspaper Coverage of Women's Executions.* Columbia: University of Missouri Press, 2002. The author examines the shifting emphasis in newspaper coverage of women's arrests, trials, and executions in the United States since the mid-19th century. Attitudes have shifted from protective (women should not be considered fully culpable) to a modern conflict between feminists' belief in equality and equal responsibility and their general opposition to the death penalty.

Articles

Abramsky, Sasha. "Taking Juveniles Off Death Row." *The American Prospect*, vol. 15, July 2004, n.p. Also available online. URL: http://www.prospect.org/web/printfriendly-view.ww?id=7877. Describes a recent trend by which courts have been limiting the application of the death penalty to certain groups of people and suggests that the Supreme Court may soon ban the death penalty for murders committed by 17-year-olds, which indeed happened in 2005. Only about a quarter of the public supports execution of minors.

Baroff, George S. "Why Mental Retardation is 'Mitigating.'" *Champion Magazine* (National Association of Criminal Defense Lawyers), August 1998, n.p. Also available online. URL: http://www.nacdl.org/CHAMPION/ARTICLES/98aug02.htm. Posted in August 1998. Explains mental retardation and differentiates it from mental illness. Baroff describes signs that attorneys should look for. He also discusses issues of competency and diminished capacity and their impact on sentencing decisions.

Bonner, Raymond, and Sara Rimer. "Executing the Mentally Retarded Even as Laws Begin to Shift." *New York Times*, August 7, 2000, n.p. Also available online. URL: http://www.deathpenaltyinfo.org/article.php?scid=17&did=439. Describes cases of mentally retarded (or allegedly retarded) prisoners on death row. Although executions continue, many states have passed laws banning execution of the mentally handicapped.

Farley, Christopher John, and James Willwerth. "Dead Teen Walking." *Time*, vol. 151, January 19, 1998, pp. 50ff. An in-depth look at the case of condemned juvenile murderer Shareef Cousin. Cousin, convicted at age 16, denies his guilt. The authors describe the situation of other juveniles on death row and debate the issue of whether juveniles should be executed. They also report possible exonerating evidence and problems with the trial procedure.

Fougerousse, Philip. "The Demise of the Death Penalty for the Mentally Retarded." *Florida Bar Journal*, vol. 77, December 2003, p. 63ff. Describes the background for the case of *Atkins v. Virginia*, in which the U.S. Supreme Court declared it unconstitutional to sentence a mentally retarded person to death. The author explains how mental retardation can have profound negative consequences for defendants from the time of their initial interrogation by police through sentencing. The judicial system does not accommodate the needs of the mentally retarded who pass the initial screening to be competent for trial.

Galati, Frank T. "Killer's Sentence Followed Law." *Arizona Republic*, September 28, 1999, p. B7. The judge who sentenced murderer Bobby Purcell to life without parole rather than death replies to critics who had insisted on the death penalty. He explains that his duty required that only the law guide him in his deliberations, and the law required that he give substantial weight to the young offender's age of 16.

George, Whitney. "Women on Death Row." *off our backs*, vol. 28, January 1998, pp. 16ff. Argues that the 47 women on death row are often ignored in debates over the death penalty because the vast majority of condemned prisoners are men. Women on death row are often denied privileges routinely given to men in the same situation.

Hitchens, Christopher. "Old Enough to Die." *Vanity Fair*, June 1999, pp. 76ff. Describes and argues against the practice of executing juveniles, a practice the United States shares only with a handful of countries, such as Iran, Yemen, Pakistan, Saudi Arabia, and Nigeria.

Lane, Charles. "Death Penalty Case Gets Skeptical Hearing." *Washington Post*, October 14, 2004, p. A09. Reports that Supreme Court justices reacted with misgivings to arguments that capital punishment of juveniles should be ruled unconstitutional. For example, Justice Anthony Kennedy suggested that exempting 16- and 17-year-olds from the death penalty might encourage gang leaders to enlist them as hit men.

Capital Punishment

Mansnerus, Laura. "Damaged Brains and the Death Penalty." *New York Times,* July 21, 2001, p. B9. Also available online. URL: http://www.deathpenaltyinfo. org/article.php?scid=17&did=432. A professor of psychiatry finds that virtually all death row prisoners she has studied have some form of organic brain damage or severe mental illness. Many had suffered beatings and sexual abuse as children. Another researcher disagrees, finding no greater incidence of child abuse in prisoners than in the general population.

Morganthau, Tom. "Condemned to Life." *Newsweek,* vol. 126, August 7, 1995, pp. 18ff. Describes the case of Susan Smith as a good example of the ambivalence with which many Americans face the decision of whether a person actually deserves death. While the majority of Americans support the death penalty, testimony about Smith's background of molestation, compulsive promiscuity, and possible mental illness led a jury to give her a sentence of life rather than death for the drowning of her two young children. Sidebar articles include a chronology, a *Newsweek* poll on attitudes toward the death penalty under various circumstances, and an account of how the trial was conducted.

Reed, Julia. "Capital Crime." *Vogue,* vol. 188, March 1998, pp. 338ff. Discusses issues raised by the case of Karla Faye Tucker (who was later executed). Issues include the role of gender in capital sentencing and the factor of possible brain damage.

Rimer, Sara, and Raymond Bonner. "Young and Condemned: A Special Report. Whether to Kill Those Who Killed As Youths." *New York Times,* August 22, 2000, p. A1. Also available online. URL: http://www.deathpenaltyinfo.org/ article.php?scid=17&did=438. Summarizes the situation of young offenders on death row and suggests that their execution expresses an extreme of the prevalent popular attitude that serious offenders should be treated as adults and receive adult consequences for their crimes.

Ross, Michael B. "Don't Execute Mentally Disturbed Killers." *The Humanist,* vol. 59, January 1999, p. 43. Argues that if as absolute a punishment as the death penalty is to be given, it must never be given to persons who lack the mental capability to understand their actions or the consequences. Ross describes the difficulty of convincing judges and juries that someone is truly mentally ill and suggests that new verdict types of "guilty but mentally ill" or "guilty but mentally retarded" together with life sentences without possibility of parole might satisfy the need for public protection and closure while preventing execution of the mentally incompetent.

Stetler, Russell. "Mental Disabilities and Mitigation." *Champion Magazine* (National Association of Criminal Defense Lawyers), April 1999, n.p. Also available online (search http://www.nacdl.org.). Introduces issues involving mentally disabled clients. Mental disabilities can be a powerful factor in avoiding conviction or mitigating sentences, but they can also make it difficult for counsel to work with clients or cause jurors to fear them and respond with harsher sentences. Stetler discusses the selection of mental health experts and the many roles they can play in investigation, in helping the client behave appropriately, and in testifying at trial. He also discusses appropriate use of physical and psychological tests and examinations.

———. "Mitigation Evidence in Capital Cases." *Champion Magazine* (National Association of Criminal Defense Lawyers). January/February 1999, n.p. Also available online. URL: http://www.nacdl.org/public.nsf/ChampionArticles/99jan04?OpenDocument. Introduces the types and purposes of mitigating evidence, starting with an overview of court decisions. Stetler discusses the many mitigating circumstances (including family background and mental illnesses and impairments) that can apply to clients facing capital punishment. He gives suggestions for approaching and interviewing witnesses who offer potential mitigating evidence.

Stettler, Russell, and Kathleen Wayland. "Capital Cases—Dimensions of Mitigation." *Champion Magazine* (National Association of Criminal Defense Lawyers), June 2004, p. 31. Also available online (search http://www.nacdl.org). Goes beyond substantial mental retardation and looks at a broad range of mental and other disabilities that might be presented in arguing for a lesser sentence than death. Includes discussion of the *Diagnostic and Statistical Manual of Mental Disorders* and prevailing medical opinion.

Stone, Alan A. "Supreme Court Decision Raises New Ethical Questions for Psychiatry." *Psychiatric Times*, September 1, 2002, p. 1. A commentary on the changing role of psychiatrists now that the Supreme Court has declared it unconstitutional to execute mentally retarded persons. The truth-telling role of forensic psychiatry that could lead to someone being found competent to be executed is in conflict with medical ethics. However, psychiatrists may find a broader role in making the public and legal system aware of the broader connections between serious mental illness and culpability for crime.

WEB DOCUMENTS

American Medical Association. Council on Ethical and Judicial Affairs. "Physician Participation in Capital Punishment: Evaluating Competence of Condemned Prisoners; Treating Condemned Prisoners to Restore Competence." Texas Medical Association. Available online. URL: http://www.texmed.org/ata/tos/ets/texmedfeb97ethcp.asp. Posted on January 1997. Discusses the ethics of doctors' participation in various parts of the capital sentencing process. The page states that physicians may testify at pretrial, sentencing, and postconviction hearings but should not be required to do so if they conscientiously oppose participation in the capital punishment system. Treating incompetent prisoners so they can become competent to be executed is a serious ethical dilemma, and states should instead automatically commute the sentence of an incompetent condemned prisoner to life imprisonment.

"The Exclusion of Child Offenders from the Death Penalty under General International Law." Amnesty International. Available online. URL: http://web.amnesty.org/library/Index/ENGACT500042003. Posted on July 18, 2003.

Summarizes the "overwhelming international consensus" against executing children, including recent action by the Inter-American Commission on Human Rights. Includes tables showing which nations still execute children, as well as status summaries for particular countries.

"Stop Child Executions! Ending the Death Penalty for Child Offenders." Amnesty International. Available online. URL: http://web.amnesty.org/library/Index/ENGACT500152004?open&of=ENG-392. Posted September 15, 2004. Calls for the ending of execution for children (generally defined as under 18 years old). Features the case of Napoleon Beazely, executed in May 2002 for a crime committed when he was 17 years old. Also includes background on U.S. Supreme Court decisions and the possible holding of child prisoners by the United States at Guantánamo Bay, Cuba.

The Question of Innocence

The issue discussed in this section is currently at the forefront of the controversy over the death penalty. Besides discussion of statistics and trends, these works include accounts of the struggle to free death row prisoners believed to have been wrongly convicted, as well as the experiences of the prisoners themselves.

BOOKS

Cohen, Stanley. *The Wrong Men: America's Epidemic of Wrongful Death-Row Convictions.* New York: Carrol & Graf, 2003. Uses the stories of more than 100 wrongfully convicted death row prisoners to illustrate the problems that have led to this "epidemic." The problems include unreliable jailhouse informants, prosecutorial misconduct, incompetent defense lawyers, and racial attitudes of police.

Edds, Margaret. *An Expendable Man.* New York: New York University Press, 2003. The author, an editorial writer for the *Virginia Pilot*, tells the story of Earl Washington, Jr., a mentally retarded black Virginia farmhand who spent nine years on death row and almost 18 years in prison for a crime that DNA evidence eventually proved he did not commit. The book emphasizes the difficulty and protracted struggle involved in proving innocence, where bureaucratic resistance is compounded by society's attitude of indifference toward marginalized people.

Frisbie, Thomas, and Randy Garrett. *Victims of Justice Revisited.* Evanston, Ill.: Northwestern University Press, 2004. An updated account of the case of Rolando Cruz and Alejandro Hernandez, who were convicted and sentenced to death for the rape and murder of a 10-year-old girl. The fight to prove their innocence eventually led to Illinois's historic moratorium on executions.

Junkin, Tim. *Bloodsworth: The True Story of the First Death Row Inmate Exonerated by DNA.* Chapel Hill, N.C.: Algonquin Books, 2004. Biography of Kirk

Bloodsworth, falsely convicted and sentenced to die for the rape and murder of a nine-year-old girl in Maryland. He struggled to survive the prison system and was finally exonerated by a DNA test.

Mello, Michael. *The Wrong Man: A True Story of Innocence on Death Row.* Minneapolis: University of Minnesota Press, 2001. Tells how the author fought for twenty years to save "Crazy Joe" Spaziano from execution for a murder he did not commit. In the course of his efforts, Mello discovered a tape of a session where police hypnotized a witness and coached him to give testimony against Spaziano that was later recanted. When authorities refused to reopen the case, Mello risked disbarment by turning to the media to expose official misconduct.

Parloff, Roger. *Triple Jeopardy: A Story of Law at Its Best—and Worst.* Boston: Little, Brown, 1996. The story of John Henry Knapp, sentenced to death for killing his two young daughters. The author covered the case as a reporter and found it to be riddled with prosecutorial misconduct, bogus testimony, and disappearing evidence. Eventually a team of lawyers used forensic evidence to prove that Knapp could not have started the fire that killed his children.

Radelet, Michael L., Hugo Adam Bedau, and Constance E. Putnam. *In Spite of Innocence: Erroneous Convictions in Capital Cases.* Boston: Northeastern University Press, 1992. Compiles the stories of more than 400 innocent Americans who were convicted of capital crimes—some of whom were executed. The authors suggest that the safeguards intended to prevent wrongful convictions are weak and unreliable, leaving the innocent to fight against forbidding odds in the hope they can eventually prove their innocence. The conclusion is that since there is no realistic way to prevent a significant number of miscarriages of justice, the death penalty should be abolished.

Scheck, Barry, Jim Dwyer, and Peter Neufeld. *Actual Innocence: When Justice Goes Wrong and How to Make It Right.* New York: Penguin USA, 2001. The authors describe how attorneys Scheck and Neufeld and the Innocence Project have freed 37 innocent people and seek to free hundreds more. Their weapons are dogged persistence, finely honed legal skills, and the science of DNA.

Simon, Taryn. *The Innocents.* New York: Umbrage Editions, 2003. A powerful book of photographs, interviews, and accounts of 45 innocent men and women whose release was won through the efforts of the Innocence Project. The book also includes commentary by Barry Scheck and Peter Neufeld of the Innocence Project.

Tucker, John C. *May God Have Mercy: A True Story of Crime and Punishment.* New York: Norton, 1997. Tells the story of Roger Coleman, convicted and executed for the brutal murder of his sister-in-law Wanda Fay McCoy. The author describes how the police quickly concluded that Coleman was guilty and how, despite the emergence of contrary evidence, the legal process moved swiftly and inexorably toward execution. The intricate maze of legal maneuvering is explained for the lay reader, revealing the complex yet arbitrary nature of the legal process.

Capital Punishment

Warden, Rob, and David L. Protess. *A Promise of Justice: The Eighteen-Year Fight to Save Four Innocent Men.* New York: Hyperion Press, 1998. Describes the cases of four young black men (the Ford Heights Four) who were wrongfully convicted of the rape and murder of a white couple in Chicago. The authors enlisted the aid of volunteer students, lawyers, and a newspaper columnist to gather evidence that eventually freed the innocent men and led to the arrest of the actual perpetrators. (Note: this book is also available online from the Center on Wrongful Convictions at http://www.law.northwestern.edu/depts/clinic/wrongful/readings/warden_protess/TOC.htm.)

Westervelt, Saundra D., and John A. Humphrey, editors. *Wrongly Convicted: Perspectives on Failed Justice.* New Brunswick, N.J.: Rutgers University Press, 2001. Distinguished criminologists, psychologists, sociologists, and legal experts discuss the causes for wrongful convictions (including death sentences), identify characteristics of people most vulnerable to such injustice, and propose reforms to the criminal justice system.

ARTICLES

Belluck, Pam. "Class of Sleuths to Rescue on Death Row." *New York Times*, February 5, 1999, p. A16. Reports the activities of a Northwestern University journalism class that was given the assignment to reinvestigate cases of persons on death row who may be innocent. A surprise stay of execution gives the class enough time to discover a new witness, who said that Illinois death row inmate Anthony Porter did not fire the fatal shots, and a possible alternative suspect as well.

Cannon, Carl W. "The Problem with the Chair: A Conservative Legal Case against Capital Punishment." *National Review*, vol. 52, June 19, 2000, p. 28. Although opposition to the death penalty is usually associated with liberals, the author, a conservative, focuses on the danger of executing the innocent as the ultimate argument against giving the state the power to kill.

"Change of Heart: The Death Penalty." *The Economist*, vol. 335, June 24, 1995, pp. 28ff. Describes how the fate of Joseph Spaziano, sentenced to die for murder, was changed by investigations by *Miami Herald* reporters that led eventually to the key prosecution witness admitting that he had made up his damning testimony.

Dowling, Claudia Glenn. "Mistaken Identity." *People Weekly*, vol. 54, August 14, 2000, p. 50ff. The poignant story of a rape victim, Jennifer Thompson, who mistakenly identified her attacker and of the man, Ronald Cotton, wrongly sent to prison who struggled to survive and win a new hearing. Finally, three years after he is freed, Thompson and Cotton have a tense, dramatic meeting, become friends, and begin to work together to help the unjustly incarcerated.

"Fixing the Death Penalty." *Chicago Tribune*, December 29, 2002, p. 22. Describes the recent groundbreaking reforms that Illinois has enacted to address problems with capital cases, including unreliable or coerced confessions and statements by jailhouse snitches, as well as prosecutorial misconduct.

Gross, Samuel R. "Lost Lives: Miscarriages of Justice in Capital Cases." *Law and Contemporary Problems*, vol. 61, Autumn 1998. Also available online. Search at http://www.law.duke.edu/journals/lcp. Rebuts arguments that miscarriages of justice on death row are "vanishingly rare." While there are many protections built into the legal system, the characteristics of capital cases that make them different from lesser cases can also contribute to an increased chance of errors. Further, even when someone's innocence is determined and they are released, there is usually no follow-up that might point officials toward similar cases.

"It's Still Not Easy: Reprieved from Execution." *The Economist* (U.S.), vol. 344, September 27, 1997, pp. 30ff. Describes the cases of Dennis Williams and other inmates who have been released from death row after their innocence had been established. The number of such cases suggests that the justice system may be rushing toward final judgment too quickly.

Kim, Alice. "Death Penalty Exposed." *The New Abolitionist*, October 2001, n.p. Also available online. URL: http://www.nodeathpenalty.org/newab021/index.html. Argues that the reasons for abolishing the death penalty grows as nearly 100 innocent persons are freed from death row. Tragically for Malcolm Rent Johnson, a reexamination of evidence came too late to save him from execution, and it is suggested that at least several other innocent persons have been executed.

Lowenstein, Tom. "121 Days Old." *The American Prospect*, vol. 15, July 2004, n.p. Also available online. URL: http://www.prospect.org/web/printfriendly-view.ww?id=7881. Nick Yarris considers his birthday to be the day he was finally freed from prison after serving 22 years on death row before a DNA test proved he was innocent. The article describes last-minute obstacles, humorous encounters with an unfamiliar world on the outside, and Yarris's continuing struggle to adjust.

Markman, Stephen. "Innocents on Death Row? Blackmun Is Convinced That Innocent People Are Likely to Be Executed. Where Is the Evidence?" *National Review*, vol. 46, September 12, 1994, pp. 72ff. Argues that the Stanford University study, which concluded that in 350 cases innocent people received death sentences, is flawed. Only 23 of the people in the study were actually executed, and some of these were clearly guilty. What the study actually reveals is the rarity of execution of the innocent.

Masters, Brooke A. "Missteps on Road to Injustice." *Washington Post*, December 1, 2001, p. A01. Describes the case of Earl Washington, Jr., whose confession to rape and murder in 1982 led to "the biggest mistake ever made by Virginia's judicial system." Washington was finally exonerated when a DNA test showed no link between him and the crime. Now the victim's widower feels betrayed by the authorities' inability to find the real perpetrator. The case has led to reform in the handling of appeals.

Radelet, Michael L., and Hugo Adam Bedau. "The Execution of the Innocent." *Law and Contemporary Problems* (Duke University), vol. 61, Autumn 1998, n.p.

Also available online. Search at http://www.law.duke.edu/journals/lcp. Describes various categories of potentially innocent defendants who might be executed, then attempts to calculate the odds that such executions have occurred—a virtual certainty given the less than 100 percent probability of guilt even in strong cases and the multiplicative effect of probabilities. Finally, the authors suggest some possible remedies.

Roberts, Paul Craig. "The Causes of Wrongful Conviction." *Independent Review*, vol. 7, Spring 2003, pp. 567–568. Suggests that the problem of wrongful conviction could bring liberals and conservatives together to abolish the death penalty. The author suggests that to be successful, however, leftists will need to forgo arguments based on race or class and focus on procedural and evidentiary reforms. A major cause of wrongful convictions is the perverse incentives and pressures caused by crusades such as the war on drugs, and respect for fundamental rights needs to be restored.

Shapiro, Joseph P. "The Wrong Men on Death Row." *U.S. News & World Report*, November 9, 1998, p. 22. Reports that one death row prisoner for every seven executed has been found innocent. Shapiro describes many causes of wrongful convictions, including hasty investigations, false confessions, and inadequate representation for defendants. Social outsiders tend to get railroaded to conviction.

Templeton, Jean M. "Shutting Down Death Row." *The American Prospect*, vol. 15, July 2004, n.p. Also available online. URL: http://www.prospect.org/web/printfriendly-view.ww?id=7862. Describes reforms that could reduce the chances of innocent persons being convicted. Sequential lineups, where persons are examined one at a time by the witness, have been shown to be more accurate than conventional lineups. Videotaping all interrogations from start to finish could reduce the number of false or coerced confessions. Illinois is leading the way with pilot programs testing the value of these and other reforms.

Turow, Scott. "To Kill or Not to Kill." *The New Yorker*, vol. 78, January 6, 2003, p. 40. Turow recounts his experience with capital cases and his service on the Illinois commission charged with reforming the state's capital punishment system after Governor George Ryan declared a moratorium on executions. Turow finds the need to respond to truly horrendous crimes to be the strongest argument for the death penalty, but finally comes down on the side of abolition. Meanwhile, he supports a variety of reforms that the commission believes will reduce the chance that innocent people will be executed.

WEB DOCUMENTS

"3,500 Groups Join the Call for a Moratorium on Executions." Quixote Center. Available online. URL: http://www.quixote.org/ej/ej_tally_of_moratorium_signers_by_st.html. Updated in August 2004. A regularly updated list of organizations that have joined the nationwide call for a moratorium on executions. Compiled by Equal Justice USA and organized by state.

Cohen, Sharon, and Deborah Hastings. "For 110 Inmates Freed by DNA Tests, True Freedom Remains Elusive." Associated Press. May 28, 2002. Available online. URL: http://www.deathpenaltyinfo.org/article.php?scid=17&did=293. Describes the hardships of 110 inmates who had collectively served more than 1,000 years in prison following false convictions. Many of them suffer from traumatic stress and bitterness, and most lack up-to-date job skills. And although the pace of exonerations is picking up, inmates seeking DNA tests still face obstacles and delays.

"The Impact of Habeas Reform on Innocent People Sentenced to Death." American Civil Liberties Union. Available online. URL: http://www.aclu.org/issues/death/death3.html. Downloaded on November 28, 1999. Describes the consequences of Supreme Court cases through April 1995 that have restricted the ability to file habeas petitions to get a new trial when there is evidence of innocence. Nine cases are discussed in detail.

Lindorff, Dave. "Unjust Executions." Salon.com. Available online. URL: http://archive.salon.com/news/feature/2003/05/06/sentencing_errors. Posted on May 6, 2003. Gives examples of sentencing errors in capital cases. Appellate courts have found such errors in about 40 percent of all capital cases since 1973, but there is no hard evidence as to how many errors actually led to people being executed or remaining on death row.

General and Miscellaneous Legal Issues

Works in this section include those that discuss a range of legal issues (including those featured in the previous sections) as well as habeas corpus and other appeals proceedings raising issues such as ineffective assistance of counsel.

BOOKS

Bigel, Alan I. *Justices William J. Brennan, Jr., and Thurgood Marshall on Capital Punishment: Its Constitutionality, Morality, Deterrent Effect, and Interpretation by the Court.* Lanham, Md.: University Press of America, 1997. A detailed study of the philosophical and legal evolution of the position that Justices Brennan and Marshall took against the death penalty during their tenure on the Court. Their opinions and arguments are placed within the context of the traditional arguments about fairness and cruelty.

Burnett, Kathleen. *Justice Denied: Clemency Appeals in Death Penalty Cases.* Northeastern University Press, 2002. The author, a sociologist and criminologist, reviews 50 clemency petitions presented to the governor of Missouri between 1977 and 2000. She details extensive evidence of police and prosecutor misconduct, incompetence and negligence by defense attorneys, and errors by trial and appellate judges. Despite all these problems there is little evidence that governors have paid serious attention to the merits of the clemency petitions, which are seldom granted.

Carter, Linda E., and Ellen Kreitzberg. *Understanding Capital Punishment Law.* New York: LexisNexis, 2004. A textbook reviewing constitutional aspects of the death penalty, recent developments, and current issues.

Coyne, Randall, and Lyn Entzeroth. *Capital Punishment and the Judicial Process.* Durham, N.C.: Carolina Academic Press, 1994. A detailed legal casebook that brings out the inconsistencies and arbitrary and unfair applications in administration of the death penalty. Coyne, a professor of law, was a member of the team that defended Oklahoma City bomber Timrothy McVeigh.

Epstein, Lee, and Joseph Fiske Kobylka. *The Supreme Court and Legal Change: Abortion and the Death Penalty.* Chapel Hill: University of North Carolina Press, 1992. Looks at capital punishment and abortion as case studies in abrupt legal change. In both cases the Supreme Court intervened decisively to change the operation of society. The authors conclude that the structure and tactics of legal argumentation is at least as important as judicial temperament and political or social pressures in determining radical legal changes.

Foley, Michael A. *Arbitrary and Capricious: The Supreme Court, the Constitution, and the Death Penalty.* Westport, Conn.: Praeger, 2003. A detailed discussion of the changing assessment of the death penalty by the Supreme Court in almost 100 decisions. The development of the jurisprudence has three phases: one, the first attempts to apply the constitution's ban on "cruel and unusual punishment"; two, the *Furman* case in 1972 that declared the death penalty to be unconstitutional as applied; and three, subsequent decisions addressing procedural questions and issues such as execution of retarded persons. The author closes with the suggestion that the final decision about capital punishment must be made by a maturing society.

Garvey, Stephen P. *Beyond Repair? America's Death Penalty.* Durham, N.C.: Duke University Press, 2003. A collection of essays on legal aspects of the death penalty, including how the threat of executing the innocent has become a central question in the debate. Other topics include the role of race, analysis of jury selection and performance, and support for abolition of the death penalty in international law.

Mello, Michael. *Against the Death Penalty: The Relentless Dissents of Justices Brennan and Marshall.* Boston: Northeastern University Press, 1996. A detailed study of the dissents written by Supreme Court justices Brennan and Marshall in more than 2,500 capital cases. Drawing on personal papers and biographical materials, the author shows how they developed their opinions, based on the Constitution (Eighth and Fourteenth Amendments) and on factors in individual cases.

———. *Deathwork: Defending the Condemned.* Minneapolis: University of Minnesota Press, 2002. The author, a capital public defender, combines autobiography with documentary and legal analysis in presenting some of his most important cases. The inherent dramatic urgency of last-minute appeals is conveyed, along with the complexity of issues such as racial inequity and the difficulty of raising evidence of innocence at a time when the legal system virtually demands closure.

———. *Dead Wrong: A Death Row Lawyer Speaks Out against Capital Punishment.* Madison: University of Wisconsin Press, 1998. The author, who worked as a counsel to convicted capital offenders, takes the reader inside the world of death row appeals and last-minute stays of execution. He argues that the lack of adequate legal resources for death row inmates coupled with the indifference of many people in the system to constitutional rights has made the legal process a travesty.

Streib, Victor L. *Death Penalty in a Nutshell.* St. Paul, Minn.: West Group, 2002. Offers a history of death penalty law in the United States, reviews constitutional and other legal issues, and explains the procedures used to try capital cases and appeals.

ARTICLES

Banner, Stuart. "The Death Penalty's Strange Career." *The Wilson Quarterly*, vol. 26, Spring 2002, pp. 70ff. The legal battle ensuing from the *Furman* case is discussed: advocates of abolition (such as Anthony Amsterdam and the Legal Defense Fund) were caught in a bind: They could not eliminate all forms of discretion in the legal system and might be forced to argue that the death penalty was inherently unconstitutional—a position the majority of the Supreme Court could not accept. The parameters of the modern legal debate are summarized, including the roles of race, age, and mental status of defendants.

Barta, Peter A. "Between Death and a Hard Place: *Hopkins v. Reeves* and the 'Stark Choice' between Capital Conviction and Outright Acquittal." *American Criminal Law Review*, vol. 37, Fall 2000, p. 1,429ff. The Supreme Court has held that a lesser included offense (if relevant) must be offered to juries as an alternative to an offense carrying the death penalty. The author explores the dilemma that arises when no such included offense is available because of how the elements of the offenses are defined and warns that states may now be free to evade the Supreme Court's *Beck* decision by effectively removing lesser included offenses from the equation.

Bright, Stephen B. "Death in Texas." *Champion Magazine*, July 1999, n.p. Also available online. URL: http://www.nacdl.org/public.nsf/championarticles/99 jul01. The director of the Southern Center for Human Rights blasts Texas courts for allowing the appointing of incompetent counsel for death penalty appeals and then punishing the clients for the results of the incompetence. Bright gives as an example the refusal of an appeals court to overturn a conviction after the defense attorney slept through much of the trial.

Bright, Taylor, and Jeb Phillips. "Execution of Justice." *Birmingham Post-Herald*, December 14–18, 2001, n.p. Also available online. URL: http://www. postherald.com/justice.shtml. A five-part comprehensive look at problems with the death penalty in Alabama. Part 1 looks at the high rate of death sentences in Talladega County and a variety of problems involving resources, race, and treatment of the mentally retarded. Part 2 looks at the cases of four inmates who were released when serious problems were found with their cases. Part 3 looks at the role played by the race of the defendant and victim in capital sentencing. Part 4 looks at the issue of executing retarded criminals. Part 5 examines the high cost (and meager resources) of defending against capital charges. This well-balanced series also describes the feelings of murder victims' families and expresses the opinions of district attorneys who feel many "innocent" defendants are just manipulating the system to stave off execution.

Bruck, David I. "A Rarefied Kind of Dread." *Journal of Appellate Practice and Process*, vol. 5, Spring 2003, p. 75ff. The author describes his feelings when he argued the case of *Skipper v. South Carolina* before the U.S. Supreme Court in 1986. There was not only the fear of losing, but the fear that the court might undermine the very rights he was arguing for. In this case the author was arguing for juries being allowed to consider all possible mitigating factors, including the defendant's good behavior in prison. He then describes his experience in giving his oral argument before the court.

Doyle, Kevin M. "Capital Cases: Heart of the Deal: Ten Suggestions for Plea Bargaining." *Champion Magazine*, November 1999, n.p. Also available online. URL: http://www.nacdl.org/public.nsf/championarticles/99nov08. Suggests a strategy for giving clients who are facing the death penalty a realistic understanding of what they can expect.

Dworkin, Ronald. "The Court's Impatience to Execute." *Los Angeles Times*, July 11, 1999, p. M1. Reports on recent cases that suggest that the Supreme Court, while having said that the death penalty requires a special level of scrutiny, has in practice been refusing to overturn death sentences even when juries receive misleading instructions or important evidence is withheld. Even if capital punishment is "right in principle," it may prove to be intolerable due to its strain on a legal system that seeks to balance efficiency and protection of rights.

Fein, Bruce. "Death Penalty Polemic Scorns Rule of Law." *Insight on the News*, vol. 10, April 4, 1994, p. 30. Argues that Supreme Court justice Harry Blackmun's renunciation of the death penalty and refusal to "tinker with the machinery of death" may be emotionally moving but lacks any reasoned argument.

Gest, Ted. "A House without a Blueprint: After 20 Years, the Death Penalty Is Still Being Meted Out Unevenly." *U.S. News & World Report*, vol. 121, July 8, 1996, pp. 41ff. A retrospective on the 20 years since the restoration of capital punishment in 1976. Torn between advocates' demand for fairness and the public's continuing demand for the death penalty, the courts preside over a system that is tangled, inefficient, and still unfair.

Kreitzberg, Ellen. "How Much *Payne* Will the Courts Allow?" *Champion Magazine*, January/February 1998, n.p. Also available online. URL: http://www.

nacdl.org/CHAMPION/ARTICLES/98jan04.htm. Discusses the decision in *Payne v. Tennessee*, which partly reversed earlier decisions in holding victim impact statements to not be in conflict with the Eighth Amendment. Kreitzberg describes kinds of victim testimony that still are not permitted (such as expressing an opinion of the crime or possible punishment) and suggests a strategy for challenging or excluding victim impact testimony.

Lindroff, David. "The Death Penalty's Other Victims." Salon.com. Available online. URL: http://www.deathpenaltyinfo.org/article.php?scid=17&did=395. Posted on January 2, 2001. Focuses on the ability of prosecutors to "death qualify" a jury—that is, to systematically remove jurors opposed to the sanction. The author believes that this practice powerfully skews the jury against the defendant. Further, because more minority jurors oppose the death penalty, juries are likely to end up with inadequate minority representation. The advantages of death-qualifying a jury may even encourage prosecutors to seek death sentences in difficult cases. However, there is no easy solution as long as the death penalty is to be used.

Norwood, Ryan. "None Dare Call It Treason: The Constitutionality of the Death Penalty for Peacetime Espionage." *Cornell Law Review*, vol. 87, March 2002, p. 820ff. Although no one has been sentenced to death for espionage since the 1950s, the threat remains, and it is sometimes used as a lever by federal prosecutors, as in the case of Robert Hanssen (who pleaded guilty and received a prison sentence) and Wen Ho Lee (whose charges were dropped). The history and relevant cases are discussed. Espionage is compared to participation of an accomplice in murder and to treason. The author concludes that the death penalty would be a disproportionate punishment for peacetime espionage.

"N.Y. High Court Voids State's Death Penalty." *The Legal Intelligencer*, June 28, 2004, n.p. A New York appeals court said that it was unconstitutional to tell jurors that if they are deadlocked between death and life without parole the defendant will be eligible for parole someday. By a 4-3 vote the court believed that such an instruction might impermissibly push jurors to join those favoring the death penalty in order to keep a dangerous defendant from ever getting back on the street.

Posner, Michael. "Life, Death, and Uncertainty." *Boston Globe*, July 8, 2001, n.p. Also available online. URL: http://www.deathpenaltyinfo.org/article.php?scid=17&did=417. The judge who presided over a lurid murder case gives an unusual perspective on how capital cases are tried, the responsibility of the jury, and how the Constitution and Supreme Court decisions are applied in practice. Both judge and jury experienced considerable personal stress in trying to deal with the complex and inconclusive evidence. After the penalty phase, the judge/author believes that both he and the jury felt that the death penalty was not "worth the price."

Ragavan, Chitra. "The Toll in Texas." *U.S. News & World Report*, vol. 127, August 16, 1999, p. 29. Reports that it is "rush hour" on the Texas death row, with the state on its way to set a new record in executions. The author argues that the biggest factor in the pace of executions in Texas is the lack of a statewide public defender system, resulting in the mostly poor defendants receiving inadequate representation.

Savage, David G. "Justices Reject Cases on Execution Delay." *Los Angeles Times*, November 9, 1999, p. A14. Reports that the Supreme Court has turned down two unusual death penalty appeals. Two inmates had argued that long delays of more than 20 years on death row constitute cruel and unusual punishment. Justice Clarence Thomas called the claim bizarre, noting that the delays were the results of the inmates' own incessant efforts to avoid execution.

Shugerman, Jed Handelsman. "Unreasonable Probability of Error." *Yale Law Journal*, vol. 111, November 2001, p. 435ff. Analyzes the Supreme Court's attempt to establish standards for effective assistance of counsel in *Strickland v. Washington* and the failure of such standards to ensure adequate representation for defendants today, particularly in capital cases. In practice, many courts require a higher standard than "reasonable probability" that the jury would have decided differently but for the defense attorney's inadequate performance. (The author suggests that "reasonable possibility" would be a better way to convey the idea.)

Stetler, Russell. "Post-Conviction Investigation in Death Penalty Cases." *Champion Magazine*, August 1999, n.p. Also available online. URL: http://www.nacdl.org/public.nsf/championarticles/99aug06. Gives suggestions for defense counsel seeking to overturn death sentences. Stetler emphasizes the need to find new facts that challenge the facts that led to the sentencing decision and the need to create empathy in judges so they will see legal errors as demanding relief. With the speeded-up death sentence appeals process in most jurisdictions, investigations must be conducted quickly yet thoroughly.

———. "Working with the Victim's Survivors in Death Penalty Cases." *Champion Magazine*, June 1999, n.p. Also available online. URL: http://www.nacdl.org/public.nsf/championarticles/99jun06. Posted in June 1999. Approaches the sensitive topic of how defense attorneys can interview survivors at various phases of the trial process. Stetler emphasizes the need to understand the experiences and feelings of survivors and their complex and sometimes conflicting feelings. It is important for defense attorneys to develop good contacts because of the significant role survivors often have in determining whether the death penalty is sought, whether the jury returns a death verdict, and sometimes whether a later appeal for clemency succeeds.

Wheelan, Dick. "Significance of *Simmons* and Future Dangerousness." *Champion Magazine* (National Association of Criminal Defense Lawyers), May 1996, n.p. Also available online. URL: http://www.criminaljustice.org/CHAMPION/ARTICLES/96may01.htm. Discusses the decision in *Simmons v. South Carolina*, where the Supreme Court ruled that if the prosecution argues that the defendant should receive the death penalty because of his or her future dangerousness, the court must allow the defense to inform the jury that the defendant is ineligible for parole. Wheelan describes strategic considerations determining whether to seek to inform the jury about life (or lengthy nonlife) sentences.

Willing, Richard, and Gary Fields. "Implementation of the Death Penalty." *USA Today*, December 20, 1999, p. 6A. Describes how the chance of someone being given the death penalty for the same sort of murder varies widely according to where the crime is committed. Thirty-eight states have the death penalty, but even among these states there is wide variation in charging and sentencing practices.

Web Documents

Cohn, Andrew. "The Death Penalty's Cloudy Future." CBSNews.com. Available online. URL: http://www.deathpenaltyinfo.org/article.php?scid=17& did=390. Posted on April 26, 2002. Although there is no direct link between recent court decisions, the Supreme Court's upcoming calendar, and the conclusions of an Illinois commission on death penalty reform, they all reflect growing misgivings and skepticism about the viability of capital punishment. The Supreme Court seems likely to begin a new round of tinkering with the system.

"Death Penalty: Uncertain Justice." *Seattle Post-Intelligencer.* Available online. URL: http://seattlepi.nwsource.com/specials/deathpenalty. Downloaded on October 4, 2004. A three-part report providing an overview of who is on death row, which sentences have been overturned and why, and the demographics of death row. Main problems focused on include inadequate legal representation, inconsistency and inequality in sentencing, and lack of resources for defense.

Dieter, Richard C. "With Justice for Few: The Growing Crisis in Death Penalty Representation." Death Penalty Information Center. Available online. URL: http://www.deathpenaltyinfo.org/article.php?scid=45&did=544. Posted in October 1995. Argues that as the number of executions in the United States continues to grow, most capital defendants receive poor legal representation from incompetent or inexperienced attorneys. States provide inadequate resources, discouraging involvement by better lawyers. A variety of illustrative cases are discussed, including that of Aden Harrison, Jr., a black man whose court-appointed counsel was 83-year-old James Venable, an Imperial Wizard of the Ku Klux Klan.

Lazarus, Edward. "A Basic Death Penalty Paradox That Is Tearing the Supreme Court Apart." Findlaw.com. Available online. URL: http://www.deathpenalty info.org/article.php?scid=17&did=296. Posted on October 31, 2002. The author suggests that Americans are increasingly torn between support for the death penalty for perpetrators of heinous crimes and dismay about the potential execution of innocent people as increasingly revealed by DNA tests. This frustration is also found within the Supreme Court itself, as justices become less willing to cooperate with one another in dealing with troubling cases, and a bitter division has ensued.

Lowenstein, Tom. "A Perfect Killing?: McVeigh Proves Why We Need a Moratorium on the Death Penalty." American Prospect Online. URL: http://www. prospect.org/print-friendly/webfeatures/2001/05/lowenstein-t-05–15.html. Posted on May 15, 2001. Suggests that if even the "perfect" death penalty case (against Timothy McVeigh, America's most notorious homegrown terrorist) can be bungled, it is time to halt executions and revamp the system. In McVeigh's case the court gave the defense only 30 days to review more than 3,000 pages of evidence that had been withheld by the state at the time of trial.

"United States of America: No Return to Execution—The U.S. Death Penalty As a Barrier to Extradition." Amnesty International. Available online. URL: http://web.amnesty.org/library/index/engAMR511712001?OpenDocument. Posted on November 29, 2001. This report suggests that as the United States faces growing isolation from world opinion on the death penalty, it will become increasingly harder for U.S. authorities to obtain extradition of criminal suspects captured abroad. Many extradition treaties and laws now have explicit language barring extradition to countries that have capital punishment. The current situation regarding a number of nations and international organizations is summarized.

POLITICAL AND CULTURAL ISSUES

Public Opinion, Laws and Legislation, and Political Developments

This section includes a variety of discussions of public opinion as expressed in polls and jury surveys, death penalty laws and proposed legislation, and political factors affecting capital punishment.

BOOKS

Bazan, Elizabeth B. "Capital Punishment: An Overview of Federal Death Penalty Statutes." Washington, D.C.: Congressional Research Service, 2001. Also available online. URL: http://www.law.umaryland.edu/marshall/ ElectronicResources/crsreports/crsdocuments/RL30962_05092001.pdf. Describes the current statutes and procedures for the federal death penalty, including the expansion of covered offenses in the Violent Crime Control and Law Enforcement Act of 1994 and the Antiterrorism and Effective Death Penalty Act of 1996.

Cole, George F., Marc G. Gertz, and Amy Bunger. *Criminal Justice System: Politics and Policies*. Belmont, Calif.: Wadsworth, 2004. This collection of classic and contemporary essays explores the relationship between politics and the formulation of criminal justice policies. Several essays focus on racial disparities and on attitudes toward the death penalty.

Cook, Kimberly J. *Divided Passions: Public Opinions on Abortion and the Death Penalty.* Boston: Northeastern University, 1998. Argues that opinions on both capital punishment and abortion are passionate but contradictory, such as abortion opponents who support the death penalty. Through a series of in-depth interviews the author seeks to identify the cultural forces that shape opinion. She concludes that both groups share an ethic of "punitiveness."

Fuhrman, Mark. "Death and Justice: An Exposé of Oklahoma's Death Row Machine." New York: HarperCollins, 2004. The controversial former detective (of O. J. Simpson case fame) turned investigative reporter accuses Oklahoma County officials of overaggressive, politically motivated capital prosecutions and mismanagement of crime lab evidence.

Hamm, Theodore. *Rebel and a Cause: Caryl Chessman and the Politics of the Death Penalty in Postwar California, 1948–1974.* Berkeley: University of California Press, 2001. Explores the wider political significance of the unsuccessful effort to save Caryl Chessman, the "Red Light Bandit," from execution. The authors explain why California governor Edmund G. Brown, a liberal opponent of the death penalty, nevertheless allowed the execution to go forward in 1960. The conflict is also placed in the broader context of the prison reform movement and other left-liberal political efforts.

Palmer, Louis J. *The Death Penalty: An American Citizen's Guide to Understanding Federal and State Laws.* Jefferson, N.C.: McFarland, 1998. An overview and summary of how capital punishment is implemented in federal and state law. A brief overview of common law is followed by sections on prosecutorial discretion and the charging mechanism, the capital penalty phase, aggravating and mitigating circumstances, appellate review, and laws relating to the execution process itself. Includes tables of death penalty provisions.

Sarat, Austin. *The Killing State: Capital Punishment in Law, Politics, and Culture.* New York: Oxford University Press, 1999. A collection of essays by scholars from various fields that seeks to explain the social and political function served by the death penalty, bringing out perversities and contradictions with cherished American values. The book generally has an abolitionist point of view. It is divided into parts dealing with political, legal, and cultural issues.

———. *When the State Kills: Capital Punishment and the American Condition.* Princeton, N.J.: Princeton University Press, 2001. An interesting political and social argument that claims that even if capital punishment were effective in deterring crime, it is intolerable to a truly democratic society. The mechanisms that decide life and death are largely hidden from the public and unaccountable. The combination of overheated political rhetoric and hidden prejudice surrounding the system guarantees that when the state kills it reflects impulses that are destructive to democracy and social stability.

Steelwater, Eliza. *The Hangman's Knot: Lynching, Legal Execution, and America's Struggle with the Death Penalty.* Boulder, Colo.: Westview Press, 2003. A history of legal and extralegal execution in the United States from executions for witchcraft in colonial times to 19th-century vigilantes and the lynchings that persisted in the South well into the 20th century. The author's work is based on extensive research into archives and her focus is on "punishment politics"—how executions were justified and the political purposes they served.

ARTICLES

Bohm, R. M., and R. E. Vogel. "Comparison of Factors Associated with Uninformed and Informed Death Penalty Opinions." *Journal of Criminal Justice*, vol. 22, 1994, pp. 125–143. Study of college undergraduates' attitudes to the death penalty. The degree of support for the death penalty was correlated with being white and accepting arguments based on deterrence, incapacitation, and revenge. Providing information about the death penalty seems to have little effect on core attitudes.

———. "Educational Experiences and Death Penalty Opinions: Stimuli That Produce Changes." *Journal of Criminal Justice Education*, vol. 2, Spring 1991, pp. 69–80. Reports the results of a study in which various stimuli were presented to college students and the effects on their opinions of capital punishment measured. The authors discuss how the last days of Earl Johnson, a black man executed in Mississippi, had a significant effect in shifting black students' opinions against the death penalty but had only a small effect on white students.

DeVries, Brian, and Lawrence J. Walker. "Moral Reasoning and Attitudes toward Capital Punishment." *Developmental Psychology*, vol. 22, 1986, pp. 509–513. Using Kohlberg's moral development theory, the authors find that university students at higher stages of moral development oppose capital punishment.

Dionne, E. J., Jr. "Karla Tucker's Legacy: The Death Penalty Debate Takes a Turn." *Commonweal*, vol. 125, February 27, 1998, pp. 9ff. Suggests that the execution of Karla Faye Tucker and the troubling emotions raised by her show of remorse may mark a turning point in public support for the death penalty.

Drinan, Robert F. "Catholic Politicians and the Death Penalty." *America*, vol. 180, May 1, 1999, p. 19. Points out the contradiction between Catholic teachings against capital punishment and the views of the 15 Catholic state governors in the United States, most of whom are in states that have the death penalty and most of whom have expressed support for the sanction. Political realities put governors who want to follow their church's teachings in a very difficult position.

———. "Catholics and the Death Penalty." *America*, vol. 170, June 18, 1994. The author, a Catholic priest, begins by acknowledging that 70 percent of Catholic laypersons support the death penalty in keeping with the attitudes of the general public. He then explains the church's position that the sanction is unnecessary and recounts facts that suggest that the death penalty is imposed in an unfair and discriminatory way, particularly with regard to racial minorities.

Garvey, Stephen P., and Paul Marcus. "Virginia's Capital Jurors." *William and Mary Law Review*, vol. 44, April 2003, p. 2,063ff. An extensive survey of the opinions and perceptions of a sample of persons who have served on Virginia capital juries. The four areas explored are general attitude toward the death penalty; understanding of the legal rules or guidelines for sentencing; the amount of weight given to the defendant's future dangerousness; and how much responsibility jurors feel for the defendant's fate. The authors suggest that the perception of future dangerousness and a juror's general underestimation of the amount of time the defendant will have to remain in prison may be especially important.

Gest, Ted. "The Law That Grief Built." *U.S. News & World Report*, vol. 120, April 29, 1996, p. 58. Describes how Oklahoma attorney general Drew Edmondson mobilized public outrage following the Oklahoma City bombing to pass a bill in Congress that curtailed the appeal rights of death row prisoners. Families of Oklahoma City bombing victims played a crucial role in this effort.

Gonzalez-Perez, Margaret. "A Model of Decision-Making in Capital Juries." *International Social Science* Review, Fall-Winter 2001, p. 79ff. Surprisingly, this study and the model derived from it found that such variables as political party or liberal/conservative identification, education, income, and religious practice did not play a significant part in predicting a juror's attitude toward the death penalty. The only variable showing a strong correlation is race, with whites favoring capital punishment significantly more often than blacks.

Harvey, O. J. "Belief Systems and Attitudes toward the Death Penalty and Other Punishments." *Journal of Personality*, vol. 54, December 1986, pp. 659–675. Explores the values and attitudes from which opinions of punishment stem.

Payne, B. K., and V. Coogle. "Examining Attitudes about the Death Penalty." *Corrections Compendium*, vol. 23, April 1998, pp. 1ff. Study examining college students' attitudes about capital punishment in order to measure possible changes as the students pursued their academic studies. Results showed that race and political affiliation correlated with attitudes toward the death penalty, while gender, academic major, and community size did not.

Rosen, Jeffrey. "Shell Game." *The New Republic*, May 13, 1996, p. 6. Attacks the Effective Death Penalty and Public Safety Act of 1996 for its crass political motivations and assault on both states' rights and the independence of the judiciary.

Rosenbloom, Joseph. "The Unique Brutality of Texas." *The American Prospect*, vol. 15, July 2004, n.p. Also available online. URL: http://www.prospect.org/web/printfriendly-view.ww?id=7883. Criticizes Texas for its continuing high volume of executions despite growing evidence of rights violations, possible execution of innocent persons, and international opposition at the highest levels. Conservative politicians seem to have a lock on the Texas judiciary and prosecutors have vastly more resources than do capital defense attorneys. Several cases are cited as showing that the system is dysfunctional.

Serrano, Richard A. "Federal Death Cases Often End with Life." *Los Angeles Times.* August 3, 1998, p. A5. Despite the increase in federal crimes for which the death penalty may be imposed, in practice the federal government sentences very few defendants to death. Although tough talk is used for political purposes, many people in the administration and career prosecutors oppose the death penalty and are reluctant to seek it.

WEB DOCUMENTS

Dieter, Richard C. "Killing for Votes: The Dangers of Politicizing the Death Penalty Process." Death Penalty Information Center. Available online. URL: http://www.deathpenaltyinfo.org/article.php?scid=45&did=260. Posted in October 1996. Discusses the use of the death penalty issue in election campaigns and how it leads to political pressure on judges and prosecutors to bring capital charges. A variety of campaigns and cases are discussed. (Some of the factors discussed may be changing in the light of recent concern about the execution of the innocent and the movement for death penalty moratoriums.)

———. "Sentencing for Life: Americans Embrace Alternatives to the Death Penalty." Death Penalty Information Center. Available online. URL: http://www.deathpenaltyinfo.org/article.php?scid=45&did=481. Posted in April 1993. Reviews public opinion on the question of the death penalty versus life without parole. When respondents are given life without parole as an alternative, it is favored more than the death penalty. Jurors are often not informed that life without parole is a sentencing alternative.

Religious, Philosophical, Ethical, and Cultural Perspectives

This final section brings together a variety of arguments and perspectives based on religious, philosophical/ethical, and cultural studies.

BOOKS

Bessler, John D. *Death in the Dark: Midnight Executions in America.* Boston: Northeastern University Press, 1997. The author, a law professor who has helped defend death row inmates, argues that executions are deliberately staged at midnight so that the public will not see the gruesome process of execution or question the rhetoric of pro–death penalty politicians. He suggests that executions be televised. The book includes an overview of capital punishment and the media in American history, starting with public hangings in colonial days and ending with the manipulation of public opinion in the age of television.

Erdahl, Lowell O. *Pro-Life/Pro-Peace: Life-Affirming Alternatives to Abortion, War, Mercy-Killing and the Death Penalty.* Minneapolis, Minn.: Augsburg Publishing House, 1986. A Lutheran bishop's call for a consistent, Christian, and "pro-life" stance on a number of issues including capital punishment.

Fisanick, Christina. *The Ethics of Capital Punishment.* San Diego, Calif.: Greenhaven Press, 2004. Focuses on the ethical and moral issues surrounding the use of the death penalty, including the rights of the condemned and the need to protect society.

Guest, David. *Sentenced to Death: The American Novel and Capital Punishment.* Jackson: University Press of Mississippi, 1997. A study of the social context of five novels in which the operation of capital punishment plays an important part: *McTeague, An American Tragedy, Native Son, In Cold Blood,* and *The Executioner's Song.*

Hanks, Gardner C. *Against the Death Penalty: Christian and Secular Arguments against Capital Punishment.* Scottsdale, Pa.: Herald Press, 1997. A concise, accessible presentation of arguments against capital punishment from a Christian perspective. Hanks places the Old Testament support for capital punishment in perspective and argues that the understanding of God and humankind developed in the New Testament compels the rejection of capital punishment. Hanks also rebuts secular justifications for capital punishment.

———. *Capital Punishment and the Bible.* Scottsdale, Pa.: Herald Press, 2002. Reviews Biblical passages about capital punishment in context and applies them to the death penalty as currently practiced, concluding that the practice is contrary to biblical values.

Kaminer, Wendy. *It's All the Rage: Crime and Culture.* Reading, Mass.: Addison-Wesley, 1995. A witty commentary on the capital punishment debate and its historical, social, legal, and ethical aspects. The author points out numerous examples of what she considers to be the irrationality of capital punishment: the media hype surrounding recent cases, the public's embrace of draconian measures such as the "three strikes" laws, and contradictions such as that between people's desire to blame others for their difficulties while holding others to the ultimate standard of responsibility.

Lifton, Robert J., and Greg Mitchell. *Who Owns Death? Capital Punishment, the American Conscience, and the End of Executions.* New York: HarperCollins, 2000. The authors explore "the reasons for America's unyielding support for executions" but clearly have an abolitionist agenda. They see support for capital punishment as largely springing from a uniquely American preoccupation with violence as a way of purging evil. The authors believe that capital punishment corrodes the sensibilities of everyone involved, including advocates, prison wardens, chaplains, and the governors who must decide whether to give clemency to the condemned.

Loney, Randolph. *Dreams of the Tattered Man: Stories from Georgia's Death Row.* Grand Rapids, Mich.: William B. Eerdmans, 2001. A Georgia pastor recounts the lessons he believed he learned from working with condemned prisoners and their families for 15 years. He believes that each individual's uniqueness and essential humanity cannot be denied.

Megivern, James J. *The Death Penalty: An Historical and Theological Survey.* New York: Paulist Press, 1997. A history of the theological, philosophical, and legal debate about capital punishment since ancient times, including teachings of the early Christian fathers, St. Thomas Aquinas, and later works. The author, a religious scholar, is abolitionist but maintains an even-handed approach.

Nathanson, Stephen. *An Eye for an Eye? The Morality of Punishing by Death.* 2d ed. Lanham, Md.: Rowman and Littlefield, 2001. An evaluation and rejection of religious arguments supporting capital punishment.

Otterbein, Keith F. *The Ultimate Coercive Sanction: A Cross-Cultural Study of Capital Punishment.* New Haven, Conn.: HRAF Press, 1986. Studies the death penalty from an anthropological viewpoint; examination of 53 tribal societies suggests that capital punishment is nearly universal.

Owens, Erik C., John D. Carlson, and Eric P. Elshtain, editors. *Religion and the Death Penalty: A Call for Reckoning.* Grand Rapids, Mich.: William B. Eerdmans, 2004. Seventeen essays exploring religious and moral aspects of capital punishment. Most but not all contributors oppose the death penalty. Contributors include Justice Antonin Scalia, former New York governor Mario M. Cuomo, Cardinal Avery Dulles, and philosopher David Novak.

Pickett, Caroll. *Within These Walls: Memoirs of a Death House Chaplain.* New York: St. Martin's Press, 2002. The author served as chaplain to death row inmates in Huntsville, Texas, for 15 years. He describes ministering to 95 men in their final hours before execution and his growing disillusionment with capital punishment.

Steffen, Lloyd. *Executing Justice: The Moral Meaning of the Death Penalty.* Cleveland: Pilgrim Press, 1999. Explores the moral theories that underlie support for the death penalty, including the right of society to defend itself from murder, the promotion of the greater good, just retribution, and a theory of just execution tested against actual practice.

Zimring, Franklin E. *The Contradictions of American Capital Punishment.* New York: Oxford University Press, 2003. The author, a leading abolitionist, sees a conflict between two deep-seated American values. On the one hand, the arbitrary and capricious administration of the justice system offends fundamental notions of fairness and due process. On the other hand, many Americans believe in the justified use of violence in dealing with crimes seen to be the ultimate challenge to the community. Zimring suggests that the greatest support for capital punishment continues to be in those areas (mainly southern) where lynching and other forms of vigilante action were most pervasive in past decades.

ARTICLES

American Medical Association. Council on Ethical and Judicial Affairs. "Physician Participation in Capital Punishment" *JAMA, Journal of the American*

Medical Association, vol. 270, 1993, pp. 365–368. Declares that medical ethics requires that physicians not participate in executions, such as by pronouncing death.

Anderson, George M. "Opposing the Death Penalty: An Interview with Helen Prejean." *America,* vol. 175, November 9, 1996, pp. 8ff. Interview with the nun whose experiences with Louisiana death row inmates were described in the book (and movie) *Dead Man Walking.*

———. "Organizing against the Death Penalty." *America,* vol. 178, January 3, 1998, pp. 10ff. Describes a gathering of religious and lay people under the title "Envisioning a World Without Violence." Sister Helen Prejean (of *Dead Man Walking* fame) was keynote speaker at the conference, which was sponsored by the Quaker group the American Friends Service Committee.

Bedau, Hugo Adam. "A Condemned Man's Last Wish: Organ Donation and a 'Meaningful' Death." *Hastings Center Report* 9, February 1979, pp. 16–17. Debate with ethicist Michael Zeik over whether a condemned man should be allowed to choose the method by which he dies so that his organs can be donated. Bedau opposes the concept while Zeik endorses it.

Boyarsky, Bill. "Don't Bar the Public Eye at Executions." *Los Angeles Times,* December 28, 1997, p. B1. Argues that the public that authorizes the death penalty should have the right—and the duty—to see what it has wrought. Claims by authorities on behalf of prisoner privacy are hypocritical.

Brownlee, Shannon, Dan McGraw, and Jason Vest. "The Place for Vengeance: Many Grieving Families Seek Comfort in the Execution of a Murderer. Do They Find It?" *U.S. News & World Report,* vol. 122, June 16, 1997, pp. 24ff. With public support for capital punishment holding steady, an examination of opinion suggests that the desire for vengeance and closure on the part of victims' families is more important to death penalty supporters than the need for deterrence and social protection. The disregard of the legal system for victims and survivors fuels this impulse. The execution, however, does not always bring the peace they sought.

"Capital Punishment 'Cruel and Unnecessary.'" *America,* vol. 180, March 20, 1999, p. 3. Discusses the commutation of the death sentence of Darrell J. Mease after intervention by Pope John Paul II and the application of the emerging Catholic opposition to the death penalty as part of a consistent "pro-life" ethic. The article also discusses the death sentence for white supremacist John William King for a brutal dragging murder of an African American and the necessity to oppose capital punishment even in such egregious cases.

"Catechism Takes Harder Line on Death Penalty." *National Catholic Reporter,* vol. 33, September 19, 1997, p. 12. Reports that the latest Latin edition of the Catholic catechism has taken a stronger position against capital punishment, reflecting Pope John Paul II's 1995 encyclical *Evangelium Vitae.* The Roman Catholic Church now accepts use of the death penalty only when there is no question of the guilt of the accused and the state has no other way to suppress the offender. This is a situation that is expected to arise seldom if ever in developed nations.

Cohen, Daniel A. "In Defense of the Gallows: Justifications of Capital Punishment in New England Execution Sermons, 1674–1825." *American Quarterly*, vol. 40, June 1988, pp. 147ff. A historical look at religious justification for the death penalty.

Dart, John. "Executing Justice." *The Christian Century*, vol. 119, February 13, 2002, p. 6. Describes growing involvement of religious leaders and scholars in capital punishment issues, including protests and calls for a moratorium on executions. Remarks by several conference speakers (including Justice Antonin Scalia) are also summarized.

Dear, John. "Mother Teresa and the Death Penalty." *America*, vol. 180, June 19, 1999, p. 20. The author, executive director of the Fellowship of Reconciliation, recounts his contacting Mother Teresa, who agreed to intervene with various state governors to stop executions. Her simple appeal, "What would Jesus do if he were in your position?" worked in some cases but not others.

"The Death March." *The Progressive*, vol. 61, August 1997, pp. 8ff. Argues that the trial of Oklahoma City bomber Timothy McVeigh typifies Americans' growing turn toward the death penalty. Victims' relatives were not allowed to testify on behalf of a lesser penalty. In recent years courts have limited the avenues of appeal for death row inmates.

"Dissent and the Death Penalty." *National Catholic Reporter*, vol. 40, July 2, 2004, p. 28. This editorial says that the death penalty is squarely against Catholic doctrine, whose latest expression is the 1995 papal encyclical *Evangelium Vitae*. Capital punishment can be used only to defend the state against extreme danger from the criminal, and modern prisons can restrain individuals and protect society, removing any justification for execution. Therefore a Catholic politician who supports capital punishment should be treated as a dissenter and presumably confronted in the same way in which orthodox Catholics would confront persons who are prochoice.

Doyle, Kevin. "No Defense." *U.S. Catholic*, vol. 64, August 1999, p. 18. A Catholic lawyer recounts his encounters with death row inmates and sums up his opposition to the death penalty in three statements: "1. Human beings are fallible. 2. Racism is mortally sinful. 3. Human life is sacred."

Elshtain, Jean Bethke. "Sacrilege." *The New Republic*, vol. 216, June 16, 1997, p. 27. Argues that capital punishment represents the prideful usurpation of ultimate power over life and death by a secular society.

"Encyclical Condemns 'Culture of Death.'" *National Catholic Reporter*, vol. 31, April 7, 1995, p. 3. Summarizes the encyclical *Evangelium Vitae* issued by Pope John Paul II. It condemns capital punishment, together with abortion and euthanasia, as part of an immoral, destructive, and dehumanizing "culture of death."

Erez, Edna. "Thou Shalt Not Execute: Hebrew Law Perspective on Capital Punishment." *Criminology*, vol. 19, 1981, pp. 25–43. Examines the Hebraic historical and legal context for capital punishment.

Annotated Bibliography

Frame, Randy. "A Matter of Life and Death: As the Number of Executions Surges, Christians Remain Divided on the Death Penalty's Morality and Purpose." *Christianity Today*, vol. 39, August 14, 1995, pp. 50ff. The growing number of executions keeps the issue of capital punishment in the spotlight, but Christian groups are deeply divided over the sanction. Some groups, such as Murder Victims' Families for Reconciliation, oppose the death penalty and seek alternative ways to prevent crime. Most major Christian denominations officially oppose the death penalty. However, 77 percent of the population supports capital punishment in recent polling. Frame also reviews biblical and theological positions as well as the secular issues of deterrence and racial bias.

Gardner, Martin R. "Mormonism and Capital Punishment, a Doctrinal Perspective, Past and Present." *Dialogue: A Journal of Mormon Thought*, vol. 12, 1979, pp. 9–26. Explores the historical context for Mormon support of the death penalty. There appears to be little evidence of doctrinal basis for that support.

Kennedy, Eugene. "Inner Peace Restored for Victims' Families When Murderer Is Executed." *National Catholic Reporter*, vol. 35, July 2, 1999, p. 21. Catholic writer challenges the church's condemnation of capital punishment. The capital punishment debate has focused mainly on the moral situation of the state and the experience of the condemned murderer, ignoring the moral stature of the crime's survivors. The author suggests that only execution of the murderer can make the victim's survivors feel whole again and that securing such restitution is a legitimate objective of government.

Kroll, Michael. "Pro-life Parents: Their Children Were Murdered. Still, They Oppose the Death Penalty." *Mother Jones*, vol. 15, February–March 1990, p. 13. Recounts parents whose "pro-life" beliefs lead them to eschew the vengeance of capital punishment.

Linebaugh, Peter. "The Farce of the Death Penalty." *The Nation*, vol. 261, August 14, 1995, pp. 165ff. Describes the political and cultural history of capital punishment since ancient times as a farcical social ritual. Today, in a supposedly enlightened time, the farce goes on, unabated and even growing.

Malcolm, Teresa. "Activists Share Strategies for Ending Death Penalty." *National Catholic Reporter*, vol. 35, April 23, 1999, p. 3. Describes a meeting of a group called Religious Organizing Against the Death Penalty. Representatives of many faiths discuss how to better communicate their opposition to capital punishment to a public (including many of their own congregants) that strongly supports the death penalty.

———. "Tucker's Death Affected Robertson Views." *National Catholic Reporter*, vol. 35, April 23, 1999, p. 4. Describes how the involvement of Pat Robertson (formerly a death penalty supporter) and Christian Coalition activists in the struggle to spare Karla Faye Tucker from execution may have made many conservative Christians a potent new force for abolition of capital punishment.

Meilaender, Gilbert. "Capital and Other Punishments." *First Things*, November 2001, p. 8ff. Suggests that Catholic moral theology has gone somewhat astray in treating capital punishment as akin to murder. This ignores the divinely established function of government in ensuring proportional justice (retribution) and the distinction between private and public action.

Paredes, J. A. "Some Anthropological Observations on Capital Punishment in the U.S.A." *International Journal of Comparative and Applied Criminal Justice*, vol. 17, Spring/Fall 1993, pp. 219–227. Suggests that the persistence of capital punishment in the United States reflects Americans' need to reassure themselves that they can cope with the nation's murder rate, which is much higher than that of other industrialized countries. The authors argues that belief in the deterrent value of executions represents magical thinking.

Pennington, Judy. "Helen Prejean." *The Progressive*, vol. 60, January 1996, pp. 32ff. Interview with Sister Helen Prejean, whose Pulitzer Prize–nominated book *Dead Man Walking* became a successful movie in 1995. Prejean recounts how she became involved in social justice work and the struggle against capital punishment.

Perl, Paul, and Jamie S. McClintock. "The Catholic 'Consistent Life Ethic' and Attitudes toward Capital Punishment and Welfare Reform." *Sociology of Religion*, vol. 62, Fall 2001, p. 275. Presents the conclusions of a survey study that suggests that the linking of abortion, capital punishment, and support for social welfare as "life issues" by Catholic leaders has met with some success, and similar links can be found even among mainline Protestants.

Prejean, Helen. "A Way out of No Way." *America*, vol. 179, August 29, 1998, p. 7. A letter from Sister Helen Prejean to her congregation describing her ministering to death row inmate Dobbie Williams on the day he was scheduled to be executed. Human touches add poignancy to the account, in which a last-minute stay of execution is granted.

Reiman, Jeffrey H. "Justice, Civilization, and the Death Penalty: Answering van den Haag." *Philosophy and Public Affairs*, vol. 14, 1985, pp. 115–148. Advocates the abolition of the death penalty and refutes pro–capital punishment arguments advanced by Ernest van den Haag.

Riga, Peter J. "The Death Chamber." *America*, vol. 172, February 18, 1995, pp. 20ff. A former prison chaplain recounts his close relationship with a decorated Vietnam veteran who had been sent to death row for the killing of two policemen, how he accompanied him to the gas chamber, remaining in eye contact with him as he died. The author believes that the "awesome and mysterious" nature of death is such that no human should have the moral power to kill another.

Rosin, Hanna. "Catholic, Jewish Leaders Target Death Penalty in National Effort; Group Aims to Abolish Practice by Raising Moral Awareness." *Washington Post*, December 6, 1999, p. A02. Reports on a new joint campaign between Catholic and Jewish activists that seeks to revive the dormant religious movement against the death penalty.

Saletan, William. "TRB From Washington: Life Time." *The New Republic*, June 19, 2000, p. 6. The author notes that many conservatives, including evangelist Pat Robertson, columnist George Will, and Illinois governor George Ryan, have all had second thoughts about the death penalty and indeed a number have come out against it. However while "pro-life" leaders stress the link between opposition to capital punishment and to abortion, the author believes that the more relevant connection is that both antiabortion laws and capital punishment put life and death decisions in the hands of a state that is ill equipped to give them individualized consideration.

Scalia, Antonin. "God's Justice and Ours." *First Things*, May 2002, p. 17ff. A Supreme Court justice gives his personal opinion on the morality of the death penalty. Scalia suggests that any judge who sincerely believes the death penalty to be immoral should resign rather than ignore the duly enacted constitution and laws. He goes on to say that the attack on the death penalty arises largely from the modern tendency to assume that the standards for moral action for the state should be no different from those for private individuals. He also disagrees with current official Catholic teaching that says that the death penalty can be imposed only if necessary to protect society, not for retribution.

Schwarzschild, Henry. "A Social and Moral Atrocity." *ABA Journal*, vol. 71, April 1985, pp. 38–42. A debate about capital punishment with proponent Ernest van den Haag.

"Speaking ex Soapbox." *National Review*, vol. 47, December 11, 1995, pp. 22ff. Argues that the moral equivalency implied in recent U.S. Catholic Conference statements condemning abortion, capital punishment, welfare reform, and sanctions against illegal aliens is not justified. The culpability of these different classes of people is quite different.

Web Documents

Cauthen, Kenneth. "Capital Punishment." Available online. URL: http://www.frontiernet.com/~kenc/cappun.htm. Posted on March 15, 1996. Originally published as a chapter in the author's *Toward a New Modernism*, this piece argues that while two valid moral principles (love and justice) can lead to opposing conclusions about the validity of capital punishment, the moral arguments against capital punishment as actually practiced in the real world are overwhelming.

Hinman, Lawrence M. "The Death Penalty." University of San Diego. Available online. URL: http://ethics.sandiego.edu/presentations/AppliedEthics/DeathPenalty/index_files/frame.htm. Posted on March 16, 2001. An online PowerPoint presentation by a professor of ethics at a Catholic university. It combines discussion of ethical and pragmatic issues involving capital punishment.

CHAPTER 8

ORGANIZATIONS AND AGENCIES

This chapter presents a selection of organizations and agencies concerned with capital punishment and related issues. The listings are broken down into four categories:

- Government and academic organizations that provide statistics and other resources. These usually do not take a position for or against capital punishment.
- National advocacy organizations, nearly all of which promote abolition of the death penalty.
- State and local organizations: these are mainly abolitionist in perspective.
- International organizations for the abolition of capital punishment.

Where available, Web (URL) and e-mail addresses have been provided in addition to phone numbers and postal addresses. A brief description of the group's focus or activities is also given for government and academic organizations and for international organizations. (Phrases in quotes are taken from the organizations' web sites.)

It should be noted that contact information for the more local or obscure groups frequently changes, and such groups often become defunct or dormant. The major resource web sites discussed in Chapter 6 are a good place to look for up-to-date information and links to organizations.

GOVERNMENT AND ACADEMIC ORGANIZATIONS

Bureau of Justice Statistics
URL: http://www.ojp.usdoj.gov/bjs
E-mail: askbjs@usdoj.gov
Phone: (202) 307-0765
810 Seventh Street, NW
Washington, DC 20001

Provides a wide range of statistics relating to the criminal justice system, including courts, sentencing, and corrections (prisons). Produces annual summary report on capital punishment in the United States.

Capital Jury Project (CJP)
URL: http://www.cjp.neu.edu
Based at Northeastern University, the CJP conducts in-depth surveys and studies of the decision-making process of jurors in capital cases. The results are analyzed to see whether they are in accordance with the standards implied by the Supreme Court's decisions starting with *Furman v. Georgia* (1972). The web site includes references to articles based on the project's research.

Cornell Law School Death Penalty Project
URL: http://www.lawschool.cornell.edu/lawlibrary/death
E-mail: deathpenalty@cornell.edu
Phone: (607) 255-7477
c/o Cornell Law School
Myron Taylor Hall
Ithaca, NY 14853-4901
Consists of a Capital Punishment Clinic offering law students the opportunity to learn about capital defense practice while helping capital defense attorneys; a program for continuing education for capital defense attorneys; and a research and data collection program.

Federal Bureau of Investigation
URL: http://www.fbi.gov
E-mail: Web forms
Phone: (202) 324-3000
935 Pennsylvania Avenue, NW
Washington, DC 20535-0001
Issues the uniform crime reports, a basic source for criminal justice research.

Federal Bureau of Prisons
URL: http://www.bop.gov
E-mail: webmaster@bop.gov
Phone: (202) 307-3198
320 1st Street, NW
Washington, DC 20534
Provides extensive information about the operation of prisons.

House Judiciary Committee
URL: http://www.house.gov/judiciary
E-mail: Judiciary@mail.house.gov
Phone: (202) 225-3951
2138 Rayburn House Office Building
Washington, DC 20515
Important source for crime and justice-related legislative developments in the House of Representatives.

Justice Research and Statistics Association
URL: http://www.jrsainfo.org
E-mail: cjinfo@jrsa.org
Phone: (202) 842-9329
777 North Capital Street, NE #801
Washington, DC 20002
Clearinghouse for state Statistical Analysis Centers (SACs); provides coordination and training for government statisticians and other researchers.

Legal Services Corporation
URL: http://www.lsc.gov
E-mail: Web form
Phone: (202) 295-1500
3333 K Street NW
3rd Floor
Washington, DC 20007-3522
Nonprofit federally funded corporation that promotes "equal justice under the law for all Americans." The corporation funds local legal services agencies for representing the poor.

National Institute of Justice
URL: http://www.ojp.usdoj.gov/
nij/
E-mail: Web form
Phone: (202) 307-2942
810 7th Street, NW
Washington, DC 20531
Research and development arm of the Department of Justice. The institute provides the NCJRS (National Criminal Justice Reference Service) abstracts database, an important source of information on criminal justice–related publications.

Senate Judiciary Committee
URL: http://judiciary.senate.gov
Phone: (202) 224-5225
224 Dirksen Senate Office
Building
Washington, DC 20510
Important source for information on pending federal criminal justice legislation.

U.S. Commission on Civil Rights
URL: http://www.usccr.gov/
index.html
E-mail: wwwadmin@usccr.gov
(webmaster)
Phone: (202) 376-8128
624 9th Street, Northwest
Washington, DC 20425
An "independent, bipartisan fact-finding agency" established to investigate civil rights violations and to collect information about civil rights problems.

U.S. Department of Justice
URL: http://www.usdoj.gov
E-mail: AskDOJ@usdoj.gov
Phone: (202) 514-2000

950 Pennsylvania Avenue, NW
Washington, DC 20530-0001
Parent organization of the Attorney General's Office, FBI, Federal Bureau of Prisons, Bureau of Justice Statistics, and other organizations.

U.S. Sentencing Commission
URL: http://www.ussc.gov
E-mail: pubaffairs@ussc.gov
Phone: (202) 273-4500
1 Columbus Circle, NE
Suite 2-500
South Lobby
Washington, DC 20002-8002
Government body charged with establishing and reviewing federal sentencing guidelines.

U.S. Supreme Court
URL: http://www.supremecourtus.
gov
Phone: (202) 479-3211
1 1st Street, NE
Washington, DC 20543
The Court's sparse web site provides some basic information and links.

NATIONAL ADVOCACY GROUPS

Abolitionist Action Committee
URL: http://abolition.org
E-mail: aac@abolition.org
Phone: (800) 973-6548
c/o Citizens United for
Alternatives to the Death
Penalty
PMB 335
2603 Dr. Martin Luther King, Jr.,
Highway
Gainesville, FL 32609

Organizations and Agencies

"An ad-hoc group of individuals committed to highly visible and effective public education for alternatives to the death penalty through nonviolent direct action." The group is a division of Citizens United for Alternatives to the Death Penalty (CUADP).

American Bar Association (ABA)
Criminal Justice Section
URL: http://www.abanet.org/
  crimjust
E-mail: crimjustice@abanet.org
Phone: (202) 662-1500
740 15th Street, NW
Washington, DC 20005-1002
Division of America's largest lawyers' organization that is concerned with criminal procedure issues.

American Civil Liberties Union
(ACLU)
Capital Punishment Project
(CPP)
URL: http://www.aclu.org/
  DeathPenalty
E-mail: Web form
Phone: (212) 549-2585
125 Broad Street
18th Floor
New York, NY 10004
The ACLU is a consistent and vigorous opponent of capital punishment on constitutional, procedural, and philosophical grounds. The CPP files "friend of the court" briefs in capital punishment cases. Their web site includes an index to ACLU materials on capital punishment, congressional action, archives, and links to other resources. There is also a searchable news database.

American Friends Service
Committee
URL: http://www.afsc.org
E-mail: afscinfo@afsc.org
Phone: (215) 241-7000
1501 Cherry Street
Philadelphia, PA 19102
National Quaker organization has a variety of local programs that work on anti–death penalty advocacy.

Amnesty International U.S.A.
Program to Abolish the Death
Penalty
URL: http://www.amnesty-usa.
  org/abolish
E-mail: aimember@aiusa.org
Phone: (212) 807-8400
5 Penn Plaza
14th Floor
New York, NY 10001
U.S. division of the worldwide human rights organization. The organization has a web page for its anti–death penalty campaign at http://www.amnesty-usa.org/abolish/index.html that provides information and a featured campaign.

Campaign to End the Death
Penalty
URL: http://www.nodeathpenalty.
  org
E-mail: Web form
Phone: (773) 955-4841
P.O. Box 25730
Chicago, IL 60625
National organization with chapters in a number of cities. Its purpose is to publicize and campaign for death penalty issues. The campaign has a newsletter, *The New Abolitionist*, which is also available at the organization's web site.

Capital Punishment Research Project
Phone: (334) 693-5225
P.O. Drawer 277
Headland, AL 36345
Maintains a massive database of information about executions in America, with over 19,000 case files.

Catholics Against Capital Punishment
URL: http://www.igc.org/cacp
E-mail: Web form
Phone: (301) 654-0925 (fax)
(no voice)
P.O. Box 5706
Bethesda, MD 20824-5706
National organization to promote abolition of capital punishment in accordance with the teachings of the Catholic Church.

Center for Constitutional Rights
URL: http://www.ccr-ny.org
E-mail: info@ccr-ny.org
Phone: (212) 614-6464
666 Broadway
7th Floor
New York, NY 10012
A general organization dedicated to advance and to protect the rights guaranteed in the U.S. Constitution and the Universal Declaration of Human Rights through advocacy and education.

Citizens for a Moratorium on Federal Executions
URL: http://www.
federalmoratorium.org
E-mail: comments@
federalmoratorium.org
Phone: (202) 675-2316
P.O. Box 92726
Washington, DC 20090

This group was formed in the mid-1990s in response to the first federal executions in nearly 40 years. The group called upon presidents George H. W. Bush and Bill Clinton to halt federal executions pending a full review of the fairness of the federal capital punishment system.

Citizens United for Alternatives to the Death Penalty (CUADP)
URL: www.cuadp.org
E-mail: cuadp@cuadp.org
Phone: (800) 973-6548
PMB 335
2603 Dr. Martin Luther King Jr. Highway
Gainesville, FL 32609
Organization that coordinates and assists anti–death penalty campaigns, working toward an eventual goal of abolishing capital punishment in the United States. Their web site provides a variety of resources and action items.

Citizens United for Rehabilitation of Errants (CURE)
URL: http://www.
curenational.org/index1.html
E-mail: Web form
Phone: (202) 789-2126
P.O. Box 2310
Washington, DC 20013-2310
A criminal justice and prison reform organization that seeks effective alternatives for the reduction of crime and humane treatment of the incarcerated. CURE has a number of state and local affiliates.

Criminal Justice Legal Foundation
URL: http://www.cjlf.org
E-mail: Rushford@cjlf.org

Phone: (916) 446-0345
P.O. Box 1199
Sacramento, CA 95812
Established in 1982, the CRLF is "dedicated to restoring a balance between crime victims and the criminally accused." Because it believes this balance has tipped too far toward the latter, the CRLF advocates and litigates for victims' rights and for making the justice system swifter and more efficient consistent with constitutional requirements. The organization is generally pro–death penalty.

Death Penalty Information Center (DPIC)
URL: http://www.deathpenaltyinfo.org
E-mail: Web form
Phone: (202) 293-6970
1320 Eighteenth Street, NW
5th Floor
Washington, DC 20036
Provides in-depth resources and briefing papers on death penalty–related issues for the media and the general public. DPIC is not explicitly abolitionist but heavily emphasizes abolitionist materials.

Death Row Support Project
URL: http://www.brethren.org/genbd/witness/drsp.htm
E-mail: cobweb@brethren.org
Phone: (260) 982-7480
P.O. Box 600
Liberty Mills, IN 46946
Primarily engaged in providing support for death row inmates and facilitating correspondence (pen pals) to keep them linked to the outside community.

Equal Justice USA
URL: http://www.quixote.org/ej
E-mail: ejusa@curixote.org
Phone: (301) 699-0042
Quixote Center
P.O. Box 5206
Hyattsville, MD 20782
A program of the Quixote Center, primarily working on a Moratorium Now! campaign to gather resolutions calling for an end to the death penalty.

Fellowship of Reconciliation
URL: http://forusa.org
E-mail: Web form
Phone: (845) 358-4601
521 North Broadway
Nyack, NY 10960
An interfaith peace and justice organization with many local affiliates. Its areas of concern include criminal justice, prisons, and opposition to the death penalty.

Friends Committee on National Legislation
URL: http://www.fcnl.org
E-mail: fcnl@fcnl.org
Phone: (202) 547-6000
245 Second Street, NE
Washington, DC 20002-5795
A Quaker organization promoting social justice through legislation. It includes abolition of the death penalty as one of its issues.

Jewish Peace Fellowship
URL: http://www.jewishpeacefellowship.org
E-mail: jpf@forusa.org
Phone: (914) 358-4601
P.O. Box 271
Nyack, NY 10960

Capital Punishment

Organization that began as a counseling service for Jewish conscientious objectors but now serves a variety of social justice issues. The organization opposes capital punishment as a violation of Jewish tradition.

Journey of Hope . . . From Violence to Healing Inc.
URL: http://www.journeyofhope.org
E-mail: bill@journeyofhope.org
Phone: (877) 924-4483
P.O. Box 210390
Anchorage, AK 99521-0390
An educational organization whose purpose is "to spotlight murder victims family members who do not seek revenge, and have chosen to promote compassion for all humanity."

Justice for All
URL: http://www.jfa.net
E-mail: info@jfa.net
Phone: (713) 935-9300
Pro–death penalty and victim's rights organization. The organization opposes appeals and paroles for murderers. Web site has news and case updates and offers a newsletter and discussion forum.

MacArthur Justice Center
URL: http://macarthur.uchicago.edu
E-mail: Web form
Phone: (773) 702-9494
University of Chicago Law School
1111 East 60th Street
Chicago, IL 60637
This nonprofit public-interest law firm is affiliated with the University of Chicago. Its litigation specialties include death penalty clemency appeals

and DNA testing petitions as well as issues concerning prison conditions, prisoner rights, and compensation for wrongfully convicted persons.

Mennonite Central Committee USA
Office on Crime and Justice
URL: http://www.mcc.org
E-mail: mailbox@mcc.org
Phone: (717) 859-1151
21 South 12th Street
P.O. Box 500
Akron, PA 17501-0500
Works on a variety of social issues including abolition of the death penalty.

Murder Victims Families for Reconciliation
URL: http://www.mvfr.org
E-mail: info@mvfr.org
Phone: (617) 868-0007
2161 Massachusetts Avenue
Cambridge, MA 02140
Organization that unites families of murder victims with families of executed persons. The organization seeks to promote healing for victims as an alternative to the death penalty and the "cycle of violence."

NAACP Legal Defense and Educational Fund
URL: http://www.naacpldf.org
E-mail: Web form
Phone: (210) 965-2200
99 Hudson Street
Suite 1600
New York, NY 10013-2897
One of the oldest and most effective civil rights litigation organizations. The organization played an important role in the legal assault on the death penalty that culminated in the *Furman v. Georgia* case in 1972.

National Association of Criminal Defense Lawyers (NACDL)
URL: http://www.nacdl.org
E-mail: assist@nacdl.com
Phone: (202) 872-8600
1150 18th Street, NW
Suite 950
Washington, DC 20036
Organization of defense attorneys promoting legal reforms and the rights of defendants. NACDL has a committee on death penalty issues.

National Bar Association
URL: http://www.nationalbar.org
E-mail: nba@nationalbar.org
Phone: (202) 842-3900
1225 W Street, NW
Washington, DC 20001-4217
Organization of (primarily African-American) attorneys, dedicated to professional development and the protection of civil rights.

National Black Police Association
URL: http://www.blackpolice.org
E-mail: NBPANATOFC@world.
net
Phone: (202) 986-2070
3251 Mt. Pleasant Street, NW
2nd Floor
Washington, DC 20010-2103
Promotes relations between police and the community and criminal justice reform.

National Coalition to Abolish the Death Penalty
URL: http://www.ncadp.org
E-mail: swisely@ncadp.org
Phone: (202) 543-9577
920 Pennsylvania Avenue, SE
Suite 104
Washington, DC 20003

Educational coalition organization whose web site provides news, alerts and links, including a link to a comprehensive directory of abolitionist organizations.

National Conference of Black Lawyers
URL: http://www.ncbl.org
Phone: (866) 266-5091
P.O. Box 80043
Lansing, MI 48908-0043
Activist civil rights legal organization. The organization advocates against the death penalty.

National Council on Crime and Delinquency
URL: http://www.nccd-crc.org
E-mail: aboldun@nccd-crc.org
Phone: (510) 208-0500
1970 Broadway
Suite 500
Oakland, CA 94612
Conducts research to develop policies to reduce crime and delinquency and to promote a fair, humane, and effective legal system. The organization opposes capital punishment as a violation of these principles.

National District Attorney's Association
URL: http://www.ndaa.org
E-mail: webmaster@ndaa-apri.
org
Phone: (703) 549-9222
99 Canal Center Plaza, #510
Alexandria, VA 22314
Formed in 1950 (originally as the National Association of County and Prosecuting Attorneys) in response to the growth of crime and the increasing demand for community protection.

National Lawyers Guild (NLG)
URL: http://www.nlg.org
E-mail: nlgno@nlg.org
Phone: (212) 679-5100
143 Madison Avenue
4th Floor
New York, NY 10016
Left-wing lawyers group that seeks to use the legal system to protect people from oppressive institutions. The NLG works on many issues including the death penalty.

National Legal Aid & Defender Association
URL: http://www.nlada.org
E-mail: info@nlada.org
Phone: (202) 452-0620
1140 Connecticut Avenue, NW
Suite 900
Washington, DC 20036
Provides training and support for lawyers who represent poor people, including death row inmates.

Parents of Murdered Children
URL: http://www.pomc.com
E-mail: Natlpomc@aol.org
Phone: (888) 818-POMC
100 East Eighth Street, B-41
Cincinnati, OH 45202
Supports families of homicide victims, assists in solving murder cases and in opposing parole for convicted murderers, advocates tougher criminal justice policies, and helps victims cope with the criminal justice system.

Partisan Defense Committee
Phone: (510) 839-0852
P.O. Box 77462
San Francisco, CA 94107
Left-wing organization that fights for issues such as opposition to the death penalty on the basis of class struggle.

Presbyterian Church (USA)
Criminal Justice Program
URL: http://pcusa.org/
    criminaljustice
E-mail: Web form
Phone: (888) 728-7228 ext. 5803
100 Witherspoon Street
Louisville, KY 40202
Part of the National Ministries Division, a ministry of the General Assembly Council, Presbyterian Church (USA). The organization examines the criminal justice system from a religious perspective.

Prison Radio
URL: http://www.prisonradio.org
E-mail: info@prisonradio.org
Phone: (415) 648-4505
P.O. Box 411074
San Francisco, CA 94141
Helps set up opportunities for prisoners to communicate with the public via radio. Death row inmates and death penalty issues are one of the organization's focuses.

Project Hope to Abolish the Death Penalty
URL: http://www.phadp.org
E-mail: beesther@earthlink.net
Phone: (334) 499-0003
P.O. Box 1362
Lanett, AL 36863
Originally founded in 1989 by Alabama death row inmates, this organization seeks to educate the public about death penalty issues and to support death row inmates and their families.

Religious Organizing Against the Death Penalty Project
URL: http://www. deathpenaltyreligious.org
E-mail: information@deathpenalty religious.org
Phone: (215) 241-7130
c/o Criminal Justice Program
American Friends Service Committee
1501 Cherry Street
Philadelphia, PA 19102
Organization dedicated to mobilizing and coordinating the efforts of the many churches that have come out against the death penalty. The organization promotes advocacy and helping faith communities minister to the needs of death row inmates, their families, and the families of crime victims.

The Sentencing Project
URL: http://www. sentencingproject.org/
E-mail: Web form
Phone: (202) 628-0871
514 Tenth Street, NW
Suite 1000
Washington, DC 20004
Independent criminal justice policy analysis, education, and research group. The project calls for a "rational debate on crime and punishment."

Southern Center for Human Rights (SCHR)
URL: http://www.schr.org/center/ index.html
E-mail: rights@schr.org
Phone: (404) 688-1202
83 Poplar Street, NW
Atlanta, GA 30303-2122
Organization that advocates for civil rights and criminal justice reform, including rights of capital defendants. SCHR also has a Death Penalty Resource Counsel provided by the National Association of Criminal Defense Lawyers.

Truth in Justice
URL: http://www.truthinjustice. org/
E-mail: truthinjusticeproject@ yahoo.com
Organization dedicated to freeing persons believed to be wholly innocent and wrongly convicted. The organization critiques misuse of forensic evidence ("junk science"). Its web site offers links to books and other resources.

Unitarian Universalists for Alternatives to the Death Penalty
URL: http://www.uuadp.org
E-mail: Web form
P.O. Box 2337
Chester, VA 23831-8445
A social activist group "seeking to bear witness to the [Unitarian Universalist] resolutions of past years calling for an end to capital punishment."

STATE AND LOCAL ADVOCACY ORGANIZATIONS

Note: States listed here represent those in which the debate over capital punishment is most active. For reasons of space, many state affiliates of national

243

organizations are not listed here nor are many local groups or branches. Contact the national organization (or see its web site) for information about local affiliates.

ALABAMA

Alabama Committee to Abolish the Death Penalty
URL: http://www.angelfire.com/al4/alajustice/news.html
E-mail: hilesjones@aol.com
P.O. Box 948
Leeds, AL 35094

Alabama New South Coalition
E-mail: vineyfig@mindspring.com
Phone: (334) 499-2380
Justice Peace Committee
11076 Country Road 267
Lanett, AL 36863

Alabama Prison Project
E-mail: addvocat@bellsouth.net
Phone: (334) 264-7416
215 Clayton Street
Montgomery, AL 36104

Equal Justice Initiative
E-mail: contact_us@ej.org
Phone: (334) 269-1803
122 Commerce Street
Montgomery, AL 36104

ALASKA

Alaskans Against the Death Penalty
URL: http://www.aadp.info
Phone: (907) 258-2296
P.O. Box 202296
Anchorage, AK 99520-2296

ARIZONA

Coalition of Arizonans to Abolish the Death Penalty
URL: http://www.azabolitionist.org
E-mail: webmaster@azabolitionist.org
Phone: (520) 325-6240
P.O. Box 42465
Tucson, AZ 85733

Sanctity of Life, People Against Executions (SOLPAE)
E-mail: norguard@earthlink.net
Phone: (520) 325-6240
4123 East Roberts Place
Tucson, AZ 85711

ARKANSAS

Arkansas Coalition to Abolish the Death Penalty
E-mail: oakleaf@aol.com
Phone: (501) 663-2414
904 West 2nd Street
Suite 1
Little Rock, AR 72205

CALIFORNIA

California Appellate Project
Phone: (800) 779-0507
One Ecker Place, Suite 400
San Francisco, CA 94105

California Coalition for Alternatives to the Death Penalty
URL: http://www.igc.apc.org/sjpc/ccadp.htm

E-mail: sjpc@sjpeace.org
Phone: (408) 297-2299

California Innocence Project
E-mail: jpb@cwest.edu
Phone: (619) 525-1485
225 Cedar Street
San Diego, CA 92101

Death Penalty Focus of California
URL: http://www.deathpenalty.org
E-mail: info@deathpenalty.org
Phone: (415) 243-0143
870 Market Street
Suite 859
San Francisco, CA 94102

COLORADO

Coloradans Against the Death
  Penalty
URL: http://www.coadp.org
E-mail: info@coadp.org
Phone: (303) 715-3163
P.O. Box 1745
Denver, CO 80201-1745

CONNECTICUT

Connecticut Network to Abolish
  the Death Penalty
URL: http://www.nadp.org/cnadp
E-mail: robertnadp@cnadp.org
Phone: (203) 206-9584
571 Farmington Avenue
Hartford, CT 06105-3051

United Students Against the
  Death Penalty
URL: http://members.tripod.com/
  ~deathpenalty
E-mail: ahinds@wesleyan.edu
Phone: (860) 685-4734
Box 4596

222 Church Street
Middletown, CT 06459-4596

DELAWARE

Delaware Citizens Opposed to
  the Death Penalty
URL: http://dcodp.org
E-mail: pinterris@aol.com
Phone: (302) 656-2721
1304 North Rodney Street
Wilmington, DE 19806-4227

FLORIDA

Florida Coalition to Abolish the
  Death Penalty
E-mail: NANSFAB@aol.com
Phone: (941) 332-3449
2363 Union Street
Fort Myers, FL 33901

Floridians for Alternatives to the
  Death Penalty
URL: http://www.fadp.org
E-mail: fadp@fadp.org
Phone: (800) 973-6548
PMB 335
2603 Dr. Martin Luther King Jr.
  Highway
Gainesville, FL 32609

GEORGIA

Georgia Resource Center
Phone: (404) 614-2014
101 Marrieta Tower, Suite 3300
Atlanta, GA 30303

Koinonia Prison and Jail Project
URL: http://www.ccda.org/g-l/
  koinonia.html
E-mail: koinonia@habitat.org
Phone: (912) 924-0391

1324 Georgia Highway 49 South
Americus, GA 31709

New Hope House
Phone: (770) 358-1148
P.O. Box 1213
Griffin, GA 30224

Prison and Jail Project
Phone: (229) 928-2080
P.O. Box 6749
Americus, GA 31709

Southern Prison Ministry
c/o The Open Door Community
Phone: (404) 874-9652
910 Ponce de Leon Avenue
Atlanta, GA 30306-4212

Team Defense Project
Phone: (404) 688-8116
P.O. Box 1728
Atlanta, GA 30301

ILLINOIS

Campaign to End the Death
 Penalty
URL: http://www.nodeathpenalty.
 org
Phone: (773) 955-4841
P.O. Box 25730
Chicago, IL 60625

Illinois Coalition Against the
 Death Penalty
URL: http://www.icadp.org
E-mail: info@icadp.org
Phone: (312) 849-2279
180 North Michigan Avenue
Suite 2300
Chicago, IL 60601-7401

Lutheran Social Services
Prisoner & Family Ministry

Phone: (708) 635-4627
1001 Touhy Avenue
Des Plaines, IL 60018

INDIANA

Indiana Citizens to Abolish
 Capital Punishment
URL: http://www.icacp.org
E-mail: info@icacp
Phone: (317) 466-7128
P.O. Box 55033
Indianapolis, IN 46205

L.O.V.(E), Inc.
Love Over Vengeance/Empathy
Phone: (219) 879-4146
P.O. Box 2151
Michigan City, IN 46361

IOWA

Criminal Justice Ministries
E-mail: cjmcure@home.com
Phone: (515) 282-0549
P.O. Box 4718
Des Moines, IA 50306-4718

Iowans Against the Death Penalty
URL: http://www.iadp.org
E-mail: iadp_iadp@hotmail.com
Phone: (515) 243-3988 ext. 12
P.O. Box 65397
West Des Moines, IA 50265-6539

KANSAS

Kansas Coalition Against the
 Death Penalty
URL: http://www.kscadp.org
E-mail: kcadp1176@aol.com
Phone: (785) 232-2272
1176 Warren
Topeka, KS 66604

246

Murder Victims Families for
 Reconciliation
Victim Services
Phone: (785) 291-3393
1176 SW Warren Avenue
Topeka, KS 66604

KENTUCKY

Kentucky Coalition to Abolish
 the Death Penalty
URL: http://www.kcadp.org
E-mail: kcadp@earthlink.net
Phone: (502) 585-2895
P.O. Box 3092
Louisville, KY 40201-3092

LOUISIANA

Bienville House Center for Peace
 & Justice
Capital Trials Project
URL: http://www.igc.apc.org/
 bhcfpj
E-mail: gesserve@aol.com
Phone: (504) 344-0405
P.O. Box 4363
Baton Rouge, LA 70821

Louisiana Association of Criminal
 Defense Lawyers
Death Penalty Committee
E-mail: jimboren@bellsouth.net
Phone: (225) 387-5796
830 Main Street
Baton Rouge, LA 70802

Louisiana Coalition to Abolish
 the Death Penalty
Pilgrimage for Life
URL: http://www.lcadp.org
E-mail: info@lcadp.org
Phone: (225) 338-0113
P.O. Box 64635
Baton Rouge, LA 70896

MAINE

Mainers Against the Death
 Penalty
E-mail: dgilpatrick@mdv.org
Phone: (207) 774-5444
P.O. Box 8703
Portland, ME 04101

MARYLAND

Maryland CASE
URL: http://www.mdcase.org
E-mail: info@mdcase.org
Phone: (410) 243-8020
P.O. Box 39205
Baltimore, MD 21212

MASSACHUSETTS

Massachusetts Citizens Against
 the Death Penalty
URL: http://www.mcadp.org
E-mail: mcadp@earthlink.net
Phone: (617) 523-3951
P.O. Box 51920
Boston, MA 02106

MICHIGAN

AFSC Michigan Criminal Justice
 Program
E-mail: pryder@afsc.org
Phone: (734) 761-7283
1414 Hill Street
Ann Arbor, MI 48104

Michigan Coalition Against the
 Death Penalty
Phone: (248) 626-7606
2128 Scotten
Detroit, MI 48209

Michigan Committee Against
 Capital Punishment

Phone: (517) 484-4165
1715 Abington Place
Lansing, MI 48910

MINNESOTA

Minnesota Advocates for Human
  Rights
Death Penalty Defense Project
URL: http://www.mnadvocates.
  org/
E-mail: hrights@mnadvocates.org
Phone: (612) 341-3302
310 4th Avenue South
Suite 1000
Minneapolis, MN 55415-1012

Minnesota Coalition to Abolish
  the Death Penalty
Phone: (651) 645-4097
1821 University Avenue, # N-392
St. Paul, MN 55104

MISSISSIPPI

Mississippians for Alternatives to
  the Death Penalty
URL: http://www.madp.us
E-mail: mcgillkenl@aol.com
Phone: (662) 416-1981
7760 Deerfield CV
Southaven, MS 38671-5014

MISSOURI

Criminal Justice Ministry
E-mail: CJM99@earthlink.net
Phone: (314) 241-0862
1408 South Tenth Street
St. Louis, MO 63104

Eastern Missouri Coalition to
  Abolish the Death Penalty
URL: http://www.mindspring.
  com/~emcadp/

E-mail: william.colbert@juno.com
Phone: (314) 241-8062
1408 South 10th Street
St. Louis, MO 63104

Missouri Coalition Against the
  Death Penalty
E-mail: linhandt@mocatholic.org
Phone: (573) 635-7239
P.O. Box 1022
Jefferson City, MO 65102

Missourians to Abolish the Death
  Penalty
URL: http://moabolition.org
E-mail: info@moabilition.com
Phone: (573) 635-7239
P.O. Box 54
Jefferson City, MO 65102

Western Missouri Coalition to
  Abolish the Death Penalty
URL: http://home.kc.rr.com/
  wmcadp
E-mail: wmcadp@spcglobal.net
P.O. Box 45302
Kansas City, MO 64171

MONTANA

Montana Abolition Coalition
URL: http://www.aclumontana.
  org/PubEd/AbolitionCoaltion
  .htm
E-mail: scottc@aclumontana.org
Phone: (406) 248-1086
P.O. Box 1663
Helena, MT 59624

Montana Ad Hoc Abolition
  Coalition
URL: http://www.helenamontana.
  com/abolition
E-mail: ambk@in-tch.com

NEBRASKA

Nebraskans Against the Death
  Penalty
URL: http://nadp.inetnebr.com
Phone: (402) 477-7787
941 O Street, Suite 725
Lincoln, NE 68508

NEVADA

Office of the Special Public
  Defender
Phone: (702) 455-6265
309 South 3rd Street
4th Floor
Las Vegas, NV 89155-2316

NEW HAMPSHIRE

New Hampshire Citizens Against
  the Death Penalty
41 A Court Street
Dover, NH 03820

NEW JERSEY

New Jerseyans for Alternatives to
  the Death Penalty
URL: http://www.njadp.org
E-mail: ksisti@njadp.org
Phone: (856) 854-3182
986 South Broad Street
Trenton, NJ 08611

NEW MEXICO

Committee to Stop Executions
Phone: (505) 827-3909
P.O. Box 1911
Santa Fe, NM 87504

New Mexico Coalition to Repeal
  the Death Penalty
URL: http://www.nmrepeal.org
E-mail: info@nmrepeal.org
Phone: (505) 986-9536
P.O. Box 8552
Santa Fe, NM 87504

NEW YORK

New York Civil Liberties
  Union
URL: http://www.nyclu.org
E-mail: nyclu@nyclu.org
Phone: (212) 344-3005
125 Broad Street
New York, NY 10004

New Yorkers Against the Death
  Penalty
URL: http://nyadp.org
E-mail: info@nyadp.org
Phone: (518) 453-6797
40 North Main Avenue
Albany, NY 12203

New York Lawyers Against the
  Death Penalty
Phone: (212) 735-2226
4 Times Square
24th Floor
New York, NY 10036-6595

New York State Defenders
  Association
URL: http://nysda.org
E-mail: info@nysda.org
194 Washington Avenue,
  Suite 500
Albany, NY 12210-2314

NORTH CAROLINA

Carolina Justice Policy Center
Phone: (919) 682-1149
P.O. Box 3092
Durham, NC 27702

Center for Death Penalty
  Litigation
Phone: (919) 956-9545
123 West Main Street, Suite 500
Durham, NC 27701

North Carolinians Against the
  Death Penalty
E-mail: geoffrey_mock@duke.edu
Phone: (919) 681-4514
1008 Lamond Avenue
Durham, NC 2770

People of Faith Against the Death
  Penalty
URL: http://pfadp.org
E-mail: info@pfadp.org
Phone: (919) 933-7567
110 Main Street, Suite 2-G
Carrboro, NC 27510

Seamless Garment Network
URL: http://www.seamless-
  garment.org
E-mail: consistentlife@aol.com
Phone: (919) 779-8766
P.O. Box 792
Garner, NC 27529

Western Carolinians for Criminal
  Justice
Phone: (704) 252-2485
P.O. Box 7472
Asheville, NC 28802

OHIO

Ohioans to Stop Executions
URL: http://www.otse.org/
E-mail: eunice@jipc-
  cincinnati.org
Phone: (614) 560-0654
9 E. Long Street, Suite 201
Columbus, OH 43215

OKLAHOMA

Death Penalty Institute of
  Oklahoma
URL: http://www.dpio.org
E-mail: Comments@dpio.org
Phone: (918) 809-7628
PMB 131
3728 South Elm Place
Broken Arrow, OK 74011

Oklahoma Coalition to Abolish
  the Death Penalty
URL: http://www.ocadp.org
E-mail: pr@ocadp.org
Phone: (405) 427-1111
P.O. Box 713
Oklahoma City, OK 73101

Oklahoma Indigent Defense
  System
Capital Post-Conviction Division
Legal Services
URL: http://www.state.ok.us/~oids
E-mail: webmaster@oids.ok.state.
  us
Phone: (405) 801-2601
P.O. Box 926
Norman, OK 73070

OREGON

Oregon Coalition to Abolish the
  Death Penalty
URL: http://members.tripod.com/
  ocadp
E-mail: ckp@open.org
Phone: (503) 249-1556
P.O. Box 361
Portland, OR 97207

PENNSYLVANIA

Center Region Coalition to
  Abolish the Death Penalty
Phone: (814) 238-1983

P.O. Box 502
State College, PA 16804

Northeast Pennsylvania Coalition
  Against the Death Penalty
Phone: (570) 342-4117
716 North Washington Avenue
Scranton, PA 18509

Pennsylvania Abolitionists United
  Against the Death Penalty
URL: http://www.pa-
  abolitionists.org
E-mail: PAUADP@aol.com
Phone: (215) 724-6120
Jeffrey Garis, Director
P.O. Box 58128
Philadelphia, PA 19102

Pennsylvania Coalition to Abolish
  the Death Penalty
Phone: (215) 564-6005 ext. 7919
c/o Pennsylvania Prison Society
2000 Spring Garden Street
Philadelphia, PA 19130

Western Pennsylvania Coalition
  Against the Death Penalty
Phone: (412) 761-4319
P.O. Box 9125
Pittsburgh, PA 15224

SOUTH CAROLINA

South Carolina Center for Capital
  Litigation
Phone: (803) 765-0650
P.O. Box 11311
Columbia, SC 29211

South Carolina Coalition to
  Abolish the Death Penalty
E-mail: pearson@earthlink.net
Phone: (803) 776-7471
6248 Yorkshire Drive
Columbia, SC 29209

SOUTH DAKOTA

South Dakota Peace & Justice
  Center
URL: http://www.sdpjc.org
E-mail: sdpjc@dailypost.com
Phone: (605) 882-2822
P.O. Box 405
Watertown, SD 57201

TENNESSEE

Tennessee Association of Crimi-
  nal Defense Lawyers
URL: http://www.tacdl.com
E-mail: office@tacdl.com
Phone: (615) 726-1225
810 Broadway, Suite 501
Nashville, TN 37203-3810

Tennessee Coalition to Abolish
  State Killing
URL: http://www.tcask.org
E-mail: tcask@earthlink.net
Phone: (615) 329-0048
Box 120552
Nashville, TN 37212

TEXAS

Texas Coalition to Abolish the
  Death Penalty
URL: http://www.tcadp.org
E-mail: pconally@earthlink.net
Phone: (713) 520-0300
3400 Montrose, Suite 312
Houston, TX 77006

Texas Death Penalty Abolition
  Movement
URL: http://www.geocities.com/
  tdpam
E-mail: AbolitionMovement@
  juno.com
Phone: (713) 523-8454
c/o SHAPE Center

3903 Almeda Road
Houston, TX 77004

Texas Defender Service
URL: http://www.texasdefender.
 org
E-mail: araceli@compassnet.com
Phone: (713) 222-7788
412 Main Street #1150
Houston, TX 77002

UTAH

Utah Association of Criminal
 Defense Lawyers
URL: http://www.uacdl.org
Phone: (801) 364-6474
P.O. Box 510846
Salt Lake City, UT 84151

VERMONT

Vermont Coalition Against the
 Death Penalty
Phone: (802) 885-3327
c/o Unitarian Universalist Church
21 Fairground Road
Springfield, VT 05156

VIRGINIA

Virginia Capital Representation
 Resource Center
E-mail: Roblee@vcrrc.org
Phone: (804) 817-2970
2421 Ivy Road, Suite 301
Charlottesville, VA 22903

Virginians for Alternatives to the
 Death Penalty
URL: http://www.vadp.org
E-mail: mail@vadp.org
Phone: (434) 960-7779
P.O. Box 4804
Charlottesville, VA 22905

WASHINGTON

Inland Northwest Death
 Penalty Abolition Group
 (INDPAG)
E-mail: pjals@icehouse.net
Phone: (509) 838-7870
35 West Main, Suite 120M
Spokane, WA 99201

Washington Coalition to Abolish
 the Death Penalty
URL: http://www.abolishdeath
 penalty.org
E-mail: info@abolishdeath
 penalty.org
Phone: (206) 622-8952
P.O. Box 3045
Seattle, WA 98114

WEST VIRGINIA

West Virginians Against the
 Death Penalty
P.O. Box 1878
Inwood, WV 25428

WISCONSIN

Wisconsin Coalition Against the
 Death Penalty
URL: http://wcadp.org
E-mail: wcadp@mailbag.com
P.O. Box 44578
Madison, WI 53744

WYOMING

Wyoming Coalition to Abolish
 the Death Penalty
E-mail: carl@newmancenter.org
(307) 745-5461
1800 East Grand Avenue
Laramie, WY 82070

INTERNATIONAL ADVOCACY ORGANIZATIONS

Amnesty International
URL: http://www.amnesty.org
E-mail: admin-us@aiusa.org
  (U.S. office)
Phone: (212) 807-8400
5 Penn Plaza, 14th Floor
New York, NY 10001
Worldwide human rights organization that has adopted abolition of the death penalty as one of its ongoing campaigns. Web page for death penalty is at URL: http://www.amnesty.org/ailib/intcam/dp/index.html.

Canadian Coalition Against the Death Penalty
URL: http://www.ccadp.org
E-mail: info@ccadp.org
Phone: (416) 686-9112
80 Lillington Avenue
Toronto, Ontario M1N-3K7
Canada
Organization of Canadians working to abolish capital punishment in the United States. They are also active on behalf of Canadians facing the death penalty in the United States.

Hands Off Cain (Nessuno Tochi Caino)
URL: http://www.handsoffcain.
  org/
E-mail: hands.off.cain@radical.it
Phone: (212) 813-1334
866 UN Plaza #408
New York, NY 10017
An Italian-based international "citizens' and parliamentarian's league" dedicated to the worldwide abolition of the death penalty. The organiza-
tion provides statistics and reports on the status of the death penalty in various nations and in international law.

Human Rights Watch
URL: http://www.hrw.org
E-mail: hrwnyc@hrw.org
Phone: (212) 290-4700
350 Fifth Avenue, 34th Floor
New York, NY 10018-3299
Although not directed explicitly toward abolition of the death penalty, the organization has an active campaign against abusive prison conditions throughout the world.

International Bannister Foundation
URL: http://maxpages.com/
  bannister
E-mail: postmaster@banfound.
  u-net.com
Phone: +44 01383 823611
28 Craigdimas Grove
Dalgety Bay
Fife, KY11 9XR
Scotland
United Kingdom
International organization founded in memory of executed death row inmate Alan Jeffrey Bannister. Describes itself as "an anti–capital punishment and pro–human rights action and support group." The organization has chapters in a number of U.S., European, and other world cities.

The Lamp of Hope
Texas Death Row Project
URL: http://www.lampofhope.org

E-mail: ksebung@lampofhope.org
P.O. Box 305
League City, TX 77574-0305
Organization in support of Texas death row prisoners. Has affiliates in Canada and several European nations.

Lifelines
URL: http://www.lifelines.org
E-mail: lifelines.secretary@ntl-
  world.com
P.O. Box 347
Darlington DL3 6WZ
United Kingdom
British-based organization that offers correspondence and support to U.S. death row prisoners.

Lifespark
Swiss Organization Against the
  Death Penalty
URL: http://www.lifespark.org

E-mail: contactus@lifespark.org
P.O. Box 4002
Basel
Switzerland
Organization emphasizes correspondence with and support services for death row inmates, lobbying, and coordination with international human rights organizations.

Moratorium 2000 International
  Campaign
URL: http://www.santegidio.org/
  en/pdm/pdm_eng.htm
E-mail: m2000@santegidio.org
International petition drive sponsored by the Communita di Sant Egidio. Its goal is for a worldwide moratorium on the death penalty and eventual abolition. Petition text is available online and the petition can be signed electronically.

PART III

APPENDICES

APPENDIX A

STATISTICS AND TRENDS FOR CAPITAL PUNISHMENT

The following selection of charts, tables, and maps gives a picture of how the death penalty has been applied in the United States in recent years. It also shows how some trends have changed over time, including public opinion about the death penalty and possible alternatives.

PERSONS SENTENCED TO DEATH

THE MURDER RATE

Because murder is essentially the only crime for which the death penalty can be given today, the murder rate is perhaps most relevant for considering any relationship between the amount of crime and the extent of use of capital punishment.

In 1984 there were 18,692 cases of murder and nonnegligent manslaughter in the United States. The total peaked at 24,703 in 1991; by 1996 it had dipped below 20,000, and it has generally continued to decline. This downward trend can be seen most clearly, however, in the number of murders per 100,000 population, as shown in the chart "Trends in the Murder Rate." Note that 2003 saw a slight increase in the murder rate for the first time in more than a decade.

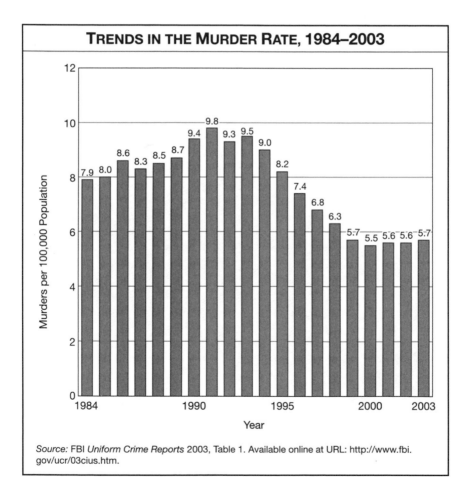

TRENDS IN THE MURDER RATE, 1984–2003

Source: FBI *Uniform Crime Reports* 2003, Table 1. Available online at URL: http://www.fbi. gov/ucr/03cius.htm.

Appendix A

NUMBER OF PERSONS ON DEATH ROW

There are two basic measures of the pervasiveness of the death penalty. The first is the total number of persons under sentence of death at the close of each year. The chart "Persons under Sentence of Death, 1953–2003" has a dip at 1972, reflecting the Supreme Court's suspending imposition of the death penalty. Death sentences resumed in 1976 after death penalty states had modified their statutes to reflect the Court's requirements.

The total number of persons under sentence of death climbed steadily through the 1980s and early 1990s. However the growth in total death sentences slowed somewhat in the late 1990s. Starting in 2000 the total number of death sentences has actually begun to decline. It is difficult to determine the cause for this decline: overall crime rates have continued to decline since the mid-1990s, but the reduction of the U.S. death row population may also reflect a slowly growing number of exonerations and a growing concern that innocent persons might be executed because of flaws in the judicial system. In 2003 an unprecedented 267 prisoners were removed from death row. Sixty percent of this decline was due to Illinois governor Ryan's commuting of all but two of the state's death sentences.

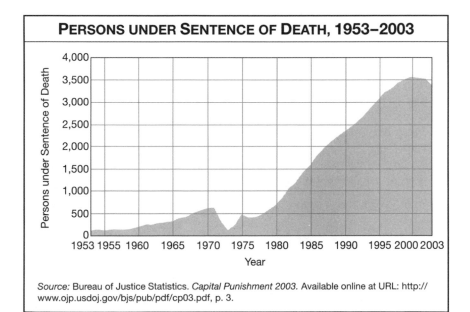

PERSONS UNDER SENTENCE OF DEATH, 1953–2003

Source: Bureau of Justice Statistics. *Capital Punishment 2003.* Available online at URL: http://www.ojp.usdoj.gov/bjs/pub/pdf/cp03.pdf, p. 3.

Capital Punishment

DEATH ROW DEMOGRAPHICS

The demographics of death row inmates are important to the death penalty rate because of the legal and moral arguments that claim that the sanction falls disproportionately on racial minorities, the poor, and the uneducated.

The chart "Persons under Sentence of Death by Race, 1968–2003" shows that blacks, who make up only about 12 percent of the U.S. population, account for a much higher proportion (about 43 percent) of death row inmates. (Hispanics, on the other hand, more closely track their percentage in the overall population.)

It is true that statistics show that blacks are about eight times as likely to commit homicides as whites. However, the milestone 1983 study by David Baldus, George Woodworth, and Charles Pulaski revealed that blacks convicted of killing whites were sentenced to death in 22 percent of capital cases, while only 3 percent of whites convicted of killing blacks received a death sentence. Minority status also tends to correlate with poverty and thus to lack of access to effective legal representation, further increasing the chance of receiving a death sentence.

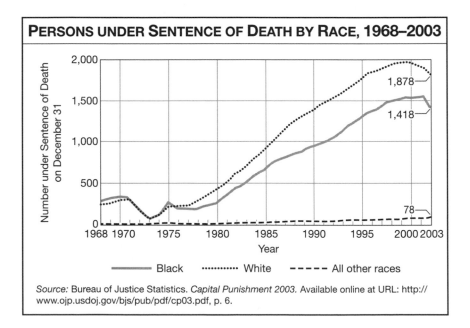

PERSONS UNDER SENTENCE OF DEATH BY RACE, 1968–2003

Source: Bureau of Justice Statistics. *Capital Punishment 2003*. Available online at URL: http://www.ojp.usdoj.gov/bjs/pub/pdf/cp03.pdf, p. 6.

The table "Demographic Characteristics of Prisoners under Sentence of Death, 2003" provides further evidence of disparities in capital sentencing. The overwhelming majority of death row inmates are male. About half of persons sentenced to death have not completed high school, and more than half of them have never been married.

DEMOGRAPHIC CHARACTERISTICS OF PRISONERS UNDER SENTENCE OF DEATH, 2003

Characteristic	Prisoners under Sentence of Death, 2003		
	Year End	Admissions	Removals
Total number under sentence of death	3,374	144	332
Gender			
Male	98.6%	98.6%	98.2%
Female	1.4	1.4	1.8
Race			
White	55.7%	63.9%	46.1%
Black	42.0	30.6	53.3
All other races*	2.3	5.5	0.6
Hispanic origin			
Hispanic	12.5%	27.0%	6.2%
Non-Hispanic	87.5	73.0	93.8
Education			
8th grade or less	15.2%	18.3%	11.6%
9th-11th grade	37.1	41.7	40.4
High school graduate/GED	38.3	35.0	37.2
Any college	9.3	5.0	10.8
Median	11th	11th	11th
Marital status			
Married	22.5%	29.1%	21.9%
Divorced/separated	20.7	17.1	20.2
Widowed	2.8	4.3	3.1
Never married	54.0	49.6	54.8

Note: Removals include persons who were executed, died naturally, were exonerated, or whose sentence was commuted. Calculations are based on those cases for which data were reported. Missing data by category were as follows:

	Year End	Admissions	Removals
Hispanic origin	416	55	44
Education	483	24	55
Marital status	333	27	40

*At year end 2002, other races consisted of 29 American Indians, 35 Asians, and 14 self-identified Hispanics. During 2003, 3 American Indians, 3 Asians, and 2 self-identified Hispanics were admitted; 1 Asian was removed; and 1 American Indian was executed.
Source: Bureau of Justice Statistics. Capital Punishment 2003. Available online at URL: http://www.ojp.usdoj.gov/bjs/pub/pdf/cp03.pdf, p. 6.

EXECUTIONS

ANNUAL TOTAL OF EXECUTIONS

The majority of death row inmates will never be executed, and many others will wait years or even decades for their final walk to the execution chamber. Indeed, the lack of timeliness and consistency in application is sometimes cited as an argument against the effectiveness of the death penalty as a deterrent.

The number of persons executed varies considerably from year to year, as shown in the chart "Persons Executed, 1930–2003." The virtual absence of executions from the late 1960s to the mid-1980s reflects the successful legal challenges to executions culminating in the Supreme Court suspending capital punishment in 1972. Even though the Court approved revised state procedures in 1976, it took nearly a decade for a significant number of executions to appear. In 2003 an apparent downward trend continued, with six fewer executions than in 2002.

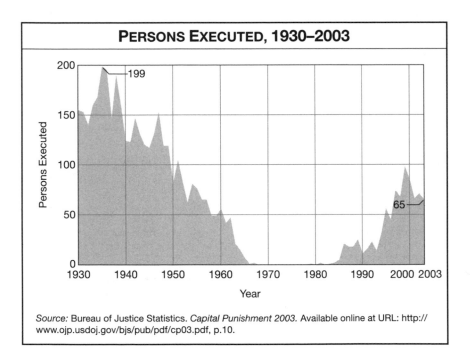

PERSONS EXECUTED, 1930–2003

Source: Bureau of Justice Statistics. *Capital Punishment 2003.* Available online at URL: http://www.ojp.usdoj.gov/bjs/pub/pdf/cp03.pdf, p.10.

Appendix A

GEOGRAPHIC DISTRIBUTION OF EXECUTIONS

As shown in the map "Distribution of Executions by State, Since 1977" executions are not evenly distributed among the states that have capital punishment, even when population is taken into account. By far the largest number of executions take place in the southern states, and Texas accounts for more than a third of the executions since 1977.

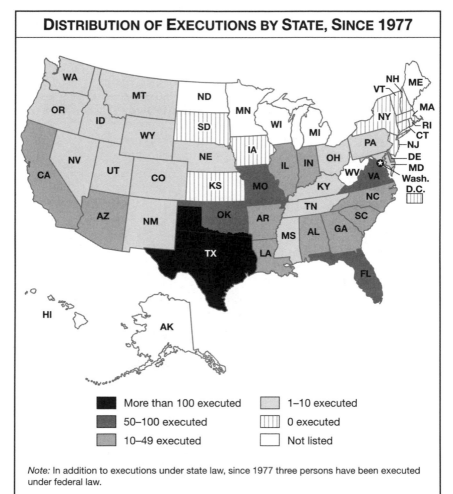

DISTRIBUTION OF EXECUTIONS BY STATE, SINCE 1977

More than 100 executed
50–100 executed
10–49 executed
1–10 executed
0 executed
Not listed

Note: In addition to executions under state law, since 1977 three persons have been executed under federal law.

Source: Based on Table 9, "Number of Persons Executed, by Jurisdiction, 1930–2003," Bureau of Justice Statistics. *Capital Punishment 2003.* Available online at URL: http://www.ojp.usdoj.gov/bjs/pub/pdf/cp03.pdf, p. 9.

Capital Punishment

DEATH ROW EXONERATIONS

The best potential outcome for a prisoner on death row is to be exonerated (found not guilty of the crime for which he or she was originally sentenced to death). As shown in the chart "Increasing Number of Exonerations, 1973–2004," the number of persons released from death row has been growing. Indeed, in 2003 there were 10 exonerations compared to 65 executions. These numbers reflect both the growing use of DNA testing and ongoing efforts by volunteer advocates on behalf of death row inmates. In turn, the growing number of exonerations seems to be lending weight to the argument that the execution of the innocent is a danger that may outweigh any value the death penalty may have as compared to life without parole.

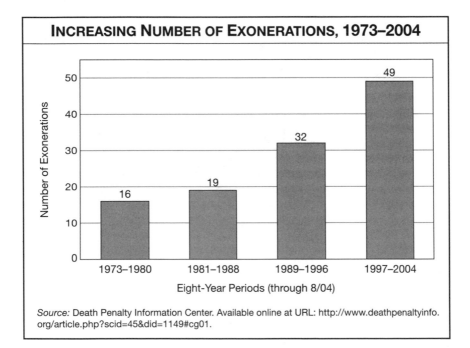

INCREASING NUMBER OF EXONERATIONS, 1973–2004

Source: Death Penalty Information Center. Available online at URL: http://www.deathpenaltyinfo. org/article.php?scid=45&did=1149#cg01.

Appendix A

PUBLIC OPINION AND THE DEATH PENALTY

The final section of this appendix looks at some trends in public opinion concerning the death penalty.

TREND IN SUPPORT FOR CAPITAL PUNISHMENT

The graph "Support for Capital Punishment, 1965–2003" suggests that while there has been some fluctuation, support for the death penalty peaked somewhere in the later 1990s and has declined a bit since.

Although concern about execution of the innocent is growing, it does not yet appear to be decisive. A July 2001 Harris poll, for example, found that 94 percent of respondents believed that innocent persons were sometimes executed. On average, they estimated that about one in eight executed persons were actually innocent. (Blacks, however estimated that almost one in four were innocent.) Only 36 percent of respondents said they would support the death penalty if a "substantial" number of innocent persons were being executed; this number had declined from that recorded in 2000 (53 percent). Apparently, however, a majority still do not believe the number of executed innocent persons is "substantial."

SUPPORT FOR CAPITAL PUNISHMENT, 1965–2003

(y-axis: Percent of Adults Participating in the Poll; x-axis: Year)

Legend: Believe in it — Opposed to it — Not sure/refused

Source: Harris Poll, "More Than Two-Thirds of Americans Continue to Support the Death Penalty," January 7, 2004. Available online at URL: http://www.harrisinteractive.com/harris_poll/index.asp?PID=431, Table 1.

Capital Punishment

THE DEATH PENALTY AS A DETERRENT

Although roughly seven in 10 Americans express generalized support for the death penalty, this support tends to erode when specific issues are raised and alternatives are offered. As the graph "Capital Punishment as a Deterrent, 1976–2003" suggests, belief in the deterrent value of the death penalty peaked sometime in the 1980s and has declined ever since. As of 2003, only 41 percent of poll respondents believed that the death penalty was an effective deterrent, about 30 percent less than the proportion of people who say they support capital punishment.

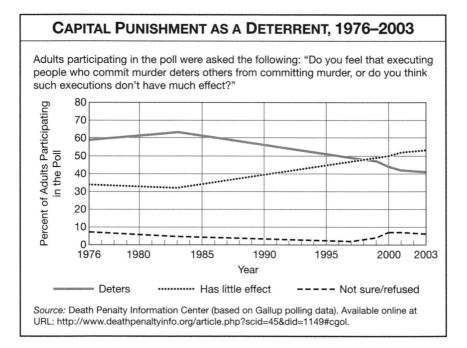

CAPITAL PUNISHMENT AS A DETERRENT, 1976–2003

Adults participating in the poll were asked the following: "Do you feel that executing people who commit murder deters others from committing murder, or do you think such executions don't have much effect?"

Legend: Deters — Has little effect — Not sure/refused

Source: Death Penalty Information Center (based on Gallup polling data). Available online at URL: http://www.deathpenaltyinfo.org/article.php?scid=45&did=1149#cgol.

Appendix A

Death vs. Life Without Parole

When poll respondents are asked to choose between death and life without parole for capital offenses, a growing number are choosing the latter. As shown in the chart "Public Views on Death Penalty versus Life Sentences, 1985–2004" today only about 5 percent more respondents favor death over life without parole. The convergence between the two percentages began in the late 1990s.

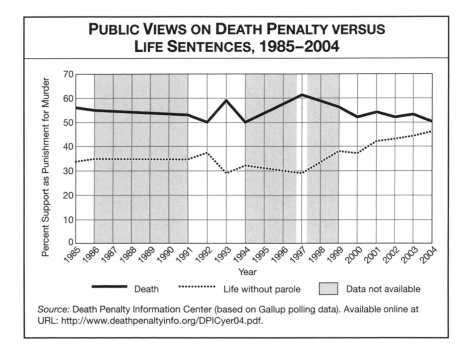

PUBLIC VIEWS ON DEATH PENALTY VERSUS LIFE SENTENCES, 1985–2004

Source: Death Penalty Information Center (based on Gallup polling data). Available online at URL: http://www.deathpenaltyinfo.org/DPICyer04.pdf.

APPENDIX B

EXTRACT FROM U.S. SUPREME COURT RULING: *FURMAN V. GEORGIA*, 1972

408 U.S. 238
FURMAN V. GEORGIA
CERTIORARI TO THE SUPREME
COURT OF GEORGIA
NO. 69-5003.

Argued January 17, 1972
Decided June 29, 1972

[Note: Selected excerpts follow, with footnotes and most references deleted.]

[PER CURIAM]
. . . Certiorari was granted limited to the following question: "Does the imposition and carrying out of the death penalty in [these cases] constitute cruel and unusual punishment in violation of the Eighth and Fourteenth Amendments?"
. . . The Court holds that the imposition . . . and carrying out of the death penalty in these cases constitute cruel and unusual punishment in violation of the Eighth and Fourteenth Amendments. The judgment in each case is therefore reversed insofar as it leaves undisturbed the death sentence imposed, and the cases are remanded for further proceedings.

So ordered.
MR. JUSTICE DOUGLAS, MR. JUSTICE BRENNAN, MR. JUSTICE STEWART, MR. JUSTICE WHITE, and MR. JUSTICE MARSHALL have filed separate opinions in support of the judgments. THE CHIEF JUSTICE,

Appendix B

MR. JUSTICE BLACKMUN, MR. JUSTICE POWELL, and MR. JUSTICE REHNQUIST have filed separate dissenting opinions.

MR. JUSTICE DOUGLAS, concurring.

... The generality of a law inflicting capital punishment is one thing. What may be said of the validity of a law on the books and what may be done with the law in its application do, or may, lead to quite different conclusions. It would seem to be incontestable that the death penalty inflicted on one defendant is "unusual" if it discriminates against him by reason of his race, religion, wealth, social position, or class, or if it is imposed under a procedure that gives room for the play of such prejudices. ...

The words "cruel and unusual" certainly include penalties that are barbaric. But the words, at least when read in light of the English proscription against selective and irregular use of penalties, suggest that it is "cruel and unusual" to apply the death penalty—or any other penalty—selectively to minorities whose numbers are few, who are outcasts of society, and who are unpopular, but whom society is willing to see suffer though it would not countenance general application of the same penalty across the board. ...

There is increasing recognition of the fact that the basic theme of equal protection is implicit in "cruel and unusual" punishments. "A penalty . . . should be considered 'unusually' imposed if it is administered arbitrarily or discriminatorily." The same authors add that "[t]he extreme rarity with which applicable death penalty provisions are put to use raises a strong inference of arbitrariness." The President's Commission on Law Enforcement and Administration of Justice recently concluded:

> *Finally there is evidence that the imposition of the death sentence and the exercise of dispensing power by the courts and the executive follow discriminatory patterns. The death sentence is disproportionately imposed and carried out on the poor, the Negro, and the members of unpopular groups. . . .*

Former Attorney General Ramsey Clark has said, "It is the poor, the sick, the ignorant, the powerless and the hated who are executed." One searches our chronicles in vain for the execution of any member of the affluent strata of this society. The Leopolds and Loebs are given prison terms, not sentenced to death. . . .

We cannot say from facts disclosed in these records that these defendants were sentenced to death because they were black. Yet our task is not restricted to an effort to divine what motives impelled these death penalties. Rather, we deal with a system of law and of justice that leaves to the uncontrolled discretion of judges or juries the determination whether defendants committing these crimes should die or be imprisoned. Under these laws no standards govern the selection of the penalty. People live or die, dependent on the whim of one man or of 12. . . .

Those who wrote the Eighth Amendment knew what price their forebears had paid for a system based, not on equal justice, but on discrimination. In those days the target was not the blacks or the poor, but the dissenters, those who opposed absolutism in government, who struggled for a parliamentary regime, and who opposed governments' recurring efforts to foist a particular religion on the people. . . . But the tool of capital punishment was used with vengeance against the opposition and those unpopular with the regime. One cannot read this history without realizing that the desire for equality was reflected in the ban against "cruel and unusual punishments" contained in the Eighth Amendment. . . .

The high service rendered by the "cruel and unusual" punishment clause of the Eighth Amendment is to require legislatures to write penal laws that are evenhanded, nonselective, and nonarbitrary, and to require judges to see to it that general laws are not applied sparsely, selectively, and spottily to unpopular groups.

A law that stated that anyone making more than $50,000 would be exempt from the death penalty would plainly fall, as would a law that in terms said that blacks, those who never went beyond the fifth grade in school, those who made less than $3,000 a year, or those who were unpopular or unstable should be the only people executed. A law which in the overall view reaches that result in practice has no more sanctity than a law which in terms provides the same.

Thus, these discretionary statutes are unconstitutional in their operation. They are pregnant with discrimination and discrimination is an ingredient not compatible with the idea of equal protection of the laws that is implicit in the ban on "cruel and unusual" punishments. . . .

I concur in the judgments of the Court.

MR. JUSTICE BRENNAN, concurring.
The question presented in these cases is whether death is today a punishment for crime that is "cruel and unusual" and consequently, by virtue of the Eighth and Fourteenth Amendments, beyond the power of the State to inflict.

II

. . . There are, then, four principles by which we may determine whether a particular punishment is "cruel and unusual." The primary principle, which I believe supplies the essential predicate for the application of the others, is that a punishment must not by its severity be degrading to human dignity. The paradigm violation of this principle would be the infliction of a torturous punishment of the type that the Clause has always prohibited. Yet "[i]t is unlikely that any State at this moment in history," would pass a law providing for the infliction of such a punishment. Indeed, no such punishment has ever been before this Court. The same may be said of the other principles. It is unlikely that this Court will confront a severe punishment that is obviously inflicted in wholly arbitrary fashion; no State would engage in a reign of blind terror. . . .

. . . The function of these principles, after all, is simply to provide means by which a court can determine whether a challenged punishment comports with human dignity. They are, therefore, interrelated, and in most cases it will be their convergence that will justify the conclusion that a punishment is "cruel and unusual." The test, then, will ordinarily be a cumulative one: If a punishment is unusually severe, if there is a strong probability that it is inflicted arbitrarily, if it is substantially rejected by contemporary society, and if there is no reason to believe that it serves any penal purpose more effectively than some less severe punishment, then the continued infliction of that punishment violates the command of the Clause that the State may not inflict inhuman and uncivilized punishments upon those convicted of crimes.

III

The question, then, is whether the deliberate infliction of death is today consistent with the command of the Clause that the State may not inflict punishments that do not comport with human dignity. I will analyze the punishment of death in terms of the principles set out above and the cumulative test to which they lead: It is a denial of human dignity for the State arbitrarily to subject a person to an unusually severe punishment that society has indicated it does not regard as acceptable, and that cannot be shown to serve any penal purpose more effectively than a significantly less drastic punishment. Under these principles and this test, death is today a "cruel and unusual" punishment. Death is a unique punishment in the United States. In a society that so strongly affirms the sanctity of life, not surprisingly the common view is that death is the ultimate sanction. This natural human feeling appears all about us. There has been no national debate about punishment, in general or by imprisonment, comparable to the debate about the punishment of death. No other punishment has been so continuously restricted, or has any State yet abolished prisons, as some have abolished this punishment. And those States that still inflict death reserve it for the most heinous crimes.

The only explanation for the uniqueness of death is its extreme severity. Death is today an unusually severe punishment, unusual in its pain, in its finality, and in its enormity. No other existing punishment is comparable to death in terms of physical and mental suffering. Although our information is not conclusive, it appears that there is no method available that guarantees an immediate and painless death. . . .

In comparison to all other punishments today, then, the deliberate extinguishment of human life by the State is uniquely degrading to human dignity. I would not hesitate to hold, on that ground alone, that death is today a "cruel and unusual" punishment, were it not that death is a punishment of longstanding usage and acceptance in this country. I therefore turn to the second principle—that the State may not arbitrarily inflict an unusually severe punishment.

The outstanding characteristic of our present practice of punishing criminals by death is the infrequency with which we resort to it. The evidence is conclusive that death is not the ordinary punishment for any crime.

There has been a steady decline in the infliction of this punishment in every decade since the 1930's, the earliest period for which accurate statistics are available. In the 1930's, executions averaged 167 per year; in the 1940's, the average was 128; in the 1950's, it was 72; and in the years 1960–1962, it was 48. There have been a total of 46 executions since then, 36 of them in 1963–1964. Yet our population and the number of capital crimes committed have increased greatly over the past four decades. The contemporary rarity of the infliction of this punishment is thus the end result of a long-continued decline. . . . When a country of over 200 million people inflicts an unusually severe punishment no more than 50 times a year, the inference is strong that the punishment is not being regularly and fairly applied. To dispel it would indeed require a clear showing of nonarbitrary infliction. . . . When there is a strong probability that an unusually severe and degrading punishment is being inflicted arbitrarily, we may well expect that society will disapprove of its infliction. I turn, therefore, to the third principle. An examination of the history and present operation of the American practice of punishing criminals by death reveals that this punishment has been almost totally rejected by contemporary society. . . .

In the United States, as in other nations of the western world, "the struggle about this punishment has been one between ancient and deeply rooted beliefs in retribution, atonement or vengeance on the one hand, and, on the other, beliefs in the personal value and dignity of the common man that were born of the democratic movement of the eighteenth century, as well as beliefs in the scientific approach to an understanding of the motive forces of human conduct, which are the result of the growth of the sciences of behavior during the nineteenth and twentieth centuries." It is this essentially moral conflict that forms the backdrop for the past changes in and the present operation of our system of imposing death as a punishment for crime. Our practice of punishing criminals by death has changed greatly over the years. . . . Our concern for decency and human dignity, moreover, has compelled changes in the circumstances surrounding the execution itself. No longer does our society countenance the spectacle of public executions, once thought desirable as a deterrent to criminal behavior by others. Today we reject public executions as debasing and brutalizing to us all.

Also significant is the drastic decrease in the crimes for which the punishment of death is actually inflicted. While esoteric capital crimes remain on the books, since 1930 murder and rape have accounted for nearly 99% of the total executions, and murder alone for about 87%. In addition, the crime of capital murder has itself been limited. . . . In consequence, virtually all death sentences today are discretionarily imposed. Finally, it is significant that nine States no longer inflict the punishment of death under any circumstances, and five others have restricted it to extremely rare crimes. Thus, although "the death penalty has been employed throughout our history," in fact the history of this punishment is one of successive restriction. What was once a common punishment has become, in the context of a continuing moral debate, increasingly rare. . . .

It is, of course, "We, the People" who are responsible for the rarity both of the imposition and the carrying out of this punishment. Juries, "express[ing] the conscience of the community on the ultimate question of life or death," have been able to bring themselves to vote for death in a mere 100 or so cases among the thousands tried each year where the punishment is available. Governors, elected by and acting for us, have regularly commuted a substantial number of those sentences. And it is our society that insists upon due process of law to the end that no person will be unjustly put to death, thus ensuring that many more of those sentences will not be carried out. In sum, we have made death a rare punishment today. . . .

The final principle to be considered is that an unusually severe and degrading punishment may not be excessive in view of the purposes for which it is inflicted. This principle, too, is related to the others. When there is a strong probability that the State is arbitrarily inflicting an unusually severe punishment that is subject to grave societal doubts, it is likely also that the punishment cannot be shown to be serving any penal purpose that could not be served equally well by some less severe punishment.

The States' primary claim is that death is a necessary punishment because it prevents the commission of capital crimes more effectively than any less severe punishment. The first part of this claim is that the infliction of death is necessary to stop the individuals executed from committing further crimes. The sufficient answer to this is that if a criminal convicted of a capital crime poses a danger to society, effective administration of the State's pardon and parole laws can delay or deny his release from prison, and techniques of isolation can eliminate or minimize the danger while he remains confined.

Capital Punishment

The more significant argument is that the threat of death prevents the commission of capital crimes because it deters potential criminals who would not be deterred by the threat of imprisonment. The argument is not based upon evidence that the threat of death is a superior deterrent. Indeed, as my Brother MARSHALL establishes, the available evidence uniformly indicates, although it does not conclusively prove, that the threat of death has no greater deterrent effect than the threat of imprisonment. The States argue, however, that they are entitled to rely upon common human experience, and that experience, they say, supports the conclusion that death must be a more effective deterrent than any less severe punishment. Because people fear death the most, the argument runs, the threat of death must be the greatest deterrent. . . .

In any event, this argument cannot be appraised in the abstract. We are not presented with the theoretical question whether under any imaginable circumstances the threat of death might be a greater deterrent to the commission of capital crimes than the threat of imprisonment. We are concerned with the practice of punishing criminals by death as it exists in the United States today. Proponents of this argument necessarily admit that its validity depends upon the existence of a system in which the punishment of death is invariably and swiftly imposed. Our system, of course, satisfies neither condition. A rational person contemplating a murder or rape is confronted, not with the certainty of a speedy death, but with the slightest possibility that he will be executed in the distant future. The risk of death is remote and improbable; in contrast, the risk of long-term imprisonment is near and great. . . .

There is, however, another aspect to the argument that the punishment of death is necessary for the protection of society. The infliction of death, the States urge, serves to manifest the community's outrage at the commission of the crime. It is, they say, a concrete public expression of moral indignation that inculcates respect for the law and helps assure a more peaceful community. Moreover, we are told, not only does the punishment of death exert this widespread moralizing influence upon community values, it also satisfies the popular demand for grievous condemnation of abhorrent crimes and thus prevents disorder, lynching, and attempts by private citizens to take the law into their own hands.

The question, however, is not whether death serves these supposed purposes of punishment, but whether death serves them more effectively than imprisonment. There is no evidence whatever that utilization of imprisonment rather than death encourages private blood feuds and other disorders. Surely if there were such a danger, the execution of a handful of criminals each year would not prevent it. The assertion that death alone is a sufficiently emphatic denunciation for capital crimes suffers from the same defect. If capital crimes require the punishment of death in order to provide moral reinforcement for the basic values of the community, those values can only be undermined when death is so rarely inflicted upon the criminals who commit the crimes. Furthermore, it is certainly doubtful that the infliction of death by the State does in fact strengthen the community's moral code; if the deliberate extinguishment of human life has any effect at all, it more likely tends to lower our respect for life and brutalize our values. . . .

In sum, the punishment of death is inconsistent with all four principles: Death is an unusually severe and degrading punishment; there is a strong probability that it is inflicted arbitrarily; its rejection by contemporary society is virtually total; and there is no reason to believe that it serves any penal purpose more effectively than the less severe punishment of imprisonment. The function of these principles is to enable a court to determine whether a punishment comports with human dignity. Death, quite simply, does not.

IV

. . . Since [the nation's founding] successive restrictions, imposed against the background of a continuing moral controversy, have drastically curtailed the use of this punishment. Today death is a uniquely and unusually severe punishment. When examined by the principles applicable under the Cruel and Unusual Punishments Clause, death stands condemned as fatally offensive to human dignity. The punishment of death is therefore "cruel and unusual," and the States may no longer inflict it as a punishment for crimes. . . .

I concur in the judgments of the Court.

MR. CHIEF JUSTICE BURGER, with whom MR. JUSTICE BLACKMUN, MR. JUSTICE POWELL, and MR. JUSTICE REHNQUIST join, dissenting.

I

If we were possessed of legislative power, I would either join with MR. JUSTICE BRENNAN and MR. JUSTICE MARSHALL or, at the very least, restrict the use of capital punishment to a small category of the most heinous crimes. Our constitutional inquiry, however, must be divorced from personal feelings as to the morality and efficacy of the death penalty, and be confined to the meaning and applicability of the uncertain language of the Eighth Amendment. . . .

II

Counsel for petitioners properly concede that capital punishment was not impermissibly cruel at the time of the adoption of the Eighth Amendment. Not only do the records of the debates indicate that the Founding Fathers were limited in their concern to the prevention of torture, but it is also clear from the language of the Constitution itself that there was no thought whatever of the elimination of capital punishment. The opening sentence of the Fifth Amendment is a guarantee that the death penalty not be imposed "unless on a presentment or indictment of a Grand Jury." The Double Jeopardy Clause of the Fifth Amendment is a prohibition against being "twice put in jeopardy of life" for the same offense. Similarly, the Due Process Clause commands "due process of law" before an accused can be "deprived of life, liberty, or property." Thus, the explicit language of the Constitution affirmatively acknowledges the legal power to impose capital punishment; it does not expressly or by implication acknowledge the legal power to impose any of the various punishments that have been banned as cruel since 1791. . . .

In the 181 years since the enactment of the Eighth Amendment, not a single decision of this Court has cast the slightest shadow of a doubt on the constitutionality of capital punishment. In rejecting Eighth Amendment attacks on particular modes of execution, the Court has more than once implicitly denied that capital punishment is impermissibly "cruel" in the constitutional sense. . . . It is only 14 years since Mr. Chief Justice Warren, speaking for four members of the Court, stated without equivocation:

> *Whatever the arguments may be against capital punishment, both on moral grounds and in terms of accomplishing the purposes of punishment—and they are forceful—the death penalty has been employed throughout our history, and, in a day when it is still widely accepted, it cannot be said to violate the constitutional concept of cruelty.*

It is only one year since Mr. Justice Black made his feelings clear on the constitutional issue:

> *The Eighth Amendment forbids 'cruel and unusual punishments.' In my view, these words cannot be read to outlaw capital punishment because that penalty was in common use and authorized by law here and in the countries from which our ancestors came at the time the Amendment was adopted. It is inconceivable to me that the framers intended to end capital punishment by the Amendment.*

Before recognizing such an instant evolution in the law, it seems fair to ask what factors have changed that capital punishment should now be "cruel" in the constitutional sense as it has not been in the past. It is apparent that there has been no change of constitutional significance in the nature of the punishment itself. Twentieth century modes of execution surely involve no greater physical suffering than the means employed at the time of the Eighth Amendment's adoption. And although a man awaiting execution must inevitably experience extraordinary mental anguish, no one suggests that this anguish is materially different from that experienced by condemned men in 1791, even though protracted appellate review processes have greatly increased the waiting time on "death row." To be sure, the ordeal of the condemned man may be thought cruel in the sense that all suffering is thought cruel. But if the Constitution proscribed every punishment producing severe emotional stress, then capital punishment would clearly have been impermissible in 1791.

However, the inquiry cannot end here. For reasons unrelated to any change in intrinsic cruelty, the Eighth Amendment prohibition cannot fairly be limited to those punishments thought excessively cruel and barbarous at the time of the adoption of the Eighth Amendment. A punishment is inordinately cruel, in the sense we must deal with it in these cases, chiefly as perceived by the society so characterizing it. The standard of extreme cruelty is not merely descriptive, but necessarily embodies a moral judgment. The standard itself remains the same, but its applicability must change as the basic mores of society change. . . .

III

There are no obvious indications that capital punishment offends the conscience of society to such a degree that our traditional deference to the legislative judgment must be abandoned. It is not a punishment such as burning at the stake that everyone would ineffably find to be repugnant to all civilized standards. Nor is it a punishment so roundly condemned that only a few aberrant legislatures have retained it on the statute books. Capital punishment is authorized by statute in 40 States, the District of Columbia, and in the federal courts for the commission of certain crimes. On four occasions in the last 11 years Congress has added to the list of federal crimes punishable by death. In looking for reliable indicia of contemporary attitude, none more trustworthy has been advanced. . . .

Counsel for petitioners rely on a different body of empirical evidence. They argue, in effect, that the number of cases in which the death penalty is imposed, as compared with the number of cases in which it is statutorily available, reflects a general revulsion toward the penalty that would lead to its repeal if only it were more generally and widely enforced. It cannot be gainsaid that by the choice of juries—and sometimes judges—the death penalty is imposed in far fewer than half the cases in which it is available. To go further and characterize the rate of imposition as "freakishly rare," as petitioners insist, is unwarranted hyperbole. And regardless of its characterization, the rate of imposition does not impel the conclusion that capital punishment is now regarded as intolerably cruel or uncivilized.

IV

Capital punishment has also been attacked as violative of the Eighth Amendment on the ground that it is not needed to achieve legitimate penal aims and is thus "unnecessarily cruel." As a pure policy matter, this approach has much to recommend it, but it seeks to give a dimension to the Eighth Amendment that it was never intended to have and promotes a line of inquiry that this Court has never before pursued. . . .

By pursuing the necessity approach, it becomes even more apparent that it involves matters outside the purview of the Eighth Amendment. Two of the several aims of punishment are generally associated with capital punishment—retribution and deterrence. It is argued that retribution can be discounted because that, after all, is what the Eighth Amendment seeks to eliminate. There is no authority suggesting that the Eighth Amendment was intended to purge the law of its retributive elements, and the Court has consistently assumed that retribution is a legitimate dimension of the punishment of crimes. . . .

Comparative deterrence is not a matter that lends itself to precise measurement; to shift the burden to the States is to provide an illusory solution to an enormously complex problem. If it were proper to put the States to the test of demonstrating the deterrent value of capital punishment, we could just as well ask them to prove the need for life imprisonment or any other punishment. . . .

V

The actual scope of the Court's ruling, which I take to be embodied in these concurring opinions, is not entirely clear. This much, however, seems apparent: if the legislatures are to continue to authorize capital punishment for some crimes, juries and judges can no longer be permitted to make the sentencing determination in the same manner they have in the past. . . .

This application of the words of the Eighth Amendment suggests that capital punishment can be made to satisfy Eighth Amendment values if its rate of imposition is somehow multiplied; it seemingly follows that the flexible sentencing system created by the legislatures, and carried out by juries and judges, has yielded more mercy than the Eighth Amendment can stand. The implications of this approach are mildly ironical. For example, by this measure of the Eighth Amendment, the elimination of death-qualified juries in *Witherspoon v. Illinois*, 391 U.S. 510 (1968), can only be seen in retrospect as a setback to "the evolving standards of decency that mark the progress of a maturing society.". . .

The Eighth Amendment was included in the Bill of Rights to assure that certain types of punishments would never be imposed, not to channelize the sentencing process. The approach of these concurring opinions has no antecedent in the Eighth Amendment cases. It is essentially and exclusively a procedural due process argument.

Appendix B

While I would not undertake to make a definitive statement as to the parameters of the Court's ruling, it is clear that if state legislatures and the Congress wish to maintain the availability of capital punishment, significant statutory changes will have to be made. Since the two pivotal concurring opinions turn on the assumption that the punishment of death is now meted out in a random and unpredictable manner, legislative bodies may seek to bring their laws into compliance with the Court's ruling by providing standards for juries and judges to follow in determining the sentence in capital cases or by more narrowly defining the crimes for which the penalty is to be imposed. . . .

Real change could clearly be brought about if legislatures provided mandatory death sentences in such a way as to deny juries the opportunity to bring in a verdict on a lesser charge; under such a system, the death sentence could only be avoided by a verdict of acquittal. If this is the only alternative that the legislatures can safely pursue under today's ruling, I would have preferred that the Court opt for total abolition. . . .

VI

Since there is no majority of the Court on the ultimate issue presented in these cases, the future of capital punishment in this country has been left in an uncertain limbo. Rather than providing a final and unambiguous answer on the basic constitutional question, the collective impact of the majority's ruling is to demand an undetermined measure of change from the various state legislatures and the Congress. While I cannot endorse the process of decisionmaking that has yielded today's result and the restraints that that result imposes on legislative action, I am not altogether displeased that legislative bodies have been given the opportunity, and indeed unavoidable responsibility, to make a thorough reevaluation of the entire subject of capital punishment. If today's opinions demonstrate nothing else, they starkly show that this is an area where legislatures can act far more effectively than courts. . . .

APPENDIX C

EXTRACT FROM U.S. SUPREME COURT RULING: *MCCLESKEY V. KEMP*, 1987

481 U.S. 279
MCCLESKEY V. KEMP, SUPERINTENDENT, GEORGIA DIAGNOSTIC AND CLASSIFICATION CENTER CERTIORARI TO THE UNITED STATES COURT OF APPEALS FOR THE ELEVENTH CIRCUIT NO. 84-6811.

Argued October 15, 1986
Decided April 22, 1987

[Note: selected excerpts given, with footnotes and most references omitted.]

JUSTICE POWELL delivered the opinion of the Court.
This case presents the question whether a complex statistical study that indicates a risk that racial considerations enter [481 U.S. 279, 283] into capital sentencing determinations proves that petitioner McCleskey's capital sentence is unconstitutional under the Eighth or Fourteenth Amendment.

I

McCleskey, a black man, was convicted of two counts of armed robbery and one count of murder in the Superior Court of Fulton County, Georgia, on October

Appendix C

12, 1978. McCleskey's convictions arose out of the robbery of a furniture store and the killing of a white police officer during the course of the robbery. . . .

In support of his claim, McCleskey proffered a statistical study performed by Professors David C. Baldus, Charles Pulaski, and George Woodworth (the Baldus study) that purports to show a disparity in the imposition of the death sentence in Georgia based on the race of the murder victim and, to a lesser extent, the race of the defendant. The Baldus study is actually two sophisticated statistical studies that examine over 2,000 murder cases that occurred in Georgia during the 1970's. The raw numbers collected by Professor Baldus indicate that defendants charged with killing white persons received the death penalty in 11% of the cases, but defendants charged with killing blacks received the death penalty in only 1% of the cases. The raw numbers also indicate a reverse racial disparity according to the race of the defendant: 4% of the black defendants received the death penalty, as opposed to 7% of the white defendants.

Baldus also divided the cases according to the combination of the race of the defendant and the race of the victim. He found that the death penalty was assessed in 22% of the cases involving black defendants and white victims; 8% of the cases involving white defendants and white victims; 1% of the cases involving black defendants and black victims; and 3% of the cases involving white defendants and black victims. Similarly, Baldus found that prosecutors sought the death penalty in 70% of the cases involving black defendants and white victims; 32% of the cases involving white defendants and white victims; 15% of the cases involving black defendants and black victims; and 19% of the cases involving white defendants and black victims.

Baldus subjected his data to an extensive analysis, taking account of 230 variables that could have explained the disparities on nonracial grounds. One of his models concludes that, even after taking account of 39 nonracial variables, defendants charged with killing white victims were 4.3 times as likely to receive a death sentence as defendants charged with killing blacks. According to this model, black defendants were 1.1 times as likely to receive a death sentence as other defendants. Thus, the Baldus study indicates that black defendants, such as McCleskey, who kill white victims have the greatest likelihood of receiving the death penalty.

II

McCleskey's first claim is that the Georgia capital punishment statute violates the Equal Protection Clause of the Fourteenth Amendment. He argues that race has infected the administration of Georgia's statute in two ways: persons who murder whites are more likely to be sentenced to death than persons who murder blacks, and black murderers are more likely to be sentenced to death

281

than white murderers. As a black defendant who killed a white victim, Mc-Cleskey claims that the Baldus study demonstrates that he was discriminated against because of his race and because of the race of his victim. In its broadest form, McCleskey's claim of discrimination extends to every actor in the Georgia capital sentencing process, from the prosecutor who sought the death penalty and the jury that imposed the sentence, to the State itself that enacted the capital punishment statute and allows it to remain in effect despite its allegedly discriminatory application. We agree with the Court of Appeals, and every other court that has considered such a challenge, that this claim must fail.

A

Our analysis begins with the basic principle that a defendant who alleges an equal protection violation has the burden of proving "the existence of purposeful discrimination." A corollary to this principle is that a criminal defendant must prove that the purposeful discrimination "had a discriminatory effect" on him. Thus, to prevail under the Equal Protection Clause, McCleskey must prove that the decisionmakers in his case acted with discriminatory purpose. He offers no evidence specific to his own case that would support an inference that racial considerations played a part in his sentence.

Instead, he relies solely on the Baldus study. McCleskey argues that the Baldus study compels an inference that his sentence rests on purposeful discrimination. McCleskey's claim that these statistics are sufficient proof of discrimination, without regard to the facts of a particular case, would extend to all capital cases in Georgia, at least where the victim was white and the defendant is black.

The Court has accepted statistics as proof of intent to discriminate in certain limited contexts. First, this Court has accepted statistical disparities as proof of an equal protection violation in the selection of the jury venire in a particular district. . . . Second, this Court has accepted statistics in the form of multiple-regression analysis to prove statutory violations under Title VII of the Civil Rights Act of 1964.

But the nature of the capital sentencing decision, and the relationship of the statistics to that decision, are fundamentally different from the corresponding elements in the venire-selection or Title VII cases. Most importantly, each particular decision to impose the death penalty is made by a petit jury selected from a properly constituted venire. Each jury is unique in its composition, and the Constitution requires that its decision rest on consideration of innumerable factors that vary according to the characteristics of the individual defendant and the facts of the particular capital offense. Thus, the application of an inference drawn from the general statistics to a specific decision in a trial and sentencing simply is not comparable to the application of an inference drawn from general statistics to a specific venire-selection or Title VII case. In those cases, the statistics relate to fewer entities, and fewer variables are relevant to the challenged decisions.

Another important difference between the cases in which we have accepted statistics as proof of discriminatory intent and this case is that, in the venire-selection and Title VII contexts, the decisionmaker has an opportunity to explain the statistical disparity. Here, the State has no practical opportunity to rebut the Baldus study. "[C]ontrolling considerations of . . . public policy," dictate that jurors "cannot be called. . . . to testify to the motives and influences that led to their verdict." Similarly, the policy considerations behind a prosecutor's traditionally "wide discretion" suggest the impropriety of our requiring prosecutors to defend their decisions to seek death penalties, "often years after they were made." Moreover, absent far stronger proof, it is unnecessary [481 U.S. 279, 297] to seek such a rebuttal, because a legitimate and unchallenged explanation for the decision is apparent from the record: McCleskey committed an act for which the United States Constitution and Georgia laws permit imposition of the death penalty.

Finally, McCleskey's statistical proffer must be viewed in the context of his challenge. McCleskey challenges decisions at the heart of the State's criminal justice system. "[O]ne of society's most basic tasks is that of protecting the lives of its citizens and one of the most basic ways in which it achieves the task is through criminal laws against murder." Implementation of these laws necessarily requires discretionary judgments. Because discretion is essential to the criminal justice process, we would demand exceptionally clear proof before we would infer that the discretion has been abused. The unique nature of the decisions at issue in this case also counsels against adopting such an inference from the disparities indicated by the Baldus study. Accordingly, we hold that the Baldus study is clearly insufficient to support an inference that any of the decisionmakers in McCleskey's case acted with discriminatory purpose.

B

McCleskey also suggests that the Baldus study proves that the State as a whole has acted with a discriminatory purpose. He appears to argue that the State has violated the Equal [481 U.S. 279, 298] Protection Clause by adopting the capital punishment statute and allowing it to remain in force despite its allegedly discriminatory application. But "'[d]iscriminatory purpose' . . . implies more than intent as volition or intent as awareness of consequences. It implies that the decisionmaker, in this case a state legislature, selected or reaffirmed a particular course of action at least in part 'because of,' not merely 'in spite of,' its adverse effects upon an identifiable group." . . . For this claim to prevail, McCleskey would have to prove that the Georgia Legislature enacted or maintained the death penalty statute because of an anticipated racially discriminatory effect. In *Gregg v. Georgia*, supra, this Court found that the Georgia capital sentencing system could operate in a fair and neutral manner. There was no evidence then, and there is none now, that the Georgia Legislature enacted the capital punishment statute to further a racially discriminatory purpose. . . .

III

McCleskey also argues that the Baldus study demonstrates that the Georgia capital sentencing system violates the Eighth Amendment. We begin our analysis of this claim by reviewing the restrictions on death sentences established by our prior decisions under that Amendment. . . .

A

In sum, our decisions since *Furman* have identified a constitutionally permissible range of discretion in imposing the death penalty. First, there is a required threshold below which the death penalty cannot be imposed. In this context, the State must establish rational criteria that narrow the decisionmaker's judgment as to whether the circumstances of a particular defendant's case meet the threshold. Moreover, a societal consensus that the death penalty is disproportionate [481 U.S. 279, 306] to a particular offense prevents a State from imposing the death penalty for that offense. Second, States cannot limit the sentencer's consideration of any relevant circumstance that could cause it to decline to impose the penalty. In this respect, the State cannot channel the sentencer's discretion, but must allow it to consider any relevant information offered by the defendant.

IV
A

In light of our precedents under the Eighth Amendment, McCleskey cannot argue successfully that his sentence is "disproportionate to the crime in the traditional sense." He does not deny that he committed a murder in the course of a planned robbery, a crime for which this Court has determined that the death penalty constitutionally may be imposed. His disproportionality claim "is of a different sort." McCleskey argues that the sentence in his case is disproportionate to the sentences in other murder cases. On the one hand, he cannot base a constitutional claim on an argument that his case differs from other cases in which defendants did receive the death penalty. On automatic appeal, the Georgia Supreme Court found that McCleskey's death sentence was not disproportionate to other death sentences imposed in the State. The court supported this conclusion with an appendix containing citations to 13 cases involving generally similar murders. Moreover, where the statutory procedures adequately channel the sentencer's discretion, such proportionality review is not constitutionally required.

On the other hand, absent a showing that the Georgia capital punishment system operates in an arbitrary and capricious manner, McCleskey cannot prove a constitutional violation by demonstrating that other defendants who may be similarly situated did not receive the death penalty. In *Gregg*, the Court confronted the argument that "the opportunities for discretionary action that are inherent in the processing of any murder case under Georgia law," specifically the opportunities for discretionary leniency, rendered the capital sentences imposed arbitrary and capricious. We rejected this contention. . . .

Because McCleskey's sentence was imposed under Georgia sentencing procedures that focus discretion "on the particularized nature of the crime and the particularized characteristics of the individual defendant," id., at 206, we lawfully may presume that McCleskey's death sentence was not "wantonly and freakishly" imposed, id., at 207, and thus that the sentence is not disproportionate within any recognized meaning under the Eighth Amendment.

B

Although our decision in *Gregg* as to the facial validity of the Georgia capital punishment statute appears to foreclose McCleskey's disproportionality argument, he further contends that the Georgia capital punishment system is arbitrary and capricious in application, and therefore his sentence is excessive, because racial considerations may influence capital sentencing decisions in Georgia. We now address this claim.

To evaluate McCleskey's challenge, we must examine exactly what the Baldus study may show. Even Professor Baldus does not contend that his statistics prove that race enters into any capital sentencing decisions or that race was a factor in McCleskey's particular case. Statistics at most may show only a likelihood that a particular factor entered into some decisions. There is, of course, some risk of racial prejudice influencing a jury's decision in a criminal case. There are similar risks that other kinds of prejudice will influence other criminal trials. . . . The question "is at what point that risk becomes constitutionally unacceptable," McCleskey asks us to accept the likelihood allegedly shown by the Baldus study as the constitutional measure of an unacceptable risk of racial prejudice influencing capital sentencing decisions. This we decline to do. . . .

C

At most, the Baldus study indicates a discrepancy that appears to correlate with race. Apparent disparities in sentencing are an inevitable part of our criminal justice system. The discrepancy indicated by the Baldus study is "a far cry from the major systemic defects identified in *Furman*." As this Court has recognized, any mode for determining guilt or punishment "has its weaknesses and the potential for misuse." . . . Specifically, "there can be 'no perfect procedure for deciding in which cases governmental authority should be used to impose death.'" . . . Where the discretion that is fundamental to our criminal process is involved, we decline to assume that what is unexplained is invidious. In light of the safeguards designed to minimize racial bias in the process, the fundamental value of jury trial in our criminal justice system, and the benefits that discretion provides to criminal defendants, we hold that the Baldus study does not demonstrate a constitutionally significant risk of racial bias affecting the Georgia capital sentencing process.

V

Two additional concerns inform our decision in this case. First, McCleskey's claim, taken to its logical conclusion, [481 U.S. 279, 315] throws into serious question the principles that underlie our entire criminal justice system. The Eighth Amendment is not limited in application to capital punishment, but applies to all penalties. Thus, if we accepted McCleskey's claim that racial bias has impermissibly tainted the capital sentencing decision, we could soon be faced with similar claims as to other types of penalty. Moreover, the claim that his sentence rests on the irrelevant factor of race easily could be extended to apply to claims based on unexplained discrepancies that correlate to membership in other minority groups, and even to gender.

Second, McCleskey's arguments are best presented to the legislative bodies. It is not the responsibility—or indeed even the right—of this Court to determine the appropriate punishment for particular crimes. It is the legislatures, the elected representatives of the people, that are "constituted to respond to the will and consequently the moral values of the people.". . . .

VI

Accordingly, we affirm the judgment of the Court of Appeals for the Eleventh Circuit.
It is so ordered.

JUSTICE BRENNAN, with whom JUSTICE MARSHALL joins, and with whom JUSTICE BLACKMUN and JUSTICE STEVENS join in all but Part I, dissenting.

I

Adhering to my view that the death penalty is in all circumstances cruel and unusual punishment forbidden by the Eighth and Fourteenth Amendments, I

Appendix C

would vacate the decision below insofar as it left undisturbed the death sentence imposed in this case. The Court observes that "[t]he *Gregg*-type statute imposes unprecedented safeguards in the special context of capital punishment," which "ensure a degree of care in the imposition of the death penalty that can be described only as unique." Notwithstanding these efforts, murder defendants in Georgia with white victims are more than four times as likely to receive the death sentence as are defendants with black victims. . . . Nothing could convey more powerfully the intractable reality of the death penalty: "that the effort to eliminate arbitrariness in the infliction of that ultimate sanction is so plainly doomed to failure that it—and the death penalty—must be abandoned altogether."

Even if I did not hold this position, however, I would reverse the Court of Appeals, for petitioner McCleskey has clearly demonstrated that his death sentence was imposed in violation of the Eighth and Fourteenth Amendments. . . .

II

. . . The Court today holds that Warren McCleskey's sentence was constitutionally imposed. It finds no fault in a system in which lawyers must tell their clients that race casts a large shadow on the capital sentencing process. The Court arrives at this conclusion by stating that the Baldus study cannot "prove that race enters into any capital sentencing decisions or that race was a factor in McCleskey's particular case." Ante, at 308 (emphasis in original). Since, according to Professor Baldus, we cannot say "to a moral certainty" that race influenced a decision, we can identify only "a likelihood that a particular factor entered into some decisions," and "a discrepancy that appears to correlate with race." This "likelihood" and "discrepancy," holds the Court, is insufficient to establish a constitutional violation. . . .

III

A

It is important to emphasize at the outset that the Court's observation that McCleskey cannot prove the influence of race on any particular sentencing decision is irrelevant in evaluating his Eighth Amendment claim. Since *Furman v. Georgia*, 408 U.S. 238 (1972), the Court has been concerned with the risk of the imposition of an arbitrary sentence, rather than the proven fact of one. Furman held that the death penalty "may not be imposed under sentencing procedures that create a substantial risk that the punishment will be inflicted in an arbitrary and capricious manner." . . . This emphasis on risk acknowledges the difficulty of divining the jury's motivation in an individual case. In addition, it reflects the fact that concern for arbitrariness focuses on the rationality of the system as a whole, and that a system that features a significant probability that sentencing decisions are influenced by impermissible considerations cannot be regarded as rational. . . .

Defendants challenging their death sentences thus never have had to prove that impermissible considerations have actually infected sentencing decisions. We have required instead that they establish that the system under which they were sentenced posed a significant risk of such an occurrence. McCleskey's claim does differ, however, in one respect from these earlier cases: it is the first to base a challenge not on speculation about how a system might operate, but on empirical documentation of how it does operate.

The Court assumes the statistical validity of the Baldus study, and acknowledges that McCleskey has demonstrated a risk that racial prejudice plays a role in capital sentencing in Georgia. Nonetheless, it finds the probability of prejudice insufficient to create constitutional concern. Close analysis of the Baldus study, however, in light of both statistical principles and human experience, reveals that the risk that race influenced McCleskey's sentence is intolerable by any imaginable standard.

B

The Baldus study indicates that, after taking into account some 230 nonracial factors that might legitimately influence a sentencer, the jury more likely than not would have spared McCleskey's life had his victim been black. . . .

Furthermore, even examination of the sentencing system as a whole, factoring in those cases in which the jury exercises little discretion, indicates the influence of race on capital sentencing. For the Georgia system as a whole, race accounts for a six percentage point difference in the rate at which capital punishment is imposed. Since death is imposed in 11% of all white-victim cases, the rate in comparably aggravated black-victim cases is 5%. The rate of capital sentencing in a white-victim case is thus 120% greater than the rate in a black-victim case. Put another way, over half—55%—of defendants in white-victim crimes in Georgia would not have been sentenced to die if their victims had been black. Of the more than 200 variables potentially relevant to a sentencing decision, race of the victim is a powerful explanation for variation in death sentence rates—as powerful as nonracial aggravating factors such as a prior murder conviction or acting as the principal planner of the homicide. . . .

C

Evaluation of McCleskey's evidence cannot rest solely on the numbers themselves. We must also ask whether the conclusion suggested by those numbers is consonant with our understanding of history and human experience. Georgia's legacy of a race-conscious criminal justice system, as well as this Court's own recognition of the persistent danger that racial attitudes may affect criminal proceedings, indicates that McCleskey's claim is not a fanciful product of mere statistical artifice. . . .

The majority thus misreads our Eighth Amendment jurisprudence in concluding that McCleskey has not demonstrated a degree of risk sufficient to raise constitutional concern. . . . It is true that every nuance of decision cannot be statistically captured, nor can any individual judgment be plumbed with absolute certainty. Yet the fact that we must always act without the illumination of complete knowledge cannot induce paralysis when we confront what is literally an issue of life and death. Sentencing data, history, and experience all counsel that Georgia has provided insufficient assurance of the heightened rationality we have required in order to take a human life.

IV

The Court cites four reasons for shrinking from the implications of McCleskey's evidence: the desirability of discretion for actors in the criminal justice system, the existence of statutory safeguards against abuse of that discretion, the potential consequences for broader challenges to criminal sentencing, and an understanding of the contours of the judicial role. While these concerns underscore the need for sober deliberation, they do not justify rejecting evidence as convincing as McCleskey has presented.

The Court maintains that petitioner's claim "is antithetical to the fundamental role of discretion in our criminal justice system." It states that "[w]here the discretion that is fundamental to our criminal process is involved, we decline to assume that what is unexplained is invidious." Ante, at 313.

Reliance on race in imposing capital punishment, however, is antithetical to the very rationale for granting sentencing discretion. Discretion is a means, not an end. It is bestowed in order to permit the sentencer to "trea[t] each defendant in a capital case with that degree of respect due the uniqueness of the individual.". . .

The Court also declines to find McCleskey's evidence sufficient in view of "the safeguards designed to minimize racial bias in the [capital sentencing] process." . . . *Gregg v. Georgia*, 428 U.S., at 226, upheld the Georgia capital sentencing statute against a facial challenge which JUSTICE WHITE described in his concurring opinion as based on "simply an assertion of lack of faith" that the system could operate in a fair manner. JUSTICE WHITE observed that the claim that prosecutors might act in an arbitrary fashion was "unsupported by any facts," and that prosecutors must be assumed to exercise their charging duties properly "[a]bsent facts to the contrary.". . .

Capital Punishment

It has now been over 13 years since Georgia adopted the provisions upheld in *Gregg*. Professor Baldus and his colleagues have compiled data on almost 2,500 homicides committed during the period 1973–1979. They have taken into account the influence of 230 nonracial variables, using a multitude of data from the State itself, and have produced striking evidence that the odds of being sentenced to death are significantly greater than average if a defendant is black or his or her victim is white. The challenge to the Georgia system is not speculative or theoretical; it is empirical. As a result, the Court cannot rely on the statutory safeguards in discounting McCleskey's evidence, for it is the very effectiveness of those safeguards that such evidence calls into question. . . .

The Court next states that its unwillingness to regard petitioner's evidence as sufficient is based in part on the fear that recognition of McCleskey's claim would open the door to widespread challenges to all aspects of criminal sentencing. Taken on its face, such a statement seems to suggest a fear of too much justice. . . .

The Court also maintains that accepting McCleskey's claim would pose a threat to all sentencing because of the prospect that a correlation might be demonstrated between sentencing outcomes and other personal characteristics. Again, such a view is indifferent to the considerations that enter into a determination whether punishment is "cruel and unusual." Race is a consideration whose influence is expressly constitutionally proscribed. We have expressed a moral commitment, as embodied in our fundamental law, that this specific characteristic should not be the basis for allotting burdens and benefits. . . .

Finally, the Court justifies its rejection of McCleskey's claim by cautioning against usurpation of the legislatures' role in devising and monitoring criminal punishment. The Court is, of course, correct to emphasize the gravity of constitutional intervention and the importance that it be sparingly employed. The fact that "[c]apital punishment is now the law in more than two thirds of our States," however, does not diminish the fact that capital punishment is the most awesome act that a State can perform. The judiciary's role in this society counts for little if the use of governmental power to extinguish life does not elicit close scrutiny.

V

It is tempting to pretend that minorities on death row share a fate in no way connected to our own, that our treatment of them sounds no echoes beyond the chambers in which they die. Such an illusion is ultimately corrosive, for the reverberations of injustice are not so easily confined. "The destinies of the two races in this country are indissolubly linked together," and the way in which we choose those who will die reveals the depth of moral commitment among the living. . . .

APPENDIX D

EXTRACT FROM U.S. SUPREME COURT RULING: *ATKINS V. VIRGINIA*, 2002

536 U.S. 304

Justice Stevens delivered the opinion of the Court.

Those mentally retarded persons who meet the law's requirements for criminal responsibility should be tried and punished when they commit crimes. Because of their disabilities in areas of reasoning, judgment, and control of their impulses, however, they do not act with the level of moral culpability that characterizes the most serious adult criminal conduct. Moreover, their impairments can jeopardize the reliability and fairness of capital proceedings against mentally retarded defendants. Presumably for these reasons, in the 13 years since we decided *Penry* v. *Lynaugh*, 492 U.S. 302 (1989), the American public, legislators, scholars, and judges have deliberated over the question whether the death penalty should ever be imposed on a mentally retarded criminal. The consensus reflected in those deliberations informs our answer to the question presented by this case: whether such executions are "cruel and unusual punishments" prohibited by the Eighth Amendment to the Federal Constitution.

I

Petitioner, Daryl Renard Atkins, was convicted of abduction, armed robbery, and capital murder, and sentenced to death. At approximately midnight on August 16, 1996, Atkins and William Jones, armed with a semiautomatic handgun, abducted Eric Nesbitt, robbed him of the money on his person, drove him to an automated teller machine in his pickup truck where cameras recorded their

291

withdrawal of additional cash, then took him to an isolated location where he was shot eight times and killed.

Jones and Atkins both testified in the guilt phase of Atkins' trial. Each confirmed most of the details in the other's account of the incident, with the important exception that each stated that the other had actually shot and killed Nesbitt. Jones' testimony, which was both more coherent and credible than Atkins', was obviously credited by the jury and was sufficient to establish Atkins' guilt. At the penalty phase of the trial, the State introduced victim impact evidence and proved two aggravating circumstances: future dangerousness and "vileness of the offense." To prove future dangerousness, the State relied on Atkins' prior felony convictions as well as the testimony of four victims of earlier robberies and assaults. To prove the second aggravator, the prosecution relied upon the trial record, including pictures of the deceased's body and the autopsy report.

In the penalty phase, the defense relied on one witness, Dr. Evan Nelson, a forensic psychologist who had evaluated Atkins before trial and concluded that he was "mildly mentally retarded." His conclusion was based on interviews with people who knew Atkins, a review of school and court records, and the administration of a standard intelligence test which indicated that Atkins had a full scale IQ of 59.

The jury sentenced Atkins to death, but the Virginia Supreme Court ordered a second sentencing hearing because the trial court had used a misleading verdict form. . . . At the resentencing, Dr. Nelson again testified. The State presented an expert rebuttal witness, Dr. Stanton Samenow, who expressed the opinion that Atkins was not mentally retarded, but rather was of "average intelligence, at least," and diagnosable as having antisocial personality disorder. The jury again sentenced Atkins to death.

The Supreme Court of Virginia affirmed the imposition of the death penalty . . . . Atkins did not argue before the Virginia Supreme Court that his sentence was disproportionate to penalties imposed for similar crimes in Virginia, but he did contend "that he is mentally retarded and thus cannot be sentenced to death." . . . The majority of the state court rejected this contention, relying on our holding in *Penry*. . . . The Court was "not willing to commute Atkins' sentence of death to life imprisonment merely because of his IQ score.". . .

Justice Hassell and Justice Koontz dissented. They rejected Dr. Samenow's opinion that Atkins possesses average intelligence as "incredulous as a matter of law," and concluded that "the imposition of the sentence of death upon a criminal defendant who has the mental age of a child between the ages of 9 and 12 is excessive." . . . In their opinion, "it is indefensible to conclude that individuals who are mentally retarded are not to some degree less culpable for their criminal acts. By definition, such individuals have substantial limitations not shared by the general population. A moral and civilized society diminishes itself if its system of justice does not afford recognition and consideration of those limitations in a meaningful way.". . .

Appendix D

Because of the gravity of the concerns expressed by the dissenters, and in light of the dramatic shift in the state legislative landscape that has occurred in the past 13 years, we granted certiorari to revisit the issue that we first addressed in the *Penry* case. . . .

II

The Eighth Amendment succinctly prohibits "excessive" sanctions. It provides: "Excessive bail shall not be required, nor excessive fines imposed, nor cruel and unusual punishments inflicted." In *Weems* v. *United States*, (1910), we held that a punishment of 12 years jailed in irons at hard and painful labor for the crime of falsifying records was excessive. We explained "that it is a precept of justice that punishment for crime should be graduated and proportioned to the offense." . . . We have repeatedly applied this proportionality precept in later cases interpreting the Eighth Amendment. . . . A claim that punishment is excessive is judged not by the standards that prevailed in 1685 when Lord Jeffreys presided over the "Bloody Assizes" or when the Bill of Rights was adopted, but rather by those that currently prevail. As Chief Justice Warren explained in his opinion in *Trop* v. *Dulles*, (1958): "The basic concept underlying the Eighth Amendment is nothing less than the dignity of man. . . . The Amendment must draw its meaning from the evolving standards of decency that mark the progress of a maturing society.". . .

Proportionality review under those evolving standards should be informed by 'objective factors to the maximum possible extent,' . . . We have pinpointed that the "clearest and most reliable objective evidence of contemporary values is the legislation enacted by the country's legislatures." Relying in part on such legislative evidence, we have held that death is an impermissibly excessive punishment for the rape of an adult woman, *Coker* v. *Georgia*, (1977), or for a defendant who neither took life, attempted to take life, nor intended to take life, *Enmund* v. *Florida*, (1982). . . .

We also acknowledged in *Coker* that the objective evidence, though of great importance, did not "wholly determine" the controversy, "for the Constitution contemplates that in the end our own judgment will be brought to bear on the question of the acceptability of the death penalty under the Eighth Amendment.". . .

Guided by our approach in these cases, we shall first review the judgment of legislatures that have addressed the suitability of imposing the death penalty on the mentally retarded and then consider reasons for agreeing or disagreeing with their judgment.

III

The parties have not called our attention to any state legislative consideration of the suitability of imposing the death penalty on mentally retarded offenders prior to 1986. In that year, the public reaction to the execution of a mentally retarded murderer in Georgia apparently led to the enactment of the first state statute prohibiting such executions. In 1988, when Congress enacted legislation reinstating the federal death penalty, it expressly provided that a "sentence of death shall not be carried out upon a person who is mentally retarded." In 1989, Maryland enacted a similar prohibition. It was in that year that we decided *Penry*, and concluded that those two state enactments, "even when added to the 14 States that have rejected capital punishment completely, do not provide sufficient evidence at present of a national consensus.". . .

Much has changed since then. Responding to the national attention received by the Bowden execution and our decision in *Penry*, state legislatures across the country began to address the issue. In 1990 Kentucky and Tennessee enacted statutes similar to those in Georgia and Maryland, as did New Mexico in 1991, and Arkansas, Colorado, Washington, Indiana, and Kansas in 1993 and 1994. In 1995, when New York reinstated its death penalty, it emulated the Federal Government by expressly exempting the mentally retarded. Nebraska followed suit in 1998. There appear to have been no similar enactments during the next two years, but in 2000 and 2001 six more States—South Dakota, Arizona, Connecticut, Florida, Missouri, and North Carolina—joined the procession. The Texas Legislature unanimously adopted a similar bill, and bills have passed at least one house in other States, including Virginia and Nevada.

It is not so much the number of these States that is significant, but the consistency of the direction of change. Given the well-known fact that anti-crime legislation is far more popular than legislation providing protections for persons guilty of violent crime, the large number of States prohibiting the execution of mentally retarded persons (and the complete absence of States passing legislation reinstating the power to conduct such executions) provides powerful evidence that today our society views mentally retarded offenders as categorically less culpable than the average criminal. The evidence carries even greater force when it is noted that the legislatures that have addressed the issue have voted overwhelmingly in favor of the prohibition. Moreover, even in those States that allow the execution of mentally retarded offenders, the practice is uncommon. . . . The practice, therefore, has become truly unusual, and it is fair to say that a national consensus has developed against it.

To the extent there is serious disagreement about the execution of mentally retarded offenders, it is in determining which offenders are in fact retarded. In this case, for instance, the Commonwealth of Virginia disputes that Atkins suffers from mental retardation. Not all people who claim to be mentally retarded will be so impaired as to fall within the range of mentally retarded offenders about whom there is a national consensus. As was our approach in *Ford* v. *Wainwright*, with regard to insanity, "we leave to the State[s] the task of developing appropriate ways to enforce the constitutional restriction upon its execution of sentences.". . .

IV

This consensus unquestionably reflects widespread judgment about the relative culpability of mentally retarded offenders, and the relationship between mental retardation and the penological purposes served by the death penalty. Additionally, it suggests that some characteristics of mental retardation undermine the strength of the procedural protections that our capital jurisprudence steadfastly guards.

As discussed above, clinical definitions of mental retardation require not only subaverage intellectual functioning, but also significant limitations in adaptive skills such as communication, self-care, and self-direction that became manifest before age 18. Mentally retarded persons frequently know the difference between right and wrong and are competent to stand trial. Because of their impairments, however, by definition they have diminished capacities to understand and process information, to communicate, to abstract from mistakes and learn from experience, to engage in logical reasoning, to control impulses, and to understand the reactions of others. There is no evidence that they are more likely to engage in criminal conduct than others, but there is abundant evidence that they often act on impulse rather than pursuant to a premeditated plan, and that in group settings they are followers rather than leaders. Their deficiencies do not warrant an exemption from criminal sanctions, but they do diminish their personal culpability.

In light of these deficiencies, our death penalty jurisprudence provides two reasons consistent with the legislative consensus that the mentally retarded should be categorically excluded from execution. First, there is a serious question as to whether either justification that we have recognized as a basis for the death penalty applies to mentally retarded offenders. *Gregg* v. *Georgia* (1976), identified "retribution and deterrence of capital crimes by prospective offenders" as the social purposes served by the death penalty. Unless the imposition of the death penalty on a mentally retarded person "measurably contributes to one or both of these goals, it 'is nothing more than the purposeless and needless imposition of pain and suffering,' and hence an unconstitutional punishment."

With respect to retribution—the interest in seeing that the offender gets his "just deserts"—the severity of the appropriate punishment necessarily depends on the culpability of the offender. Since *Gregg*, our jurisprudence has consistently confined the imposition of the death penalty to a narrow category of the most serious crimes. For example, in *Godfrey* v. *Georgia*, (1980), we set aside a death sentence because the petitioner's crimes did not reflect "a consciousness materially more 'depraved' than that of any person guilty of murder." If the culpability of the average murderer is insufficient to justify the most extreme sanction available to the State, the lesser culpability of the mentally retarded offender surely does not merit that form of retribution. Thus, pursuant to our narrowing jurisprudence, which seeks to ensure that only the most deserving of execution are put to death, an exclusion for the mentally retarded is appropriate.

With respect to deterrence—the interest in preventing capital crimes by prospective offenders—"it seems likely that 'capital punishment can serve as a deterrent only when murder is the result of premeditation and deliberation.'" . . . Exempting the mentally retarded from that punishment will not affect the "cold calculus that precedes the decision" of other potential murderers. Indeed, that sort of calculus is at the opposite end of the spectrum from behavior of mentally retarded offenders. The theory of deterrence in capital sentencing is predicated upon the notion that the increased severity of the punishment will inhibit criminal actors from carrying out murderous conduct. Yet it is the same cognitive and behavioral impairments that make these defendants less morally culpable—for example, the diminished ability to understand and process information, to learn from experience, to engage in logical reasoning, or to control impulses—that also make it less likely that they can process the information of the possibility of execution as a penalty and, as a result, control their conduct based upon that information. Nor will exempting the mentally retarded from execution lessen the deterrent effect of the death penalty with respect to offenders who are not mentally retarded. Such individuals are unprotected by the exemption and will continue to face the threat of execution. Thus, executing the mentally retarded will not measurably further the goal of deterrence.

The reduced capacity of mentally retarded offenders provides a second justification for a categorical rule making such offenders ineligible for the death penalty. The risk "that the death penalty will be imposed in spite of factors which may call for a less severe penalty," *Lockett* v. *Ohio*, (1978), is enhanced, not only by the possibility of false confessions, but also by the lesser ability of mentally retarded defendants to make a persuasive showing of mitigation in the face of prosecutorial evidence of one or more aggravating factors. Mentally retarded defendants may be less able to give meaningful assistance to their counsel and are typically poor witnesses, and their demeanor may create an unwarranted impression of lack of remorse for their crimes. As *Penry* demonstrated, moreover, reliance on mental retardation as a mitigating factor can be a two-edged sword that may enhance the likelihood that the aggravating factor of future dangerousness will be found by the jury. Mentally retarded defendants in the aggregate face a special risk of wrongful execution.

Our independent evaluation of the issue reveals no reason to disagree with the judgment of "the legislatures that have recently addressed the matter" and concluded that death is not a suitable punishment for a mentally retarded criminal. We are not persuaded that the execution of mentally retarded criminals will measurably advance the deterrent or the retributive purpose of the death penalty. Construing and applying the Eighth Amendment in the light of our "evolving standards of decency," we therefore conclude that such punishment is excessive and that the Constitution "places a substantive restriction on the State's power to take the life" of a mentally retarded offender.

The judgment of the Virginia Supreme Court is reversed and the case is remanded for further proceedings not inconsistent with this opinion.

It is so ordered.

INDEX

Locators in **boldface** indicate main topics. Locators followed by *c* indicate chronology entries. Locators followed by *b* indicate biographical entries. Locators followed by *g* indicate glossary entries.

Index

Index

301

Index

305

Index

impaired capacity 47
impartial hearing 59
impartial jury 58
incapacitation 147*g*
incarceration 7. *See also* prisons
incompetence (mental). *See*
 mental incompetence
Increasing Number of
 Exonerations, 1973–2004
 264
"incremental deterrence" 15
Indiana **52**, 123*c*
Indiana Citizens to Abolish the
 Capital Punishment 246
indigent defendants 34, 89–90,
 118*c*, 122*c*, 125*c*
"individualized determination"
 34
individualized sentence 68
Indonesia 126*c*
INDPAG (Inland Northwest
 Death Penalty Abolition
 Group) 252
informants 26, 45, 49
Ingle, Joe 138*b*
injurious articles 49
Inland Northwest Death
 Penalty Abolition Group
 (INDPAG) 252
inmates 50, 97–98
innocence. *See* actual innocence
innocence phase. *See* guilt
 phase
In re Kemmler 108*c*
insanity 32, 43, 81–82, 99,
 121*c*
institutionalized violence 18
institutional racism 33
intent 74
International Bannister
 Foundation 253
International Bill of Rights
 111*c*
International Convenant on
 Civil and Political Rights
 39
international convention 4–5
International Court of Justice
 (World Court) 130*c*, 131*c*
international issues and law
 38–39, 123*c*, 126*c*, 130*c*. *See
 also* extradition
 death penalty **55–57**

Medellín v. Dretke
 104–105, 131*c*
Roper v. Simmons 103
international precedent 32
interpretation of the law 26
interstate commerce 25
Iowans Against the Death
 Penalty 246
Iran 39
Iraq 39
irrevocability 147*g*

J

Jackson, Roscoe 110*c*
Jackson v. Georgia 60
Jewish Peace Fellowship
 239–240
Jews 24
Johans, Mike 127*c*
John, Gee 109*c*
John Paul II (pope) 24, 119*c*,
 121*c*, 125*c*, 127*c*
Johnson administration 114*c*
Journey of Hope...From
 Violence to Healing Inc. 240
judges 114*c*
 Clemons v. Mississippi 93
 and common law 25
 and death sentences 40,
 50
 and international opinion
 39
 murder of 45, 48
 Ring v. Arizona 100, 129*c*
judicial review 27, 29
Jurek v. Texas 63
jurors 108*c*
 Adams v. Texas 60
 Deck v. Missouri 104
 McCleskey v. Kemp 83
 murder of 45, 48
 removal of 60
 "scrupled" 58–60
 selection of 59
 Wainwright v. Witt 60
jury(-ies) 113*c*–115*c*, 121*c*,
 122*c*, 126*c*, 127*c*, 129*c*
 and aggravating and
 mitigating factors 44
 Beck v. Alabama 69–70,
 118*c*
 Booth v. Maryland 86
 Clemons v. Mississippi 93

death-qualified jury 59,
 145*g*
discretion of 64
Furman v. Georgia 62
grand jury 147*g*
and mitigating evidence 69
and option of life without
 parole 34
the role of the **28–29**
and the "scrupled juror"
 58–60
selection of 28
and social class 22
standards for 62–64
Witherspoon v. Illinois 114*c*
Woodson v. North Carolina
 64–66
jury(-ies), as sole capital
 sentencer 42, 130*c*
 Apprendi v. New Jersey 100
 Ring v. Arizona 40, 50, 93,
 99–101, 129*c*
 Summerlin v. Stewart
 100–101
 Walton v. Arizona 100
jury instructions 78–79, 120*c*
jury override 147*g*
jury qualifications
 Adams v. Texas 60
 Davis v. Georgia 59
 Lockett v. Ohio **67–69**, 71,
 91, 117*c*
 Wainwright v. Witt 60
 Witherspoon v. Illinois
 58–60, 114*c*
justice, society's sense of 17
Justice Department, U.S. 119*c*,
 122*c*, 127*c*, 128*c*, 236
Justice for All 240
Justice Research and Statistics
 Association 235
juveniles (minors) 110*c*, 120*c*,
 121*c*, 123*c*, 130*c*
 culpability of 31–32
 and death penalty 42
 deviant sexual behavior
 with a 45
 Roper v. Simmons 50, 89,
 102–103, 130*c*
 Stanford v. Kentucky 123*c*
 Thompson v. Oklahoma
 88–89, 122*c*
 Wilkins v. Missouri 123*c*

Index

315